Zdenka Mansfeldová, Heiko Pleines (eds.)

Informal Relations from Democratic Representation to Corruption

Case Studies from Central and Eastern Europe

CHANGING EUROPE

Edited by Dr. Sabine Fischer, Dr. Heiko Pleines and
Prof. Dr. Hans-Henning Schröder

ISSN 1863-8716

Zdenka Mansfeldová, Heiko Pleines (eds.)

INFORMAL RELATIONS FROM DEMOCRATIC REPRESENTATION TO CORRUPTION

Case Studies from Central and Eastern Europe

ibidem-Verlag
Stuttgart

Bibliographic information published by the Deutsche Nationalbibliothek

Die Deutsche Nationalbibliothek lists this publication in the Deutsche Nationalbibliografie; detailed bibliographic data are available in the Internet at http://dnb.d-nb.de.

Bibliografische Information der Deutschen Nationalbibliothek

Die Deutsche Nationalbibliothek verzeichnet diese Publikation in der Deutschen Nationalbibliografie; detaillierte bibliografische Daten sind im Internet über http://dnb.d-nb.de abrufbar.

ISSN: 1863-8716

ISBN-13: 978-3-8382-0173-3

© *ibidem*-Verlag / *ibidem* Press

Stuttgart, Germany 2011

Contents

List of Figures

List of Tables

Preface

This book presents a selection of the papers discussed at the Changing Europe Summer School on 'Informal Networks, Clientelism and Corruption. Case Studies from Central and Eastern Europe' held in Prague at the Institute of Sociology of the Academy of Sciences of the Czech Republic in August 2010. Organised since 2006 by the Research Centre for East European Studies (Forschungsstelle Osteuropa) at the University of Bremen, the Changing Europe Summer School has every year invited twenty to thirty young academics from different disciplines of the social sciences and the humanities to share their research on Central and Eastern Europe. Our main goal is to give them a chance to present and discuss their research projects as well as to help them become more integrated into the academic community. Participants are selected by means of an anonymous review process that is kindly supported by the members of our international review panel (for more information on the Changing Europe Summer Schools, see www.changing-europe.de). The results of each Summer School are published in this book series.

It goes without saying that this book would not have been possible without ample support. First of all, our thanks go to the participants themselves, whose enthusiasm and knowledge made the Summer School a truly worthwhile event. We would also like to thank all the referees who aided us in the selection process for appropriate participants. We are additionally grateful to all those who helped to organize the Summer School and the book production, namely Hilary Abuhove (language editing), Nozima Akhrarkhodjaeva (bibliography), Alzbeta Bernardyova (organizational support), Christopher Gilley (language editing), Petra Guasti (organizational support), Judith Janiszewski (style editing), Matthias Neumann (layout), Ksenia Pacheco (organizational support) and Pavla Vamberova (organizational support).

Last but certainly not least, we want to express our gratitude to the Volkswagen Foundation for its generous support of the Changing Europe Summer Schools.

Prague and Bremen, February 2011
The Editors

Heiko Pleines

1. Introduction

Informal relations have been one of the major research topics of the social sciences since the 1990s. Above all in the non-Western context, informality has been seen as a negative, pre-modern phenomenon which explains the failure of societies to develop modern democracies and market economies. In line with the distinction by Max Weber, the Western legal-rational model of the organisation of state and society has been contrasted with the pre-modern patrimonial model based on personal relations of a clientelistic type, kinship and arbitrary rule. As today's transforming societies cannot simply be described as pre-modern, the concept of neo-patrimonialism has been developed in order to describe a hybrid system, where the formal rules are based on Western legal-rational principles, while, at the same time, patrimonialism determines many interactions in politics and society informally.

However, the range of informal relations categorized in the context of neo-institutional concepts is much wider than the usual research suggests. In the neo-institutional understanding, informal practice refers to acts which are not regulated by formal rules, where formal rules are those supported by the state's monopoly of power. However, informal rules are not necessarily illegitimate or illegal; they may just complement the formal rules. As formal rules cannot cover every aspect of life, and are not intended to do so, informal rules are common in functioning democracies, too.

In this context, Helmke/Levitsky distinguish four types of relations between formal and informal rules:

> Our typology is based on two dimensions. The first is the degree to which formal and informal institutional outcomes converge. The distinction here is whether following informal rules produces a substantively similar or different result from that expected from a strict and exclusive adherence to formal rules. [...] The second dimension is the effectiveness of the relevant formal institutions, that is the extent to which rules and procedures that exist on paper are enforced and complied with in practice. [...] Where formal rules and procedures are ineffective, actors believe the probability of enforcement (and hence the expected cost of violation) will be low.[1]

These two dimensions produce a fourfold typology. In the case of effective formal institutions, the informal ones can be complementary (in the case of convergence) or accommodating (in the case of divergence). In the case of ineffective formal institutions, the informal ones can be substitutive (in the case of convergence) or competing (in the case of divergence).

According to this understanding, informal practices are only illegitimate when they challenge the proper functioning of the formal rules, i.e. when they are competing,

---

[1]   Helmke, Gretchen/ Levitsky, Steven: Informal Institutions and Comparative Politics: A research Agenda, in: Perspectives on Politics, 2004 (vol. 2),pp. 725–740, here: p. 728.

although they are only illegal when the law covers the form of behaviour in question. This perspective facilitates an integration of the research on informal relations into broader social science theories.

The negative side of informal relations is linked to theories of clientelism and corruption. In the analysis of modern societies, the research focuses on the perversion of constitutional (often democratic) and law-based regulation by informal relations. This negative concept of informal relations, which sees them as influential, traditional and perverting the formal rules of democracy, also prevails in studies on the post-socialist societies of Central and Eastern Europe, particularly in those focusing on the former Soviet Union and the Western Balkans.

The positive side of informal relations is linked to theories of social capital. Generalized (interpersonal or social) trust and institutional trust are seen as major factors contributing to the establishment and maintenance of efficient democratic political systems. The former refers to trust in unknown people and is assumed to be the foundation for collective political activity for the public good (as opposed to lobbying for the interests of narrow and closely knit circles). The latter refers to trust in the major institutions[2] of the state and civil society, which are vital for the functioning of the democratic system, most notably state organs (such as the government, parliament, courts, state administration and police), collective representatives of society (for example, political parties and different types of associations) and the channels of information (most notably mass media). As democratic decision-making relies on participation and compromise, trust in the relevant actors is vital for the functioning and legitimacy of the political system. With regard to informal relations, the argument is that generalized trust leads to open and transparent informal networks and collective action focused on the public good, while a lack of generalized trust promotes the formation of closed circles focused on narrow interests.

One of the best known and most concise versions of the claim that generalized trust creates both social capital in the form of an active civil society and high levels of institutional trust, which in turn promotes democratic development, is presented by Putnam[3], who analysed Northern and Southern Italy. Similarly, for example, Belson

---

2   It is important to note that in this context institutions refer to state bodies or organizations as collective actors and not to rules (as in the neo-institutionalist concepts). However, in democratic societies, the respective collective actors are strongly embedded in specific rules regulating their behaviour. Accordingly, it can be argued that institutional trust refers not only to the specific persons representing the collective actors, but at least as much to the system of rules governing their behaviour. Trust in parliament or, even more obviously, trust in the police does not just emerge from trust in a specific deputy or policeman, but from trust in the correct functioning of parliament or the police.

3   Putnam, Robert: Making Democracy Work: Civic Tradition in Modern Italy, Princeton: Princeton University Press, 1993.

and Loncko[4] state, based on an analysis of popular attitudes in new democracies, that there is a positive relationsip between trust and democratic consolidation. Rothstein[5] in a volume on social trust in transition states holds that such trust is a precondition for the establishment of efficient institutions.

Following this line of argument, several authors have pointed to low levels of trust in order to explain a perceived democratic deficit in the post-socialist countries of Central and Eastern Europe nearly two decades after the end of socialism. However, the causal direction is not obvious, as it can also be argued, as do e.g. Fidrmuch and Gërxhani,[6] that the poor performance of institutions leads to (justified) low levels of institutional trust.

Accordingly, low levels of trust and the low quality of public institutions can be mutually reinforcing and thus create a vicious circle. At the same time, high levels of trust and high quality of public institutions can also be reinforcing and thus stabilize democracies. This means that trust has a relatively high predictive power concerning democratic development as it takes a long time to build (or destroy) high levels of generalized and institutional trust in a society. Trust levels are, therefore, at least from a theoretical perspective, long-term explanatory factors for democratic development.[7]

The negative and positive perspectives on informal relations are clearly separated in academic research as they are integrated into different theoretical concepts and look at different actors and institutional settings. However, the rationale of this book is that, from an empirical point of view, the distinction is not so clear-cut and that it is, therefore, important to bring the two perspectives together. This can be demonstrated using the issue of democratic representation.

The normative aim of democratic representation is to allow all interested groups in society equal access to democratic decision-making processes in a transparent way.[8] At the same time, decision-makers should be authorized by the relevant constituencies and should be held accountable for their decisions and actions. Next to this for-

---

4   Belson, Molly/ Loncko, Lukas: Trust and Democratic Consolidation: A Comparative Analysis of Post-Communist Europe and Latin America, Paper presented at the Annual meeting of the International Studies Association, Hilton Hawaiian Village, Honolulu, Hawaii, March 05, 2005, available at http://www.allacademic.com/meta/p72171_index.html, accessed 23 November 2010.

5   Rothstein, Bo: Social Trust and Honesty in Government: A Causal Mechanisms Approach, in: Kornai, Janos/ Rothstein, Bo/ Rose-Ackerman, Susan (eds.): Creating Social Trust in Post-Socialist Transition, N.Y.: Palgrave Macmillan, 2004.

6   Fidrmuch, Jan/ Gërxhani, Klarita: Mind the Gap! Social Capital, East and West, William Davidson, 2007, Working Paper 888 (Ann Arbor, MI).

7   See, for example, the discussions in Mishler, William/ Rose, Richard: What are the Origins of Political Trust? Testing Institutional and Cultural Theories in Post-Communist Societies, in: Comparative Political Studies, 2001 (vol. 34), no. 1, pp. 30–62 and Dimitrova-Grajzl, Valentina/ Simon, Eszter: Political Trust and Historical Legacy. The Effect of Varieties of Socialism, in: East European Politics & Societies, 2010 (vol. 24), no. 2, pp. 206–228.

8   The relevant analytical framework is developed in the chapter by Petra Guasti in this volume.

malistic aspect of representation, Hanna Pitkin also points to the descriptive, symbolic and substantive aspects, which refer respectively to the resemblance between constituency and representative, the subjective belief in the representative link and the actual actions by the representative in support of the constituency.[9]

If we now look at the role informal relations and institutions can play in democratic representation, we can see a continuum where open and transparent civil society networks involved in democratic decision-making processes are placed at one end and corrupt insider deals perverting democratic norms are placed at the other. However, in-between there are relatively closed networks engaging in lobbyism on the basis of formal democratic rules and political parties acting not only according to democratic principles but also based on clientelism. In the terminology of Helmke/Levitsky, one end of the continuum would be characterized as informal institutions complementing democratic representation (with those accommodating or replacing it further down the line), while informal institutions competing with democratic representation (and thus manipulating or perverting it) would be at the other end of the continuum.

In order to allow for meaningful comparisons between different combinations of the positive and negative effects of informal relations on democratic representation, all the chapters in this book focus on post-socialist Central and Eastern Europe as a particular region where formal democratic rules have been established but competing informal rules are still strong. The first section discusses a broad spectrum of related analytical concepts from different perspectives and from different academic disciplines. The second part then goes on to analyse empirical cases of the relationship between informal relations and democratic representation. The contributions span the whole continuum, as we perceive it, from civil society networks seen as supporting democratic representation to the perversion of democratic representation through political corruption. The final part of the book then takes a closer look at corruption through four case studies from Russia which allow a broader examination of the negative effects of informal relations in different social settings within the same country.

The first two chapters in this book introduce concepts which cover the full range of positive and negative aspects related to informal relations. Eelco Jacobs looks at the governance of public services. He argues that

> by definition, the governance of public service delivery in those states where the government is not able or willing to deliver basic public goods and services […] does not conform to [the] legal-rational ideal type. In fact, in such cases the social contract is broken. This does not imply that governance in the wider definition ceases to exist but rather that informal and often more particularistic governance institutions play a stronger role.

Accordingly, actual governance mechanisms are a hybrid combination of formal and informal elements and the performance of, for example, public services depends on

---

9   See the chapter by Andreea Carstocea for an elaboration of this concept.

their interaction. As the formal institutions are weak in such circumstances, Jacobs argues that the informal institutions often compete with them—to use the terminology of Helmke/Levitsky—because

> in these cases, neo-patrimonial forms of rule dominate, which reproduce societal inequalities in the public sphere. Clientelist relations and other personalistic modes of governance become essential for access to education, health care and clean water.

Whereas Jacobs looks at the interplay between the formal and the informal in public service provision and, therefore, focuses on governance mechanisms and power relations at the macro level of states and societies, Piotr Stankiewicz and Stanislaw Burdziej investigate the individual, thereby adding a micro perspective. Their presentation of the concept of conflict of interest offers an analytical framework for a normative, legal and sociological analysis of situations where the individual can either follow the formal rules in support of the public good or pursue personal interests in violation of such rules.

Next, Marco Zanella and Mi Lennhag examine typical competing informal institutions in more detail. The chapter by Zanella offers a broad overview of criminal provisions for corruption in Central and East European states. He demonstrates that despite the European efforts towards harmonization, the legal definition of the illegality of informal rules still differs between countries even within the EU. Thus, his contribution offers, on the one hand, a concise summary of different forms of competing informal relations which are deemed illegal and, on the other, demonstrates that an informal act that is defined as illegal corruption in one country can be legal (though still informal) in another. The problem of different legal definitions thus poses a considerable challenge to comparative research beyond the legal realm. The chapter by Lennhag, therefore, presents sociological approaches to informal relations, which focus not on legal regulations but on established routines, path-dependent developments and informal norms. In doing so, she returns to the neo-institutional analytical framework sketched out above.

The second part of the book then presents empirical cases of the impact of informal relations on democratic representation in a declining order from the supportive best cases to the perverting worst scenarios.

Petra Guasti discusses the contribution by civil society networks to the legitimacy of the EU polity. She offers an introduction to the academic debate on whether the involvement of civil society actors can reduce the perceived democratic deficit of the EU. She then goes on to describe the methodological approach to the related network analysis and illustrates the theoretical and methodological aspects with a case study of the role and strategies of civil society actors in the political communication about Europe in the case of the failed Treaty Establishing a Constitution for Europe. Although the involvement of civil society is seen by many as improving the democratic credentials of the EU, Guasti points out that the lack of formal procedures related to the participation of non-state actors in political decision-making processes at the EU level leads to a lack of transparency and unequal access, which in turn result in unequal democratic representation. This means that even in the best cases of informal relations in a democratic setting, a tension emerges between the importance of participation by organised civil society and the normative desire to ensure transparent proceedings and the fair representation of all relevant interests in democratic policy-making processes.

Tomasz Gabor continues this theme with a quantitative analysis of the capacity for cooperation of civil society organisations in three Central East European countries. He concludes that

> large, professionalized organizations that have received the biggest share of EU Structural Funds tend to maintain collaborative ties exclusively with higher tiers of government. Since these organizations are not accountable to other nonprofits, their intensive involvement in regional governance bears the risk of clientelism.

Further down the continuum running from informal institutions complementing democratic representation to those competing with it, Veronika Pasynkova, looks at the informal relationship between those socialist political parties and trade unions that are successors to communist organizations. In her view, the socialist legacies are still shaping this relationship, which is aimed at cooperation in the political field. The successor parties recruit the trade unions for their election campaigns and in return offer preferential treatment in labour and social policy-making. However, whereas this relationship has been formalized in some countries through electoral alliances and the establishment of a social dialogue, it has remained informal in other countries. In the latter case, clientelistic links exclude other participants and thus restrict democratic representation intentionally.

The case of some political parties claiming to represent small ethnic minorities in Romania shows a clear and intentional perversion of the basic rules of democratic representation. As Andreea Carstocea demonstrates in her chapter, these parties were exploited by political entrepreneurs who wanted to gain access to power. Carstocea explicitly links her empirical results to Hanna Pitkin's concept of representation in order to categorize the substantial impact of the strategies of these political entrepreneurs on democratic representation.

But, whereas the minority parties studied form only a small part of the Romanian political system, the analysis of Bosnia-Herzegovina and Kosovo presented by Maja Nenadović looks at two countries where informal relations have perverted the formal democratic political system on a large scale. She also demonstrates that international administrations have approached corruption in a half-hearted manner and have even taken advantage of it for their own policy aims, because in Bosnia-Herzegovina, those willing to cooperate with the international community could do as they pleased, while those opposing the international administration's policies invited investigation.

However, competing informal relations do not only have an impact on democratic representation, but also on all spheres of society. The third part of the book, therefore, looks at examples of the role which corruption—as an informal institution—plays in business, education and the administration of condominiums.

Elena Denisova-Schmidt demonstrates that informal practices have a fundamental impact on businesses in Russia and have been standardized to a large degree. At the same time, the formal rules are enforced selectively, not only as a result of weak governance structures, but also partly as a conscious strategy by state actors to put pressure on specific companies.

Eduard Klein and Elvira Leontyeva then examine informal relations and corruption in Russian universities, which they describe as omnipresent. Both highlight the routine aspect of bribing university teachers. Though individual informal relations between students and teachers change regularly as students advance to other courses, the informal rules governing the relationship between student and teacher are quite stable.

Finally, the chapter by Dilorom Akhmedzhanova looks at collective action challenges in the case of responsibility for common goods. In her case study of condominiums with a huge number of flat owners, she demonstrates that the formal rules fail to provide sufficient governance mainly due to a lack of participation. As a large proportion of the owners stays away, minorities can not only dominate decision-making, but they can also engage in manipulations of the formal rules and outright corruption because they are unsupervised.

The contributions in the third section demonstrate that the different spheres of society face similar challenges from the presence of competing informal institutions. Formal governance mechanisms are perverted and, as a result, they fail to deliver common goods, be it democratic decision-making, a law-based business environment, knowledge-based education or efficient housing management. In all cases, actors profiting from the informal institutions develop routines which make related interactions predictable and reduce the moral hurdle for engagement in such interactions.

Although competing informal institutions by definition violate the formal rules, some actors even succeed in getting formal approval for their actions. For this, the formal rules are either intentionally enforced only selectively, thus granting some actors implicit immunity from the application of formal rules, or the formal rules are used to create a situation in which the competing informal rules are not legitimized as such, but the respective actors are locked in. A good example is the political entrepreneurs exploiting ethnic minority rights in Romania. Although their practices are not in line with the ideal of democratic representation, they have changed legislation on ethnic minorities in a way which ensures that they remain the only political representatives of the ethnic minorities, as Andreea Carstocea details in her chapter.

If we finally return to the idea of a continuum running from informal institutions complementing democratic representation to those competing with it, then the case studies in this collection provide ample evidence that any sustainable change in situations marked by high degrees of manipulation and corruption is unlikely to occur overnight as a result of one reform; instead, it is more likely to take place gradually as either the formal rules are strengthened, so that the informal ones become increasingly accommodating, or the informal rules are gradually brought in line with the spirit of the formal ones, so that the former become substitutive.

Part I. Concepts

Eelco Jacobs

2. Basic Public Services and Informal Power: An Analytical Framework for Sector Governance

2.1. Introduction

Since the 1980s, increasing awareness of the severe governance challenges that exist in the public sectors of many developing countries and their effect on human development have thrust state capacity into the spotlight as a new sphere of interest in research.[1] This has provided new ideas of *what* is required to strengthen basic service delivery[2] in specific areas in terms of information transparency, expenditure tracking, management capacity and oversight control. However, the question of *why* these improvements frequently fail to appear, even when seemingly straightforward solutions are available, needs to be further explored. Often these shortcomings are attributed to the black box of political will, but what precisely constitutes this *will*, i.e. the power context[3] that affects public sectors, needs further research in relation to sector governance. This article will seek to offer analytical tools to study this power context with explicit consideration of the role of informal institutions and networks.

This paper argues that informal dimensions of power need to be included in the analysis of sector governance, especially—but not exclusively—in developing countries. An exclusive focus on state structures and bureaucracy, based on the classical Weberian[4] framework of governance with its strict distinction between public and private spheres, cannot address many of the challenges facing the delivery of basic public services. In many developing countries, states lack the institutional and operational

---

1 Evans, Peter B./ Rueschemeyer, Dietrich/ Skocpol, Theda (eds.): Bringing the State Back in. Cambridge: Cambridge University Press, 1985.

2 This paper is concerned with basic services that are partly or wholly delivered, financed or regulated by public agencies. The theory and methodological tools provided therefore mainly, but not exclusively, apply to the water, education and health sectors, which are commonly understood to be the most crucial services for human welfare.

3 Unsworth, Sue: Understanding Pro-Poor Change: a discussion paper. London: Department for International Development, 2001

4 Based on Max Weber's legal-rational ideal type of authority, whereby the public and private realms, with their own guiding principles, are strictly separated. Weber's other ideal type of authority, patrimonialism, which is based on a pre-modern model of power, is heavily dependent on one person in power rather than officeholders. It assumes the presence of a personal, patriarchal ruler whose authority over his followers is unlimited by formal rules and procedures but based on tradition. In contrast to the legal-rational bureaucracy no distinction between private and public domains with due roles or responsibilities exists: 'the system is held together by the oath of loyalty or by kinship ties (often symbolic and fictitious) rather than by a hierarchy of administrative grades and functions'. Clapham, Christopher: Third World Politics: An Introduction. London: Routledge, 1985.

capability to consistently and effectively enforce policy decisions and, more generally, the rule of law throughout the entire national territory.[5] In these cases, there is no sharp distinction between public and private roles.[6] This is a cause for concern because not only does ineffective public, or formal, governance affect the performance of service delivery and ultimately human welfare, but the absence or poor quality of services can also undermine a state's legitimacy in the long term.[7] Given the great significance for both human welfare *and* state legitimacy, the case for a governance approach that incorporates those dimensions of power beyond the formal structures is strong.

This article uses the definition of governance put forth by Brinkerhoff and Bossert[8], who argue that 'Governance is about the rules that distribute roles and responsibilities among societal actors and that shape the interactions among them'. These rules can also be understood as institutions as defined by Douglass North: any form of constraint that human beings devise to shape interaction.[9] It is essential to understand that the rules that shape the game can be both formal(ized) and informal, public or private. Informal and formal institutions co-exist and interweave with one another in all political and bureaucratic systems, albeit to varying degrees. Based on North's definition, institutions shape power relations and their consequences, including '*will*'. This article views accountability as central to power relations. Following this interpretation, formal and informal normative frameworks, to which institutions can be reduced, provide incentives and constraints on action that influence to whom accountability is exercised.

To understand the core of what constitutes accountability, this article uses Kelsall's definition,[10] which implies a relationship between two actors in which A is accountable to B if A takes into account B's wishes, while B can hold A responsible if A ignores B's wishes. This occurs when B relinquishes some degree of power, status or resources to A, which B may withdraw in order to enforce A's responsiveness. Accountability, just like the institutions that guide it, can be formal or informal. Based on this premise, accountability within an ideal type legal-rational institutional framework can be understood along the pillars of delegation, answerability and enforceability. This can be further disaggregated by considering the adequate financing that comes with delegating

---

5   The World Wide Governance Indicators give a good indication of this: Kaufmann, Daniel/ Kraay, Aart/ Mastruzzi, Massimo: Governance Matter VIII: Aggregate and Individual Governance Indicators, 1996–2008. World Bank Policy Research Working Paper 4978, 29 June 2009.

6   Rose-Ackerman, Susan: Corruption and Government: Causes, Consequences and Reform. Cambridge: Cambridge University Press, 1999: p. 91.

7   OECD DAC: Service Delivery in Fragile Situations. Key Concepts, Findings and Lessons, in: Journal of Development, 2008, (vol. 9), no. 3.

8   Brinkerhoff, Derick W./ Bossert, Thomas J.: Health Governance: Concepts, Experience, and Programming Options, Bethesda: Abt Associates Inc. 2008, p. 3.

9   North, Douglass Cecil: Institutions, institutional change, and economic performance. Cambridge University Press, 1990, p. 4

10   Kelsall, Tim: Going with the grain in African development? Africa Power and Politics Programme, 2008, Discussion Paper 1, p. 3

tasks and performance monitoring to judge responsibility.[11] Part of the social contract that defines the cadre mediating accountability between state and society is the delegation of decision-making powers and tax money to politicians with the expectation that basic services are provided. Citizens can sanction their governments—by voting them out of office or, in more extreme cases, by withholding tax payments—in the case of non-compliance.

By definition, the governance of public service delivery in those states where the government is not able or willing to deliver basic public goods and services,[12] despite citizens' expectations and promises in national poverty reduction strategies or during elections, does not conform to this legal-rational ideal type. In fact, in such cases the social contract is broken. This does not imply that governance in the wider definition ceases to exist but rather that informal and often more particularistic governance institutions play a stronger role. Understanding the influence of the accountability relationships that arise from these informal institutions helps to identify stakeholders in sector governance and can explain why people behave differently than what might be expected in ideal type formal governance settings.

An exclusive focus on institutions, however, is not sufficient to explain accountability relations. In cases where (formal and informal) normative frameworks overlap or compete, the mere existence of different institutions does not explain their degree of influence on human action. Institutional and stakeholder analysis should therefore be complemented by the analytical perspective that choice theory offers.[13] This gives insight into the motivation for the choices of norms that humans make.

The central question of this article is therefore: what is the best way to analyse accountability relations in the governance of basic service delivery while taking full account of the mix of informal and formal power that is so typical in these contexts?

To address this question, the article first sketches out the structural features of many developing countries with special reference to the concepts of neo-patrimonialism and clientelism. The role of basic service delivery, which is key to the social contract between the state and society, is given particular consideration with regard to these concepts. Second, suggestions for a model to assess the governance of public services are given. The contours of a multi-step assessment framework involving institutional and stakeholder analysis are drawn and consideration is given to the insights

---

11　Baez-Camargo, Claudia. Accountability for Better Health Care Provision: a framework and guidelines to define, understand and assess accountability in health systems, Basel Institute on Governance Working Paper 10.

12　OECD DAC: Service Delivery in Fragile Situations. Key Concepts, Findings and Lessons, in: Journal of Development, 2008, (vol. 9), no. 3.

13　Booth, David: Elites, Governance and the Public Interest in Africa: Working with the Grain? Africa Power and Politics Programme, 2009, Discussion Paper 6, p. 15.

that rational choice theory offers to come to a closer understanding of stakeholder behaviour.

2.2. Understanding Informal Institutions in Sector Governance

While the fields of political sociology and economy recognize the importance of informal institutions and actors, the nascent health systems literature,[14] as an example of one of the most crucial basic services, has been predominantly concerned with (good) governance, defined in terms of the formal rules and procedures that are associated with effectively carrying out health policy. The literature has provided sophisticated and detailed knowledge of the ways in which the various levels of formal governance can be analysed. With an instrumental perspective on governance mechanisms, it has refined the conceptualization of formal health governance. In addition, serious attention has been paid to the diverse manifestations of corruption that plague the sector, and possible ways to address corruption in terms of technical solutions. Brinkerhoff and Bossert[15] rightly note that the role of non-state actors needs to be considered more closely in the governance of health systems, particularly in contexts where the state fails in its task of providing, regulating or financing basic services. Nevertheless, what is often termed the *political context* (versus the technical dimension) of sector governance remains to be further explored, as an evaluation of donor good practice highlights.[16] This paper attempts to fill that void by outlining an analytical framework that explicitly considers the role of informal institutions, networks and actors in sector governance.

Understanding the importance of informal institutions and their impact on governance in developing countries requires a closer look at the historical and structural development of their states. Without delving into the various ways in which colonization took place across the world, it can be generalized that the process of decolonization in much of the developing world in the past half-century—from Ghana in

---

14   Ruger, Jennifer Prah: Global Health Governance and the World Bank, in: The Lancet, 2007, (vol. 370), no. 9597, pp. 1471–1474; Savedoff, William D.: Transparency and Corruption in the Health Sector: A Conceptual Framework and Ideas for Action in Latin America and the Caribbean. Inter-American Development Bank. Health Technical Note 03/2007; Lewis, Maureen: Governance and Corruption in Public Health Care Systems, Working Paper 78, Center for Global Development, Washington, 2006. Lewis M./ Pettersson, G.: Governance in Health Care Delivery: Raising Performance, Unpublished draft, July 2009; Roberts, Marc, J. et al. Getting Health Reform Right, Oxford: Oxford University Press, 2002; De Savigny, Don/ Adam, Taghreed, (eds.): Systems thinking for health systems strengthening. World Health Organization, Geneva, Switzerland, 2009; Brinkerhoff, Derick W./ Bossert, Thomas, J.: Health Governance: Concepts, Experience, and Programming Options. Bethesda: Abt Associates Inc., 2008; Vian, Taryn: Review of corruption in the health sector: theory, methods and interventions. Health Policy and Planning, 2008.

15   Brinkerhoff, Derick W./ Bossert, Thomas J.: Health Governance: Concepts, Experience, and Programming Options. Bethesda: Abt Associates Inc. 2008.

16   Vlan, Taryn. Corruption in the Health Sector. U4, 2008, no. 10, pp. 31–41.

1957 to the former Soviet republics in 1990–1991—opened up the state as a prize for domestic political competition. With either a scant industrial base or a state monopoly on much of the economy, state control became the quickest route to wealth accumulation. In this process of elite state capture and the *de facto* privatization of many state institutions, the boundary between state and society became largely blurred;[17] this nebulousness has since become a common feature in many developing countries.

Migdal's categorisation of strong societies and weak states[18] captures the seemingly paradoxical situation in many low-income countries effectively. While many states do not effectively enforce their own legislation, their societies (or elements thereof) have strongly resisted state domination or have even managed to infiltrate the state with institutions based on particularism. In effect, the situation can be described as a conflict between (elements of) the state and societal institutions. This leads to a situation characterized as 'dual governance systems'.[19] While the formal system is based on legal-rational provisions, such as judicial structures and constitutions, the informal system is 'based on implicit and unwritten understandings'.[20] Some of the characteristics of this informal system are captured by the concept of 'economy of affection',[21] which highlights the particularist and reciprocal nature of the system:

> Because governance there is extensively reliant on informal relations [...] power does not stem from occupying official positions alone. It comes from the ability to create personal dependencies, from mastering a clientelist form of politics.[22]

Chabal and Daloz reason that because the state in Africa has never actually been institutionalized, 'its formal structure has ill-managed to conceal the patrimonial and particularistic nature of power'.[23] Some even contend that in some African countries the state is not only infiltrated by informal institutions that promote illegal behaviour, but

---

17 Clapham, Christopher: Third World Politics: An Introduction. London: Routledge, 1985.
18 Migdal, Joel S.: Strong Societies and Weak States: State–Society Relations and State Capabilities in the Third World, Princeton: Princeton University Press, 1988.
19 Brinkerhoff, Derick W. and Goldsmith, Arthur A. Clientelism, Patrimonialism and Democratic Governance: An Overview and Framework for Assessment and Programming. Prepared for USAID by Abt Associates Inc. December 2002.
20 Ibid.
21 Hyden, Goran: Informal Institutions, Economy of Affection, and Rural Development, in: Tanzanian Journal of Population Studies and Development, Special Issue: African Economy of Affection, 2004, (vol. 11), no. 2.; Hyden, Goran. Beyond Governance: Bringing Power into Development Policy Analysis, paper presented to the Danida/GEPPA Conference on Power, Politics and Change in Weak States, Copenhagen, 1–2 March 2006, online at www.geppa.dk/files/activi ties/Conference%202006/Goran%20Hyden.pdf; Hyden, Goran: African Politics in Comparative Perspective. Cambridge: Cambridge University Press, 2006; Hyden, Goran: Governance and Poverty Reduction in Africa, 2007, PNAS, (vol. 104), no. 43, pp. 16751–16756; Hyden, Goran: Institutions, Power and Policy Outcomes in Africa. Africa Power and Politics Programme, 2008, Discussion Paper 2.
22 Hyden, Goran Governance and Poverty Reduction in Africa. 2007 PNAS 104 (43): 16751–16756.
23 Chabal, Patrick/ Daloz, Jean-Pascal: Africa Works: Disorder as Political Instrument. Bloomington, Indiana University Press, 1999.

has itself become a vehicle for organized crime.[24] Although much of the relevant literature is centred on Africa, examples can also be found across the newly independent countries of the former Soviet Union as well as in other parts of the world. The predatory elite behaviour and the strong influence of patronage networks on governments found across Central Asia[25] are exemplary.

This brings the argument to the concept of neo-patrimonialism, or modern patrimonialism, which has become commonly used in political science over the past three decades to denote the nature of many contemporary states in the developing world, particularly in Africa.[26] Derived from Weber's ideal types of authority, the term refers to the coexistence of patrimonial and legal-bureaucratic elements constituting the state. Its manifestation can take different forms depending on the local context and is not a typology of political freedom, yet its character typically excludes most liberal democracies. Many neo-patrimonial features can also be found in the large gray hybrid zone of political systems, including many of the 'new polyarchies', but also in some long-enduring polyarchies in Asia, Southern Europe and Latin America.[27] Due to this broad applicability, the term is often criticized for being too much of a catchall concept. However, in this framework it serves to describe a general state of politics in which informal power, often defined by clientelist relations, thrives.[28] Essentially, a

---

24   Bayart, Jean Francois/ Ellis, Stephen/ Hibou, Beatrice: The Criminalization of the State in Africa. Bloomington: Indiana University Press, 1999. See also: Bayart, Jean Francois: The State in Africa: The Politics of the Belly. New York: Longman, 1993.

25   Buisson, Antoine: State-Building, Power-Building and Political Legitimacy: The Case of Post-Conflict Tajikistan, in: China and Eurasia Forum Quarterly, 2007, (vol. 5), no. 4, pp. 115–147; Ilkhamov, Alisher: Neopatrimonialism, interest groups and patronage networks: the impasses of the governance system in Uzbekistan, in: Central Asian Survey, 2007, (vol. 26), no. 1, pp. 65–84; International Crisis Group 2009, Tajikistan: On the Road to Failure. Asia Report 162; Matveeva, Anna: The Perils of Emerging Statehood: Civil War and State Reconstruction in Tajikistan. An Analytical Narrative on State-Making. Crisis States Research Centre 2009, Working Paper 46; Radnitz, Scott: It takes more than a village: mobilisation, networks and the state in Central Asia. PhD Thesis Massachusetts Institute of Technology February, 2007.; Radnitz, Scott/ Wheatly, Jonathan/ Zürcher, Christopher: The Origins of Social Capital. Evidence from a Survey in Post-Soviet Central Asia, in: Comparative Political Studies, 2009, (vol. 42), pp. 707–732.

26   Bratton, Michael/ Van de Walle, Nicolas (eds.): Democratic Experiments in Africa: Regime Transitions in Comparative Perspective, Cambridge: Cambridge University Press, 1997; Brinkerhoff, Derick W./ Goldsmith, Arthur A. Clientelism, Patrimonialism and Democratic Governance: An Overview and Framework for Assessment and Programming. Prepared for USAID by Abt Associates Inc. December 2002; Clapham, Christopher: Third World Politics: An Introduction. London: Routledge, 1985; Eisenstadt, Shmuel N.: Traditional Patrimonialism and Modern Neopatrimonialism. Beverly Hills: Sage Publications, 1973.

27   O'Donnell, Guillermo: Illusions About Consolidation, in: Journal of Democracy, 1996, (vol. 7), no. 2, pp. 34–51; O'Donnell, Guillermo/ Schmitter, Phillipe C.: Transitions from Authoritarian Rule: Tentative Conclusions about Uncertain Democracies. Baltimore: Johns Hopkins University Press, 1986. OECD DAC: Service Delivery in Fragile Situations. Key Concepts, Findings and Lessons, in: Journal of Development, 2008, (vol. 9) no. 3.

28   Brinkerhoff, Derick W./ Goldsmith, Arthur A.: Clientelism, Patrimonialism and Democratic Governance: An Overview and Framework for Assessment and Programming. Prepared for

neo-patrimonial state possesses the basic structures of a modern bureaucracy (albeit often partly symbolic or redundant) but is strongly pervaded by informal networks and traditional rather than legal-rational institutions. The term also helps to explain how formal rules and procedures in the public sector do not always lead to the predicted outputs relevant to human welfare. In many societies based on strong interpersonal relations, the very idea of separating public roles and responsibilities from private obligations—which involve ties of loyalty, friendship and kinship— seems unnatural and impractical.[29] Understanding this challenge is essential because it underpins one of the basic problems that characterize service delivery in many developing countries: weak formal governance.

Because the state and its institutions were originally imposed on many colonized countries from outside and mainly used for the benefit of a small elite group, no 'merging between state and society as common expressions of a set of shared values'[30] took place. The assumption that state institutions such as health systems 'are not only producers of health or health care but they are also the purveyors of a wider set of societal values and norms'[31] therefore does not hold in these contexts. Ideally, 'people value health and welfare systems both because they satisfy their own interests through them and because such systems allow them to contribute to the social good'.[32] However, in a context where the state is viewed with suspicion and (the revenues for) its institutions are regularly manipulated by private interest, entities such as health or water systems lose their role of a cherished public service. This scenario is especially common in states where the government seriously lacks legitimacy among and accountability toward the general population and service delivery is grossly inadequate.[33] These shortcomings also constitute the heart of state fragility, which 'arises primarily from weaknesses in the dynamic political process through which citizens' expectations of the state and state expectations of citizens are reconciled and brought into equilibrium with the state's capacity to deliver services'.[34] Jones, Chandran et al. argue that this social contract, i.e. the interplay between capacity, will and legitimacy, is the key to understanding state fragility. Basic services are a chief component of this social contract. It therefore stands to reason that governance concerns in this field have wider

---

USAID by Abt Associates Inc. December 2002, p. 6
29	Rose-Ackerman, Susan: Corruption and Government: Causes, Consequences and Reform. Cambridge: Cambridge University Press, 1999, p. 106.
30	Clapham, Christopher: Third World Politics: An Introduction. London: Routledge, 1985, p. 42.
31	Gilson, Lucy: Trust and the development of health care as a social institution, Social Science & Medicine, 2003, (vol. 56), no. 7, p. 1461.
32	Ibid.
33	Conversely, one could argue that improving basic services can contribute to state-building and the enhancement of state legitimacy. See: OECD DAC: Service Delivery in Fragile Situations. Key Concepts, Findings and Lessons. Journal of Development, 2008, (vol. 9), no. 3.
34	Jones, B./ R. Chandran, et al. Concepts and Dilemmas of State Building in Fragile Situations: From Fragility to Resilience. OECD/DAC, 2008, Discussion Paper.

implications for the resilience of states, as failing public service delivery may serve to further undermine trust in formal institutions and thus perpetuate a downward spiral of deteriorating state performance and legitimacy.

As 'clientelism is indeed the application of the principles of neo-patrimonialism to relationships between superiors and inferiors',[35] this particular phenomenon requires extra attention. The concept of clientelism implies dyadic, inherently unequal but reciprocal relationships between public office holders and followers, supporters or dependents. They may be legal or not, may involve more dynamic and complex networks with more than two actors involved, may be semi-institutionalized and strictly clan-based, or may be merely motivated by political and/or economic interests. However, according to Kaufman,[36] clientelist relations always exhibit the following characteristics:

> (a) the relationship occurs between actors of unequal power and status;
> (b) it is based on the principle of reciprocity; that is, it is a self-regulating form of interpersonal exchange, the maintenance of which depends on the return that each actor expects to obtain by rendering goods and services to the other and which ceases once the expected rewards fail to materialize;
> (c) the relationship is particularistic and private, anchored only loosely in public law or community norms.

In essence, clientelism and accountability share a strong element of reciprocity in power relations. Therefore, some clientelist relations can be considered to contain elements of informal and particularistic vertical accountability. In line with the basic definition of accountability in this article,[37] the degree of accountability in patron-client relationships depends on the degree of extortion and space for withdrawal or choice on the side of the client (the exit option in accountability[38]). Clearly, many clientelist relations that are unequal by definition, merely function under heavy intimidation and the lack of choices on the side of the client. Still, cases of competitive clientelism,[39] whereby clients 'choose' their patron and patrons compete for client support, suggest that clientelist networks can be centred around principles of accountability. Seeing clientelism as a potential form of vertical accountability can serve to explain how accountability

35 Clapham, Christopher: Third World Politics: An Introduction. London: Routledge, 1985, p. 55.
36 Kaufman, Robert: The Patron-Client Concept and Macro-Politics: Prospects and Problems, Comparative Studies in Society and History, 1974, (vol. 16), no. 3, p. 285.
37 A relationship between two actors in which A is accountable to B if A takes into account B's wishes, while B can hold A responsible if A ignores B's wishes. This occurs when B relinquishes some degree of power, status or resources to A, which B may withdraw in order to enforce A's responsiveness..
38 For an excellent conceptual analyses on accountability and its voice and exit options, see: Paul, S.: Accountability in Public Services: Exit, Voice and Control, in: World Development, 1992, (vol. 20), no. 7, pp. 1047–1060; Baez-Camargo, Claudia: Accountability for Better Health Care Provision: A Framework and Guidelines to Define, Understand and Assess Accountability in Health Systems, Basel Institute on Governance Working Paper 10.
39 Denissen, Ingeborg: New Forms of Political Inclusion: Competitive Clientelism. The case of Iztapalapa, Mexico City. MinBuZa: A Rich Menu for the Poor: Food for Thought on Effective Aid Policies Essay Series, 19 June 2009, no. 33.

can be skewed beyond relations that are formal, public and for all to see. The inherently unequal relationship between the (potential) user and provider makes public services especially vulnerable to the influence of clientelist networks, often described as corruption.[40] In fact, clientelist networks can so deeply pervade politics and society that they often come to be regarded as the only means to access supposedly public services. In an ethnographic study[41] on the effect of clientelism on basic service delivery in Argentina, Auyero described how urban slum dwellers depend on their clientelist relationships for physical survival. State provisions, such as the *Programa Materno-Infantil*, are interpreted as a favour granted by benefactors or a tool through which to win support rather than a rights-based service for which officeholders can be held accountable based on their position. The expectation that personal ties are indeed crucial for meeting even basic needs helps to explain the resilience of such clientelist networks.

The impact of clientelist networks on the governance of basic services can have a substantial effect at all levels. At the macro level, an example would be the allocation of more spending for basic services to a particular district in which an important official has a strong constituency or political interest. This type of clientelism, which concerns the more general implementation of policy, can distort the allocation of resources according to national poverty reduction strategies or stand in the way of public sector reform. At the micro level, clientelism could take the form of preferential access to a health facility or school as a result of good relations with the relevant doctor/teacher in exchange for support in the community. In this case, those involved aim for direct private gain and a one-on-one link between patron and client can be discerned. Taking into account these and other examples given later, it becomes clear that clientelist networks can pervade democratic procedures and negatively affect basic services' influence on responsiveness, efficiency and equity. In addition, these networks can play a crucial role in explaining specific sector outcomes that are governance related. For instance, although there have been several studies on informal payments or other manifestations of corruption in water, education and health, relatively little attention has been paid to clientelism as an underlying mechanism. Various types of informal payments could be a possible manifestation of a patron–client relationship. Because informal payments are at the discretion of the service provider, variation can take the form of who is charged and by how much. A long-term doctor–patient or student–teacher relationship may lend itself to a more subtle type of reciprocity that is common in clientelist relations. This could help to explain how those who cannot afford informal or co-payments in regular healthcare, education or water services are still able to obtain access to medical help, education or water; conversely, those who might have

---

40   For a good analysis of the reasons for the high corruption vulnerability of the Health Sector, see: Vlan, Taryn. Corruption in the Health Sector. U4, 2008, no. 10, p. 5.

41   Auyero, Javier: The Logic of Clientelism in Argentina: An Ethnographic Account, in: Latin American Research Review, 2001, (vol. 35), no. 3, pp. 55–81.

the financial means for treatment might lack the proper connections and thus fail to gain adequate access to the best doctors, schools or water resources because patron–client relationships are ultimately more important than money. Clientelist networks can also underlie corruption in drug procurement, tendering, payment and supply,[42] as a case study in China illustrates.[43] In education, licensing, grading, passing and even entry to schools are often dependent on informal relations.[44] Another way in which informal networks can facilitate corruption or infringe equity of access to health care for patients is through referral by health workers to benefactors within the network, as witnessed in a Kazakh case.[45] In the water sector, comparable phenomena have been observed in terms of informal payments and illegal connections[46]

Although informal institutions in neo-patrimonial states can be very influential, this does not dictate whether their aggregate effect on basic service delivery is positive or negative per se. In fact, informal institutions are oftentimes deeply rooted in local values and can be more acceptable and hence effective in reaching societal goals. Despite their shortcomings, the traditional reconciliation rituals that have followed many of the civil wars in Sub-Saharan Africa constitute cases of informal institutions offering a framework for justice, peacemaking or addressing war trauma that is often more effective and acceptable than formal channels such as the judiciary or investigative committees.[47] Donor agencies have even started to use mahallas, traditional community councils in Tajikistan, to strengthen governance of basic services at the local level from the bottom up.[48] As extensive research in anthropology suggests,[49] the custom of gift-giving can play an important role in human interactions

42   Lewis, Maureen: Governance and Corruption in Public Health Care Systems, Center for Global Development, 2006, Working Paper 78.

43   Bloom, Gerard/ Han, Leiya/ Li, Xiang: How health workers earn a living in China, Brighton: Institute for Development Studies, 2000, IDS Working Paper 108, p. 24.

44   Heyneman, S. P.: Education and Corruption, in: International Journal of Educational Development, 2004, (vol. 24), no. 6, pp. 637–648.

45   Thompson, R./ Rittmann, J.: A Review of Specialty Provision: Urology Services, in: Thompson, Ensor, Tim/ J. Rittmann (eds.): Health Care Reform in Kazakstan, compendium of papers prepared for the World Bank Health Reform Technical Assistance Project, 1995–1996, 1997.

46   Davis, Jennifer: Corruption in Public Service Delivery: Experience from South Asia's Water and Sanitation Sector, in: World Development, 2004, (vol. 32), no. 1, pp. 53–71.

47   Huyse, Luc/ Salter, Mark: Traditional Justice and Reconciliation after Violent Conflict: Learning from African Experiences, Stockholm: IDEA, 2008.

48   For one of the longest lasting and most intensive projects with community development in Tajikistan, see: Aga Khan Development Network. Rural Development Activities in Tajikistan. http://www.akdn.org/tajikistan_rural.asp accessed 30 November 2010. Freizer, Sabine. Tajikistan local self governance: a potential bridge between government and civil society. In di Martino, Luigi (2004) Tajikistan at a Crossroads: the Politics of Decentralisation. Cimera: Geneva.

49   Komter, Aafke: Social Solidarity and The Gift, Cambridge: Cambridge University Press, 2004; Lévi-Strauss, Claude: The Principle of Reciprocity, in: Komter, Aafke (eds.): The Gift: An Interdisciplinary Perspective, Amsterdam: Amsterdam University Press, 1996, (Orig. pub. 1949.); Mauss, Marcel: The Gift: The Form and Reason for Exchange in Archaic Societies. London: Routledge. 1990 (Orig. pub. 1923.).

across different societies. Its exact implications for the functioning of the public sector are varied; in the private sector, gift-giving and the cherishing of important relations that it symbolizes is common and often well accepted.[50] In the often partly privatized health, education and water sectors, the same activities are therefore often not questioned, even when the sector is publicly regulated. One of the commonly used words for bribe in Tanzania, *asante*, sums up the confusion: the word also means 'thank you' in Kiswahili. Ultimately, distinguishing between a gift, a bribe and a tip depends considerably on how explicit or direct the reciprocity is in the relationship; the implications may be very subtle. The appeasement of diverse groups in a country and communication between 'centre and periphery' or a powerholder and his base can be seen as the positive effects of clientelism, as a classic case study in Senegal shows. [51] Moreover, clientelism does not necessarily exclude legal-rational or democratic institutions from having voice and participation. In its essence, constituent services performed by congressmen in the United States are an example of *de facto* institutionalized clientelism. Informal institutions and networks operating within them can, however, challenge the democratic principles in decision-making by virtue of their exclusive, particularistic and parochial character. Such institutions are based on personalist or parochial interests rather than universal principles and are less clear, transparent and reliable. Because of this, clientelist relations are easily manipulated and the client can suffer exploitation.[52] Informal institutions should therefore be taken into account in efforts to strengthen basic service delivery as intervening variables that can offer alternative routes for accountability; however, they may also skew existing formal channels of voice and participation. In any case, it must be recognized that informal institutions are part of the governance mechanism in many developing countries and are often very persistent and durable. While recognizing their importance, it might also be possible to find informal institutions that are conducive to development;[53] building upon their potential might be the most productive approach to strengthening the public sector in these contexts.

---

50   Rose-Ackerman, Susan. Corruption and Government: Causes, Consequences and Reform. Cambridge: Cambridge University Press, 1999, p. 91

51   Coulon, Christian/ Cruise O'Brien, Donal B.: Senegal, in: Cruise O'Brien, Donal B./ Dunn, John/ Rathbone, Richard (eds.): Contemporary West African States, Cambridge: Cambridge University Press, 1989, here: p. 150.

52   Brinkerhoff, Derick W./ Goldsmith, Arthur A.: Clientelism, Patrimonialism and Democratic Governance: An Overview and Framework for Assessment and Programming. Prepared for USAID by Abt Associates Inc. December, 2002, pp. 5, 9.

53   Booth, David: Elites, Governance and the Public Interest in Africa: Working with the Grain? Africa Power and Politics Programme 2009, Discussion Paper 6; Kelsall, Tim: Going with the Grain in African development? Africa Power and Politics Programme 2008, Discussion Paper 1; Kelsall, Tim: Game-theoretic Models, Social Mechanisms and Public Goods in Africa: A Methodological Discussion. Africa Power and Politics Programme 2009 Discussion Paper 7. De Sardan, Olivier/ Pierre, Jean: Researching the Practical Norms of Real Governance in Africa. Africa Power and Politics Programme 2009, Discussion Paper 5.

It should be clear that in many developing countries, governance does not solely take place through formal institutions. Neo-patrimonial forms of governance often have a considerable and distorting impact on the functioning of bureaucracies and the delivery of basic services. Informal institutions and networks are relevant to the assessment of the quality of governance because they may adversely affect the equity, responsiveness and efficiency of basic service delivery by reproducing societal inequalities within the public sector, which is officially designed to work in an anonymous, egalitarian way. Clientelism is one of the more pronounced manifestations of neo-patrimonialism, especially in the case of basic services, where unequal relations are inevitable and the costs—both human and financial—are high. Clientelist relations are often behind many symptoms of problematic governance, such as informal payments, false accreditation, drug leakages, overprescription in health care and procurement fraud. To address these challenges, it is therefore crucial to be aware of these underlying, informal networks of reciprocity to which clientelism can be reduced. Moreover, understanding the interplay between formal and informal power institutions, networks and actors yields insight into the dynamics of accountability in the public sector; this information can be useful for designing interventions. However, the question remains: what the best way is to assess the quality of sector governance?

2.3. Assessing Sector Governance and Informal Dimensions of Power: A Discussion of Methodology and Approach

Institutions and actors beyond those that are formal(ized) matter greatly, but they are by definition difficult to assess openly. Not only is their place in society not formally regulated, but it is also fluid, dynamic and particularistic. Informal power institutions, actors and networks are best mapped in combination with their formal counterparts because the two inevitably interact with, pervade or serve as alternatives for each other. This approach yields a more comprehensive picture of governance challenges than does an analysis that merely concentrates on capacity gaps. More practically, this paper suggests an approach using institutionalism combined with rational choice to gain insight into the crucial interplay between social structures and human actions in the field of sector governance.

By considering the strengths and weaknesses of different perspectives, each of which places a different emphasis on institutions and agents, it is possible to capitalize on the value that they can bring to an understanding of governance in practice. This ultimately requires a multi-step process that recognizes the different analytical loci of each approach. Such a multi-step assessment framework would enable an understanding of institutions that either guide or constrain behaviour; it would also provide insight into the motivation of different actors for the choice of particular norms/

rules/institutions in the governance of basic services, including their variation across time and space. This combination of approaches can ultimately provide the points of entry for strengthening the accountability relations that are productive in the delivery of basic public services such as education, health care and water.

Governance and accountability in settings where the legal-rational concept of the state does not apply, can be analysed from different perspectives. The frameworks that are used in such analyses in political sociology typically emphasize social structures and functions, such as 'institutions', or individual actions and agency, captured in methodological individualism and choice theory. Many scholars, for example Parssons[54] (1951) and Giddens[55] (1984) to name just two, have attempted to overcome this dichotomy, and the debate will continue to develop in sociology.[56] For the study of governance, it is important to consider the differences in the theoretical traditions if methodological inconsistency is to be avoided. Likewise, a clear conceptual delineation must be made between institutions, stakeholders and actors—along with an understanding of the connections between them.

Referring back to North,[57] an institution can be defined as a framework that places normative constraints and incentives on the behaviour of agents. Agents, in turn, can be human individuals or organizations/networks pursuing particular interests.[58] If decision-making on a particular issue concerns them, agents can become stakeholders—literally, agents who hold a certain interest (stake), big or small, in the issue. One institution can theoretically be dominant in constraining and incentivizing the behaviour of a whole organization and thereby set the norms for accountable behaviour in a certain setting. However, as has been argued before, in reality the variation within organizations is often large and multiple, formal and informal institutions play a role in the variety of accountable relations between people.

Attempts at constructing more comprehensive governance mapping tools have come from both academia and the donor community, with varying degrees of practical applicability. With different purposes in mind, the premises, emphasis, focus and scope of the given analytical frameworks differ, as well as the degree to which they

---

54 Parssons, Talcott/ Shills, Edward E.: Toward a General Theory of Action. Theoretical Foundations for the Social Sciences. New Brunswick, NJ: Transaction Publishers, Abridged edition, 2001.

55 Giddens, Anthony: The Constitution of Society, Cambridge: Polity Press, 1984.

56 This article does not aim to explicitly position itself in this debate, nor re-evaluate Emile Durkheim's structuralist-functionalism, Weber's social action theory or the large body of sociological theory that these classics in sociology have inspired. However, the continuing, albeit often latent, influence of their approaches must be recognized and considered in the search for theoretically consistent tools to assess governance of basic services in general and health systems in particular.

57 North, Douglass Cecil: Institutions, Institutional Change, and Economic Performance. Cambridge University Press, 1990.

58 Warrener, Debbie: The Drivers of Change Approach. Overseas Development Institute. November, 2004, Synthesis Paper 3, p. 8.

strive at an objective or normative assessment. Lastly, the use of these tools for comparative or case study research also varies.[59]

A distinction between mapping tools for entire countries and those that are more applicable to sectoral analysis can be made, although some tools can be used for both purposes. Examples of the tried and tested tools best equipped for country-level analysis are USAID's Governance and Democracy Assessment and the World Bank's Governance Matters, CPIA and Country Diagnostic Tools. These provide valuable insight into a country's structural situation, within which basic service delivery functions, and into the institutional features that shape the rules of the game. Their methodology is fixed and systematic, which yields results on institutional patterns that are easily comparable.[60] However, because the results are so broad, further research is needed to answer in greater detail the questions of *why* sectors operate the way they do and *who* holds influence over this process. This requires a closer look first of all at the character of institutions and secondly at the positioning of stakeholders in relation to the institutions as well as to each other.

Examples of analytical tools from the donor community that pay specific attention to the functions of institutions, both formal and informal, include DFID's Drivers of Change,[61] the EU's Sector Governance[62] and SIDA's Power Analysis.[63] The analytical frameworks of these tools are methodologically flexible, incorporating relevant results from different types of studies; this approach increases the understanding of specific contexts but can hinder comparative analysis.[64]

A common feature of many institutional approaches is a functionalist interest in the sources of power. Where and how is it exercised?[65] It takes governance functions as its starting point, which facilitates an analysis of the role that different, state and non-state, actors play in fulfilling them. Furthermore, there is recognition that governance functions are contested, specifically when it comes to public services, even

---

59   Nash, Robert/ Hudson, Alan/ Lutrell, Cecilia: Mapping Political Content: A Toolkit for Civil Society Organisations, Overseas Development Institute, 2006.
60   Schiffer, Eva/ Waale, Douglas: Tracing Power and Influence in Networks, IFPRI 2008, Discussion Paper 00772, p. 2.
61   Warrener, Debbie: The Drivers of Change Approach. Overseas Development Institute, November 2004, Synthesis Paper 3, p. 9.
62   Boesen, Niels: Analysing and Addressing Governance in Sector Operations. European Commission, November 2008, Tools and Methods Series. Reference Document 4.
63   Bjuremalm, Helena: Power Analysis—Experiences and Challenges, Swedish International Development Agency (SIDA), Stockholm, 2006.
64   Schiffer, Eva/ Waale, Douglas: Tracing Power and Influence in Networks, IFPRI 2008, Discussion Paper 00772, p. 2.
65   Boesen, Niels: Analysing and Addressing Governance in Sector Operations. European Commission, November 2008, Tools and Methods Series, Reference Document 4.

within Europe and North America. This leads to the case for a view of non-state governance actors as equal to state actors in fulfilling governance functions.[66]

In the study of informal institutions, there is a risk of falling into the primordialist, culturalist or traditionalist trap[67] by generalizing about a whole region or viewing institutions as hereditary, fixed and constant over time. In reality, institutions are not static, but vary across time and space. Even though institutions centred on ethnicity, family and religion play a large role in many societies and have proven durable over time,[68] their degree of construction and instrumentalization by elites[69] must also be considered. Accordingly, some scholars use the distinction between official and practical norms to analyse the situation being studied with a greater sensitivity to the normative diversity that can exist in societies.[70] While official norms are based on formal institutions, practical norms can be the particular applications of informal institutions to any decision that an agent encounters in a situation. Interestingly, however, even intricate knowledge of the character of institutions does not fully explain its influence or the ultimate normative choices that agents make and neither does it yield an understanding into the ways in which the agents' actions have shaped the character of the institutions. Ultimately, an analysis of institutions tends to remain largely descriptive. The central questions remaining beyond this analysis are therefore: what motivates actors' choice of norms and how do their actions shape institutional outcomes?

Any attempt to answer the question of why actors choose to follow particular norms needs to be grounded in an understanding of individual behaviour, or *action*. Stakeholder mapping and analysis can help to illuminate the foundations of this action. This approach can be described as a set of tools to discover who the most relevant formal and informal actors are with regards to a specific situation or issue by carefully considering their interests, intentions and inter-relations. This mapping allows one to 'develop an understanding of—and possibly identify opportunities for influencing—how decisions are taken in a particular context'[71] and thus provides insight into actor behaviour. Choice and political economy theory exercises, such as game-theo-

---

66   Draude, Anke: How to Capture Non-Western Forms of Governance. In Favour of An Equivalence Functionalist Observation in Areas of Limited Statehood, SFB Working Paper Series 2, January 2007, pp. 1–16.

67   Booth, David: Elites, Governance and the Public Interest in Africa: Working with the Grain? Africa Power and Politics Programme 2009, Discussion Paper 6, p. 15.

68   Kelsall, Tim: Going with the grain in African development? Africa Power and Politics Programme 2008, Discussion Paper 1.

69   Chabal, Patrick / Daloz, Jean-Pascal: Africa Works: Disorder as Political Instrument. Bloomington: Indiana University Press, 1999, p. 2.

70   De Sardan, Olivier/ Pierre, Jean: Researching the Practical Norms of Real Governance in Africa, Africa Power and Politics Programme 2009, Discussion Paper 5.

71   Brugha, R./ Varvasovsky, Z.: Stakeholder Analysis: A Review. Health Policy and Planning, 2000, (vol. 15), no. 3, p. 239. Brugha, R./ Varvasovsky, Z.: How to do (or not to do)… A Stakeholder analysis, in: Health Policy and Planning, 2000, (vol. 15), no. 3, pp. 338–345.

retical models, can be included in order to examine the choices made by stakehold-ers more closely.[72] The element of perceived costliness in choices, whether material, psychological, social or moral, is at the heart of choice theory in the social sciences, which assume that individuals will always choose the least costly route to satisfy their perceived self interest.

The element of perception in the definition of self-interest and the possibility of self-interest involving more than just material gain necessarily complicate the appli-cability of the theory. Furthermore, the rational choice assumptions that 1) individ-uals are forward-looking in their behavioural choices and 2) individuals act consist-ently over time[73] can be challenged in some instances, as can all general approaches to human action. Nevertheless, when complemented by a thorough understanding of the relevant normative frameworks, careful consideration of choice theory's under-lying principles regarding human action can yield deep insight into power relations.

Stakeholder mapping and analysis can help to gain firsthand insight into the rel-evant power relations at play. This approach can be described as a set of tools to dis-cover who the most relevant formal and informal actors are with regard to a specific situation or issue by carefully considering their interests, intentions and inter-rela-tions. This mapping allows one to 'develop an understanding of—and possibly iden-tify opportunities for influencing—how decisions are taken in a particular context'[74] and thus provides an insight into actor behaviour. Oft-used elements of stakeholder mapping are game-theoretical models. Game-theoretical analysis has its origin in applied mathematics and is part of choice theory in social science research. The value of applying mathematical models in an effort to understand societal phenomena is that they can map strategy based on the combination of choices that exist for a vari-ety of agents. For example, in Nash equilibriums, one of the classic game situations, the goal of achieving maximum gain is a choice between competition or cooperation with trust as an important element.

However, many real-life situations are too complex to map in a mathematical model, particularly when the situation concerns a choice for rules or institutions.[75] This is the paradox of game theory, which ultimately wants to understand how a game works given a variety of structural rules. Still, it is possible to put some of the underly-

---

72   World Bank website, On Stakeholder Analysis. Last Accessed 31 May 2010: http://web.world
     bank.org/WBSITE/EXTERNAL/TOPICS/EXTPUBLICSECTORANDGOVERNANCE/EXTANTICORRUP
     TION/0,,contentMDK:20638051~pagePK:210058~piPK:210062~theSitePK:384455~isCURL:Y,00.
     html
73   Becker, G.: Nobel Lecture: The Economic Way of Looking at Behavior, in: The Journal of Political
     Economy, 1993, (vol. 101), no. 3, p. 402.
74   Brugha, R./Varvasovsky, Z.: Stakeholder analysis: a review, in: Health Policy and Planning, 2000,
     (vol. 15), no. 3, p. 239. Brugha, R./Varvasovsky, Z.: How to do (or not to do)... A Stakeholder anal-
     ysis, in: Health Policy and Planning, 2000, (vol. 15), no. 3, pp. 338–345.
75   Ostrom, E.: Understanding Institutional Diversity. Princeton, NJ: Princeton University Press: 2005.

ing principles to use in the analysis of power relations. In short, the argument is that the degree of difficulty of exclusion of use and the subtractability of a good are the axes along which four types of goods can be classified: toll goods, private goods, public goods and common pool resources.[76]

Subtractability refers to the extent to which one person's use of a good or resource limits its use by others. If a good or resource is scarce, its subtractability is generally higher than when it is seemingly abundant or unlimited. Excludability is the extent to which people can be prevented from using a good or resource. These two factors largely determine the stake that people perceive themselves as having in a given situation as well as the extent to which they (can) compete for influence. For example, official positions high up in the hierarchy of a low-income country's bureaucracy allow for potentially greater access to scarce financial resources. If internal, or managerial, accountability within a sector is weak, it becomes easy to withhold these resources from the public, i.e. to adhere to the official institutional norm, but to reserve the public resources for personal or parochial use.

Given the high excludability and subtractability of financial resources in a low-income country, competition for (access to people in) high official positions is intense. This not only explains elite state capture, and the subsequent organization of state apparatuses as milk cows, but also sheds light on society's perceptions of clientelism and patronage, which can even take on a formally institutionalized shape. In the case of water services, their high subtractability but low excludability leads to the free rider or tragedy of the commons problem that is associated with common-pool resources. Unless strict monitoring and enforcement systems, in other words elements of excludability, are built in, it remains more beneficial to free-ride than to follow the formal regulations and pay for a service or good. A factor heavily influenced by excludability is the direction in which accountability is exercised. On the assumption that people faced with multiple choices would opt for the one that best satisfies their own perceived self-interest, it follows that people exercise accountability to those who hold most power over their status, career, access to resources or remuneration in a job, which does not necessarily need to be their official boss or the primary stakeholder. A doctor whose salary and position depends on the patient's satisfaction is more likely to be responsive to their needs than one whose salary and position is unquestioned and secured by a political friend in the ministry of health. Similarly, if child benefits depend on school attendance, teachers acquire a very strong position, and parents will be willing to relinquish power or resources to them in exchange for access to the benefits. This element of excludability also highlights the importance of clientelism, potentially skewing accountability away from those formally outlined. The actor with

---

76   Ostrom, E.: Understanding Institutional Diversity. Princeton, NJ: Princeton University Press: 2005: p. 24.

the power to exclude potential (groups of) care seekers or users from accessing a service holds great power. In turn, clients can also lever their power, especially when political competition is at stake.[77] The potential 'excluder' should therefore be considered as the strong power wielder, especially in cases of conditional cash transfers that are gaining in popularity among donors and policymakers. These examples illustrate how subtractability and excludability can help identify stakeholders in a given situation, including how they exercise accountability with each other, and facilitate an understanding of the prominence and character of the relevant institutions.

Stakeholder mapping and analysis has its roots in management and programmatic decision-making[78] and is applied in a wide variety of disciplines and situations. Because of the consequent absence of a single methodology, its results can be mixed and greatly depend on the purpose, time and context. A good research design needs to clarify these factors from the start, however. Because institutions and stakeholders cannot be strictly separated, their mappings and analyses should complement one another. Networks or organizations that function within institutional norms as a unit can, especially in an analysis with a large scope, be considered stakeholders. However, it must be stressed again that individual actors working within the normative framework of a single formal institution often still respond to other, possibly informal, institutions. In sum, an awareness of the normative frameworks at play is crucial because it sets the parameters within which stakeholders act.

The composition of a definite framework for a stakeholder analysis will have to depend on the institutional mapping that needs to be included and, most importantly, the precise issue under scrutiny. In this kind of problem-driven research, methodological adaptability is always a must.

2.4. Conclusions

Many developing countries do not approximate the ideal type of legal-rational governance. However, many donors working on sector governance continue to merely focus on formal governance institutions and actors in their attempts to understand the existing challenges in the governance of basic services. Informal dimensions of power remain under-researched and are insufficiently recognized in donor policy. This article constitutes an attempt to contribute to this debate with a framework of the analysis of sector governance.

---

77   Denissen, Ingeborg: New Forms of Political Inclusion: Competitive Clientelism. The case of Iztapalapa, Mexico City. MinBuZa: A Rich Menu for the Poor: Food for Thought on Effective Aid Policies Essay Series, 2009, no. 33.

78   Nash, Robert/ Hudson, Alan/ Lutrell, Cecilia: Mapping Political Context: A Toolkit for Civil Society Organisations. Overseas Development Institute, 2006.

As governance can be conceptualized in terms of the formulation and operationalization of rules and procedures that facilitate and constrain societal interaction, it should be clear that governance can be both formal and informal. Because of their large impact on the quality of human life, basic services are seen as a public—and therefore formal—good in most countries. Since states in many developing countries fail in the governance of this basic service, the importance of informal institutions and actors is even greater. In these cases, neo-patrimonial forms of rule dominate, which reproduces societal inequalities in the public sphere. Clientelist relations and other personalistic modes of governance become essential for access to education, health care and clean water. An understanding of these mechanisms is therefore crucial to acquiring a full picture of the challenges in the governance of basic services.

Any sector governance assessment needs to focus on both institutions and agents, with the recognition that these can be both formal and informal. Formal and informal dimensions of power are best analysed in combination because both kinds of institutions often interweave or compete, and agents can perform different roles at the same time. An understanding of the relevant informal institutions in addition to the formal rules and procedures reveals much about the underlying causes for the performance of systems set up for basic service delivery, but ultimately does not suffice to explain fully the behaviour of actors in different settings. Therefore, a consideration of the principles of choice theory can be instrumental in analysing the composition of stakeholder networks and the nature of the individual relations within them.

The discussion on sector governance and informal dimensions of power presented in this article represents an initial effort to sketch the contours for an analytical framework. The practical utility of such a framework in assessing governance-related problems in basic service delivery requires empirical research, which will undoubtedly generate new hypotheses on the role of (informal) institutions and actors in different settings.

3. Conflict of Interest as a Research-Analytical Category

3.1. Introduction

Contrary to common understanding, a conflict of interest (COI) is not a situation in which two different actors have conflicting interests. According to one of the best-known definitions, offered by Michael Davis,

> [a] conflict of interest is a situation in which some person P (whether an individual or corporate body) stands in a certain relation to one or more decisions. On the standard view, P has a conflict of interest if, and only if, (1) P is in a relationship with another requiring P to exercise judgment in the other's behalf and (2) P has a (special) interest tending to interfere with the proper exercise of judgment in that relationship.[1]

More succinctly, Nobel Prize-winning economist George J. Stigler defines COI as arising 'whenever one man is an agent for another'.[2] Put differently, whenever one person or institution is charged with acting in the interest of another party, the temptation to pursue private or third party interests will emerge. COI can thus arise whenever people are forced to trust each other, and trust can always be violated. It is also possible to think of COI as a situation of 'double loyalty', whereby one 'should pursue goals which in the given circumstances cannot be achieved simultaneously'.[3]

The aim of this article is to offer a critical review of the concept of COI, primarily as it is understood and applied in the field of legal studies. We argue that when couched in strictly legal terms, COI loses much of its power and promise as a research-analytical category. A more nuanced, sociological view would broaden the conceptual scope and help to uncover obvious and potentially destructive conflicts of interest that the narrow legal definition would fail to detect. In this vein, we try to establish a link between COI and the phenomena of corruption, nepotism, illegal lobbying and the revolving-door syndrome. Finally, we develop the concept of a structural COI involving key state institutions and attempt to apply it to the study of contemporary countries in Central Eastern Europe.

---

1   Davis, Michael: Introduction, in: Davis, Michael/ Stark, Andrew (eds.): Conflict of Interest in the Professions, Oxford, New York: Oxford University Press, 2001, pp. 3–19, here: p. 8.
2   Stigler, George J.: The Economics of Conflict of Interest, in: Journal of Political Economy, 1967 (Vol. 75), no. 1, pp. 100–101, here: p. 100.
3   Lewicka-Strzałecka, Anna: Teoretyczne i praktyczne aspekty identyfikacji i ograniczania konfliktu interesów, in: Węgrzecki, Adam (ed.): Konflikt interesów – konflikt wartości, Cracow: Wydawnictwo Akademii Ekonomicznej, 2005, pp. 7–23, here: p. 7.

3.2. Legal Definitions of COI

At the beginning of this brief discussion, it is necessary to distinguish between actual and potential COI. Again, Michael Davis offers a useful definition of the two forms:

> A conflict of interest is potential if, and only if, P has a conflict of interest with respect to a certain judgment but is not yet in a situation where he must (or, at least, should) make that judgment. Potential conflicts of interest, like time bombs, may or may not go off. A conflict of interest is actual if, and only if, P has a conflict of interest with respect to a certain judgment and is in a situation where he must (or, at least, should) make that judgment.[4]

Although potential COI may seem more innocuous than actual COI, it can be just as destructive. For example, it is equally capable of undermining trust in public institutions.

The legal difficulties in pinning down the nature of COI stem mainly from the elusive character of the phenomenon. Two factors contribute to the conceptual haziness: first, merely acting in the circumstances of a COI cannot be treated and sanctioned as wrong per se; numerous COI can and are solved with the common good in mind. This, however, is strictly related to the second difficulty: a COI is a state of mind, a psychological construct, rather than a concrete, tangible entity.[5] Obviously, mental perceptions and intentions cannot be scrutinized by any external authority.

However, even a third party's *perception* that an agent, e.g. a public official, has conflicting interests can have real consequences, similar or identical to the consequences of an actual COI. Many authors think that a possible (or potential) COI is in fact tantamount to an actual COI in terms of its negative consequences.[6] By this logic, a COI could be said to exist even when there is merely a *possibility* that a public official could pursue private interests instead of performing his or her duties, regardless of what actually occurs. A way to solve this dilemma would be to talk in terms of acting *in the situation* of a COI, or *in the circumstances* of a COI, rather than of actual or potential COI.

The elusive nature of COI is reflected in the legal approach toward regulating it. Michael Davis argues that much of the legal thinking about COI is based on the notion that one cannot be punished merely for acting in a situation where there are conflicting interests: 'Having a conflict of interest is not like being a thief or holding a grudge. One can have a conflict of interest without being in the wrong. To have a conflict of interest is merely to have a moral problem.'[7] People cannot be 'prohibited' from having conflicting interests, because they are often thrust into ethically murky situations

---

4   Davis, Michael: Introduction, in: Davis, Michael/ Stark, Andrew (eds.): Conflict of Interest in the Professions, Oxford, New York: Oxford University Press, 2001, pp. 3–19, here: p. 15.
5   Stark, Andrew: Conflict of Interest in American Public Life, Cambridge/MA: Harvard University Press, 2000, p. 22.
6   Lewicka-Strzałecka, Anna: Teoretyczne i praktyczne aspekty identyfikacji i ograniczania konfliktu interesów, in: Węgrzecki, Adam (ed.): Konflikt interesów – konflikt wartości, Cracow: Wydawnictwo Akademii Ekonomicznej, 2005, pp. 7–23, here: p. 10.
7   Davis, Michael: Introduction, in: Davis, Michael/ Stark, Andrew (eds.): Conflict of Interest in the Professions, Oxford, New York: Oxford University Press, pp. 3–19, 2001, here: p. 13.

through no fault of their own (e.g. when a policeman pursuing drug dealers finds himself forced to arrest his own son or a municipal clerk has to make a decision that affects family or friends). For these reasons, as we shall see, most legal regulation focuses on ensuring that COI are managed in such a way so as to avoid the very appearance of the COI or—when it cannot be avoided—increase the probability that it will be sorted out to the benefit of the public interest. That is why most of these regulations are prophylactic: instead of prohibiting the COI (whatever that might entail) and punishing those who breach it, the law concentrates on preventing the emergence of situations leading to COI in the first place. This entails devising institutional conditions that will minimize the risk of their occurrence or reduce their negative consequences.

The above-mentioned approach excludes a number of phenomena related to COI merely because they are not illegal. This shortcoming calls for a sociological approach, which could help to conceptualize and study other dimensions of COI apart from purely legal considerations. Other COI angles worthy of study might include the social costs (such as decreasing social trust), the undermining of civil society, the expansion of economic grey areas, the increased costs of running a market economy, etc.

3.3.　Types of Legal Regulation

Given the difficulties discussed above, most legal regulation of COI is preventive rather than punitive. Andrew Stark put it this way:

> Conflict-of-interest law ultimately does, then, focus on external acts, but on those acts that give rise to encumbered states of mind, not the ultimate acts which flow from them. [...] Because we cannot prohibit officials from becoming mentally beholden to those who give them gifts, we prohibit the very act of receiving gifts under certain kinds of circumstances.[8]

In effect, there are three main legal avenues for dealing with COI: classic regulation, 'soft law' and no regulation at all. The first revolves around a supposedly precise definition of a COI, usually as part of anti-corruption legislation meant to regulate the financing of electoral campaigns, the expenditure of public money, and the combination of employment in public offices with other jobs. Traditional regulation also contains laws against fraud, tax crimes, nepotism, etc. This approach is probably the most effective of the three, but it views every COI as inherently negative and suspect. 'Soft law', on the other hand, includes 'rules of conduct with no legal binding and not accompanied by sanctions, which should, however, cooperate, or harmonize with classic regulation'.[9] All sorts of internal codes of ethical conduct and intra-institutional policies against COI fall into this category. For example, public officials or candidates for

---

8　　Stark, Andrew: Conflict of Interest in American Public Life, Cambridge/MA: Harvard University Press, 2000, p. 23.

9　　Suwaj, Patrycja Joanna: Konflikt interesów w administracji publicznej, Warsaw: Wolters Kluwer Polska, 2009, p. 78.

public office can be required to disclose their funding sources, and scholars publishing articles in medical journals are expected to disclose (or not to have) any financial ties to the producers of the substances or drugs described in their papers.[10] The third avenue, no legal regulation, can work in systems with other means of detecting and regulating COI, such as close monitoring of the electoral process by the media and non-governmental watchdog institutions.

Another approach, discussed by Michael Davis, lists three mechanisms for dealing with COI.[11] First, one can decide to overcome the situation of COI, e.g. by granting someone else the power to decide on a particular issue. One can also terminate a private interest conflicting (potentially or actually) with one's current job, e.g. by selling stocks in a company that does business in the area which one is supposed to regulate or control. However, 'removing' the COI is not always an option: in such a situation one can instead disclose it, as when candidates for the municipal council declare their sources of income. Disclosure does not remove a COI, of course, but helps to control it. Finally, one can manage the conflicting situation; depending on the circumstances, this may include a broad range of measures:

- choosing non-action if it is determined that the potential conflict is minimal and mere disclosure will be enough to control it;
- informing the parties involved that the conflict was disclosed and is under control;
- engaging a third party, e.g. an independent auditor, to investigate the threat of conflict of interest;
- co-opting additional participants in the decisional process engaging persons in a conflict of interest;
- identifying parties that could be harmed by the conflict and seeking their opinion;
- restricting access to confidential or secret information to people having a conflict of interest;
- removing people in the situation of conflict of interest from debating or voting on certain issues;
- barring a given person from performing certain duties;
- moving the person to a different department;
- in serious cases, convincing the person to resign.[12]

---

10   See Górski, Andrzej: Tendencje do komercjalizacji w nauce i dydaktyce wymagają pilnych uregulowań administracyjno-prawnych, Forum Akademickie, 2002, no. 2; Krimsky, Sheldon: Science in the Private Interest: Has the Lure of Profits Corrupted Biomedical Research?, Lanham: Rowman and Littlefield, 2003.

11   Davis, Michael: Introduction, in: Davis, Michael/ Stark, Andrew (eds.): Conflict of Interest in the Professions, Oxford, New York: Oxford University Press, pp. 3–19, 2001, here: p. 13.

12   Lewicka-Strzałecka, Anna: Teoretyczne i praktyczne aspekty identyfikacji i ograniczania konfliktu interesów, in: Węgrzecki, Adam (ed.): Konflikt interesów – konflikt wartości, Cracow: Wydawnictwo Akademii Ekonomicznej, 2005, pp. 7–23, here: p. 20.

A number of legal and extra-legal devices can help detect and regulate COI. Instruments for regulation range from instituting internal ethical codes, mandating the disclosure of COI, setting up watchdog institutions, and assuring public access to information to introducing regulation concerning the incompatibility of certain offices with certain other jobs. None of these devices will be completely efficient, though, if core state institutions are ineffective, ignore the problem or even actively counter such efforts. The above-mentioned devices could generally be called preventive; however, instruments for detecting and investigating COI are also necessary. 'Whistle-blowing' is one example: when all internal controlling mechanisms fail, an insider (usually an employee) can inform external actors, typically the media, non-governmental organizations or state institutions, about the problem. This 'disloyalty' is associated with significant psychological costs, so institutional regulation is necessary to facilitate such decisions and to protect the informant later on. A striking example is the story of a medium-level manager in a German cartel operating for 50 years in the construction business, providing road signs for highways. The manager had a very hard time getting his findings to the police and the courts, where he was repeatedly ignored, and in the meantime he was fired by his company.[13] According to Erwin Scheuch, whistle-blowing is one of the most effective tools in combating complex corruption networks.[14] He cites the case of Opel, where a corrupt system lasted for 20 years and implicated over 60 people.[15]

3.4. Inadequacy of Legal Definitions

As we have noted before, it is mostly lawyers and legal scholars who make use of the concept of COI. Alison L. Gash and Christine Trost[16] argue that in effect, most of the existing literature focuses on two areas: (1) analyses of legal regulations pertaining to COI in various countries which take into account local circumstances and solutions, attempt cross-cultural comparison, and study the evolution of this jurisprudence; (2) assessments of the effectiveness of different legal solutions. This second area seems to be sociologically relevant, but when it is framed in legal discourse, scholars tend to explain the efficiency or inefficiency of the law as resulting from incorrectly shaped regulation, without taking the influence of social factors into account. The lack of empirical

---

13　Bannenberg, Britta: Korruption in Deutschland und ihre strafrechtliche Kontrolle, Neuwied: Luchterhand, 2002, pp. 109–111.

14　Scheuch, Erwin Kurt: Die Mechanismen der Korruption, in: von Arnim, Hans Herbert/ Bannenberg, Britta (eds.): Korruption. Netzwerke in Politik, Ämtern und Wirtschaft, München: Droemer Knaur, 2003, pp. 31–75, here: p. 53.

15　Scheuch, Erwin Kurt: Korruption als Teil einer freiheitlichen Gesellschaftsordnung. Oder: die Kriminogenese eines kommunalen »Klüngels«, in: Kriminalistik, 2002, (vol. 56), no. 2, pp. 79–91, here: p. 82.

16　Trost, Christine/ Gash, Alison L.: Conflict of Interest and Public Life. Cross-national Perspectives, Cambridge: Cambridge University Press, 2008, p. 3.

research on COI leaves a gap in our knowledge regarding its forms, mechanisms, institutional factors that favour or hamper it, and the influence of social, cultural and ethical contexts. This gap is especially troublesome when one particular consequence of the prevailing legal-administrative discourse is stressed: its focus on decision-makers acting in the situation of a COI. This means that the entities that put those decision-makers in such situations in the first place remain in the shadows. For lawyers, a corrupted official is naturally more interesting than the corrupting businessman; ought sociologists to look more closely at 'the perpetrators' rather than at 'the victims' of COI?

The legalistic approach to COI also has significant consequences for the public debate and the ways for dealing with COI in it. COI is often associated—or even equated—with financial interest. As Karen Getman and Pamela S. Karlan observed, a great deal of legal regulation in California is predicated on this equation, with the result of weakening the impact of laws by excluding all cases in which private interest is not overtly financial or material (or when it simply cannot be proven).[17] Indeed, many legal systems around the globe simply dismiss COI cases in which no financial gain can be proven. A case in point is the story of a municipal clerk in Torun, Poland, who was exonerated when the court decided it could not prove that he had divulged plans for a new bridge to a female friend, who immediately bought a lot in a relevant location and can now resell it to the city at a significantly higher price. In the verdict we read that 'It was not possible to verify the hypothesis that any municipal officials received any material or personal reward in return for their behaviour.'[18] Note that while reward here was understood broadly, i.e. not only in the material sense, the mere fact that the receipt of such a reward was not proven was enough to dismiss the charges against the clerk. Obviously, from a legal point of view, this was probably a perfectly logical decision, but how did the public perceive the proceedings? Undoubtedly, this case concerned a profound COI, even though the court was unable to determine the nature of the private interest involved when the clerk disclosed the confidential information to his friend. Regardless of whether a kickback, which could not be proven, or platonic love was at play, this was a textbook case of COI (which, we might add, was resolved with a great loss for the public interest). However, the message from the court to the public was unequivocal: If no money changed hands, then no crime was committed.

We have no problem with the legal approach as such, but when it is the *dominant* approach to resolving a COI, the social perception of the phenomenon will be severely distorted. The resulting reduction of all COI to the financial dimension can

---

17   Getman, Karen/ Karlan, Pamela S.: Pluralists and Republicans, Rules and Standards. Conflict of Interest and the California Experience, in: Trost, Christine/ Gash, Alison L. (eds.): Conflict of Interest and Public Life. Cross-National Perspectives, Cambridge: Cambridge University Press, 2008, pp. 56–74, here: pp. 64–65.

18   Quoted in: Dolecki, Karol: Działo się przy toruńskim moście. Oj, działo, in: Gazeta Wyborcza Toruń, 11 January 2010.

in turn be instrumentalized in public debate: many of the commentators on the so-called gambling affair of 2009 (which implicated a number of important Polish politicians) stressed that there was no proof that any of the politicians were materially rewarded for their 'help'. Therefore, since no material gains could be proven to have changed hands, the judge in the case ruled that the anti-corruption law had not been violated. The same argument has been used as a justification for lobbying politicians.

Conflict of interest can assume both legal and illegal forms, just as lobbying can—and the legalization of lobbying has by no means prevented COI; it simply puts them on a legal playing field. Thus, we have forms of corruption which are not punishable by law, such as the cooperation between scientists and businesses (in fact, such cooperation is strongly encouraged in the Lisbon Strategy of the EU) and the fully legal circulation of people between politics and business (with certain exceptions concerning so-called post-employment). When we add to this list the phenomena of nepotism, protectionism, clientelistic and informal networks, which are almost completely immune to legal judgment, it becomes clear that COI cannot be understood merely in legal terms or in the light of administrative regulations.

3.5. Conflict of Interest in Psychological and Ethical Discourse

To forge a broader perspective of COI, it is necessary not only to go beyond the legal point of view, but also to transcend the ethical and psychological discourses, which seem to frame COI in a way that obscures rather than clarifies it. The scholarly penchant for psychological explanations and ethical individualism masks COI's social dimension. With respect to the various codes of ethical conduct adopted by public institutions, the corresponding discourse focuses on the public official as the chief or sole actor; his or her interests and motivations are perceived as the causes for the COI and are thought to determine the way it is resolved. This approach neglects the various forces that impact the official's behaviour, as well as the broader social context (in psychology, this tendency is called the 'attribution error'). Corruption is often portrayed as an inherent feature of one's character rather than the product of diverse pressures and temptations flooding in from the outside world. These external factors include the huge gap between the earnings of the corrupters and the corruptees, the low social prestige of many public offices, inadequate working conditions, political pressures, etc. All of these circumstances facilitate corruption, and their combined force can outweigh the power of moral principles. Put differently, the sociological imagination teaches us that institutions often shape their personnel, and not the other way round; likewise, our system of justice produces judges and is not produced by them.

Similarly, in Poland we often hear complaints about the 'low political culture' in the country; this culture is tacitly understood as the way particular politicians behave (it is said that 'we have such politicians as we have been able to educate and elect').

However, there is much more to political culture than just the moral (in)sensibility of the political elite. Structural conditions, including the existence and attitude towards COI, are at least as important. Of course, ethical sensibility can be a significant factor in countering the numerous temptations that crop up in the work of public officials. Codes of conduct, seminars aiming at increasing their morale, etc. can prove to be effective tools of 'soft power'; however, it would be naive to rely exclusively or predominantly on these tools.

3.6. Structural Conflict of Interest

To address the insufficiency of both the legal and ethical-psychological discourses, we would like to briefly discuss the concept of structural conflict of interest. First introduced by Andrzej Zybertowicz, the concept refers to COI that affect core institutions, whose proper functioning is crucial for the health of the state.[19] These include the parliament, the executive branch, the system of justice, police and secret services, and the media. In sum, these institutions are strategically important, and if COI is widespread in any one of them, state capture becomes possible.[20]

Another feature of structural COI is its prevalence. Conflicts of interest can be systemic (or structural) even if they occur in areas not defined above as crucial for the state, e.g. in sports. Press releases on corruption in Polish football point to a widespread COI in the industry. Structural COI can therefore be said to exist when key state institutions are involved and/or when it is so widespread that it becomes the standard way of doing business in a given field.

Structural COI triggers a destructive snowball effect: the less it is addressed by the law and/or condemned by public opinion, the more it reshapes political culture. The classic mechanism of self-fulfilling prophecy seems to be in place: conditions for public service are increasingly defined by the widespread presence of COI. A popular expression of such a 'definition of situation'—in Poland, at least—is the proverbial belief that 'you have to steal the first million'.[21] This snowball effect is not merely symbolic, however: one of its consequences is that it paves the way for more COI situations. Knowledge of an existing COI can provide others with a 'hook' to engage in blackmail, thus perpetuating the cycle of favouring private interest over public interest.

Antoni Z. Kamiński summarized the origins of this mechanism when he wrote: 'The strategy of privatization that was adopted in Poland—through full acceptance,

---

19 Zybertowicz, Andrzej: Strukturalny konflikt interesów jako kategoria analizy uwarunkowań przemian instytucjonalnych w Polsce po r. 1989, unpublished paper, 2009.

20 Grzymala-Busse, Anna: Beyond Clientelism. Incumbent State Capture and State, in: Comparative Political Studies, 2008 (Vol. 41), no. 4/5, pp. 638–673.

21 Numerous examples could be cited from other countries, too; see e.g. Della Porta, Donatella/ Vannucci, Alberto: Corrupt Exchanges. Actors, Resources, and Mechanisms of Political. Corruption, New York: Aldine de Gruyter, 1999, for a description of the Italian case.

or even conscious evoking of situations of the conflict of interest—created fertile soil for corruption'.[22] This suggests that structural conflicts of interest were created consciously to facilitate the creation of COI situations in other areas. Having launched a chain of cooperation generating ever new conflicts of interest, entrepreneurs of the so-called 'enfranchised nomenclature', the former communist elite among the early winners of the free market transformation in Poland, created and thrive in precisely such a system.

Reproduction of COI via the snowball effect results in a systematic loss of self-regulative and self-controlling capacity in the political system. This can be illustrated by the different impact exerted by economic-political affairs and scandals in the West and in the East. Western scholars point to the regulative function of such affairs for public life.[23] Detection of scandals sends a signal that something is not functioning properly, e.g. that there are either gaps in the legal system, in regulations concerning party financing, or in the state of public debate. Exposing a scandal thereby helps to close these loopholes by triggering better regulation, circulation of the elites, changes in social practices and sensibility, or the establishment of new institutions. As Bruce E. Cain, Alison L. Gash and Mark J. Oleszek observed, 'Most major conflict-of-interest innovations occur in the wake of a highly publicized political scandal for one simple reason: scandals put the political system on the defensive'.[24] For example, the famous Watergate affair of the 1970s drew public attention to the 'revolving door' problem in the US political system and brought about complex legal rules concerning the movement of individuals between big business and politics.[25]

The so-called Rywin affair (2002–2003), the largest corruption scandal in recent Polish history, initially seemed to have launched a renewal of political life in Poland. Although no new regulations were adopted in its wake (apart from the comeback of parliamentary investigation committees), public opinion became more sensitive to cases of COI, and the media started looking more closely at other scandals at the intersection of politics and business. The scandal did, however, result in the creation of the Central Anti-Corruption Bureau in 2005. Nevertheless, the subsequent scandals that surfaced after 'Rywingate' no longer seemed to have this salutary effect on

---

22 Kamiński, Antoni Z.: Korupcja jako system instytucjonalnej niewydolności państwa i zagrożenie dla rozwoju polityczno-gospodarczego polski, in: Popławska, Ewa (ed.): Dobro wspólne, władza, korupcja. Konflikt interesów w życiu publicznym, Warsaw: ISP, 1997, pp. 23–74, here: p. 53.

23 Trost, Christine/ Gash, Alison L.: Conflict of Interest and Public Life. Cross-national Perspectives, Cambridge: Cambridge University Press, 2008, pp. 4–5.

24 Cain, Bruce E./ Gash, Alison L./ Oleszek, Mark J.: Conflict-of-Interest Legislation in the United States. Origins, Evolution, and Inter-Branch Differences, in: Trost, Christine/ Gash, Alison L. (eds.): Conflict of Interest and Public Life, Cambridge: Cambridge Univ. Press, 2008, pp. 101–123, here: p. 102.

25 Green, Jeffrey: History of Conflicts Law, in: Hamline Law Review, 2002 (vol. 26), no. 3, pp. 556–600, here: p. 555.

Polish public life. In 2009 alone we learned about several major political-economic scandals (the so-called annex affair, as well as gambling, shipyard, and wiretapping affairs), and over the past several years it was also revealed that major political figures (including the vice-prime minister; ministers of public health, sports, justice, internal affairs, defence, and treasury; and the chief of one of the secret services), were involved in COI situations. These revelations somehow failed to spark any systemic reactions (and sometimes, not even individual sanctions) that could prevent the emergence of COI in the future. We seem to be witnessing the same mechanism that has operated in lustration cases: news about the collaboration of ever more public figures with the communist secret services does not meet with public condemnation.

This situation illustrates the 'corrosive effect' of structural COI, i.e. when subsequent cases of COI that make headlines cease to contribute to the reform of the system and instead intensify the snowball effect. We already mentioned one consequence of this corrosive effect—the creation of new COI situations; another would be the undermining of public trust in the state and its representatives, as well as in other public figures. Interestingly, while many scholars discuss the importance of social trust for the quality of democracy and governance, it is not easy to find analyses that take the existence of COI and reactions to it into account.[26] The justice system, the media, the public health system, moral authorities and pundits, state authorities, and the scholarly community all require a certain level of public trust; all of them are also repeatedly involved—in different ways—in various COI situations.

In the legal arena, COI is usually defined as a relationship between two and only two actors: the decision-maker and the agent to whom the former is loyal at the expense of the public interest. In fact, COI can be a much more complex tangle of relationships and mutual dependency. What is more, in treating the phenomena of corruption, nepotism, and illegal lobbying separately, one neglects what unites and largely explains them: COI situations. In other words, each particular instance of COI (e.g. corruption) can be just one element of a more complicated operation, which might consist of forgery, fraud, tax extortion, false evidence, and so on. Treating each case of COI as a discrete dual scheme of good vs. evil or victim vs. perpetrator obscures the network character of COI.

Most scholars (and lawmakers) dealing with COI assume that actors are individuals. Cases where formal institutions can be implicated in COI thus tend to be pre-emptively excluded. A number of scholars stress the need to examine situations in which COI involves whole institutions or their segments.[27] This advice is especially important in the context of structural COI, which by definition affects key state institutions.

---

26   A notable exception is Della Porta, Donatella/ Vannucci Alberto: Corrupt Exchanges. Actors, Resources, and Mechanisms of Political Corruption, New York: Aldine de Gruyter, 1999.

27   See Emanuel, Ezekiel J./ Steiner, Daniel: Institutional Conflict of Interest, in: New England Journal of Medicine, 1995 (vol. 332), no. 4, pp. 262–268.

Research on institutional COI concentrates mainly on the study of science, particularly medicine and pharmacology. Nils Hasselmo, who investigates institutional COI in regard to American universities, suggests the following definition:

> An institutional financial conflict of interest may occur when the institution, any of its senior management or trustees, or a department, school, or other sub-unit, or a related organization (such as a university foundation) has an external relationship or financial interest in a company that itself has a financial interest in a faculty research project. Senior managers or trustees may also have conflicts when they serve on the boards of (or otherwise have an official relationship with) organizations that have significant commercial transactions with the university. The existence (or appearance) of such conflicts can lead to actual bias, or suspicion about possible bias, in the review or conduct of research at the university. If they are not evaluated or managed, they may result in choices or actions that are incongruent with the missions, obligations, or the values of the university.[28]

Hasselmo's definition pertains to COI in the academic world but could also be applied to other milieus affected by institutional COI. Universities are just one example of institutions that can be taken over and made to pursue other interests than those publicly declared. This take-over process could be called 'third degree control'[29], whereby a given institution's resources and personnel can be mobilized toward goals that foster private interests of a group or individual that are inconsistent with this institution's declared purpose. A model example would be using 'friendly' tax control officials to fight business competition with prolonged, overly detailed inquiries. Third degree control can also arise within the institution itself, resulting in the emergence of informal cliques, interest groups and networks among its members. In effect, this institution ceases to fulfil its statutory function and becomes subservient to the strongest interest groups.

3.7. Structural Conflict of Interest in Central and Eastern Europe

Regardless of the antipathy that public administrations might harbour toward attempts at establishing external norms and institutions to control their work and counter possible COI, European countries are slowly moving away from the idea of self-control and internal evaluation systems and replacing them with specialized institutions.[30] Examples of this tendency include the Lithuanian Investigative Service (STT), founded

---

28   Hasselmo, Nils: Individual and Institutional Conflict of Interest. Policy Review by Research Universities in the United States, in: Science and Engineering Ethics, 2002 (vol. 8), no. 3, pp. 421–427, here: p. 425.

29   Zybertowicz, Andrzej: Kontrola społeczna trzeciego stopnia, in: Kwaśniewski, Jerzy/ Winczorek, Jan (eds.): Idee naukowe Adama Podgóreckiego, Warsaw: Wydawnictwo UW, 2009, pp. 152–178.

30   Suwaj, Patrycja Joanna: Konflikt interesów w administracji publicznej, Warsaw: Wolters Kluwer Polska, 2009, p. 41.

in 1997; the Corruption Prevention and Combating Bureau (KNAB), established in 2002 in Latvia; and the Polish Central Anti-Corruption Bureau (CBA), founded in 2006.[31]

In Poland, the CBA's activities are supported by the Supreme Chamber of Control, the Ombudsman, courts, the prosecutor's office, and a number of other controlling institutions. Coordination of their activities is especially important in Poland, as well as in other CEE countries, because of the particular nature of existing conflicts of interest there. As noted above, they assume a structural character, and—unlike in the West— share another important feature: they are often based on informal ties dating back to the communist era. As Andrzej Zybertowicz wrote, these ties are characterized by 'high invisibility [...] and cannot be detected with standard institutions and controlling procedures of the democratic social system'.[32] Elsewhere he observed that among top Polish politicians of at least the ministerial level, between 1989–2000,

> at least 18 people had to take into account the activities of past and present secret services or some other informal structures, which had at their disposal information gathered by those services. We are talking here about two presidents, six out of eight prime ministers, two vice-prime ministers, four out of nine ministers of justice, two ministers of foreign affairs and a secretary of state in the cabinet of one prime minister.[33]

How does the existence of these ties influence the citizens' trust in their representatives? It is not hard to see that politicians with such a background could easily be 'hooked'.

A narrowly legalistic approach has proven insufficient for detecting all cases of COI; a more nuanced, sociological view would broaden the conceptual scope and greatly improve diagnostic capacity. Only by taking into account their complex nature and various forms—not only those where illegality or financial gain is involved—can these structural conflicts of interest be successfully explored and regulated.

---

31   For a survey of anti-corruption bureaus in Central Eastern Europe see Dionisie, Dan/ Checchi, Francesco: Corruption and Anti-Corruption Agencies in Eastern Europe and the CIS. A Practitioners' Experience, 2008, http://ancorage-net.org/content/documents/dionisie-checchi-corruption_in_ee.pdf

32   Zybertowicz, Andrzej: Strukturalny konflikt interesów jako kategoria analizy uwarunkowań przemian instytucjonalnych w Polsce po r. 1989, unpublished paper, 2009.

33   Zybertowicz, Andrzej: Demokracja jako fasada. Przypadek III RP, in: Mokrzycki, Edmund/ Rychard, Andrzej/ Zybertowicz, Andrzej (eds.): Utracona dynamika? O niedojrzałości polskiej demokracji, Warsaw: Wydawnictwo IFiS PAN, 2002, pp. 173–214, here: pp. 175–176.

Marco Zanella

4. Evaluating the Harmonization of Criminal Provisions on Corruption in Central and Eastern Europe

4.1. Anti-Corruption in Transition. The Way Toward a Common Approach

Corruption has always been present in human history[1]. However, interest in anti-corruption strategies surged dramatically in the late 1980s, when the increasing recognition of the damaging effects of such a crime on social stability and economic growth have triggered national and international interventions. Reforms and anti-corruption campaigns have particularly targeted the so called transition countries, such as those in Central and Eastern Europe (CEE). These nations, in fact, have undergone dramatic changes over the last 20 years. Most CEE countries have modified their political orientation, trading communism for a more liberal system. This political reform has in turn had an impact on national economies, which have moved toward a privatization process based on the transfer of ownership of enterprises and agencies from the public to the private sector. In addition, CEE countries have also been affected by changes and reforms in neighbouring countries, from the fall of the former Soviet Union to the establishment of the European Union and the Single European Market. In the weak socio-political context of the CEE countries, 'the simultaneous processes of (…) designing new political and social institutions and redistributing social assets have created fertile ground for corruption'.[2] Corruption has, in fact, been addressed as a central impediment to progress in many CEE countries.

Especially in the wake of EU enlargement, corruption became an important issue, and 'has figured prominently in political campaigns, and has been a key concern of

---

1   See, *inter alia*, Fornasari, Gabriale/ Luisi, Demetrio (eds.): La Corruzione. Profili Storici, Attuali, Europei e Sopranazionali, Padova: CEDAM, 2003; Tiihonen, Seppo (ed.): The History of Corruption in Central Government, Amsterdam: IOS Press, 2003; Brioschi, Alberto: Breve Storia della Corruzione. Dall'Età Antica ai Giorni Nostri, Milano: TEA, 2004.

2   World Bank: Anticorruption in Transition. A Contribution to the Policy Debate, Washington D.C.: World Bank, 2000, here: p. vii. In this regard see also Savona, Ernesto U./ Curtol, Federica: The Contribution of Data Exchange Systems to the Fight against Organised Crime in the See Countries, Transcrime Reports no. 10, Trento: Transcrime, 2004; Shelley, Louise: Crime and Corruption. Enduring Problems of Post-Soviet Development, in: Demokratizatsiya, 2003 (vol. 11), no. 1, pp. 110–114; Shelley, Louise: Can Russia Fight Organized Crime and Corruption, in: The Tocqueville Review, 2002 (vol. XXIII), no. 2, pp. 37–55; Shelley, Louise: Organized Crime and Corruption in Ukraine. Impediment to the Development of a Free Market Economy, in: Demokratizatsiya, 1998 (vol. 6), no. 4, pp. 648–663.

citizens, businesses, and international organizations alike'.[3] Under the umbrella of the anti-corruption strategies that have been undertaken in these transition countries, which in most cases have taken a page out from those proposed by international institutions, an important role is played by reforms concerning the criminal justice system. These reforms include the establishment of common approaches in dealing with corruption and the enforcement of harmonized criminal definitions aimed at ensuring the 'co-ordinated criminalisation of national and international corruption'.[4] In this regard, the Council of Europe and the Group of States against Corruption (GRECO)—among other international actors—have played a remarkable role since the adoption of the Criminal Law Convention on Corruption of 1999 (CLCC) and the Additional Protocol of 2003 (AP).[5]

This chapter seeks to understand the extent to which a co-ordinated criminalization of corruption in the *public sector* in CEE countries currently exists. Consequently, this chapter endeavours to provide a preliminary answer to the following questions: (1) what is the degree of harmonization of national definitions on corruption in the *public sector* with respect to the CLCC and the AP? (2) Are there additional national definitions that are not in the CLCC or the AP but that may deserve consideration in the international arena?

To investigate these issues, the chapter commences with the description of the methodology employed in carrying out the comparison and it then proceeds to compare anti-corruption definitions in CEE according to two comparative criteria, i.e.: (1) the analysis of the harmonization of national provisions with those of the CLCC and the AP and (2) the analysis of those definitions that are present in specific criminal justice systems though not defined within the CLCC and the AP. Some conclusions are finally drawn, discussing the degree of harmonisation of criminal provisions on corruption in the CEE and the need for future research in this domain.

---

3   Anderson, James/ Gray, Cheryl: Anticorruption in Transition 3. Who Is Succeeding … And Why? Washington D.C.: World Bank, 2006, here: p. xi. For an introduction regarding the interventions of the Council of Europe and the European Union with regard to anti-corruption policies in the EU accession process see: European Commission: Background Documentation, in: European Commission (ed.): Annual Forum on Combating Corruption in the EU 2010. Incorporating Anti-corruption Policy into the EU Accession Process, Brussels: European Commission, 2010; Vachudova, Milada A.: Corruption and Compliance in the EU's Post-Comunist Members and Candidates, in JCMS, 2009 (vol. 47), Annual Review, pp. 43–62; Börzel, Tanja A./ Stahn, Andreas/ Pamuk, Yasemin: The European Union and the Fight Against Corruption in its Near Abroad: Can it Make a Difference?, in: Global Crime, 2010 (vol. 11), no. 2, pp. 122–144.
4   As stated under the second guiding principle for the fight against corruption under Resolution (97) 24 of the Committee of Ministers of the Council of Europe.
5   For an assessment of the performance in Eastern Europe of the international anticorruption instruments see: Wolf, Sebastian: Assessing Eastern Europe's anti-corruption performance: views from the Council of Europe, OECD, and Transparency International, in Global Crime, 2010 (vol. 11), no. 2, pp. 99–121.

4.2. Methodological Note

In this section the methodology employed in comparing criminal law provisions on corruption is explained. While focusing exclusively on corruption in the *public sector*, the comparative analysis proposed in this chapter has a specific *geographical scope*. The study covers all CEE countries, i.e. Albania, Bosnia-Herzegovina, Bulgaria, Croatia, Czech Republic, Estonia, Hungary, Latvia, Lithuania, Macedonia, Montenegro, Poland, Romania, Serbia, Slovakia and Slovenia. Most CEE countries have acceded to the European Union (EU): the Czech Republic, Estonia, Hungary, Latvia, Lithuania, Poland, Slovakia and Slovenia joined the EU in May 2004, while Bulgaria and Romania joined in January 2007.

The evaluation of the harmonization is carried out by means of a comparative analysis of the national provisions on corruption in the *public sector*. Two criteria form the basis of the evaluation.[6]

As a *first comparative criterion*, the CLCC and the AP are selected as benchmarks for carrying out the comparison of the national provisions for combating corruption. This allows for a better understanding of the symmetries and asymmetries present within each national criminal justice system and the degree of harmonization that the national provisions have achieved with respect to the international standards indicated in these instruments. The CLCC and the AP have been chosen as benchmarks because all CEE countries are members of the Council of Europe and are monitored by the GRECO concerning their compliance with Council of Europe anti-corruption standards.[7] In addition, due to their 'European' spectrum, these international instruments enable a better understanding and comparison of criminal provisions deriving from different legal traditions[8] (Civil Law *vs.* Socialist Law) that are now part of the wider

---

6   In this regard see Vettori, Barbara/ Zanella, Marco: Tra Nuove e Vecchie Fattispecie Penali, in: Di Nicola, Andrea (ed.): Contro la Criminalità Organizzata in Europa. Una Prima Valutazione delle Politiche Penali ed Extra-penali, Milano: Franco Angeli, in press.

7   'The Group of States against Corruption (GRECO) was established in 1999 by the Council of Europe to monitor States' compliance with the organisation's anti-corruption standards. GRECO's objective is to improve the capacity of its members to fight corruption by monitoring their compliance with Council of Europe anti-corruption standards through a dynamic process of mutual evaluation and peer pressure. It helps to identify deficiencies in national anti-corruption policies, prompting the necessary legislative, institutional and practical reforms. GRECO also provides a platform for the sharing of best practice in the prevention and detection of corruption.' GRECO: What is Greco, in: coe.int, http://www.coe.int/t/dghl/monitoring/greco/general/3.%20 What%20is%20GRECO_en.asp, accessed 17 May 2010.

8   See, *inter alia*, Ajani, Gianmaria: Il Modello Post-Socialista, Torino: G. Giappichelli Editore, 2008; Zweigert, K./ Kötz, H.: Introduction to Comparative Law, Broadbridge: Clarendon Press, 1998; Ajani, Gianmaria: Diritto dell'Europa Orientale, Torino: Utet, 1996; Ajani, Gianmaria: Chance and Prestige. Legal Transplants in Russia and Eastern Europe, in: The American Journal of Comparative Law, 1995 (vol. 43), no. 1, pp. 93–117; Ajani, Gianmaria: La Circulation de Modèles Juridiques Dans le Droit Post-socialiste, in: Revue Internationale de Droit Comparé, 1994, no. 4, pp. 1087–

                                     Marco Zanella

and more flexible area of the Western Legal Tradition, where differences among legal systems are mitigated by supra-national legislation (e.g. EU Law, International Law).[9]

As a *second comparative criterion*, considering that individual countries may criminalize further illicit behaviours, the analysis focuses on those definitions that are present in national criminal justice systems but not defined in the CLCC and AP. This comparison takes all these corruption-related offences—whether criminalized by only one or by more CEE countries—into account. This is because one way to proceed with the enforcement of common measures against corruption may be to criminalize at a supra-national level acts that were previously punished only within individual countries.

Any comparative study that considers a wide number of criminal justice systems is intrinsically affected by *limits*, especially related to language barriers.[10] The present analysis benefits from the usage of official English translations of the national legislation and criminal codes as provided by the Council of Europe and by the GRECO. In addition, information on national legislation has been collected from official documents prepared by the Support and Improvement in Governance and Management (SIGMA)[11] and by the Regional Anti-corruption Initiative (RAI).[12]

    1106; David, René/ Brierley, John E.C.: Major Legal Systems in the World Today. An Introduction to the Comparative Study of Law, New York: Free Press, 1985.

9   Ajani, Gianmaria: Il Modello Post-Socialista, Torino: G. Giappichelli Editore, 2008; Goldman, David B.: Globalisation and the Western Legal Tradition. Recurring Patterns of Law and Authority, Cambridge: Cambridge University Press, 2007; Haveman, Roelof/ Kavran, Olga/ Nicholls, Julian: Supranational Criminal Law. A System *Sui Generis* (vol. 1), Schoten: Intersentia, 2003; de Sousa Santos, Boaventura: Toward a New Legal Common Sense. Law, Globalization, and Emancipation, Cambridge: Cambridge University Press, 2002; Berman, Harold J.: Law and Revolution. The Formation of the Western Legal Tradition, Harvard: Harvard University Press, 1983.

10   See, *inter alia*, Pradel, Jean: Droit Pénal Comparé, 3rd edn., Paris: Dalloz, 2008; Galdia, Marcus: Comparative Law and Legal Translation, in: The European Legal Forum, 2003 (vol. 1), pp. 1–4. For a philosophical perspective: Santambrogio, Marco: Introduzione alla Filosofia Analitica del Linguaggio, Bari: Laterza, 1992; Casalegno, Paolo: Introduzione alla Filosofia del Linguaggio, Firenze: Carrocci, 1997.

11   'SIGMA is a joint initiative of the European Union (EU) and the Organisation for Economic Co-operation and Development (OECD), principally financed by the EU. SIGMA was launched in 1992 by the OECD and the European Commission's Phare Programme to support the Czech Republic, Hungary, Poland, Slovakia and Slovenia implement public administration reforms. In parallel with further EU enlargement and the expansion of the Stabilisation and Association Process, SIGMA support has since been extended to other partners, including all ten 2004 EU entrants and to the two 2007 entrants, Bulgaria and Romania. In 2009, SIGMA is working with the 3 EU candidate countries—Croatia, the former Yugoslav Republic of Macedonia, and Turkey—and with the 5 EU potential candidates—Albania, Bosnia and Herzegovina, Montenegro, Serbia, and Kosovo under UNSCR 1244/99.' SIGMA: About SIGMA, in: sigmaweb. org, http://www.sigmaweb.org/document/45/0,3343,en_33638100_33638163_34842669_1_1 _1_1,00.html, accessed 20 April 2010.

12   'The Regional Anti-corruption Initiative (RAI) was initially adopted in Sarajevo in February 2000, as Stability Pact Anti-corruption Initiative (SPAI), to address corruption—one of the most serious threats to the recovery and development of the South East European countries. Currently the Initiative consists of 9 member countries from the region—Albania, Bosnia and Herzegovina, Bulgaria, Croatia, Macedonia, Moldova, Montenegro, Romania and Serbia and

4.3. Comparing the Definitions of Corruption in the Public Sector Across CEE Countries

Comparing CEE countries' definitions regarding corruption in the *public sector*, this section revolves around the analysis of the national legislation on corruption and is organized according to the above-mentioned *comparative criteria*.

4.3.1. The CLCC, the AP and National Definitions. The First Comparative Criterion

As mentioned above, CEE countries are first compared to each other using the definitions provided in the CLCC and the AP[13] as a benchmark. Definitions are as follows:

- *Active bribery of domestic public officials* (Article 2):

  […] when committed intentionally, the promising, offering or giving by any person, directly or indirectly, of any undue advantage to any of its public officials, for himself or herself or for anyone else, for him or her to act or refrain from acting in the exercise of his or her functions.

- *Passive bribery of domestic public officials* (Article 3):

  […] when committed intentionally, the request or receipt by any of its public officials, directly or indirectly, of any undue advantage, for himself or herself or for anyone else, or the acceptance of an offer or a promise of such an advantage, to act or refrain from acting in the exercise of his or her functions.

- *Bribery of members of domestic public assemblies* (Article 4):

  […] the conduct referred to in Articles 2 and 3, when involving any person who is a member of any domestic public assembly exercising legislative or administrative powers.

- *Bribery of foreign public officials* (Article 5):

  […] the conduct referred to in Articles 2 and 3, when involving a public official of any other State.

---

one observer—UNMIK, providing all of them with a general framework for coordination, optimization of efforts and permanent dialogue with the partner community involved in the fight against corruption.' RAI: Historical Background, in: rai-see.org, http://www.rai-see.org/about-us/historical-background.html, accessed 20 April 2010.

13   For an introduction see: de Boer Buquicchio, Maud: Legislative Measures of the Council of Europe to Adress Corruption and Money-Laundering in the International Financial System, in: UNODC (ed.): Global Action against Corruption. The Mérida Papers, Vienna: United Nations, 2004, pp. 109–112; Locati, Giovanni: Le Convenzioni del Consiglio d'Europa in Materia di Lotta alla Corruzione e gli Adempimenti di Alcuni Stati ad esse Aderenti, Liuc Papers no. 123, Serie Impresa e Istituzioni, 2003; Henning, Peter J.: Public Corruption A Comparative Analysis of International Corruption Conventions and United States Law, in: Arizona Journal International & Comparative Law, 2001 (vol. 18), no. 3, pp. 793–846; Huber, Barbara: La Lotta alla Corruzione in Prospettiva Sovranazionale, in: Rivista Trimestrale di Diritto Penale dell'Economia, 2001 (vol. 2), no. 3, pp. 475–489.

- *Bribery of members of foreign public assemblies* (Article 6):

  [...] the conduct referred to in Articles 2 and 3, when involving any person who is a member of any public assembly exercising legislative or administrative powers in any other State.

- *Bribery of officials of international organizations* (Article 9):

  [...] the conduct referred to in Articles 2 and 3, when involving any official or other contracted employee, within the meaning of the staff regulations, of any public international or supranational organisation or body of which the Party is a member, and any person, whether seconded or not, carrying out functions corresponding to those performed by such officials or agents.

- *Bribery of members of international parliamentary assemblies* (Article 10):

  [...] the conduct referred to in Article 4 when involving any members of parliamentary assemblies of international or supranational organisations of which the Party is a member.

- *Bribery of judges and officials of international courts* (Article 11):

  [...] the conduct referred to in Articles 2 and 3 involving any holders of judicial office or officials of any international court whose jurisdiction is accepted by the Party.

- *Trading in influence* (Article 12):

  [...] when committed intentionally, the promising, giving or offering, directly or indirectly, of any undue advantage to anyone who asserts or confirms that he or she is able to exert an improper influence over the decision-making of any person referred to in Articles 2, 4 to 6 and 9 to 11 in consideration thereof, whether the undue advantage is for himself or herself or for anyone else, as well as the request, receipt or the acceptance of the offer or the promise of such an advantage, in consideration of that influence, whether or not the influence is exerted or whether or not the supposed influence leads to the intended result.

In addition to the definitions provided in the CLCC, in 2003 an Additional Protocol to the Criminal Law Convention on Corruption (AP) was adopted that criminalizes the following activities belonging to the macro-area of 'corruption in the public sector':

- *Active bribery of domestic arbitrators* (Article 2):

  [...] when committed intentionally, the promising, offering or giving by any person, directly or indirectly, of any undue advantage to an arbitrator exercising his/her functions under the national law on arbitration of the Party, for himself or herself or for anyone else, for him or for her to act or refrain from acting in the exercise of his or her functions.

- *Passive bribery of domestic arbitrators* (Article 3):

  [...] when committed intentionally, the request or receipt by an arbitrator exercising his/her functions under the national law on arbitration of the Party, directly or indirectly, of any undue advantage for himself or herself or for anyone else, or the acceptance of an offer or promise of such an advantage, to act or refrain from acting in the exercise of his or her functions.

- *Bribery of foreign arbitrators* (Article 4):

  [...] the conduct referred to in Articles 2 and 3, when involving an arbitrator exercising his/her functions under the national law on arbitration of any other State.

- *Bribery of domestic jurors* (Article 5):

  [...] the conduct referred to in Articles 2 and 3, when involving any person acting as a juror within its judicial system.

- *Bribery of foreign jurors* (Article 6):

  [...] the conduct referred to in Articles 2 and 3, when involving any person acting as a juror within the judicial system of any other State.

4.3.1.1. Active and Passive Bribery of Domestic Public Officials

Both active and passive bribery/corruption of domestic public officials represent the backbone of the criminalisation of corruption and are meant to protect the public administration from private interests and to ensure that public bodies and actors operate in an impartial and transparent manner while following public interests.

Although all the CEE countries criminalize these practices, asymmetries in the national definitions still remain and full coordination has not yet been achieved, especially concerning the concept of 'undue advantage'. In fact, the different legal drafting techniques as well as the interpretations provided by the national courts have created some gaps and differences with reference to this concept. Some countries under analysis provide a broad definition of 'undue advantage'. In Croatia, for example, authorities indicate that this term covers both material and immaterial benefits.[14] The same is the case in Latvia, where Sections 320 and 323 of the Criminal Code do not explicitly use this term, but instead refer in their heading to 'bribes', which is in both Sections defined as 'material value, property or benefits of another nature'.[15] Slovakia also belongs to this group of countries. The concept of 'advantage' is not used there in the provisions on bribery and has been replaced by the term 'bribe', which is defined under Section 131(3) of the Criminal Code as 'a thing or other transaction of property or non-property nature to which there is no legal entitlement'.

Differently, other countries provide a narrower definition of the concept of 'undue advantage', excluding 'minor benefits' or 'gratuity'. This is the case, for example, in Albania, where the concept of 'undue advantage' applies to 'any irregular benefit'

---

14   GRECO: Third Evaluation Round Evaluation Report on Croatia Incriminations (ETS 173 and 191, GPC 2) (Theme I), Strasbourg: Council of Europe, 2009, pp. 5–6.

15   GRECO: Third Evaluation Round Evaluation Report on Latvia Incriminations (ETS 173 and 191, GPC 2) (Theme I), Strasbourg: Council of Europe, 2008, p. 7. In this context, the Latvian authorities refer to paragraph 6 of the decision of the Supreme Court of the Republic of Latvia No. 7 of 1993, titled 'On court practice in bribery cases', which appears to be a judicial doctrine based on the practice of the courts and which explains that a bribe can include 'money, securities, food products, non-consumable goods, service of a different nature, rights to property, deposits in the name of a bribe-taker, processing of fictitious contracts, payment of unwarranted bonuses or allowances, intentional gambling losses in favour of the bribe-taker, gifts for the bribe-taker's family members or friends, involvement in a profitable job etc.'

both material and immaterial, with the exception 'for very minor permissible bene-fits which a public official may accept without being obliged to declare them if they do not exceed the value of 1,000 ALL/8 EUR'.[16] Also Estonia makes a similar distinction between the concepts of 'bribe' and 'gratuity'.[17]

Finally, a third group of countries excludes immaterial advantages from its defini-tion of 'undue advantage'. The most interesting example here is the one of Lithuania. In the Lithuanian criminal justice system, in fact, even though any kind of illegally obtained property benefit can constitute a bribe, according to the national courts immaterial advantages, like honorary positions or titles, are not considered to be included in the concept of a bribe.[18]

4.3.1.2. Bribery of Members of Domestic Public Assemblies

This crime represents a specification of the crime of corruption of domestic public offi-cials. It is meant to extend the control over the members of domestic public assem-blies (i.e. parliaments or elected councils of all governance levels) who often do not fall under the label of 'public officials'.

All of the countries under study criminalize bribery of public assemblies. In this regard most CEE countries specifically criminalize corruptive practices (both active and passive) carried out by officials elected or appointed to representative/legislative bodies. Those countries that do not provide for a specific definition criminalize these practices by including the concept of 'member of domestic public assemblies' under the umbrella of the general definition of 'public official'. This is the case, for example, in Estonia and Lithuania. In Estonia, in fact, members of domestic public assemblies like members of Parliament or members of local assemblies are covered by Section 288(1) of the Criminal Code and, according to the local courts, since they represent the state or the local authority they are to be considered 'officials' for the purpose of bribery offences (Sections 293 to 298).[19] Similarly, in Lithuania, members of domestic public assemblies are considered to be 'public servants' as defined in Article 230 of the Criminal Code.[20]

---

16   GRECO: Third Evaluation Round. Evaluation Report on Albania on Incriminations (ETS 173 and
      191, GPC 2) (Theme I), Council of Europe: Strasbourg, 2008, here: p. 5.
17   Estonia Supreme Court Decision n. 3-1-1-118-06, p. 16.
18   GRECO: Third Evaluation Round Evaluation Report on Lithuania Incriminations (ETS 173 and
      191, GPC 2) (Theme I), Strasbourg: Council of Europe, 2009, pp. 5–6.
19   GRECO: Third Evaluation Round. Evaluation Report on Estonia on Incriminations (ETS 173 and
      191, GPC 2) (Theme I), Strasbourg: Council of Europe, 2008, p. 9.
20   This broad interpretation of the concept of 'public servant' was stressed in a 2005 case (SCL
      ruling of 11 October 2005) in which two persons were convicted for 'organising an attempt to
      bribe' and one person for attempting to bribe a member of the Vilnius City Municipality Council
      to vote for one of the candidates in the elections of the mayor (see decision of 10 February
      2009, Criminal Case No. 2K-7-48/2009); GRECO: Third Evaluation Round Evaluation Report on

Most CEE countries do not merely criminalize corruption practices where members of national legislative bodies are involved, but also criminalize corrupt acts committed by members of local public assemblies. This is the case, for example, in Latvia, where Section 316(1) of the Criminal Code refers to 'representatives of state authority', which includes 'persons exercising legislative power', and thus covers 'members of the *Saeima*' (i.e. the national Parliament) as well as persons performing duties in local government service or members of local councils like mayors and deputy mayors.[21] In Slovenia members of domestic public assemblies are also considered public officials according to Article 126(2)1) of the Criminal Code, which defines as public officials also 'a National Assembly deputy, a member of the National Council, or a member of a local or regional representative body'.[22]

4.3.1.3. Bribery of Foreign Public Officials

The crime of bribery of foreign public officials has been the object of several interventions at a supranational level and is explicitly defined in the CLCC, since with

> the globalisation of financial structures and the integration of domestic markets into the world-market, decisions taken on capital movements or investments in one country may and do exert effects in others.[23]

All CEE countries criminalize both active and passive corruption involving foreign public officials. Such a harmonized approach is related to the fact that in the last few years several corruption-related provisions have been subject to legal amendments aimed at aligning national legislation with the requirements of the CLCC. Most of the countries adapted their national legislation by amending the concept of 'public official' or of 'public servant' in order to include also foreign public officials. Few countries, like Slovakia, introduced *ad hoc* crime definitions explicitly criminalizing passive and active bribery of foreign public officials.[24] The only partial exception to this process of

---

Lithuania Incriminations (ETS 173 and 191, GPC 2) (Theme I), Strasbourg: Council of Europe, 2009, pp. 8–9.

21   GRECO: Third Evaluation Round Evaluation Report on Latvia Incriminations (ETS 173 and 191, GPC 2) (Theme I), Strasbourg: Council of Europe, 2008, p. 10.

22   GRECO: Third Evaluation Round Evaluation Report on Slovenia Incriminations (ETS 173 and 191, GPC 2) (Theme I), Strasbourg: Council of Europe, 2009, p. 7.

23   Council of Europe: Explanatory Report, in: conventions.coe.int, http://conventions.coe.int/treaty/en/Reports/Html/173.htm, accessed 20 May 2010.

24   *Section 330 Passive bribery of a foreign public official*
(1) Any person, who as a foreign public official, for himself or for another person, receives, requests or accepts the promise of a bribe in connection with his/her official duties, either directly or through an intermediary, in order to provide or maintain an undue advantage in an international business transaction, shall be punished by imprisonment for a term of five to twelve years.
(2) The offender shall be punished by imprisonment for a term of ten to fifteen years if he/she commits the offence referred to in paragraph 1 on a large scale.

harmonization of national definitions to the standards of the CLCC is Albania, where no specific reference to 'foreign public officials' is present in Sections 244, 245, 259, 260, 319 and 319/a of the Criminal Code.[25]

4.3.1.4. Bribery of Members of Foreign Public Assemblies

The crime of bribing members of foreign public assemblies as defined under Article 6 of the CLCC is a specification of the crime of bribery of foreign public officials (Article 5 CLCC) and is essentially based on the need for protecting democratic institutions, independently of whether they are national or foreign in character. In this regard 15 out of 16 CEE countries explicitly criminalize both active and passive corruption of members of foreign public assemblies.

For example, in Latvia, members of foreign public assemblies are considered to be 'public officials' pursuant to Section 316(3) of the Criminal Code, which provides that also the members of foreign public assemblies (institutions with legislative or executive functions) are to be considered as public official.[26] Similar legislation exists in Slovenia, where, according to Article 126(2)5) of the Criminal Code, members of foreign public assemblies are addressed as 'public officials' and are defined as

> any person who performs a legislative, executive or judicial function or any other official duty in a foreign country and at any level, and who fulfils the conditions indicated in points 1, 2 or 3 of Article 126(2).[27]

As in the previous case, within the Albanian criminal justice system, there is no explicit reference to members of foreign public assemblies in the provisions dealing with corruption, even though national courts consider members of foreign public assemblies as 'high State officials' or 'locally elected persons' for the purpose of bribery offences (Sections 245 and 260 of the Criminal Code).[28]

Section 334 Active bribery of a foreign public official
(1) Any person who gives, offers or promises a bribe to a foreign public official or to another person, either directly or through an intermediary, in connection with the official duties of the foreign public official with the aim to obtain or maintain an undue advantage in an international business transaction, shall be punished by imprisonment for a term of two to five years.
(2) The offender shall be punished by imprisonment for a term of five to twelve years if he/she commits the criminal offence referred to in paragraph 1 on a large scale.

25 GRECO: Third Evaluation Round. Evaluation Report on Albania on Incriminations (ETS 173 and 191, GPC 2) (Theme I), Strasbourg: Council of Europe, 2008, p. 7.
26 GRECO: Third Evaluation Round Evaluation Report on Latvia Incriminations (ETS 173 and 191, GPC 2) (Theme I), Strasbourg: Council of Europe, 2008, pp. 10–11.
27 GRECO: Third Evaluation Round Evaluation Report on Slovenia Incriminations (ETS 173 and 191, GPC 2) (Theme I), Strasbourg: Council of Europe, 2009, p. 8.
28 GRECO: Third Evaluation Round. Evaluation Report on Albania on Incriminations (ETS 173 and 191, GPC 2) (Theme I), Strasbourg: Council of Europe, 2008, p. 7.

4.3.1.5.   Bribery of Officials of International Organizations and Bribery of Members of International Parliamentary Assemblies

The need for criminalizing corrupt practices in the international sphere has been stressed not just in the framework of the Council of Europe, but also within the EU with the adoption of the Protocol[29] to the EU Convention on the protection of the European Communities' financial interests and that of the Convention on the Fight against Corruption involving officials of the European Communities or officials of EU member states. This EU interest had an important impact on national legislation since most CEE countries are now members of the EU and thus are part of several legislative reforms aiming at strengthening the fight against corruption in the international context.

In this section, attention is devoted to the crimes of *bribery of officials of international organizations* (Article 9 CLCC) and *bribery of official of international parliamentary assemblies* (Article 10 CLCC). Their protected legal interest in general is the transparency and impartiality of the decision-making process of public international organizations and, with reference to Article 10 of the CLCC, the fight against corruption within those assemblies that perform legislative, administrative or advisory functions on the basis of the statute of the international organization which created them.[30]

The attention and commitment that emerged at a supranational level led to an increasing harmonization in CEE countries with regard to the definitions of corruption in the international sphere. The harmonization is higher for the crime of bribery of officials of international organizations. A lower degree of harmonization is found with respect to the crime of bribing officials of international parliamentary assemblies. In fact, 4 countries out of 16 do not explicitly criminalize this practice. These countries are Albania, Bulgaria, Estonia and Macedonia. In Estonia, Section 288 of its Criminal Code defines 'public officials' as persons who hold office in a state agency or body and who represent state authority; Subsection 3 extends this definition to include officials working in international organizations. However, there is no explicit reference to members of international parliamentary assemblies under Subsection 3.[31] The case is similar in Bulgaria and Macedonia, where Article 122(4)f) of the Criminal Code refers to a 'representative of [...] international organizations' but does not mention the members of international organizations' parliamentary assemblies. Finally, in Poland, Article 93 (n.15) of the Criminal Code defines the duties of 'foreign officials' as consisting of a

---

29   Official Journal of the European Communities No. C 313 of 23. 10. 96.

30   Council of Europe: Explanatory Report, in: conventions.coe.int, http://conventions.coe.int/treaty/en/Reports/Html/173.htm, accessed 20 May 2010.

31   GRECO: Third Evaluation Round. Evaluation Report on Estonia on Incriminations (ETS 173 and 191, GPC 2) (Theme I), Strasbourg: Council of Europe, 2008, p. 10.

'job or commission assigned by an international organization', but, in this case again no explicit reference to international parliamentary assemblies is made.

4.3.1.6. Bribery of Judges and Officials of International Courts

With reference to the protection of the international sphere, Article 11 of the CLCC specifies the crime of bribery of judges and officials of international courts. This definition, which is intrinsically linked to those provided under Articles 2, 3 and 9 of the CLCC, includes 'judges' in international courts—like the European Court of Human Rights—as well as other officials or members of the clerk's office.[32]

When analyzing the degree of harmonization, it has to be noted that 6 out of 16 CEE countries—Bulgaria, Estonia, Macedonia, Montenegro, Poland and Romania—do not specifically criminalize bribery of judges and officials of international courts. On the other hand, 12 CEE countries do criminalize this form of bribery, albeit according to different definitional techniques. For example, in Slovenia judges and officials of international courts are considered public officials according to Article 126(2)7) of the Criminal Code, which refers to 'any person who performs a judicial, prosecutorial or other official duty or function in an international court'.[33] A similar definition is provided for under Section 137(3)d) of the Hungarian Criminal Code, in which specific mention is devoted to a

> member of an international court that is vested with jurisdiction over the territory or the citizens of the Republic of Hungary, and any person serving in such international court, whose activities form part of the court's activities.

In contrast, a less specific definition in which prosecutors are not mentioned is provided under Article 2(7) of the Criminal Code of Bosnia-Herzegovina, where only 'judge[s] or other official[s] of an international court' are included among 'foreign official persons'.

A different definitional technique is used in countries such as Slovakia, where active and passive bribery of judges and officials of international courts is covered by the extension of the provisions on bribery of foreign public officials in international business transactions (Sections 330, 334, 331 and 335 of the Criminal Code). This is possible since according to Section 128(2) of the Criminal Code foreign public officials are defined as

> any person holding an office [...] in an international organization established by states or another subject of public international law, if the performance of their office also includes

---

32   Council of Europe: Explanatory Report, in: conventions.coe.int, http://conventions.coe.int/treaty/
       en/Reports/Html/173.htm, accessed 20 May 2010.
33   GRECO: Third Evaluation Round Evaluation Report on Slovenia Incriminations (ETS 173 and 191,
       GPC 2) (Theme I), Strasbourg: Council of Europe, 2009, p. 12.

the competencies for running public affairs, and the criminal offence has been committed in connection with such competencies.[34]

4.3.1.7.   Trading in Influence

The inclusion of the crime of 'trading in influence' in the CLCC is the result of the comprehensive approach that guided the Council of Europe when criminalizing 'trilateral corrupt relationships'. The case of trading in influence differs from the one of corruption in terms that in such a case a person trades his/her real or supposed influence in exchange for an undue advantage from someone seeking this influence.[35]

A wide range of legislative reforms[36] (both on the national and supra-national level) has dealt with this phenomenon and highlighted the need for its criminalization. As a result of the international attention devoted to the criminalization of trading in influence, all 16 CEE countries now criminalize this offence, but with some particularities.

In this regard 9 of 16 CEE Countries criminalize 'trading in influence' both in its active and passive form: Albania (Section 245/1 of the Criminal Code); Bulgaria (Article 304b of the Criminal Code); Croatia (Section 343 of the Criminal Code); Latvia (Section 326.1 of the Criminal Code); Poland (Sections 230 and 230a of the Criminal Code); Romania (Article 312 of the Criminal Code); Serbia (Article 366 of the Criminal Code); Slovakia (Section 366 of the Criminal Code); and Slovenia (Articles 269 and 269a of the Criminal Code).

---

34   GRECO: Third Evaluation Round Evaluation Report on Slovakia Incriminations (ETS 173 and 191, GPC 2) (Theme I), Strasbourg, Council of Europe, 2008, pp. 15–16.

35   'This provision criminalises a corrupt trilateral relationship where a person having real or supposed influence on persons referred to in Articles 2, 4, 5, and 9–11, trades this influence In exchange for an undue advantage from someone seeking this influence. The difference, therefore, between this offence and bribery is that the influence peddler is not required to "act or refrain from acting" as would a public official. The recipient of the undue advantage assists the person providing the undue advantage by exerting or proposing to exert an improper influence over the third person who may perform (or abstain from performing) the requested act. "Improper" influence must contain a corrupt intent by the influence peddler: acknowledged forms of lobbying do not fall under this notion. Article 12 describes both forms of this corrupt relationship: active and passive trading in influence. As has been explained (see document GMC (95) 46), "passive" trading in influence presupposes that a person, taking advantage of real or pretended influence with third persons, requests, receives or accepts the undue advantage, with a view to assisting the person who supplied the undue advantage by exerting the improper influence. "Active" trading in influence presupposes that a person promises, gives or offers an undue advantage to someone who asserts or confirms that he is able to exert an improper over third persons'. Council of Europe: Explanatory Report, in: conventions.coe.int, http://conventions.coe.int/treaty/en/Reports/Html/173.htm, accessed 20 May 2010.

36   For example, the United Nations Convention against Corruption criminalizes the offence of 'trading in influence as a crime involving the using of one's real or supposed influence to obtain an undue advantage for a third person from an administration or public authority of the State' under Article 18. See UNODC: Legislative Guide for the Implementation of the United Nations Convention against Corruption, Vienna: UNODC, pp. 101 ss.

On the contrary, the remaining CEE countries criminalize trading in influence only in its *passive* form: Bosnia-Herzegovina (Article 382 of the Criminal Code); Estonia (Section 298.1. of the Criminal Code), Hungary (Section 256 of the Criminal Code); Lithuania (Article 226 of the Criminal Code); Moldova (Article 326 of the Criminal Code); and Montenegro (Article 422 of the Criminal Code).

4.3.1.8. Active/Passive Bribery of Domestic Arbitrators and Bribery of Foreign Arbitrators

During the final stages of the Convention negotiations, several scholars mentioned the problem of the corruption of arbitrators, i.e. persons who by virtue of an arbitration agreement are called upon to render a legally binding decision in a dispute submitted by the parties to the agreement. The need to address this offence was stated to be related to the importance of their tasks and the similarity of their activities with those of judges.[37] Due to these concerns, three new measures to be taken at the national level were defined under Articles 2, 3 and 4 of the Additional Protocol (AP) of 2003 to combat the following offences: active bribery of domestic arbitrators, passive bribery of domestic arbitrators and bribery of foreign arbitrators.

While looking at the harmonization of national definitions with those provided under Articles 2 and 3 of the AP, 5 out of 16 CEE countries (namely: Albania, Estonia, Poland, Romania and Slovakia) are still not in line with the international benchmark. In Albania, authorities claim that domestic (and foreign) arbitrators are covered by Sections 319 and 319/a of the Criminal Code, but there is no explicit reference to them in the Criminal Code. In Estonia, authorities have stated that even if the functions of arbitrators are similar to those of judges under Estonian law, the definition of public official as provided in the Criminal Code seems not to cover arbitrators.[38] Polish statutes also lack a specific reference to arbitrators (both national and foreign), as do those of Romania and Slovakia. Only under particular circumstances are arbitrators included in the case law under the broader concept of public official in these countries.[39]

A lower degree of harmonization is present with regard to the crime of *bribery of foreign arbitrators*, with 9 out of 16 CEE countries presenting gaps and asymmetries

---

37   Council of Europe: Explanatory Report, in: conventions.coe.int, http://conventions.coe.int/treaty/
      en/Reports/Html/173.htm, accessed 20 May 2010.
38   GRECO: Third Evaluation Round. Evaluation Report on Estonia on Incriminations (ETS 173 and
      191, GPC 2) (Theme I), Strasbourg: Council of Europe, 2008, p. 13.
39   For example, 'according to the national authorities of Poland, bribery of foreign arbitrators is
      possibly covered by the bribery provisions, on the condition that such arbitrators can be con-
      sidered to be performing 'public functions in a foreign State' in the meaning of sections 228(6)
      and 229(5) of the Criminal Code'. GRECO: Third Evaluation Round Evaluation Report on Poland
      Incriminations (ETS 173 and 191, GPC 2) (Theme I), Strasbourg: Council of Europe, 2009, p. 14.

in their definitions: Albania, Bulgaria, Estonia, Latvia, Macedonia, Poland, Romania, Serbia and Slovakia.

4.3.1.9. Bribery of Domestic Jurors and Bribery of Foreign Jurors

In line with the need for guaranteeing the transparency and impartiality in the decision-making process within the judiciary, next to the criminalization of corruption of judges and arbitrators, Articles 5 and 6 of the AP criminalize passive and active corruption of national and foreign jurors. A juror is understood, according to the minimum standard defined under Article 1(3) of the AP, as a 'lay person acting as a member of a collegial body which has the responsibility of deciding on the guilt of an accused person in the framework of a trial'.

While considering that such a definition is intrinsically connected with the structure of the national criminal justice system, 6 out of 16 CEE countries do not criminalize the bribery of jurors. This includes Lithuania, where no definition is provided for the offence due to the fact that the concept of trial by jury is not known in the national legal system.[40] Other countries that do not specifically criminalize corruption of domestic and foreign jurors are Albania, Estonia, Romania, Slovakia and Slovenia. In Albania, according to the national courts the concept of 'judges, prosecutors and employees of the judicial bodies' as employed by sections 319 and 319/a CC covers also domestic and foreign jurors, even though these categories of persons are not explicitly mentioned in the Criminal Code.[41] Similarly, in Croatia, authorities indicate that domestic and foreign jurors are included in the notion of 'official person' in the sense meant in the Croatian bribery provisions and referred to in the definition in Section 89(3) of the Criminal Code.[42] The same applies to the case of Poland, where domestic jurors are covered by section 115 §§ 19 and 13 (clause 3) of the Criminal Code which explicitly include lay judges in the concept of 'a person performing public functions'.[43]

---

40   GRECO: Third Evaluation Round Evaluation Report on Lithuania Incriminations (ETS 173 and 191, GPC 2) (Theme I), Strasbourg: Council of Europe, 2009, p. 13.

41   GRECO: Third Evaluation Round. Evaluation Report on Albania on Incriminations (ETS 173 and 191, GPC 2) (Theme I), Strasbourg: Council of Europe, 2008, p. 10.

42   In addition it should be considered that 'the Croatian legal system considers the concept of lay judges as members of a judicial panel trying criminal cases at first instance and that any Croatian citizen of full age worthy of performing the duty of a lay judge may be appointed as a lay judge' GRECO: Third Evaluation Round Evaluation Report on Croatia Incriminations (ETS 173 and 191, GPC 2) (Theme I), Strasbourg: Council of Europe, 2009, p. 11.

43   GRECO: Third Evaluation Round Evaluation Report on Poland Incriminations (ETS 173 and 191, GPC 2) (Theme I), Council of Europe: Strasbourg, 2009, p. 14.

4.3.2.   Further National Definitions. The Second Comparative Criterion

The *second comparative criterion* relates to those illicit behaviours that are not defined in the CLCC and the AP, even though they may be subsumed under the label of 'corruption in the public sector'. This section takes all these further offences—whether criminalized by only one or by more CEE countries—into account.

National definitions are grouped in four macro-areas: (1) intermediation in corruption, (2) corruption in professional sporting events, (3) corruption in voting and (4) illegal influence on witnesses.

4.3.2.1.   Intermediation in Corruption

The first macro-area of national definitions relates to the crime of intermediation in corruption. From a criminological perspective the introduction of such a crime seems to be of a particular interest since it allows to tackle most of the gate keepers (e.g. lawyers, accountants, notaries) of the corruptive agreements. These people, though external to the actual corruptive deal, intermediate between private and public actors and, by employing their specific know-how and know-who, tend to reduce the detection risks[44]. Intermediation in corruption is explicitly criminalized in Estonia, Latvia and Bulgaria.

In Estonia, for example, under Section 295 of the Criminal Code the crime of *Arranging the receipt of gratuities* 'is punishable by a pecuniary punishment or up to one year of imprisonment' or 'by a pecuniary punishment or up to 3 years' imprisonment' if the crime is committed 'at least twice, or by taking advantage of an official position'. The same punishments are provided for under Section 296 of the Criminal Code for those involved in *arranging a bribe*. The Latvian Criminal Code under Section 322 punishes with the deprivation of liberty for a term not exceeding 6 years those involved in cases of *intermediation in bribery*, i.e. in 'the acts manifested in the providing of a bribe received from the giver of the bribe to a person accepting the bribe, or the bringing together of these persons'. The punishment is even tougher (deprivation of liberty for a term of not less than 3 and not exceeding 10 years, with or without confiscation of property) if 'commission (…) is repeated or is by a public official'. On the same line the Bulgarian Criminal Code under Art. 305a. (New, SG 28/82) punishes by imprisonment of up to 3 years 'all those who mediate the giving or receiving of a bribe'.

---

44   On this specific issue see *inter alia* Guzin, Bayar: Corruption and Intermediaries—A Game Theoretical Approach, in Middle East Technical University Studies in Development, 2009 (vol. 36), no. 1, pp. 25–49.

4.3.2.2. Corruption in Professional Sporting Events

The second macro-area of national definitions relates to the crime of corruption in professional sporting events. Such a crime is related to match-fixing practices which caused scandals in the last few years and lead the major sport institutions in Europe, like the Union of European Football Associations, to take measures against such a practice.

As far as the CEE are concerned the case of Poland is of a particular interest. The Polish Criminal Code, in fact, in addition to the general bribery provisions under section 296b criminalizes the acceptance of undue advantages as well as the giving of a benefit,

> when organising a professional sporting competition or taking part in such a competition, of a material or personal benefit or a promise thereof in exchange for unfair behaviour or abandonment, which can affect the outcome of the competition.[45]

4.3.2.3. Corruption in Voting

The third macro-area of national definitions relates to the crime of corruption in voting or in elections, i.e. in one of the most characteristic elements of democratic political systems.

Section 250a of the Polish Criminal Code criminalizes corruption in voting with reference to the acceptance and the request of a benefit in return for voting in a certain way as well as the giving of a benefit to such a person for having voted.[46] Similar definitions are provided for within the Criminal Codes of Bosnia-Herzegovina, Macedonia, Romania and Serbia. The Criminal Code of Bosnia-Herzegovina under Article 195(1) defines the crime of *violating the free decision-making of voters*. Punishing with a fine or imprisonment for a term not exceeding 3 years

> whoever, during elections for the institutions in the Federation or a recall vote or at a referendum, forces a voter in the Federation by use of force, serious threat, bribery or by taking advantage of his poor material position, or in any other illegal way, to vote for or against a particular candidate or for or against a list of candidates, or for or against the recall, or for or against a proposal to be decided upon at the referendum, or not to vote at all.

A narrower definition is provided for under the Macedonian Criminal Code, Article 162 (Bribery at elections and voting) which criminalizes offering, giving or promising

> a present or some other personal benefit to a person with voting right, with the intention of attracting this person to perform or not to perform the voting right, or to perform it in a certain sense,

---

45   GRECO: Third Evaluation Round Evaluation Report on Poland Incriminations (ETS 173 and 191, GPC 2) (Theme I), Strasbourg: Council of Europe, 2009, p. 4.
46   Ibid.

as well as requesting or receiving 'a present or some other benefit, (…) in order to perform or not to perform the voting right, or to perform it in a certain sense'. In Romania the Criminal Code under Article 303 punishes the

> act of promising, offering or giving money or other benefits in order to determine an elector to vote or not to vote for a certain list of candidates or for an independent candidate or to vote or not to vote in a referendum, as well as their receipt by the elector, for the same purpose.

Similarly, in Serbia Article 156 of the Criminal Code criminalizes *giving and accepting bribes in connection with voting* with fine or imprisonment of up to 3 years.

4.3.2.4. Illegal Influence on Witnesses

The fourth macro-area of national definitions relates to witnesses in court cases. They are of great relevance since they often provide the major evidence in court proceedings. In this regard the most interesting example derives from the Macedonian legal experience. The Criminal Code of Macedonia provides a specific definition of *illegal influence on witnesses* as stipulated by Article 368-a which punishes with imprisonment of 1 to 3 years whoever

> will influence some person to appear or not to appear as a witness in a procedure in front of a court or in administrative procedure or is called as a witness to give or not to give statement in a certain sense, using threats on the life or the body or on the property in greater scope, offering a bribe, disruption or any other means.

4.4. Conclusions

This chapter was aimed at understanding to what extent a co-ordinated criminalization of corruption exists in the *public sector* in CEE countries. In this regard, despite the diversity among national criminal justice systems and legislation, a high degree of harmonization and approximation of criminal definitions on corruption has emerged especially with reference to those definitions provided for in the CLCC. A lower degree of harmonisation has been reached regarding the definitions introduced in 2003 with the AP. However, several legal reforms related to corruption are currently under discussion in most of the CEE counties. In addition, while looking at the specific national experiences, the analysis of the anti-corruption legislation in the CEE has also highlighted interesting definitions that may deserve attention in the international arena. This is particularly true in the case of intermediation in corruption and the illegal influence on witnesses.

The move toward a common approach in anti-corruption in the CEE has begun, but still needs concrete efforts at an international and national level. In this regard scholars have pointed out the overall importance in the *short term* of the international actors (e.g. the Council of Europe and the GRECO) and their activities in monitoring the national legislation as well as the 'EU conditionality's impact during the accession process[47], which provide incentives for legal reforms and revisions. However, in the *long term* these guiding forces need to be sustained and integrated through processes of national 'social learning'[48] and by 'domestic sources of reform'[49] deriving from social movements and governmental machines[50] able to provide an actual and concrete application of these anti-corruption reforms in the national everyday life.

This chapter has mainly focused on the formal elements of the definitions provided at the national level and, in some cases, by means of case law or information provided by national authorities, on *how* national provisions on corruption are actually applied in the national case law. However, further research should be carried out in this domain. Using Roscoe Pound's[51] terminology, research ought to be aimed, in fact, at combining in a more specific manner the study of the anti-corruption 'law in the books' (i.e. the legal texts), with the anti-corruption 'law in action', that is, the concrete enforcement of the law. Such an approach would help in tailoring *ad hoc* national policies able to provide concrete changes by looking at the *micro* dimension of each nation.

---

47 Pridham, Geoffrey: The EU's Political Conditionality and Post-Accession Tendencies: Comparisons from Slovakia and Latvia, in Journal of Common Market Studies, 2008 (vol. 46), no. 2, pp. 365–387, here: p. 386. Similarly, while looking at the specific case of Poland Gadowska argues that 'from among the many initiatives undertaken by various international institutions combating corruption in Poland, the most effective was found to be pressure exerted by the European Union' Gadowska, Kaja, National and international anti-corruption efforts: the case of Poland, in Global Crime, 2010 (vol. 11), no. 2, pp. 178–209. For the specific example of Bulgaria and Romania see: Ivanov, Kalin: The 2007 accession of Bulgaria and Romania: ritual and reality, in Global Crime, 2010 (vol. 11), no. 2, pp. 210–219.
48 Pridham, Geoffrey: The EU's Political Conditionality and Post-Accession Tendencies: Comparisons from Slovakia and Latvia, in JCMS, 2008 (vol. 46), no. 2, pp. 365–387.
49 Batory, Agnes: Post-accession malaise? EU conditionality, domestic politics and anticorruption policy in Hungary, in Global Crime, 2010 (vol. 11), no. 2, pp. 178–209, here:: p. 164.
50 Moroffa, Holger/ Schmidt-Pfister, Diana: Anti-corruption movements, mechanisms, and machines—an introduction, in Global Crime, 2010 (vol. 11), no. 2, pp. 89–98. See also Sampson, Steven: The anti-corruption industry: from movement to institution, Global Crime, 2010 (vol. 11), no. 2, pp. 261–278.
51 Pound, Roscoe: Law in Books and Law in Action, in American Law Review (vol. 44), no. 12, pp. 12–18.

4.5. Appendix: Corruption in CEE Countries—Comparative Table

State	Art. 2 CLCC	Art. 3 CLCC	Art. 4 CLCC	Art. 5 CLCC	Art. 6 CLCC	Art. 9 CLCC	Art. 10 CLCC	Art. 11 CLCC	Art. 12 CLCC	Art. 2 AP	Art. 3 AP	Art. 4 AP	Art. 5 AP	Art. 6 AP
Albania	√	√	√	O	O	O	O	√	√	O	O	O	O	O
Bosnia-Herzegovina	√	√	√	√	√	√	√	√	√	√	√	√	√	√
Bulgaria	√	√	√	√	√	√	O	X	√	√	√	O	√	O
Croatia	√	√	√	√	O	√	√	√	√	√	√	√	√	√
Czech Rep.	√	√	√	√	√	√	√	√	√	√	√	√	√	√
Estonia	√	√	O	√	O	√	O	O	√	X	X	X	O	O
Hungary	√	√	√	√	√	√	√	√	√	√	√	√	√	√
Latvia	√	√	√	√	√	√	√	√	√	√	√	O	√	O
Lithuania	√	√	O	√	√	√	√	√	√	√	√	√	X	X
Macedonia	√	√	√	√	O	√	O	O	√	√	√	O	√	O
Montenegro	√	√	√	√	√	√	√	X	√	√	√	√	√	√
Poland	√	√	√	√	√	√	√	O	√	O	O	O	√	√
Romania	√	√	√	√	√	√	√	X	√	O	O	O	O	O
Serbia	√	√	√	√	√	√	√	√	√	√	√	O	√	√
Slovakia	√	√	√	√	√	√	√	√	√	O	O	O	O	O
Slovenia	√	√	√	√	√	√	√	√	√	√	√	√	O	O

Legend:

√   the definition of the respective crime is in line with the definition provided in the CLCC or AP

O   national authorities claim that the conduct is punishable in their criminal justice system but there is no specific legal definition

X   lack of a specific definition or presence of a definition that is not in line with the one provided in the CLCC or AP

Last updated in November 2010.

Mi Lennhag

5. Understanding Post-Soviet Petty Corruption. Informal Institutions, Legitimacy, and State Criticism

5.1. Introduction

Almost 20 years have passed since the collapse of the Soviet Union, and a new market-based order has been introduced. Alena Ledeneva's book *Russia's Economy of Favours—Blat, Networking and Informal Exchange*[1] described the Soviet phenomenon of *blat* as an informal economic (but mostly non-monetary), non-hierarchical, network-based channel for transactions, parallel to the state, that has existed since the 1930s.

Despite new economic routines and the not negligible time that has passed since the Soviet period, it is worth exploring the legacy of 70 years of time-consuming, informal economic strategies that dominated everyday life during the communist period.

During a field study conducted in Ukraine and Belarus in the spring of 2009, this topic was examined through 33 qualitative, semi-structured interviews. This field study will be treated here as a pilot study, and the basis both for my future qualitative interviews and for my later quantitative research. The pilot study is also a good take-off point for how to theoretically understand, discuss and explain petty corruption.[2]

The first of two research questions during the pilot study investigated whether the *Soviet phenomenon of* blat *had disappeared, continued or changed and adapted to new circumstances in post-Soviet Ukraine and Belarus.* The second question focused on *the reasons for the changes in, or continuity of,* blat *as an informal institution in the eyes of 'ordinary' citizens.* The main objective was, however, to examine citizens' *perceptions* of the reasons for taking part in the contemporary informal economy.

The most interesting results were to be found in how the everyday economic behaviour was presented, justified and explained by citizens. Many of the 'models of explanation' focus on the relationship to the state.

The continuous existence of *blat*—albeit adapted to new socio-economic circumstances—is evident from the interview material. Today's *blat* constitutes a channel for giving bribes or guaranteeing good social services. It involves even more money and an increasing number of autonomous bribe collectors demanding bribes during contact with civil servants. Individuals justify their participation in these informal activities by placing the blame on the existence of dysfunctional laws, heavy bureaucracy, lack of state control, illicit acts by other citizens or by the state officials and politicians, and

---

1   Ledeneva, Alena V.: Russia's Economy of Favours—Blat, Networking and Informal Exchange, Palantino: Cambridge University Press, 1998.
2   *Petty corruption* is frequently called 'street level corruption' or 'low level corruption'.

on a low identification with the (immoral) state. Respondents also present an ongoing preference for informal solutions as a better way of solving many everyday problems.

This paper is, however, a theoretical discussion on how to understand today's post-Soviet petty corruption and not a report on field research. It presents a theoretical framework which aims to provide a deeper understanding of both the characteristics of today's petty corruption and of individuals' models of explanation. The focus is on informal economic practices, institutional path dependence and the relationship between individuals and the post-Soviet state.

This introduction is followed by a section on *blat* as a phenomenon and area of research.[3] Then, after the theoretical framework, the last section offers some concluding thoughts in.

5.2.   Blat as a Concept and Field of Research

Several researchers have described Soviet *blat*,[4] which Ledeneva defines as 'the use of personal networks and informal contacts to obtain goods and services in short supply and to find a way around formal procedures'.[5] One of my respondents in Ukraine described Soviet *blat*[6] as 'getting something without competition, without standing in a public queue', which illustrates how *blat* has existed beside—and employed different rules than—the official economy.

Blat was a widespread and time-consuming response to shortages, control and hierarchies. The purpose was to find channels besides the dysfunctional formal queuing system and thereby gain faster and cheaper access to, for example, consumer goods, eminent jobs, apartments, dental care or university education.

Blat is often described in relation to the state and, thus, as a natural reaction to the dysfunctional official state. Rasma Karklins calls *blat* a 'response to the inadequa-

---

3   It is worth mentioning that I initially did not expect people to talk about *blat* as a feature in a post-Soviet context.

4   Examples of such descriptions are: Humphrey, Caroline: The Unmaking of Soviet Life. Everyday Economies After Socialism, London: Cornell University Press, 2002, pp. 128–139; Karklins, Rasma: The System Made Me Do It: Corruption in Post-Communist Societies, New York: M.E. Sharp, 2005, pp. 77–80; Easter, Gerald: Reconstructing the state: personal networks and elite identity in Soviet Russia, Cambridge: Cambridge University Press, 1999, pp. 52ff; Zimmerman, William: Mobilized participation and the nature of the Soviet dictatorship, in Millar, James (ed.): Politics, work, and daily life in the USSR, Cambridge: Cambridge University Press, 1987; Fitzpatrick, Sheila: Everyday Stalinism: Ordinary Life in Extraordinary Times: Soviet Russia in the 1930s, New York: Oxford University Press, 1999; Holmes, Leslie: Rotten states?, Durham: Duke University Press, 2006. A similar investigation from the case of Poland: Wendel, Janine: The Private Poland. Oxford: Oxford University Press, 1986.

5   Ledeneva, Alena V.: Russia's Economy of Favours—Blat, Networking and Informal Exchange, Palantino: Cambridge University Press, 1998, p. 1.

6   Translated literally, *blat* means 'useful connections' or 'to pull'.

cies' of the formal political and economical system,[7] Alena Ledeneva sees *blat* as the 'reverse side of an over controlling centre',[8] and Leslie Holmes refers to it as a 'second economy'.[9]

Citizens associated Soviet *blat* transactions with the precarious circumstances that forced them to engage in informal exchange. They regarded *blat* as a necessary survival strategy and part of Soviet daily life. This way of thinking made it possible to 'excuse' one's own informal acts, which often were made at the expense of state property (such as when people 'gave away' state goods).

People did, however, not lack money, and money was not the focus of *blat* within the Soviet informal economy. Power emanated from holding an office that controlled desirable resources or from having friends in strategic places. Blat was based on connections beyond the individuals you associated with, in an expanded circle of acquaintances where people constantly 'collected' and spent time ingratiating themselves with potentially useful contacts.

Alena Ledeneva and Thomas Borén also regard *blat* as a social and cultural phenomenon, and not simply an economic one. Blat relations were often non-hierarchical, and trust was an important component. Distinguishing this 'grey' economy from the 'black' one perhaps reveals the role of informal trust. Friendship acquired a special meaning, considered in terms of 'usefulness',[10] 'functional friendship'[11] or 'useful people'[12] and was driven by self-interest and mutual benefit. Ledeneva describes individuals as 'simultaneously social and calculating', generating an 'instrumental use of personal networks'.[13]

Blat made the Soviet system tolerable, while also subverting and maintaining it by offering informal solutions to distribution problems. The prohibited was possible and kept as an open secret since the state depended on informal solutions. Ledeneva

---

7   Karklins, Rasma: The System Made Me Do It: Corruption in Post-Communist Societies, New York: M.E. Sharp, 2005, p. 79.

8   Ledeneva, Alena V.: Russia's Economy of Favours—Blat, Networking and Informal Exchange, Palantino: Cambridge University Press, 1998, p. 3.

9   Holmes, Leslie: Rotten states?, Durham: Duke University Press, 2006, p. 26.

10   Borén, Thomas: What are Friends for? Rationales in Informal Exchange in Russian Everyday Life, in Arnstberg, Karl-Olov/ Borén, Thomas (eds.): Everyday Economy in Russia, Poland and Latvia, Stockholm: Södertörns högskola, 2003, p. 25.

11   Karklins, Rasma: The System Made Me Do It: Corruption in Post-Communist Societies, New York: M.E. Sharp, 2005, p. 79.

12   Ledeneva, Alena V.: Blat and Guanxi: Informal Practices in Russia and China, in: Comparative Studies in Society and History, 2008 (vol. 50), no. 1, p. 121.

13   Ledeneva, Alena V.: Blat and Guanxi: Informal Practices in Russia and China, in: Comparative Studies in Society and History, 2008 (vol. 50), no. 1, p. 120. cf. Humphrey, Caroline: The Unmaking of Soviet Life. Everyday Economies After Socialism, London: Cornell University Press, 2002, p. 139; Borén, Thomas: What are Friends for? Rationales in Informal Exchange in Russian Everyday Life, in Arnstberg, Karl-Olov/ Borén, Thomas (eds.): Everyday Economy in Russia, Poland and Latvia. Stockholm: Södertörns högskola, 2003, p. 22.

argues that this eventually led to a situation where 'loyalty to one's connections means more than loyalty to the state'.[14]

Soviet *blat* is often distinguished from corruption as something with positive societal outcomes, as non-monetary, non-hierarchical and based on trust, while also not obviously violating the law.[15]

The ideas on what has happened to *blat* in the post-Soviet context differ. Some scholars see *blat* as an outdated term replaced by corruption; others see a transformation and re-orientation of the phenomenon. In later works, Ledeneva argues that there still is a 'tradition of give and take practices in Russia', with negative outcomes for society.[16]

Existing research on *blat* mainly focuses on the Soviet period or the time just afterwards, and most often on the Russian case.[17] Contemporary studies of the post-communist, informal economy also mainly concentrate on Russia's high level corruption (among oligarchs)[18] or bribery in the sphere of business.[19]

Despite this, our everyday informal behaviour has a great impact. Our informal acts affect the creation of formal institutions and limit state authority.[20] Widespread informality and the persistence of parallel economies can in some forms (the most common being corruption) be regarded as threats to (weak) states. It can also be an illus-

---

14 Ledeneva, Alena V.: Russia's Economy of Favours—Blat, Networking and Informal Exchange, Palantino: Cambridge University Press, 1998, p. 214. cf. Borén, Thomas: What are Friends for? Rationales in Informal Exchange in Russian Everyday Life, in Arnstberg, Karl-Olov/ Borén, Thomas (eds.): Everyday Economy in Russia, Poland and Latvia. Stockholm: Södertörns högskola, 2003, p. 22; Karklins, Rasma: The System Made Me Do It: Corruption in Post-Communist Societies, New York: M.E. Sharp, 2005, pp. 87f; Ledeneva, Alena V.: Blat and Guanxi: Informal Practices in Russia and China, in: Comparative Studies in Society and History, 2008 (vol. 50), no. 1, pp. 118–144, here: p. 123.
15 Compare this to Jan Teorell's definition of *petty corruption* as 'exchanges made during everyday interactions between low-level public officials and citizens'. Teorell, Jan: Corruption as an Institution: Rethinking the Nature and Origins of the Grabbing Hand, QoG Working Papers Series, The Quality of Government Institute, 2007.
16 Ledeneva, Alena V.: Blat and Guanxi: Informal Practices in Russia and China, in: Comparative Studies in Society and History, 2008 (vol. 50), no. 1, pp. 118–144, here: p. 120.
17 For example, see: Piirainen, Timo: Learning to Live with the Market. Urban Households in Russia and the Official and Informal Economies, in Månson, Per (ed.): East Europe Ten Years After Communism. Transforming Power and Economy, Forskning om Europafrågor, no. 9, 2000; Rose, Richard: Living in an Anti-Modern Society, in: East European Constitutional Review, 1999 (vol. 8), no. 1–2, pp. 68–75.
18 For example, see: Johnston, Michael: Syndromes of Corruption: Wealth, Power, and Democracy, Cambridge: Cambridge University Press, 2005, p. 59; Ledeneva, Alena V.: How Russia really works, Ithaca: Cornell University Press, 2006; Lovell, S./ Ledeneva, A./ Rogachevskii, A.: Bribery and Blat in Russia: Negotiating Reciprocity from the Early Modern Period to the 1990s, Houndmills, Basingstoke: Macmillan Press Ltd, 2000; Karklins, Rasma: The System Made Me Do It: Corruption in Post-Communist Societies, New York: M.E. Sharp, 2005.
19 For example, see: Wästerfors, David: Berättelser om mutor, Eslöv: Symposion, 2004.
20 For example, see: Helmke, Gretchen/ Levitsky, Steven: Informal Institutions and Comparative Politics: A research Agenda, in: Perspectives on Politics, 2004 (vol. 2), pp. 725–740, here: p. 726.

tration of a government's failure to incorporate or even consider existing social and cultural systems of norms. Finally, it might also be a sign that a state is too weak to be able to adopt new practices or exert control over its own citizens.

One of my assumptions in the following theoretical discussion is that informality to a large extent is maintained by citizens' attitudes, by deeply rooted norms and by public opinion of what is rational—and that this affects both society and economy considerably. There are several reasons for highlighting the relationship between individuals and the state, and individuals' subjective feelings about this relationship. This paper examines *one* aspect of how informal economic institutions are developed and accommodated, yet also retained. It is therefore a case study of ongoing informal economic behaviour.

One should also bear in mind that some countries in the post-Soviet region have expressed the hope of joining the EU, which could eventually lead to demands for reforms in order to 'fix' the informal economy, with the intention of conforming to the European market. I find it important that we dare to consider the impact of informal attitudes on development and integration, especially since the situation—from the outside and an economic point of view—seems to be a sub-optimal state of equilibrium.[21]

5.3. Informal Institutions and Change

The economist Douglass North—who places particular emphasis on the concepts of norms and path dependence—defines institutions as 'humanly devised constraints that structure political, economic and social interaction [and] consist of both informal constraints [...] and formal rules'.[22] In institutional theory, institutions constitute the framework that defines, enables, limits and simplifies decision-making. Repeated interaction might form a pattern and establish common expectations and mutual trust.[23] North emphasizes that institutions are invented 'to create order and reduce uncertainty in exchange'.[24]

Another economist, Oliver Williamson, further developed North's reasoning and neoclassical criticism by extending institutionalism to focus on the underlying

---

21   Cf. North, Douglass C.: Institutions, in: The Journal of Economic Perspectives, 1991 (vol. 5), no. 1, pp. 97–112, here: p. 109.
22   Ibid., p. 97.
23   See, for example, Pierson, Paul: Politics in Time. History, institutions, and Social Analysis, Princeton: Princeton University Press, 2004; Hedlund, Stefan: Institutionell teori: ekonomiska aktörer, spelregler och samhällsnormer, Lund: Studentlitteratur, 2007, p. 134.
24   North Douglass C.: Institutions, in: The Journal of Economic Perspectives, 1991 (vol. 5), no. 1, pp. 97–112, here: p. 97.

social and legal norms and rules that affect economic activity.[25] To fully understand *blat*, I believe, it is crucial to include underlying norms, which are not always clearly articulated. Williamson presents[26] four levels of analysis, of which I find the two upper ones most useful for my research. The highest level describes *'social embeddedness'*: norms, habits and other deeply rooted patterns of behaviour. On this level, change occurs very slowly. The second level—the more concrete *'institutional environment'*— includes laws and rules associated with the political arena.

Gretchen Helmke and Steven Levitsky, for example, argue that 'many "rules of the game" that structure political life are informal,' defining them as 'socially shaped rules, usually unwritten, that are created, communicated, and enforced outside of officially sanctioned channels'.[27]

Helmke et al. make an interesting distinction between 'competing informal institutions', such as corruption, and 'substitutive informal institutions', which 'achieve what formal institutions were designed, but failed, to achieve'.[28] Keith Darden[29] argues against such a dichotomy and stresses that graft can also be seen as an institution organized by the state itself.[30]

Informal institutions are consequently often seen as having a close relationship with formal ones. This can be seen, for example, when Helmke et al. argue that informal institutions appear when: 1) formal institutions are *incompatible*, 2) informal institutions are the *'second best'* for actors who would prefer to, but cannot, find a formal solution or means to change the formal institutions, and 3) the formal institutions are *ineffective* and lack credibility.

Darden mentions that it might even be 'impossible to follow the law in many situations'.[31] Informal procedures could, therefore, be acceptable. Helmke et al. say that informal institutions can be seen both as 'dysfunctional, or problem creating' and as 'functional, problem solving' depending on the circumstances.[32] Soviet-era *blat* mainly correlates to the aspect of problem solving, but the situation might be different when it comes to today's *blat*.

---

25   Williamson coined the term 'New Institutional Economics' (see Hedlund, Stefan: Institutionell teori: ekonomiska aktörer, spelregler och samhällsnormer, Lund: Studentlitteratur, 2007, p. 61, 245).

26   Williamson, Oliver E.: The New Institutional Economics: Taking Stock, Looking Ahead, in: Journal of Economic Literature, 2000 (vol. 38), pp. 595–613.

27   Helmke, Gretchen/ Levitsky, Steven: Informal Institutions and Comparative Politics: A research Agenda, in: Perspectives on Politics, 2004 (vol. 2), pp. 725–740, here: p. 727.

28   Ibid., p. 729.

29   Darden, Keith: The integrity of corrupt states: Graft as an informal state institution, in: Politics & Society, 2008 (vol. 36), pp. 35–59.

30   This idea of integrated and officially 'accepted' corruption is further developed below.

31   Darden, Keith: The integrity of corrupt states: Graft as an informal state institution, in: Politics & Society, 2008 (vol. 36), p. 38.

32   Helmke, Gretchen/ Levitsky, Steven: Informal Institutions and Comparative Politics: A research Agenda, in: Perspectives on Politics, 2004 (vol. 2), p. 728.

Ledeneva—employing a culture-based analysis—argues that informal practices cannot only be seen as reactions to constraints, but also as historical and cultural products.[33] Helmke et al., on the other hand, choose to highlight 'shared expectations' and leave out the more culturally 'shared values'.[34] My analysis will not be a culture-based one, but I should emphasize that cultural circumstances might be stressed by my respondents as the motivations for informal acts.

Besides the man-made origin of institutions emphasized by North, there appear to exist other aspects of social interaction that eventually lead to the creation of visible (and lasting) patterns. Path dependence means stability over time in actions and patterns of thought, and institutions that 'maintain' themselves by being stable, repetitive and sometimes self-reinforcing. An overarching idea is that history matters; the past is relevant and is the backdrop that influences and limits actors in making consistent, enlightened decisions today that maximize utility. This historical influence on the present is well captured by the expression that past events keep a 'grip on the mind'.[35]

Paul Pierson is a political scientist whose works highlight path dependence and the importance of seeing institutional development as a long-term process. He puts forward some suggestions concerning actors' roles in institutional development which will be useful for understanding respondents' ideas on their continuing informal activities. Regarding the ability of actors to create change, he points out that 'institutions, once in place, may "select" actors'.[36] This means that actors, over a long period, have adapted to institutional arrangements. An unofficial economy sanctioned by the state, such as Soviet *blat*, might constitute such an institutional arrangement.

This 'arrangement' includes high initial costs that create an increasing resistance to change, even when that change might bring greater future benefits. Citizens have invested too much knowledge and time adapting and making contacts to make change their first choice. In the case of Soviet *blat*, individuals spent an increasing amount of time on maintaining good relations with 'useful people', making the possibility of a new social order increasingly remote. This feature is well captured in North's idea of 'pirates' who will go on investing in becoming better pirates—i.e. more corrupt—in a society that lacks incentives for them to abandon their behaviour.[37]

---

33   Ledeneva, Alena V.: Blat and Guanxi: Informal Practices in Russia and China, in: Comparative Studies in Society and History, 2008 (vol. 50), no. 1, p. 119.

34   Helmke, Gretchen/ Levitsky, Steven: Informal Institutions and Comparative Politics: A research Agenda, in: Perspectives on Politics, 2004 (vol. 2), p. 728.

35   cf. Hedlund, Stefan: Institutionell teori: ekonomiska aktörer, spelregler och samhällsnormer, Lund: Studentlitteratur, 2007, pp. 133, 239–251.

36   Pierson, Paul: Politics in Time. History, institutions, and Social Analysis, Princeton: Princeton University Press, 2004, p. 152.

37   In a more economic context, this is called 'massive increasing returns'. See North, Douglass C.: Institutions, in: The Journal of Economic Perspectives, 1991 (vol. 5), no. 1, p. 109.

Informal institutions have several features relevant to an understanding of *blat*'s post-Soviet survival. Firstly, North argues that informal institutions remain stable even when formal institutions change. Secondly, he argues that informal institutions will be much more resilient to intentional political actions because they are deeply embedded in traditions and patterns of behaviour.[38]

5.4. Informal Economic Practices

5.4.1. The Gift

Glenn Sjöstrand[39] argues that the gift as an institution works through strong informal and institutionalized norms, and can be an integrated part of the economy. The gift may be freely offered—without demands of reciprocity—but, in reality, giving often includes social restrictions and obligations. Gifts, in some situations, can therefore be 'virtually required'.[40]

The political scientist Jan Teorell describes a situation when '[g]ifts in return for favors are commonplace'.[41] Important in this context, as the sociologist David Wästerfors has pointed out, is that the bribe was originally often a part of everyday life that was taken for granted by those involved, who therefore did not have to justify it.[42] The gift can consequently be seen as the origin of the bribe.[43]

Glenn Sjöstrand argues that a gift immediately reciprocated cannot be regarded as a gift.[44] Wästerfors has a similar idea: when something is expected in return, it should be considered a bribe rather than a gift.[45] This does not imply that my respondents make the same distinction by regarding the 'demanded gift' a bribe.

5.4.2. Bribery

According to Michael Johnston, bribery is—if it includes extortion, i.e. when an official demands payment—the most common form of corruption. This, however, does not

38   North, Douglass C.: Institutions, in: The Journal of Economic Perspectives, 1991 (vol. 5), no. 1, pp. 97–112. North, Douglass C.: Institutions, Institutional Change and Economic Performance. Cambridge: Cambridge University Press, 1990, p. 6.
39   Sjöstrand, Glenn: Gåvoinstitutionen i det moderna samhället, in: Sociologisk Forskning, 2001, no. 2, pp. 44–66.
40   Holmes, Leslie: Rotten states?, Durham: Duke University Press, 2006, p. 17. cf. Wästerfors, David: Berättelser om mutor, Eslöv: Symposion, 2004, p. 39
41   Teorell, Jan: Corruption as an Institution: Rethinking the Nature and Origins of the Grabbing Hand, QoG Working Papers Series, The Quality of Government Institute, 2007, p. 1.
42   Wästerfors, David: Berättelser om mutor, Eslöv: Symposion, 2004, p. 32.
43   Noonan, John T.: Bribes, New York: Macmillan, 1984.
44   Sjöstrand, Glenn: Gåvoinstitutionen i det moderna samhället, in: Sociologisk Forskning, 2001, no. 2, p. 47.
45   Wästerfors, David: Berättelser om mutor, Eslöv: Symposion, 2004, pp. 40f.

include corrupt transactions such as nepotism,[46] 'where considerable time may elapse between receiving quid and repaying quo'.[47] Caroline Humphrey distinguishes the bribe—'immediate deals' outside personal networks—from Soviet *blat*.[48] We should bear in mind that respondents perhaps might not call these immediate deals bribery.

Bribery crimes occur if a bribe is offered, accepted or demanded; it does not have to imply economic gain.[49] Black's Law Dictionary[50] describes bribery as the 'offering, giving, receiving, or soliciting of any item of value to influence the actions of an official'. However, some researchers choose to include in the definition—following Thorsten Cars[51]—the situation where someone working in sales or the service industry breaks the rules in relation to a superior. Bribes can thus even occur in the private sphere.

Wästerfors argues that bribes and corruption are part of a society's juridical as well as its social and moral spheres; even if bribery is forbidden by formal rules, it might be legitimate within an operational code.[52] This will be developed later on as the special relationship between moral and illegal acts.

5.4.3.   Corruption

Leslie Holmes makes a distinction between bribery that 'may occur between two private individuals'[53] and corruption, which does 'not necessarily involve any exchange'.[54] Transparency International (TI) defines corruption as 'the abuse of entrusted power for private gain'.[55]

A definition might be difficult, as Holmes says, when 'many actions or non-actions are not clearly forbidden by law'.[56] This is important to keep in mind when collecting respondents' opinions on what qualifies as bribery.

Andrei Shleifer and Robert Vishny[57] discuss the special case of corruption 'with theft' when bribe-takers in official positions keep the whole fee for services that per-

---

46   Sometimes called 'favouritism'.
47   Johnston, Michael: Syndromes of Corruption: Wealth, Power, and Democracy, Cambridge: Cambridge University Press, 2005, p. 36.
48   Humphrey, Caroline: The Unmaking of Soviet Life. Everyday Economies After Socialism, London: Cornell University Press, 2002, p. 129.
49   Cars, Thorsten: Mutbrott, bestickning och korruptiv marknadsföring: corruption in Swedish law. Stockholm: Norstedts juridik, 2001, pp. 18–43; Wästerfors David: Berättelser om mutor, Eslöv: Symposion, 2004, pp. 47f.
50   The most widely used legal dictionary in the United States.
51   Cars, Thorsten: Mutbrott, bestickning och korruptiv marknadsföring: corruption in Swedish law. Stockholm: Norstedts juridik, 2001.
52   Wästerfors David: Berättelser om mutor, Eslöv: Symposion, 2004, p. 11.
53   Holmes, Leslie: Rotten states?, Durham: Duke University Press, 2006, p. 22.
54   Ibid., p. 29.
55   Transperency International: http://www.transparency.org/news_room/faq/corruption_faq
56   Holmes, Leslie: Rotten states?, Durham: Duke University Press, 2006, p. 17.
57   Shleifer, Andrei/ Vishny, Robert: Corruption, in: The Quarterly Journal of Economics, 1993 (vol. 108), no. 8, pp. 601f.

haps should be free of charge, or to speed up the process, or by simply 'selling' things cheaper than the official price. This corruption reduces costs for individuals and is therefore more attractive and gives few 'incentives to expose the corrupt officials'.[58] As a consequence, corruption persists and spreads. In the long run everyone will 'need' to use the cost-reducing corruption 'with theft' to be able to compete with others in society.

TI further differentiates between two types of corruption. The first one, 'according to rule' corruption, is when the bribe 'is paid to receive preferential treatment for something that the bribe receiver is required to do by law'.[59] Keith Darden calls this 'a second salary'.[60] The other case is 'against the rule' corruption, when the bribe gives access to services the bribe receiver is prohibited from providing.[61]

Shleifer et al. argue that in the Soviet monopolistic and centralized system of collecting bribes ('mafia-style') it was 'always clear who needs to be bribed and by how much'.[62] Now, Shleifer et al. see a system in Russia with decentralized 'toll-booth' corruption, with many potentially corrupt actors in each sector acting independently by selling governmental goods, meaning that both the level and amount of bribes are 'rising to infinity'.[63]

A similar reflection is made by Karklins about the 'self-sustaining system of corruption' in which officials seek bribes and citizens are willing to pay, or even offer them of their own free will.[64] Even if *blat*, as defined above, cannot be regarded as bribery, some of the self-sustaining characteristics of corruption might help us understand the persistence of *blat*.

Shleifer et al. also illustrate the insecurity of informal transactions in Russia by describing a common situation when 'numerous bureaucrats need to be bribed [...] and bribing one does not guarantee that some other bureaucrat or even the first one does not demand another bribe'.[65]

Darden argues against always correlating graft and low state capacity positively. Instead, graft might be informally institutionalized as 'state-strengthening graft' that reinforces rather than undermines formal state institutions. A result might be a state

---

58   Shleifer, Andrei/ Vishny, Robert: Corruption, in: The Quarterly Journal of Economics, 1993 (vol. 108), no. 8, p. 604.
59   http://www.transparency.org/news_room/faq/corruption_faq. 101230.
60   Darden, Keith: The integrity of corrupt states: Graft as an informal state institution, in: Politics & Society, 2008 (vol. 36), p. 42.
61   Transperency International: http://www.transparency.org/news_room/faq/corruption_faq
62   Shleifer, Andrei/ Vishny, Robert: Corruption, in: The Quarterly Journal of Economics, 1993 (vol. 108), no. 8, pp. 599–617, here: p. 605.
63   Ibid, p. 611.
64   Karklins, Rasma: The System Made Me Do It: Corruption in Post-Communist Societies, New York: M.E. Sharp, 2005, p. 43.
65   Shleifer, Andrei/ Vishny, Robert: Corruption, in: The Quarterly Journal of Economics, 1993 (vol. 108), no. 8, p. 600.

that 'functions largely trough informal institutions'.[66] I think that Soviet *blat*, as we have seen it described by several researchers, is a typical case where a state to a large extent functions on the basis of informal solutions. Karklins presents a similar idea of 'good' or 'useful' corruption that is functional as it 'reduces bureaucratic rigidity'.[67] Shleifer et al. present corruption as desirable in some cases, since 'bureaucrats might be more helpful when paid directly' and it 'enables entrepreneurs to overcome cumbersome regulations'.[68]

Darden points out that graft can be an 'allowed [...] part of an informal agreement or contract', and bribe-taking can become 'a convention' in contact with officials.[69] He thereby treats deeply embedded rules, enforced by the state itself or widely rooted in expectations among citizens and officials, as an institution rather than a behavioural pattern.[70] Teorell points out how leaders might not at all be interested in curbing corruption.[71] Control can also be limited, both because corrupt officials are legitimized by other corrupt officials above them, or, as often described in the case of post-communist Russia, because the central government is too weak to be able to penalize its officials.[72] All together, these factors might create an ongoing post-Soviet *blat* that is expected, seen as legitimate and regarded as an integrated part of the state.

5.5. Citizens' Relations to the State

5.5.1. Identification, Trust & Legitimacy

The idea that Soviet citizens 'enjoyed beating the system' is often mentioned as a feature of the Soviet period,[73] inspired by the perception of citizens as being outside

---

66   Darden, Keith: The integrity of corrupt states: Graft as an informal state institution, in: Politics & Society, 2008 (vol. 36), p. 38. Wästerfors presents a similar idea, arguing that the system might even depend on the opportunities to make exceptions (Wästerfors, David: Berättelser om mutor, Eslöv: Symposion, 2004, p. 30).

67   Karklins, Rasma: The System Made Me Do It: Corruption in Post-Communist Societies, New York: M.E. Sharp, 2005, p. 15.

68   Shleifer, Andrei/ Vishny, Robert: Corruption, in: The Quarterly Journal of Economics, 1993 (vol. 108), no. 8, p. 600.

69   Darden, Keith: The integrity of corrupt states: Graft as an informal state institution, in: Politics & Society, 2008 (vol. 36), p. 41.

70   Cf. Teorell, Jan: Corruption as an Institution: Rethinking the Nature and Origins of the Grabbing Hand, QoG Working Papers Series, The Quality of Government Institute, 2007.

71   Teorell, Jan: Corruption as an Institution: Rethinking the Nature and Origins of the Grabbing Hand, QoG Working Papers Series, The Quality of Government Institute, 2007, p. 4.

72   See Shleifer, Andrei/ Vishny, Robert: Corruption, in: The Quarterly Journal of Economics, 1993 (vol. 108), no. 8, pp. 601ff.

73   E.g. Borén, Thomas: What are Friends for? Rationales in Informal Exchange in Russian Everyday Life, in: Arnstberg, Karl-Olov/ Borén, Thomas (eds.): Everyday Economy in Russia, Poland and Latvia. Stockholm: Södertörns högskola, 2003, p. 25; Holmes, Leslie: Rotten states?, Durham: Duke University Press, 2006, p. 177.

of, not represented by, the state. Holmes says that most Soviet citizens had a clearly defined concept of 'them'—the party and state authorities—and 'us', the fellow citizens.[74] The Soviet planned economy is said to have encouraged a lack of respect for formal institutions, created cryptic laws and rules, and a public feeling that 'institutions cannot be designed to serve the public good'.[75] This led to a broad understanding among citizens 'who would never contemplate stealing from their fellow citizens [but] had far less compunction about helping themselves to state property'.[76] This also remains important in post-Soviet societies as it relates to the constancy of informal institutions as a result of deeply embedded norms described in the existing literature.

Trust, feelings of legitimacy and identity are, however, difficult to implement. Jon Elster describes states that are bi-products, meaning that some mental conditions cannot be evoked directly by an effort of will or on command, but are the results of positive experiences. This provides an interesting contrast to Williamson's above-mentioned highest level of analysis (social embeddedness) where change occurs very slowly.[77]

5.5.2.   Presenting the Immoral as Moral

Karklins argues that the (post-Soviet) system *makes* people participate in the informal economy. Essentially, individuals see acting according to the rules as irrational and personal contacts as better than formal institutions. This causes actors' inventiveness to focus on coping with the everyday, despite—rather than thanks to—the state.[78]

Eventually, citizens might blame their own behaviour on an immoral state. Karklins stresses that the 'view of the detrimental role of the state is crucial in legitimizing personal corrupt acts'.[79] This is interesting in relation to respondents' perceptions, since Ukraine is a relatively new state, and the Ukrainian national movement was strong during the Soviet period. Even if informal economic acts, such as *blat*, are forbidden according to the written laws, they might, as mentioned before, be considered *jus-*

---

74   Holmes, Leslie: Rotten states?, Durham: Duke University Press, 2006, p. 184.
75   Karklins, Rasma: The System Made Me Do It: Corruption in Post-Communist Societies, New York: M.E. Sharp, 2005, p. 15. cf. Holmes, Leslie: Rotten states?, Durham: Duke University Press, 2006, p. 186.
76   Holmes, Leslie: Rotten states?, Durham: Duke University Press, 2006, p. 184.
77   Hedlund, Stefan: Institutionell teori: ekonomiska aktörer, spelregler och samhällsnormer, Lund: Studentlitteratur, 2007, p. 35, 225; Holmes, Leslie: Rotten states?, Durham: Duke University Press, 2006, p. 197. Johnston also talks about the importance of 'social ownership' to create working institutions: Johnston, Michael: Syndromes of Corruption: Wealth, Power, and Democracy, Cambridge: Cambridge University Press, 2005, pp. 2f.
78   Hedlund, Stefan: Institutionell teori: ekonomiska aktörer, spelregler och samhällsnormer, Lund: Studentlitteratur, 2007, p. 135, 189ff; Teorell, Jan: Corruption as an Institution: Rethinking the Nature and Origins of the Grabbing Hand, QoG Working Papers Series, The Quality of Government Institute, 2007, p. 14.
79   Karklins, Rasma: The System Made Me Do It: Corruption in Post-Communist Societies, New York: M.E. Sharp, 2005, p. 69f.

tified or at least *understandable* according to some public perceptions of morality. Stefan Hedlund discusses the situation where pirates finally manage to rationalize their behaviour as acceptable, turning the immoral into something moral.[80] Taking it one step further, actors might, as Karklins describes, see themselves as smart, knowing how to survive in a tough environment. They thereby turn illegal coping strategies into an element of civic pride.[81]

Finally, we should remember that informal acts are also regulated by the risk of being exposed and penalized. Hedlund describes a negative spiral set in motion when individuals identify a game which has no referee and consequently begin to violate laws—eventually encouraging others to follow.[82] Being honest is, in the end, not the best position. Teorell encapsulates this with the phrase that 'corruption becomes the rules of the game'.[83] At the same time, the state might choose to ignore the citizens' immoral acts, thereby creating an environment for 'necessary' ingenious, private transactions.[84]

5.5.3. Soviet Legacy in the Individual-State Relationship

Hedlund identifies a substantial resistance to change that forces many cultures—with post-Soviet Russia as a typical case—to rely on informal networks to such a great extent.[85] The idea of a special *Soviet legacy*[86] is a widely discussed concept.[87] While I do not explain individuals' acts in terms of culture alone, I highlight the Soviet legacy because it might be a notion that respondents refer to.

---

80 Hedlund, Stefan: Institutionell teori: ekonomiska aktörer, spelregler och samhällsnormer, Lund: Studentlitteratur, 2007, pp. 190, 253; Wästerfors, David: Berättelser om mutor, Eslöv: Symposion, 2004, pp. 10–30.
81 Karklins, Rasma: The System Made Me Do It: Corruption in Post-Communist Societies, New York: M.E. Sharp, 2005, p. 70. cf. Wästerfors, David: Berättelser om mutor, Eslöv: Symposion, 2004, p. 34.
82 Hedlund, Stefan: Institutionell teori: ekonomiska aktörer, spelregler och samhällsnormer, Lund: Studentlitteratur, 2007, p. 134.
83 Teorell, Jan: Corruption as an Institution: Rethinking the Nature and Origins of the Grabbing Hand, QoG Working Papers Series, The Quality of Government Institute, 2007, p. 2.
84 cf. Wästerfors, David: Berättelser om mutor, Eslöv: Symposion, 2004, pp. 10f; Hedlund, Stefan: Institutionell teori: ekonomiska aktörer, spelregler och samhällsnormer, Lund: Studentlitteratur, 2007, p. 198.
85 Hedlund, Stefan: Institutionell teori: ekonomiska aktörer, spelregler och samhällsnormer, Lund: Studentlitteratur, 2007, p. 148.
86 'Historical determinism' is *not* the same as 'path dependence' (see Hedlund, Stefan: Institutionell teori: ekonomiska aktörer, spelregler och samhällsnormer, Lund: Studentlitteratur, 2007, p. 240).
87 By Klas-Göran Karlsson, Kristian Gerner, Stefan Hedlund, Martin Malia et al. Richard Pipes represents an extreme position with his 'continuity theory', arguing that the Soviet period follows the patterns of Russian history, meaning that post-Soviet Russia is afflicted with the same problems (see Hedlund, Stefan: Institutionell teori: ekonomiska aktörer, spelregler och samhällsnormer, Lund: Studentlitteratur, 2007, p. 87).

One of Karklins' central arguments in her culture-based analysis is that citizens in post-Soviet countries display a particular pattern of thought and behaviour, and that the past will continue to exert considerable influence within these societies. Karklins argues that 'everyday life under communism shaped political habits and attitudes that focused on personal concerns and unofficial methods of accomplishing things'.[88] This reasoning is well captured by the term 'culture of collectivism'.[89] According to Karklins, these circumstances led to the fact that these countries 'tend to have a special relationship between formal and informal institutions, with the latter often being decisive'.[90] Holmes, on the other hand, wants to 'avoid creating the impression that only system-related factors explain corruption in post-communist states'.[91]

5.6. Final Remarks

A crucial starting point for my theoretical framework is the goal of creating a better means of understanding the *ongoing existence* of *blat* as an informal institution.

The phenomenon of *blat* has—based on the replies from the 33 respondents in the pilot study—*transformed* and *adapted* to new socio-economic circumstances and needs. The similarities with the Soviet era are, however, considerable. Blat is still described in relation to a system that *forces* people into informal acts. Even if many of the *blat* transactions described by my respondents would be regarded as bribery according to the definition presented in this paper, I think it is useful to refer to this phenomenon as 'contemporary *blat*' or 'today's *blat*'. The main reasons for this standpoint are: 1) respondents themselves use the concept of *blat*; 2) the networks for informal transactions are still constructed in a similar way as before and include elements of trust and social relations, and 3) *blat* is still primarily defined as a response to the official state.

The ideas in the theoretical discussion above serve to explain the existence of contemporary *blat*. The first idea is that path dependence appears to be more visible regarding informal than formal institutions and that actors tend to choose the already existing contract they have adapted to. The second idea is Darden's discussion of corruption as functional, widely demanded and sometimes the best option. The third aspect is individuals' perceptions of morality and legitimacy in their relationship to the state and how one might 'excuse' informality by blaming the state.

A final remark that should be made is that it is important to not see everyday corruption as being primarily the result of citizens' lack or morality, but as a result of the

---

88   Karklins, Rasma: The System Made Me Do It: Corruption in Post-Communist Societies, New York: M.E. Sharp, 2005, p. 59.
89   Ibid., p. 65.
90   Ibid., p. 15.
91   Holmes, Leslie: Rotten states?, Durham: Duke University Press, 2006, p. 176.

way the official state is constructed, of a history of a low level of public identification with the state and an 'officially sanctioned unofficial economy', and of bureaucracy and the contradictory laws that often exist in post-Soviet societies today.

Part II. Personal Relations and Democratic Representation

Petra Guasti

6.   Civil Society and the Legitimacy of the EU Polity. Using Network Analysis to Analyse Linkages Among Actors

6.1.   Introduction

Since the beginning of the 1990s, the EU institutions have progressively acknowledged the need to include and represent civil society in the European project in order to decrease public, political and institutional criticism of the EU's efficiency and, above all, its lack of democratic legitimacy. More than 15 years of both academic and political discussion of what has been labelled the 'democratic deficit' has led to changes in the formal and informal inclusion of organized civil society in the policy-making and everyday functioning of the Union. However, 15 years and numerous political documents and academic analyses later, the problems remain; a stalemate has been reached.

During these years, the European Commission and other European institutions, acknowledging the EU's democratic deficit, have repeatedly called for the democratization of European governance by increasing citizens' participation both directly and via civil society:[1]

> The Commission considers that civil society plays an important role in the development of Community policies. It will continue to encourage the activities of non-governmental organizations, the social partners and civil society in general. (…) the Economic and Social Committee should give its opinions before rather than after proposals have been transmitted to the legislature, in order to contribute more towards shaping policies[2].

and more recently after the failure of the French/Dutch referenda:

> The current crisis can be overcome only by creating a new consensus on the European project, anchored in citizens' expectations[3].

---

1   For further details, see the summary of the argument by the EU Civil society Contact Group in a recent report 'Civil Dialogue: Making it Work Better, 2006' by Fazi, Elodie/ Smith, Jeremy, a legal analysis by Obradovic, Daniela: Civil Society and the Social Dialogue in European Governance. in: Yearbook on European Law, 2005 (vol. 24), pp. 261–328. For a critique of the current passive nature of EU citizenship, see Bellamy, Richard: The 'Right to Have Rights': Citizenship Practice and the Political Constitution of the EU. in Bellamy, Richard., Warleigh, Alex (eds.): Citizenship and Governance in the European Union. London: Continuum, 2001, pp. 41–70. For a thorough assessment of the EU democratic deficit and possible solutions, see Schmitter, Philippe: How to Democratize the EU … and why Bother?, Oxford: Rowman & Littlefield Publishers, 2000.
2   European Commission: European governance—A white paper. COM(2001) 428 final—Official Journal No 287 of 12.10.2001, 2001.
3   European Commission Communication: The Commission's contribution to the period of reflection and beyond: Plan-D for Democracy, Dialogue and Debate, COM 494, Brussels, 2005.

> Civil society organizations have a very important role to play in raising public awareness of European issues and policy debates, and in encouraging people to take an active part in those debates[4].

Based on numerous political discourses, some of which are documented above, and recent theoretical contributions to the research on the nature of legitimacy of European governance[5], this paper examines the potential for civil society to contribute to the legitimacy of the emerging European polity. Therefore, while building on the current literature on both civil society and legitimacy theory, the aim of this work is not to theorize on these matters, but rather to asses the existing gaps between theoretical perspectives, discourses and practices.

The work is organized into three parts—theory, empirical analysis and conclusions. The first part defines (1.) the space within which the processes analyzed take place; (2.) the actors—civil society organizations, EU institutions[6] and citizens, and (3.) the processes taking place—or connections—between these actors. Based on the existing literature, I distinguish three criteria for legitimacy, elaborate on the relationship between legitimacy and constitutionalization and, most importantly, on the interaction between EU legitimacy and civil society, and, finally, identify the plurality of the EU's official discourses on legitimacy. I then review the current research on civil society, social and civil dialogue, and compare the EU's institutional discourses on civil society with civil society's critical perspective on EU legitimacy and its own role in this process.

The second part of this paper presents a brief summary of some empirical research concentrating on the application of network analysis as a means of analyzing the connections between actors. Using ConstEPS interview data, the paper also analyzes the connections between civil society and other actors. Here, the network analysis shows that civil society organizations mainly concentrate on contacts with EU institutions and parties rather than those with citizens and among themselves.

---

4   Wallström, Margot: A Note, in: Fazi, Elodie/ Smith, Jeremy: Civil Dialogue—Making it work better, Brussels: Civil Society Contact Group, 2006. p. 2.

5   For example, Héretier, Adrienne: Elements of democratic legitimation in Europe: an alternative perspective. in: Journal of European Public Policy, 1999 (vol. 6), no. 2, pp. 269–282; Beetham, David/ Lord, Christopher: Legitimizing the EU: Is there a Post-Parliamentary Basis for its Legitimation?. in: Journal of Common Market Studies, 2001 (vol. 39) no. 3. pp. 433–462; Magnette, Paul/ Lequesne, Christian/ Jabko, Nicolas/ Costa, Olivier: Conclusion: Diffuse Democracy in the European Union: The Pathologies of Delegation. Journal of European Public Policy, 2003 (vol. 10) no. 5, pp. 834–840; Føllesdal, Andreas: The Seven Habits of Highly Legitimate New Models of Governance. NEWGOV Paper, 2004. Available online http://www.follesdal.net/ms/Follesdal-2005-Leg-nmg-NEWGOV.pdf (last visited 18.10.2010); Kohler-Koch, Beate/ Rittberger, Berthold (eds.). Debating the Democratic Legitimacy of the European Union. Lanham: Roman and Littlefield, 2007; Paolini, Giulia: The Legitimacy Deficit of the European Union and the Role of National Parliaments. Fiesole: EUI Dissertation, 2007; Hix, Simon: What's Wrong with the European Union and How to Fix it. Cambridge: Polity, 2008; Kohler-Koch, Beate/ Larat, Fabrice: Efficient and Democratic Governance in the European Union. CONNEX Report series no. 9, Mannheim: MZES, 2008.

6   For the sake of brevity, we concentrate mainly on the European Commission, which is the major actor that shapes discourses and practices vis-à-vis civil society.

The conclusion relates the empirical findings back to the theoretical starting point of the research and suggests policy recommendations for two types of actors—EU institutions and civil society actors.

6.2. Theoretical Model and Analytical Framework

Given the gaps between theoretical perspectives, discourses and practices, this paper centres around the following questions: Can civil society enhance the legitimacy of the EU? Under what conditions can it do this? What type of legitimacy does the emerging European polity requires? This is conceptualized with three research questions: 1. Is there a dominant discourse on civil society and its role in the emerging democratic European polity? 2. What is the role of civil society in the constitutionalization process at the domestic and European levels? Is civil society an active or passive actor? Are we witnessing the emergence of a transnational European civil society? 3. What are the conditions under which civil society can enhance the legitimacy of the emerging polity? These questions are tied to the most relevant criteria in assessing the legitimacy of a given polity—inclusion, transparency, representation, consent and performance[7].

As a framework for this work, I introduce a model of viable civic participation in the European political arena (Figure 6-1.) For analytical purposes, I distinguish between the national and European level; however, as the diagram indicates, both processes (arrows) and actors cross this boundary as they often operate within or their actions have implications for both national and European arenas. I understand processes to mean networks of communication, interaction and cooperation. Regarding the actors, the paper distinguishes between citizens, EU level institutions, civil society organizations (encompassing both economic actors, such as employer associations and trade unions, and civil society actors) and EU-level civil society organizations, the so-called umbrella organizations (such as ETUC).

---

7   Paolini, Giulia: The Legitimacy Deficit of the European Union and the Role of National Parliaments. Fiesole: EUI Dissertation, 2007; and also Lord, Christopher: Democracy in the European Union. Sheffield: Sheffield Academic Press, 1998; Sharpf, Fritz: Governing in EU: Effective and democratic? Oxford: Oxford University Press, 1999; Majone, Giandomenico: Deficit Democratico: Instituzioni Non-Maggioritarie ed il Paradosso dell'Integrazione Europea. in: Stato e Mercato, 2003 (vol. 67), no. 1, pp. 3–38; Schmitter, Philippe: Organized Labor between the Practice of Democracy and the Prospect of Democratization of Europe. in Magnusson, Lars/ Ottosson, Jan (eds.): Europe—One Labour Market?, Bruxelles: PIE- Peter Lang, 2002; Schmitter, Philippe: Democracy in Europe and Europe's Democratization. In: Journal of Democracy, 2003 (vol. 14), no. 4, pp. 71–85.

Figure 6-1:   Model of Viable Civic Participation in the European Political Arena

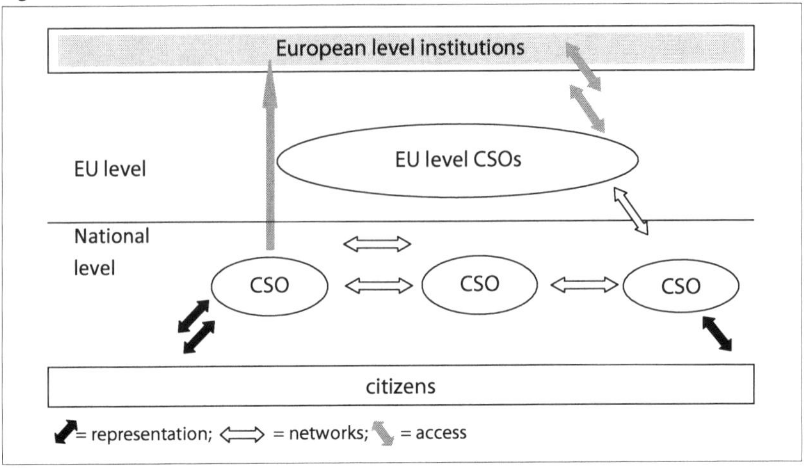

Source: Author.

6.3. Operationalization

The research questions are operationalized in the following hypothesis. The analysis of empirical data will further disentangle this into several working hypotheses, re-integrating them during the summary of the argument. With regard to discourses, I regard discursive plurality and the abstract nature of the discourses vis-à-vis civil society and its role in solving the democratic deficit as an obstacle to the enhancement of the EU's democratic legitimacy. Equally, regarding the role of civil society, the vague conceptualization of civil society's role and the failure to fulfil the basic criteria for its involvement—inclusion, transparency and representation—are also impediments to the enhancement of EU's legitimacy.

If verified, these hypotheses point to concrete gaps in civil society's potential to contribute to an increase in the EU's legitimacy:

1. The criteria of inclusion are undermined by unequal access to decision-making processes between NGOs and economic organizations, by qualitative differences in status and the nature of civil and social dialogue, as well as the inclusion of civil society in the TCE and EU governance in general[8].

---

8   Kohler-Koch, Beate/ De Biévre, Dirk/ Maloney, William: Opening EU Governance to Civil Society—Gains and Challenges, CONNEX Report Series, (vol. 5), 2008; Kohler-Koch, Beate/ Larat, Fabrice: Efficient and Democratic Governance in the European Union. CONNEX Report series no. 9.

2. The criteria for transparency are weakened by the lack of formal procedures to include civil society and the absence of an assessment of civil society's democratic credentials[9].

3. The criteria for representation are undermined by unequal access among federalist civil society organizations to EU decision-making, as well as the preferential access for transationalized civil society organizations to EU institutions.

The importance of these criteria for each of the three types of legitimacy of the European polity—inclusion, transparency and representation—is summarized in Table 6-1.

Table 6-1:   Types of Legitimacy and the Relevant Criteria

Type of legitimacy/ criteria	A. inclusion	B. Representation	C. Transparency
Input	X	X	x
Output	x	x	X
procedural	X	X	X

Note: x = important, X= crucial
Source: Author.

6.4. Methodology

The following section describes the methodology, briefly outlining the case selection and describing the data and types of analysis employed in the research.

The empirical data analysed in this work was produced in the course of the ConstEPS research project[10] during the period of constitutional ratification and failure (2004–2007). Data was collected by the members and collaborators of the ConstEPS research team in the following countries: the Czech Republic, Estonia, France, Germany, Poland and the UK. The selection of a period of intense public debate and the inclusion of old and new member states with a range of actors and diverse attitudes towards the European polity allowed the project to test the hypothesis outlined above. This research project is not primarily looking for differences between East and West, but rather for distinct patterns across the East–West divide, as well as other divides across Europe.

Mannheim: MZES, 2008.; Erne, Roland: European Unions: Labors' Quest for Transnational Democracy. Ithaca: Cornell University Press, 2008.

9   Fazi, Elodie/ Smith, Jeremy: Civil dialogue: making it work better, Brussels: Civil Society Contact Group, 2006; Obradovic, Daniela: Civil Society and the Social Dialogue in European Governance, in: Yearbook on European Law, 2005 (vol. 24), pp. 261–328.

10   The full title of the ConstEPS project is 'Citizenship, Publics and the Constitution for Europe. The Czech Republic, Germany, Latvia and Poland in European Integration'. It is based at the Jean Monnet Centre for European Studies at the University of Bremen, directed by Prof. Ulrike Liebert (2005–8) and funded by Volkswagen Foundation.

The starting point of the empirical research is a discourse analysis of 21 selected EU documents. These documents were chosen according to their relevance for the issues of legitimacy and civil society as revealed by the literature review. They include treaties (for example, the constitutional treaty), green and white papers, communiqués, declarations, action plans and opinions from the years between 1992 and 2006. The documents were analyzed with a comparative discourse analysis. A coding scheme was developed and applied using the computer package Atlas.ti. Aside from the basic information about the document, the coding scheme included information on the following categories and subcategories of code: (1.) **type of legitimacy**—divided into the following subcategories *input, output* and *procedural*; (2.) **type of democracy**—divided into the following subcategories—*liberal, republican* and *deliberative*; (3.) **criteria for legitimacy**—here three subcategories were identified—*inclusion, representation* and *transparency,* and (4.) **evaluation**—*positive, negative* and *neutral*. The unit of analysis is the discursive element of the statement. Therefore, it is possible to identify more than one discourse in one statement. The length of statement varies between a phrase, sentence, several sentences or, in some cases, a paragraph.

In this work, discourse is defined as 'a language use relative to the social, political, and cultural formations—it is language reflecting social order but also language shaping social order, and shaping individuals' interaction with society'. The use of discourse analysis allows us to deconstruct and interpret practices which constitute the perceptions of legitimacy, civil society and their interaction in the European polity and to test the first hypothesis regarding the level of discursive plurality with respect to civil society and legitimacy. Our aim is, therefore, not to provide detailed analysis of the selected documents, but to concentrate solely on identifying and understanding the discourses of legitimacy and civil society.

The empirical analysis also examined the ConstEPS media sample covering the period between October 2004 and October 2005. The set consisted of 8,540 articles selected from 36 printed media and a sample of 185 articles was chosen for a qualitative analysis of all six ConstEPS countries—Poland, Estonia and the Czech Republic from the new member states and France, Germany and the UK from the old member states. The qualitative sample for the comparative discourse analysis is representative with regard to following criteria: (1.) the overall coverage by month; (2.) the share of the periodicals over time, and with the preceding two criteria in mind, (3.) coverage of key events in the ratification debate.

For the purpose of the comparative discourse analysis,[11] the ConstEPS research team developed and applied a coding scheme using the computer package Atlas.ti.

---

11 Within the ConstEPS project, 'Political discourse analysis determines how political elites and mass media construct public opinion—and, hence, potentially, how the social constituencies of the emerging European polity conceptualize the EU, its legitimacy, and the roles and competences of member governments, citizens and civil society'. Liebert, Ulrike: The European

Aside from the basic information about the article (title, author, and origin of actor, etc.), the coding scheme includes information on the following categories and sub-categories of code: (1.) actors; (2.) topics—divided into the following subcategories—*substantive topics, the constitution as such* and *procedure*; (3.) argumentative strategies—here four major subcategories of statements were distinguished—*definitive, designative, evaluative* (positive, negative and neutral) and *advocative*, as well as different *elements of style*; (4.) justifications—distinguishing four major subcategories of justification—*interest, ideas, democracy* and *political ideologies*; objections to justifications were also included; (5.) interactions and relationships, and (6.) domestic context. A further category that cut across these divisions was the place of origin, which was ascertained for actors, topics, justifications and context.

The analysis of the ConstEPS qualitative sample will provide answers to the working hypothesis regarding the criteria of inclusion, transparency and representation; the presence/absence of the civil society actors will be analysed, as well as their positions in the mainstream media. The ConstEPS data shows that due to the highly polemical character of a media debate dominated by political parties (for example, in the Czech Republic), CSOs used other channels of communication rather than the formal process of negotiating the constitution. This included other forms of communication such as internet campaigns, informal campaigns, social partnership dialogue and political consultation at the national and European levels. Thus, rather than utilizing the intermediary communicative role of the print media, CSOs used direct channels of communication to reach both decision makers and citizens. Furthermore, the data confirms the fact that CSOs preferred activities aimed directly at national and European institutions rather than communicating to the public via the media.

The paper then analyzes the ConstEPS interview data, which was collected by ConstEPS team members and collaborators between February and June 2007. In each country, approximately 24 semi-structured interviews were undertaken with NGOs, political parties and economic organizations. In addition to selecting actors present in the ConstEPS media sample, the construction of the sample followed both a bottom–up and top–down principle—organizations with links to the EU-level umbrella organizations, and or represented in the European Social and Economic Council, were selected (top–down), as well as organizations influential at the national level (bottom–up).A set of 95 interviews with both European and national level CSOs (NGOs and economic organizations such as trade unions and employers' associations) from both new and old member states—the Czech Republic, Estonia, Poland, France, Germany and the UK—was constructed and analyzed qualitatively and quantitatively, employing, for example, statistical and network analysis.

---

citizenship paradox: Renegotiating equality and diversity in the New Europe. in: Siim, Birte/ Squires, Judith (eds.): Contesting Citizenship. London: Routledge, 2008.

Furthermore, a statistical analysis of the Eurobarometer data from the ratification period was used to further support the findings of the media analysis; this incorporated the attitudinal level of stakeholders' opinions. While the media analysis concentrated on the criteria of transparency and representation, the network analysis, which was utilized to identify connections between civil society actors, European institutions and citizens, sheds light on the criteria of inclusion and representation.

Finally, as a summary of the argument, the ConstEPS interview data was supplemented with macro data in order to evaluate the four criteria of democratic legitimacy that delineate the kind of legitimacy which organized civil society provides the EU polity. The method employed for this final assessment of the four criteria of democratic legitimacy is critical discourse analysis (CDA). CDA is an interdisciplinary approach to the study of discourse. It views 'language as a form of social practice'[12], and its essential elements are patterns of access to discourse and communicative events. The use of critical discourse analysis will allow us to 'examine the structure of spoken and written texts in search of politically and ideologically salient features which are constitutive of the (re)produced power relations without often being evident to the participants'[13].

The combination of quantitative and qualitative data using ConstEPS and other data sources allows us to present a theoretically grounded and empirically sound argument regarding the possible contributions of civil society to the democratic legitimacy of the European polity. However, this paper will concentrate on the use of network analysis; the empirical results of other types of analyses will not be presented.

6.5. Theory

It is first necessary to introduce our understanding of the nature of the European polity[14] and its legitimacy deficit. Both of these concepts are complex and variegated. We understand the European political order as a multilevel polity in the making[15] or a European would-be polity[16]. Understanding the EU as a polity in flux/the making helps us, as Smith states, to 'better capture patterns of contestation and their impli-

---

12   Fairclough, Norman: Language and Power, London: Longman, 1989, here: p. 20.
13   Jaworski, Adam/ Coupland, Nikolas (eds.): The Discourse Reader, London: Routledge, 1999, here: p. 497.
14   In this work, we understand 'polity' in its original meaning—i.e. the political organization of a group.
15   Smith, Michael, E.: Toward a Theory of EU Foreign Policy Making: Multi-level Governance, domestic Politics, and national Adaptation to Europe's Common foreign and security Policy, in: Journal of European Public Policy 2004 (vol. 11), no. 4, pp. 740–758.
16   For a further discussion see Liebert, Ulrike: The European citizenship paradox: Renegotiating equality and diversity in the New Europe. in: Siim, Birte/ Squires, Judith (eds.): Contesting Citizenship. London: Routledge, 2008.

cations for legitimacy'[17]. To summarize, this work accepts that some terms that apply to national political systems[18] can (to a certain degree) also be applied to EU, without asserting that the EU is a state[19]. This allows us to expect the EU polity to meet the standards of legitimation similar to a state[20].

There are various different theoretical approaches to the democratic deficit of the European polity, which will be discussed below. The theoretical understanding of the democratic deficit is rooted in the conceptualization of the EU as a political entity. According to Erne, the EU is more sensitive to democratic criticism because it cannot build upon the historical legitimacy of an established state. Thus, tensions between democratic norms and undemocratic practice causes more concerns in relation to the EU because the EU is not deeply ingrained in the mindsets of its citizens[21].

The intergovernmentalist approach is generally sceptical about the existence of a democratic order in Europe and thus is less interested in the democratic deficit. Andrew Moravcik, one of the major proponents of intergovermentalism, puts forward an argument that can be summarized in four steps/constraints: 1. the concept of EU political capacity as being subject to heavy procedural constraints and the division of power among individual institutions delimits power among interdependent EU institutional actors; 2. the multi-level structure of decision-making and implementation represents a further guarantee against the concentration of powers; 3. the lack of fiscal, administrative and legislative capacity, and 4. at the national level, delegation is controlled by democratically appointed institutions[22]. Thus, the intergovernmental approach conceptualizes the EU as being legitimized indirectly by national actors and

---

17 Smith, Michael, E.: Toward a Theory of EU Foreign Policy Making: Multi-level Governance, domestic Politics, and national Adaptation to Europe's Common foreign and security Policy, in: Journal of European Public Policy 2004 (vol. 11), no. 4, pp. 740–758.

18 In this work, we define 'political system' as a part of complex social system encompassing politics and government.

19 Paolini, Giulia: The Legitimacy Deficit of the European Union and the Role of National Parliaments. Fiesole: EUI Dissertation, 2007; Beetham, David/ Lord, Christopher: Legitimizing the EU: Is there a Post-Parliamentary Basis for its Legitimation?, in: Journal of Common Market Studies, 2001 (vol. 39) no. 3. pp. 433–462; for a counterargument, see Schmitter, Philippe: Democracy in Europe and Europe's Democratization. In: Journal of Democracy, 2003 (vol. 14), no. 4, pp. 71–85.

20 Beetham and Lord further state that legitimation is a matter of public expectations, the kind of choices the EU makes on behalf of its citizens and the extent to which the EU has final rule-making authority. Furthermore: 1. both public opinion and the EU leadership have high expectations of the EU's democratic legitimacy; 2. the EU engages in modes of collective choice similar to a state's; 3. the EU not only undertakes so called 'regulatory functions', but also redistributive ones. Thus, one can expect it to meet the standards of democratic legitimacy [2001: 445–450]. Hix further supports this point by stating that from a legal standpoint, ultimate rule-making authority across a wide range of areas has moved from the state to the EU. See Hix, Simon: What's Wrong with the European Union and How to Fix it. Cambridge: Polity, 2008.

21 Erne, Roland: European Unions: Labors' Quest for Transnational Democracy. Ithaca: Cornell University Press, 2008, here: p. 201.

22 Moravcsik, Andrew. In Defence of the Democratic Deficit: Reassessing Legitimacy in European Union. in: Journal of Common Market Studies, 2002 (vol. 40), no. 4, pp. 603–624.

does not see any need for further legitimacy of the EU, which Moravcik understands as an intergovernmental structure.

Regulatory theorists such as Majone go one step further towards conceptualizing the EU as a polity, but arrive at a similar conceptualization of EU legitimacy. For Majone, the EU is an administrative and regulatory agency that cannot provide its own legitimacy; thus it derives legitimacy only from the principals of delegation, i.e. from the governments of the member states. Aside from this indirect legitimacy, EU also possesses, firstly, procedural legitimacy derived from the fact that regulatory tasks are delegated and their implementation controlled by both EU institutions and the governments of the member states, and, secondly, the EU also has substantive legitimacy, which refers to the efficiency and effectiveness of the activity of regulatory agencies[23]. Majone does not speak about democratic deficit but uses the term 'credibility deficit' arising from the lack of transparency and accessibility in EU policy-making[24].

Neo-constructivists, such as Ernst Haas, tend to conceptualize the EU as an international organization with its legitimacy resting on two pillars: 1. the open and prolific participation of voluntary interest groups in decision-making, and 2. the effective performance of functions perceived as being crucial by its units[25]. More recently, the focus on participation has been revitalized by Schimitter's proposal to formulate the system of EU inclusion of aggregated interests through European governance arrangements as policy 'sites' where stakeholders and knowledge-holders would negotiate the definition of policies with the supervision provided by the EU institutions[26]. While they attempt to enhance the democratic and participatory legitimacy of the EU, neofunctionalists cease to question the effectiveness of indirect legitimacy.

Multilevel and poly-centric governance theorists view legitimacy as a patchwork of different standards. Legitimacy is conceived as a product of the interaction of all main sources of control and among decision-makers—horizontal, vertical, oblique and put out. The participation of policy networks emphasizes the increased participation of organized interests and stakeholders[27]. However, Schmitter and Follesdal note that

---

23 Majone, Giandomenico: Federation, Confederation, and Mixed government: A EU–US Comparison. in Menon, Anand/ Schain, Martin A. (eds.): Comparative Federalism: The European Union and the United States in Comparative Perspective, Oxford: Oxford University Press, 2007. pp. 121–46.

24 Paolini, Giulia: The Legitimacy Deficit of the European Union and the Role of National Parliaments. Fiesole: EUI Dissertation, 2007.

25 Haas, Ernst. B.: Beyond the Nation State. Functionalism and International Organizations. Stanford: Stanford University Press, 1964, pp. 195–196.

26 Schmitter, Philippe: How to Democratize the EU … and why Bother?, Oxford: Rowman & Littlefield Publishers, 2000.

27 Héretier, Adrienne: Elements of democratic legitimation in Europe: an alternative perspective. in: Journal of European Public Policy, 1999 (vol. 6), no. 2, pp. 269–282.

input side democratic procedures and participation need to be improved[28]. According to Banchoff and Smith, new modes of governance add to the traditional channels of democratic vertical accountability, but do not replace them, thus providing output legitimacy in addition to legitimacy 'borrowed' from the national level[29].

Federalist theorists conceptualize the EU as a polity evolving in the direction of a supranational state, meaning that an ever increasing share of political and administrative competencies once held by the nation state are being transferred to the EU and its institutions. EU institutions thus ought to have high levels of democratic legitimacy. According to the federalists, the EU decision-making process currently does not meet these standards, thereby creating a legitimacy deficit[30]. As a result, the federalist theorists are most critical of the current state of legitimacy of the EU polity and propose possible solutions, such as increasing the authority of the European parliament, introducing a directly elected commission etc.

All five approaches outlined above share one important aspect—they all seem to rely on an assumption concerning the effectiveness of the indirect sources of legitimacy. National governments are held accountable for their activity at the EU level. The pillar of EU legitimacy is the Council of Ministers (intergovernmentalist and regulatory theorists consider it to be the ultimate source of legitimacy; multilevel/polycentric theorists and federalists see it as an implied condition for the deployment of other legitimacy channels)[31].

At the same time, these approaches provide distinct frameworks for the incorporation of civil society[32]. Hüller and Kohler-Koch describe these approaches as three ideal-typical concepts. First, the 'participatory governance' approach stresses the re-establishment of the EU's steering capability, the enhancement of problem-solving (effectiveness) by including non-state actors (civil society). This approach stresses the role of civil society as a key actor in the inclusion of stakeholders in decision-making processes. The trade-off of this approach is the fact that inclusion and openness without restriction can in practice reduce effectiveness. Thus, this approach, favoured by governance as well as normative theorists, has an inherent contradiction—the inclusion and openness that aim to enhance effectiveness can in practice decrease it.

---

28   Schmitter, Philippe: How to Democratize the EU ... and why Bother?, Oxford: Rowman & Littlefield Publishers, 2000; Føllesdal, Andreas: The Seven Habits of Highly Legitimate New Models of Governance. NEWGOV Paper, 2004. Available online http://www.follesdal.net/ms/Follesdal-2005-Leg-nmg-NEWGOV.pdf (last visited 18.10.2010).
29   Banchoff, Thomas/ Smith, Mitchell: Legitimacy and European Union: The Contested Polity, London: Routledge, 1999, here: p. 15.
30   Beetham, David. Lord, Christopher: Legitimizing the EU: Is there a Post-Parliamentary Basis for its Legitimation?. in: Journal of Common Market Studies, 2001 (vol. 39) no. 3. pp. 433–462.
31   Paolini, Giulia: The Legitimacy Deficit of the European Union and the Role of National Parliaments. Fiesole: EUI Dissertation, 2007.
32   Kohler-Koch, Beate/ De Biévre, Dirk/ Maloney, William: Opening EU Governance to Civil Society—Gains and Challenges, CONNEX Report Series no. 5, 2008.

Second, the 'federalist' approach emphasizes the currently evolving character of the European polity—accentuating the simultaneous processes of polity building and social constituency building. Here, not only civil society but also the emerging transnational European civil society is perceived as a necessary condition for the successful establishment of a legitimate European polity. Authors such as Fossum and Trenz—following Juergen Habermas's notion of a political public sphere—bind together European civil society and the European public sphere[33]. According to Habermas, civil society has a strategic significance for the public sphere, constituting its very basis[34]. Unlike the first approach, which regards civil society in more abstract terms, the second approach makes an important distinction between civil society and lobby groups. Nonetheless, both key elements of this approach—European civil society and the European public sphere—are currently contested[35].

The third concept, proposed by Hüller and Kohler-Koch themselves, conceptualizes the EU as a political system which performs governmental functions without having a government and cooperates with civil society organizations. They regard civil society, which they conceptualize as a 'wide range of voluntary associations that follows "a logic of action" that is distinct from that of the state or the market or the private sphere'[36], as a possible remedy for the democratic deficit. This approach emphasizes three normative standards for the assessment of the democratic quality of civil society's involvement—reciprocity, transparency/publicity and responsiveness/accountability. The authors conclude that at the moment 'involving civil society does not live up to the promises rendering the EU more democratic'. Although newly implemented instruments provide stakeholder access to decision-making and improved transparency, they stress that the citizens' impact on outcomes is still deficient[37].

While Hüller and Kohler-Koch remain sceptical, and other authors such as Hix propose alternative solutions for democratic legitimacy by enhancing direct and indirect political participation at the European level[38], others, such as Erne, remain optimistic and view the emergence of transnational trade union networks as a possible contribution to a more democratic EU[39]. However, the contribution of organized labour

---

33 Fossum, John E./ Trenz, Hans-Joerg: The EU's Fledgling Society: From Deafening Silence to Critical Voice in European Constitution Making. in: Journal of Civil Society, 2006 (vol. 2), no. 1, pp. 57–77.

34 Habermas, Juergen: Between Facts and Norms: Contributions to the Discourse Theory of Law and Democracy. Cambridge: MIT, 1996, here: p. 240.

35 Delanty, Gerard/ Rumford, Chris: Rethinking Europe. Social theory and the implications of Europeanization. London and New York: Routledge, 2005.

36 Kohler-Koch, Beate/ De Biévre, Dirk/ Maloney, William: Opening EU Governance to Civil Society—Gains and Challenges, CONNEX Report Series no. 5, 2008, here: p. 164.

37 Ibid., p. 173.

38 Hix, Simon: What's Wrong with the European Union and How to Fix it. Cambridge: Polity, 2008.

39 Erne, Roland: European Unions: Labors' Quest for Transnational Democracy. Ithaca: Cornell University Press, 2008.

to the future of democracy, according to Erne, depends on the choices of organized labour itself[40].

Furthermore, civil society itself (in particular, civil society organized at the European level) in the form of the Civil Society Contact Group (CSCG) highlights the following critical issues which continue to shape the democratic life of the Union: 1. there is a lack of awareness of the general principles and minimum standards for consultation, which are therefore applied inconsistently, undermining the consultative framework as a whole; 2. some EU institutions and national governments question the value of organized civil society having an input in EU policy-making; 3. horizontal coordination is problematic; 4. in the ongoing debate, there is a lack of both clarity and transparency with regard to the selection of actors and stakeholders, and finally 5. there has been no critical assessment of the contribution by organized civil society[41].

The solution, according to the CSCG, lies in addressing the following four challenges: 1. providing and enabling a structure that can promote concrete outcomes; establishing an efficient and effective structure that will allow civic dialogue to make a difference; 2. recognizing the need for better horizontal coordination and equal access and strengthening the degree of cooperation between different actors; 3. strengthening trust and mutual understanding between NGOs and EU institutions—due to lack of horizontality there is a greater need for transparency and accountability among the actors involved in the process, and 4. recognizing the need for an inclusive approach— in the confrontation between efficiency and inclusion, inclusiveness should be strengthened in order to ensure the inclusion of the voices of unheard social groups[42].

6.5.1.　Legitimacy

In recent years, the literature on legitimacy—and EU legitimacy in particular—has flourished[43]. This section outlines, summarizes and evaluates critically the basic arguments encountered in the literature.

40　Ibid.
41　Fazi, Elodie/ Smith, Jeremy: Civil dialogue: making it work better, Brussels: Civil Society Contact Group, 2006.
42　Ibid., pp. 86–87.
43　Føllesdal, Andreas: The Seven Habits of Highly Legitimate New Models of Governance. NEWGOV Paper, 2004. Available online http://www.follesdal.net/ms/Follesdal-2005-Leg-nmg-NEWGOV. pdf (last visited 18.10.2010); Beetham, David. Lord, Christopher: Legitimizing the EU: Is there a Post-Parliamentary Basis for its Legitimation?. in: Journal of Common Market Studies, 2001 (vol. 39) no. 3. pp. 433–462; Lord, Christopher/ Harris, Erika: Democracy in the New Europe. London: Palgrave Macmillan, 2006; Duff, Andrew. A Liberal Reaction to the European Convention and the Intergovernmental Conference. Federal Trust Papers, July. London: Federal Trust, 2003; Kohler-Koch, Beate/ Rittberger, Berthold (eds.). Debating the Democratic Legitimacy of the European Union. Lanham: Roman and Littlefield, 2007; Bellamy, Richard: The 'Right to Have Rights': Citizenship Practice and the Political Constitution of the EU. in Bellamy, Richard., Warleigh, Alex (eds.): Citizenship and Governance in the European Union. London: Continuum, 2001,

Legitimacy is, above all, a matter of whether citizens have trust that both citizens and the authorities will comply with institutions that they believe normatively deserve their obedience in the future. Negative popular responses and legal challenges to the Maastricht treaty were the first important symptoms of a legitimacy deficit creating challenges for future integration and enlargement (i.e. both the deepening and broadening of the union). Crucial flaws in the EU outlined in the literature are: the lack of a common language, media and public discussion among a European citizenry that lacks a shared identity and functioning political parties.

Four basic concepts of legitimacy are: legitimacy as legality, legitimacy as compliance, legitimacy as problem-solving and legitimacy as justifiability. These can be achieved through four mechanisms (institutional arrangements): legitimacy through participation, legitimacy through democratic rule, legitimacy through actual consent and legitimacy through output. The current changes within the EU (integration and enlargement) may involve shifts in all four concepts of legitimacy in that they threaten the widespread support for the political community and the political order of the EU, thus requiring a serious review of the mechanisms of legitimacy.

The literature outlines three basic functions of legitimacy: 1. performance (output) legitimacy—the ability to enhance or stabilize (the capacity of a given polity to deliver goods effectively and efficiently); 2. regime legitimacy—the extent to which justice is achieved within the polity's institutions vis-à-vis representation, protection of individual and minority interests, etc., and 3. polity legitimacy—the overall support for and the stability of the polity as an 'autonomous political community'. In the political arena, all these functions are interlinked and separated in the research for analytical purposes only.

6.5.2. EU Legitimacy and Civil Society

Lord considers the wider problem of how political systems manage fundamental disagreement with regard to the requirements for their legitimation by first looking at how the issue of legitimacy needs to be understood and studied (depending on whether a political system articulates an agreed principle of legitimation or mediates disagreements between several principles), then scrutinizing the diversity of beliefs

---

pp. 41–70; Bellamy, Richard/ Castiglione, Dario: Between Cosmopolis and Community: Three Models of Rights and Democracy within the European Union, in: Archibugi, Daniele/ Held, David/ Koehler, Martin (eds.): Reimagining Political Community: Studies in Cosmopolitan Democracy, Oxford: Polity Press, 1998, pp. 152–178; Walker, Neil: Constitutionalising Enlargement, Enlarging Constitutionalism, in: European Law Journal, 2003 (vol. 9), no. 3, pp. 365–385; Schmitter, Philippe: Organized Labor between the Practice of Democracy and the Prospect of Democratization of Europe, in: Magnusson, Lars/ Ottosson, Jan (eds.): Europe—One Labour Market?, Bruxelles: PIE-Peter Lang, 2002; Schmitter, Philippe: Democracy in Europe and Europe's Democratization. In: Journal of Democracy, 2003 (vol. 14), no. 4, pp. 71–85.

about EU legitimacy, analysing the ways in which the EU deals with the issue of diversity and finally linking the disagreements on the EU's legitimacy and the elaboration of the convention method. Lord concludes that the use of a deliberative convention was an understandable response to the challenge of contentious constitutionalization[44].

Lord describes four vectors of EU legitimation (understood not in absolute terms, but rather as ideal types):

1. *indirect* (legitimacy of the Union and its institutions is indirect and derivative as it depends on the legitimacy of the Union's component states, on its respect for their sovereignty and on its ability to serve the states' purposes);
2. *parliamentary* (EU policies and institutions are best legitimated by a combination of elected parliamentary bodies and member states, thus serving the purpose of a number of people: a citizenry divided along the lines of cultural identity);
3. *technocratic* (EU institutions are best legitimated via their ability to offer solutions to problems);
4. *procedural* (legitimacy may be positively related to the observance of certain procedures—such as transparency, balancing interests, proportionality, legal certainty and consultation of the stakeholders).

Lord's use of the term 'vectors' is justified by two facts: First, they are commonly articulated as suppositions about the general directions in which the legitimation of the Union ought to be headed rather than as fully developed theories;, second, like vectors, they can both reinforce or pull against each other (at different times). Based on this differentiation, Lord presents input and output legitimacy according to the four vectors described above.

Lord further outlines three types of general relationships between the vectors: 1. each vector has elements of both compatibility and exclusivity in its relations with the others; 2. the boundaries of conflict and compatibility between the vectors are unlikely to be static, and 3. supporters of different approaches to the legitimation of the EU policies and institutions are unlikely to divide along clear lines of cleavage (thereby contradicting the two theoretical perspectives of Kantian and principal-agent theory).

Lord thus concludes that the multilevel governance structure of the EU, characterized by the absence of hierarchical relationships between the institutions and the absence of a centre, is itself an incentive for constitutional deliberation.

This work concentrates on the criteria for legitimacy vis-à-vis inclusion, transparency and representation—which are regarded as impediments to the enhancement of the EU's legitimacy.

---

44   Lord, Christopher/ Magnette, Paul: E Pluribus Unum? Creative Disagreement about Legitimacy in the EU. in: Journal of Common Market Studies, 2004 (vol. 1), no. 42, pp. 183–202.

6.5.3.   Conceptual Framework

The concept of civil society is a very common one and is used in professional literature, the media and in private life. However, it is very difficult to define—in theoretical
literature, the term has been used for centuries,[45] but during this period it has gone
through conceptual and connotative changes, which have been widely discussed by
specialists,[46] and which have led to political battles.[47]

An extensive review of the literature reveals that civil society is a term that delineates the area between the private sphere of interest and the state. It is an area of voluntary association outside the spheres of the market, state and private lives, in which

---

45   The theoretical literature finds the origins of the term 'civil society'—societas civilis—in antiquity
     Arato, Andrew/ Cohen, Jean, L.: Civil Society and Political Theory. Cambridge and London: MIT,
     1990, pp. 84–86, also Müller, Karel: Koncept občanské společnosti: konceptualizace, dilemata a
     nebezpečí. in: Politologická revue, 2001, no. 1, pp. 3–26, here: p. 3.
46   The concept is a very lively one, which can be demonstrated by the fact that the definitions
     and concept of civil society are the subject of professional discussion, for example between
     Christoph Bryant and Krishan Kumar in The British Journal of Sociology [Kumar 1993; Bryant,
     Christopher., G.A: Social Self-Organisation, Civility and Sociology: A Comment on Kumar's 'Civil
     Society'. in: The British Journal of Sociology, 1993 (vol. 44), no. 3, pp. 397–401; Kumar 1994; Bryant
     1994; Neocleous, Mark: From Civil Society to the Social. In: The British Journal of Sociology, 1995
     (vol. 46), no. 3, pp. 395–408; Keane, John: Democracy and Civil Society. London: Verso, 1988;
     Gellner, Ernest: Civil Society in Historical Context. in: International Social Science Journal, 1991
     (vol. 129), pp. 415–510 ; Seligman, Adam. B.: The Idea of Civil Society, New York: Free Press, 1992;
     Alexander, Jeffrey: The Paradoxes of Civil Society. in: International Sociology, 1997 (vol. 12), no. 2,
     pp. 115–133; Waltzer, Michael: The Concept of Civil Society in: Waltzer, Michael (ed.) Towards
     a Global Civil Society, Providence: Berghahn Books, 1998, pp. 7–27; Habermas, Juergen: The
     Future of Human Nature. Oxford: Polity Press, 2003.
47   Green, Andrew, T : Občanská společnost, ideje a utváření politiky. in : Sociologický časopis, 1997
     (vol. 33), no. 3, pp. 309–320. The global discussion about the character and the role of civil soci-
     ety in a democratic political system at the beginning of the 1990s was strongly influenced by a
     dispute between the then Czech President Václav Havel and the current Czech President (and
     at that time Prime Minister) Václav Klaus. At the core of the dispute was an intermingling of civil
     society and politics, i.e. the question of whether civil society actors at the macro-level should
     try to influence politics actively. Whereas Václav Havel (and also Petr Pithart) were considered
     to be in favour of the active intertwining of civil society and politics, Václav Klaus adopted a
     diametrically opposed position in this discussion. In his view, not only does civil society have
     negative connotations, but the liberal understanding of society also makes an active partici-
     pative civil society superfluous because elections already guarantee participation, see, Klaus,
     Vaclav. Predmluva. in Coughlan, Anthony/ Louzek, Marek et al. Krach evropske ustavy: Sbornik
     textu. Praha: Centrum pro ekonomiku a politiku, 2005. The substance of the dispute is more
     complicated: it is about the definition of the relationship between the state and civil soci-
     ety, which in post-communist countries especially is considered to be essentially inconsistent;
     based on historical experience, civil society is regarded as the opposition to state power, see,
     Arato, Andrew/ Cohen, Jean, L.: Civil Society and Political Theory. Cambridge and London: MIT,
     1990. According to Seligman, civil society has often been the only ideological alternative to for-
     eign hegemony in Central Europe, see Seligman, Adam. B.: The Idea of Civil Society, New York:
     Free Press, 1992; similarly cf. Waltzer, Michael: The Concept of Civil Society in: Waltzer, Michael
     (ed.) Towards a Global Civil Society, Providence: Berghahn Books, 1998, pp. 7–27; Nardin, Terry:
     Private and Public Role in Civil Society, in: Waltzer, Michael (ed.): Towards a Global Civil Society.
     Providence: Berghahn Books, 1998, pp. 29–33.

we realize how interrelated our world is. According to Jean Cohen, modern civil society is formed and reproduced by means of varying forms of collective activities and is institutionalized on the basis of law and particularly by subjective rules, which play an important role in stabilizing social differentiation[48].

As the sociologist Radim Marada explains,

> the idea of civil society—as a symbol of certain types of social and public sensitivity, approaches, behaviors and thinking, or ethical reasoning—does not aim at criticizing the institutional basis of NGOs. [...] the idea of civil society as the sphere of a civilized behavior of free, moral and rational individuals may (and probably should) pose limits to these spheres (the author has in mind the spheres of market and family; note by the author[49].

To sum up the theoretical and historical work on civil society, one can conclude that civil society exists as the result of a democratic political system based on the direct participation of citizens who can influence public affairs. As mentioned above, despite its long tradition and topicality, the term 'civil society' is rather abstract and is used today mainly in theoretical and conceptual contexts, whereas empirical research related to civic society uses the practical and concrete concept of NGOs, which are an institutionalized form and, as a subset of civil society, a part of civil society. The non-profit sector and its synonyms—civil sector or third sector—generally denote NGOs.[50] Some of the issues resulting from the current inaccurate use of the term civil society have been identified, for example by the American sociologist Jeffrey Alexander[51].

6.5.4. The Emerging European Civil Society

Within the study of emerging European citizenship[52], authors such as Waltzer and Meehan recognize civil society as a useful framework as part of the notion of active (European) citizenship. Nonetheless, it is exactly the state of European civil society and the overall weakness of the European public sphere which Meehan identifies as

---

48 Arato, Andrew/ Cohen, Jean, L.: Civil Society and Political Theory. Cambridge and London: MIT, 1990.

49 Marada, Radim: Civil Society: Adventures of the Concept before and after 1989. in: Czech Sociological Review, 1997 (vol.5), no. 1, pp. 3–22, here: p. 20, cf. Kumar, Krishan: Civil Society: An Inquiry into the Usefulness of the Historical Term, in: The British Journal of Sociology, 1993 (vol. 44), no. 3, pp. 375–395.

50 The Italian political scientist Amitai Etzioni introduced the notion of the third sector, i.e. the sector between the state and the economic spheres, in the 1970s to refer to a set of private organizations providing public services sponsored by the state, see Etzioni, Amitai: The Third Sector and Domestic Missions, in: Public Administration Review 1973 (vol. 33), no. 1, pp. 314–323.

51 Alexander, Jeffrey: The Paradoxes of Civil Society. in: International Sociology, 1997 (vol. 12), no. 2, pp. 115–133.

52 Meehan, Elizabeth: Europeanization and Citizenship of European Union. in: Harmsen, Robert/ Wilson, Thomas, M.: Yearbook of European Studies, 2000 (vol. 14), pp. 157–177; Bellamy, Richard/ Warleigh, Alex (eds.): Citizenship and Governance in the European Union. London: Continuum, 2001; Delanty, Gerard/ Rumford, Chris: Rethinking Europe. Social theory and the implications of Europeanization. London and New York: Routledge, 2005.

the barrier hindering the emergence of European citizenship. This view is further supported by Richard Delanty and Charles Rumford, who define European civil society as being predominantly rooted in individual national civil societies. Predominantly national civil society serves as a protection against economic globalization, establishing a basis for the maintenance of the integrity of the nation state[53].

For Meehan, the supranational rather than domestic arena confers democratic citizenship, which, however, is currently torn between the notion of market citizenship, regarding citizens predominantly as producers and consumers (hence the stress on labour and the consumer protection within the EU framework) and a liberal or libertarian notion of privatized citizenship[54]. Based on her examination of the civil and social dialogue in European governance, the Dutch lawyer Daniela Obradovic confirms the dominance of the economic dialogue over civil society in the European Union[55].

From an analysis of numerous EU documents (including, for example, white papers, regular and special reports, and Council decisions) against the yardstick of political theory Obradovic states that

> participatory democracy requires that parties who are affected by legal provisions should be involved in the opinion-forming process at the earliest possible stage and should be given the opportunity to bring their wishes to bear in this process and to put forward their proposals[56].

Thus, the goal of governance is to establish structures for the participation of stakeholders (those affected by decisions) in the decision-making process via civil dialogue.

Obradovic concludes that the boundaries between social and civil dialogue in Europe are blurred, even though the Commission supports the involvement of civic groups in European governance[57] in order to increase its efficiency. However, most of these programmes have been carried out without a legal basis and were rather problematic. Obradovic concludes that currently the involvement of the interest groups in various processes of EU governance does not dramatically increase the efficiency of EU governance. Civil society, unlike social partners, is perceived as being a diffuse,

---

53 Delanty, Gerard/ Rumford, Chris: Rethinking Europe. Social theory and the implications of Europeanization. London and New York: Routledge, 2005.
54 Meehan, Elizabeth: Europeanization and Citizenship of European Union. in: Harmsen, Robert/ Wilson, Thomas, M.: Yearbook of European Studies, 2000 (vol. 14), pp. 157–177
55 Although, as Obradovic points out, the civil dialogue was launched to counterbalance the involvement of the productive sphere in European governance, the current prevailing notion of civil dialogue is complementary rather than contradictory to the social dialogue. See, Obradovic, Daniela: Civil Society and the Social Dialogue in European Governance, in: Yearbook on European Law, 2005 (vol. 24), pp. 261–328, here: 322.
56 Ibid., p. 262
57 There are numerous organizations (over 160) and around 1,500 interest groups involved in regular consultations with the Commission, but this is mainly in the pre-drafting phase of legislation, see, Obradovic, Daniela: Civil Society and the Social Dialogue in European Governance. in: Yearbook on European Law, 2005 (vol. 24), pp. 261–328.

unstable partner[58]. This is also supported by the current findings of Ruzza et al., who call for the further establishment of sectoral umbrella organizations as credible partners in the European governance process.[59]

To summarize: within the system of European governance, civil society is a normative project aimed at improving both governance (efficiency) and democracy (legitimacy). This brings us towards the paradoxes of both the study and the practice of EU citizenship. As Richard Bellamy and Alex Warleigh point out, European citizenship is essentially normative—its major purpose was to make the EU more legitimate. They argue that EU citizenship is thus mainly composed of formal entitlements provided by the treaties, as well as a matter of institutional practices and structures[60]. Furthermore, in its current state—as a catalogue of entitlements—, EU citizenship is passive and not capable of providing legitimacy to the EU elite-driven process[61].

Several authors criticize the insufficient participation of civil society in the constitutional process and the marginal attention paid to its demands. According to Andreeev, citizens and civic organizations were somehow forgotten and marginalized during the work of the most recent convention. Although there were several public hearings and online forums, organized either by the various working groups of the convention or the convention itself, there was no clear link between the proposals made by the citizens' organizations and the content of the draft constitutional treaty[62]. Similarly, Della Porta and Caiani state that the more top-down the process of Europeanization, the less civil society actors seem to have access to the public sphere[63].

---

58   Ibid.

59   Ruzza, Carlo et. al outlines the following roles of organized civil society in European governance: 1) raising support for decision-making activities (the enhancement of output legitimacy)—organized civil society can have a relevant input in a number of policy functions, above all in their role as information gatherers and monitors; 2) mediation and conflict resolution—this role is particularly relevant at the EU level, where initiatives such as the open method of co-ordination encourage 'soft' negotiated solutions to policy conflicts, and other structures which involve civil society as a counterbalance to organized interests, and 3) enhancement development of new forms of civil society aggregation, see, Ruzza, Carlo et all : Final report of the project 'Organized Civil Society and European Governance'. Trento: Universita degli studii Trento, 2005.

60   Warleigh, Alex: Purposeful Opportunists? EU Institutions and the Struggle over European Citezenship, in: Bellamy, Richard/ Warleigh, Alex (eds.): Citizenship and Governance in the European Union. London: Continuum, 2001, pp. 19–40.

61   Bellamy, Richard: The 'Right to Have Rights': Citizenship Practice and the Political Constitution of the EU, in: Bellamy, Richard., Warleigh, Alex (eds.): Citizenship and Governance in the European Union. London: Continuum, 2001, pp. 41–70.

62   Andreev, Svetlozar: What is the Convention Method? London: Centre for the Study of Democracy, University of Westminster, 2006, here: p. 7.

63   Della Porta, Donatella/ Caiani, Manuela: The Europeanization of Public Discourse in Italy: A top-down Process. in: European Union Politics, 2006 (vol. 7), no. 1, pp. 77–112.

Obradovic and Vizcaino[64] criticized not only the unsatisfactory level of participation by civil society in the constitutional process, but also the missing link between national and European associations. They came to the conclusion that many major groups and platforms which regularly submit contributions to the Commission's consultation process have not undertaken any measures to promote the participation of their members or supporters in the preparation of those submissions. According to them and another authors[65], the internal governance systems of European-level interest organizations are even more detached from their supporters. Almost all European associations are organized as confederations, i.e. associations of national organizations that do not admit individuals as members. This entails a structural remoteness from the grass roots interests that they represent.

In conclusion, it can be said that the interplay between citizenship and civil society points to the need to incorporate the notion of the state into the analysis. In this paper, I understand the state in functional terms—as providing the legal framework for civil society. This operationalization also allows an understanding of the structure of European governance as the framework in which the emerging transnational European civil society functions.

6.5.5.　The Public Sphere as the Arena of Civil Society

The previous section outlined the view of participation and civil society as elements of active citizenship; the following section looks at the European[66] as well as domestic public sphere.

According to Eriksen[67], the public sphere is the place where civil society is linked to the power structure of the state. The public sphere (PS) is an arena where civil society and social movements raise new questions, problems and issues. It is a counter-

---

64　Obradovic, Daniela/ Alonso Vizcaino, Jose M: Good Governance Requirements for the Participation of Interest Groups in EU Consultations, in: Pleines, Heiko (ed.): Participation of Civil Society in New Modes of Governance. The Case of the New EU Member States. Part 3: Involvement at the EU Level, Forschungsstelle Osteuropa an der Universität Bremen. Arbeitspapiere und Materialien, no. 76, 2006, pp. 19–44.

65　Greenwood, Justin: Interest Representation in the European Union, New York: Palgrave Macmillan, 2003, here: p. 77.

66　Within the constitutionalization process, this issue is strongly connected to the issue of legitimacy—the debate on civil society is shaped by the legitimacy discourse. Generally, civil society can provide alternative forms of legitimacy (which can be seen as a substitute for the legitimacy provided by representative government at the level of the nation state, see Ruzza, Carlo et. al: Final report of the project 'Organized Civil Society and European Governance'. Trento: Universita degli studii Trento, 2005. Furthermore participation is understood as a means of improving legitimacy and efficiency, see Magnette, Paul: Will the EU be More Legitimate after the Convention?, in: Shaw, Jo/ Magnette, Paul/ Hoffman, Lutz/ Vergés Bausili, Anna. The Convention on the Future of Europe Working Towards and EU Constitution. London: The Federal Trust, 2003.

67　Eriksen, Erik, O./ Fossum, John, E: Europe in Search of its Legitimacy: The Strategies of Legitimation Assessed. International Political Science Review, 2004 (vol.25), no. 4, pp. 435–459.

balance to the state and precondition for the realization of popular sovereignty as—in principle—it entitles everybody to speak without any limitations on subject matter, participation, questions, time or resources. As a concept, PS signifies that equal citizens form a public and set their own agenda through open communication, thereby providing the sort of deliberative arrangement that meets the requirement of discourse theory, namely that a norm is deemed legitimate only when all those affected have accepted it in a free and rational debate. In conceptual terms, PS is non-coercive, secular and rational; it is established through rights arising from rational debate that protect citizens from state intrusion. The result of PS is unpredictable in a strictly mono-causal scientific sense (the explanatory factor is the quality not the outcome of the interaction).

The European public sphere ranges beyond and below the national public spheres and consists of the following three categories of actors –speakers attempting to convince, addressees assessing what the speakers say and third parties acting as listeners[68]. The key element of the public discussion is the authority established in the course of the debate. In this way, the public sphere alters the power holders' basis of legitimacy as citizens are equipped with rights against the state. Consequently, in order to justify their decisions and gain support, decision-makers are compelled to enter the public arena.

The communitarian perception (as opposed to the thin conception of the public sphere) sees PS as a communication network (a social space created by communicating operators who are the representatives of opinions and interests) based on informal streams of communication. However, both communitarian and thin concepts can work next to each other—PS should be seen as presupposing a certain level of solidarity and norms of tolerance, as well as making up a liberal democratic culture conductive to reflective identity (a self-confident identity that also recognizes difference).

The link between the public sphere and civil society is established through the framework of active citizenship, which defines the public sphere as a space where active citizenship is realized through active civic and political participation. Here, I find the two models elaborated by Marc M. Howard in his work on Central and East European civil society very useful[69].

In Figure 6-2, Howard provides a graph presenting the separation between family and friendship networks, on the one hand, and civil society and the other four arenas, on the other. In Howard's definition, the public sphere rests on legal institutions and organizing principles which provide the essential core of any modern democratic system. The key part of the scheme for the notion of active citizenship is the centre,

---

68   Ibid., pp. 7–8.
69   Howard, Marc M: The Weakness of Civil Society in Post-Communist Europe, Cambridge: Cambridge University Press, 2003.

which consists of concrete organizations which shape and define the particular character of the democratic system[70]. As pointed out above, there is a vibrant interplay between the spheres. Their division in Figure 6-2 should thus be mainly perceived in conceptual terms.

Here, *political society* refers to elite politics, political leadership and the competition for political power and office, *economic society* refers to business organizations pursuing profit, and *civil society* refers to the sphere of organizations, groups and associations that are formally established, legally protected, autonomously run and voluntarily joined by ordinary citizens[71].

Figure 6-2: The Arenas of Democratization

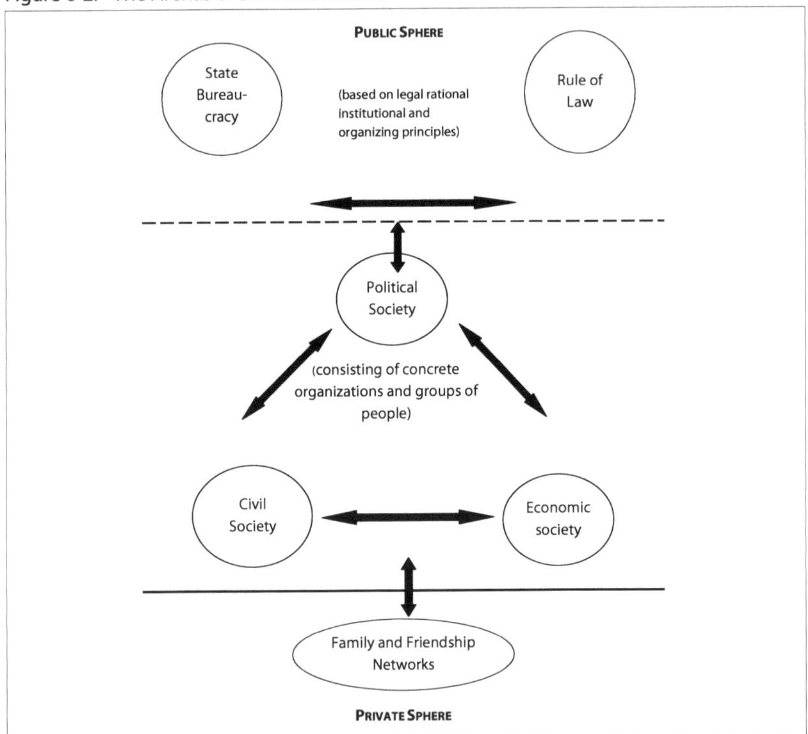

Source: Howard, Marc M.: The Weakness of Civil Society in Post-Communist Europe.

---

70   See also Mansfeldová, Zdenka: Interest Representation in Post-Communist Democracies, lecture presented at the PhD Summer School 2006 on Governance and Democracy in Central Eastern Europe, Lüneburg, 22 August 2006.

71   Howard, Marc M: The Weakness of Civil Society in Post-Communist Europe, Cambridge: Cambridge University Press, 2003, here: pp. 34–35.

To summarize: the concepts of legitimacy and participatory democracy provide the framework of my research, thus incorporating the concepts of participation and civil society. For the purpose of the empirical analysis civil society is operationalized as based on both organized and individual forms of civic and political participation.

6.6.　Empirical Results

The second part of the paper presents the empirical results of the network analysis of the connections between actors. Our task is to highlight what type of legitimacy the civil society organizations currently involved in the European public sphere provide. The working hypotheses (WH) state:

WH 1: In order to provide input legitimacy, civil society organizations need to be linked to both European institutions and citizens. In this way, the European institutions achieve additional legitimacy by involving civil society actors.

WH 2: In order to provide procedural legitimacy, civil society actors form linkages with all three types of actors—among each other, with European institutions and with citizens.

WH 3: In contrast to the view of civil society held by European Institutions, civil society organizations might not see themselves as actors crucial to the legitimating process and thus form linkages to best represent the interests of their members. In this case, dominant linkages will be found between civil society organizations and European institutions, as well as between civil society organizations and political parties.

6.6.1.　Networks of Cooperation[72]

In this part, our aim is to analyse the existence of vertical and horizontal networks among civil society organizations. This analysis will concentrate on horizontal transnational networks and divide the civil society organizations under study into NGOs (NGOs and think tanks) and economic organizations (trade unions and employers). The analysis compares the networks of these two types of organizations at the domestic and transnational levels. Data is available for the Czech Republic, Estonia, France, Germany, Poland and the UK. As an example, and for the sake of brevity, the paper only presents network analysis results for the Czech Republic and the UK, thereby taking cases that represent both old and new member states.

In the Czech Republic (see Figures 6-3, 6-4, 6-5 and 6-6 on pp. 116–119), two well connected actors can be found; one think tank—AMO, and one foundation responsible for the distribution of EU funds to civil society actors. In contrast, all the other

---

72　I would like to thank Ewelina Pawlak for her help in creating the network analysis matrixes as well as the graphs.

actors are less inter-connected. Interestingly, three actors show no network links with organizations at the EU level. As for Czech economic organizations, they are, in general, better connected than NGOs and think tanks. Trade unions tend to maintain relationships with their EU-level counterparts and other organizations, while employers have numerous links to both their European counterparts and to EU-level political actors. Czech employers tend to have stronger political links than Czech NGOs and think tanks.

Polish NGOs are better connected than their Czech counterparts. However, Polish economic actors are less well connected than Czech trade unions and employers' organizations and possess fewer links to EU-level political actors. In Estonia, as in the Czech Republic, economic organizations have stronger links at the EU level than the other types of organization.

If a comparison is made between the density of the networks from the Czech Republic, Estonia and Poland, stronger vertical links between national and EU-level organizations can be found in Poland and in the Czech Republic than in Estonia. In addition, Estonian organizations show a stronger tendency toward bilateral rather than multilateral networks.

Turning our attention now to the old member states, in Germany a similar pattern can be detected to that observed in the Czech Republic– with regard to civil society actors, there are two well-connected actors and several less well-connected ones. However, German economic organizations do not tend to have stronger networks than their NGO counterparts.

In the UK (see Figures 6-3, 6-4, 6-5 and 6-6 on pp. 116–119), both NGOs and economic actors have established multilateral networks. In contrast to the other countries examined, British NGOs, and especially think tanks, tend to be well connected with political actors at the EU level. As for economic actors, both trade unions and employers have established transnational networks rather than strong multilateral networks of cooperation. Significantly, British economic actors have less contact with political party groupings in the European Parliament than their counterparts in other member states.

As with the UK, in France and Germany, a network analysis points to the establishment of multilateral domestic as well as transnational networks among both civil society actors and economic actors. In general, in the old member states, the analysis identifies a larger differentiation of the networks. In France, both economic organizations and civil society actors concentrate on their relationships with European political parties and transnational civil society and economic actors. In Germany both economic and civil society actors tend to have a preference for institutional partners. German economic organizations have the strongest links to EU-level institutions—the European Commission and European Parliament, as well as German civil society actors with domestic institutions such as the Bundestag and the Government. In the UK, both economic organizations and organized civil society actors have strong transnational civil society links and links to transnational economic actors (such as the ETUC). The UK civil society actors also maintain relationship with European party groups.

The evidence presented in this section may be summarized as follows: 1) economic organizations are generally better connected than NGOs; 2) both employers and trade unions are often part of multilateral transnational networks; 3) economic organizations often have horizontal links to European political partiers; and 4) looking in more detail at NGOs, it can be stated that think tanks tend to be better connected than other NGOs.

On the basis of these empirical results, it seems reasonable to conclude that the second hypothesis is partially false; as the transnational comparative analysis of organized civil society actors (NGOs, think tanks, and economic organizations) demonstrates, national civil society organizations tends to have bilateral, and multilateral links to EU-level organizations and party groupings in the European Parliament.

### 6.6.2.	Activities Aimed at Institutions Versus Those Directed at the Public

In order to corroborate and explain the findings of the network analysis, the following section provides an additional analysis of the ConstEPS interview data, concentrating on the activities directed at citizens and activities aimed at national and EU institutions. The goal is to examine the third working hypothesis outlined above.

As Figure 6-7 on p. 120 shows, there are two different patterns: 1) in countries such as Estonia, Germany, Poland, the UK and at the EU level, the economic organizations were more often involved in citizen-related activities; 2) in the Czech Republic and France, the NGOs were more involved in this area. The general intensity of the involvement also varies: whereas on average more than 80 percent of civil society organizations in Estonia and at the EU level claim to be involved in citizen-related activities, more than 40 percent of civil society organizations claim to be involved in these activities in the UK and the Czech Republic and this figure is more than 30 percent in Germany and Poland.

This involvement took two major forms—direct and indirect (through umbrella organizations and transnational structures). When asked the reasons for non-involvement, the answers can be classified according to the following categories: 1) no interest—involvement was not part of an organization's priorities (for example, producer organizations, employer organizations and some NGOs); 2) opposition to the activities (some Euro-sceptic groups); 3) no invitation to participate (some Euro-critical and Euro-sceptic groups and trade unions); 4) no domestic debate—the end of the domestic debate after the ratification failure (some economic organizations).

Figure 6-3:   Network Analysis of the Non-Governmental Organizations—the Czech Republic

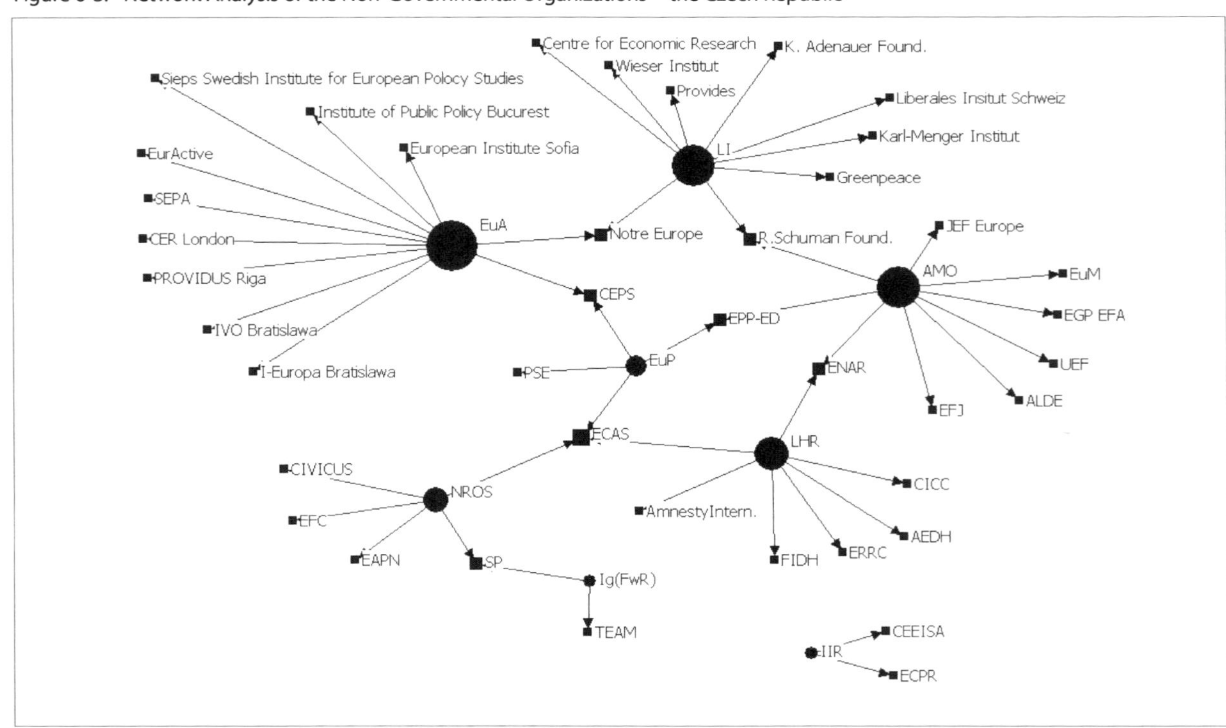

Sources: Ewelina Pawlak for ConstEPS.
Note: grey circle: national organizations, black square: EU-level organizations.

Figure 6-4:   Network Analysis of the Non-Governmental Organizations—the UK

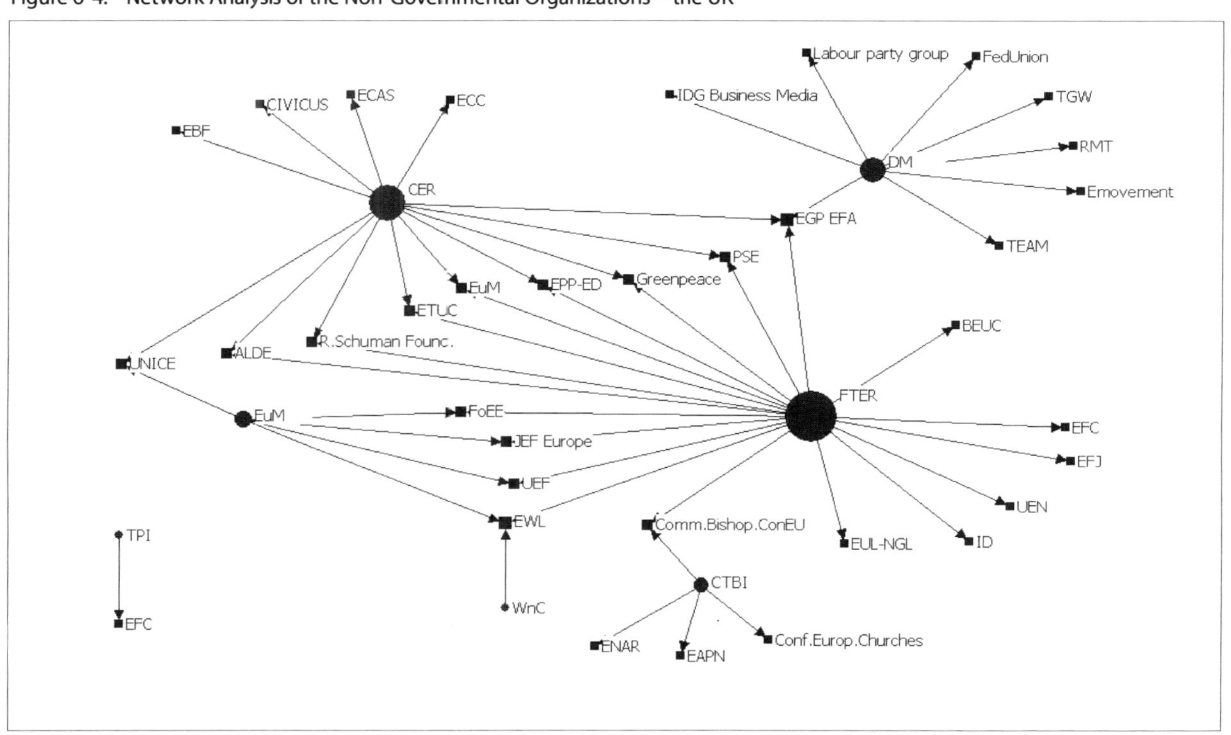

Figure 6-5: Network Analysis of Economic Organizations—the Czech Republic

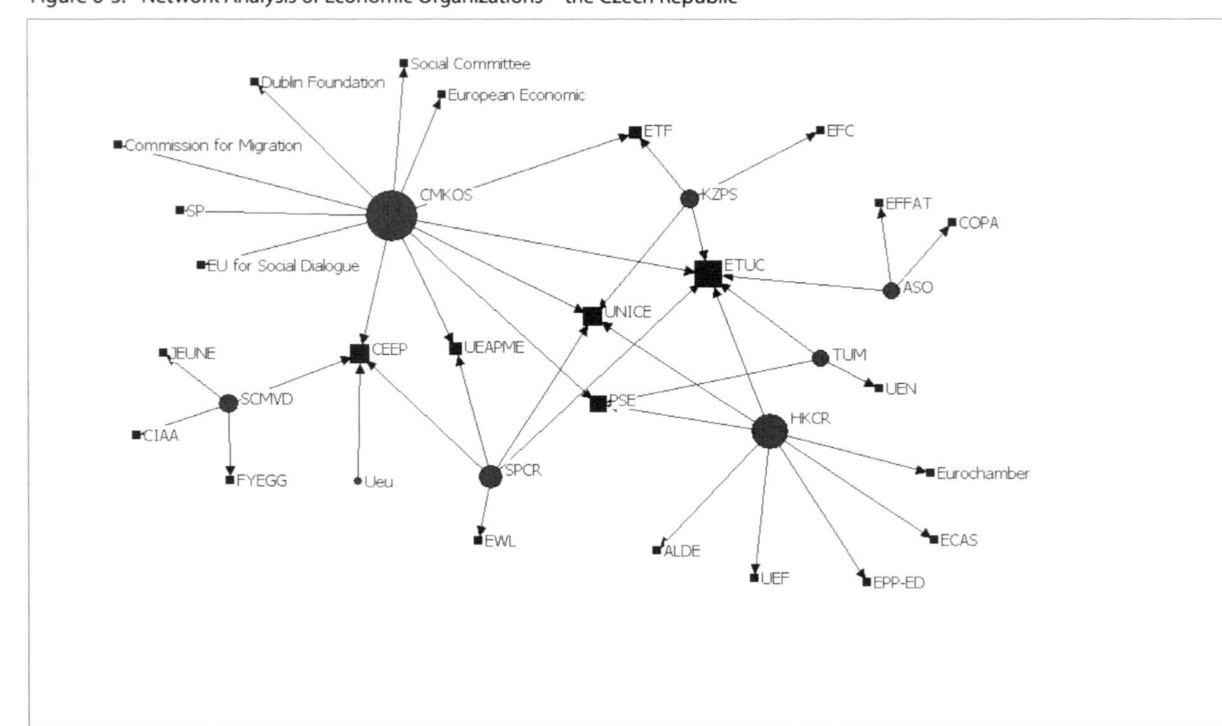

Sources: Ewelina Pawlak for ConstEPS
Note: grey circle: national organizations, black square: EU-level organizations.

Figure 6-6: Network Analysis of Economic Organizations—the UK

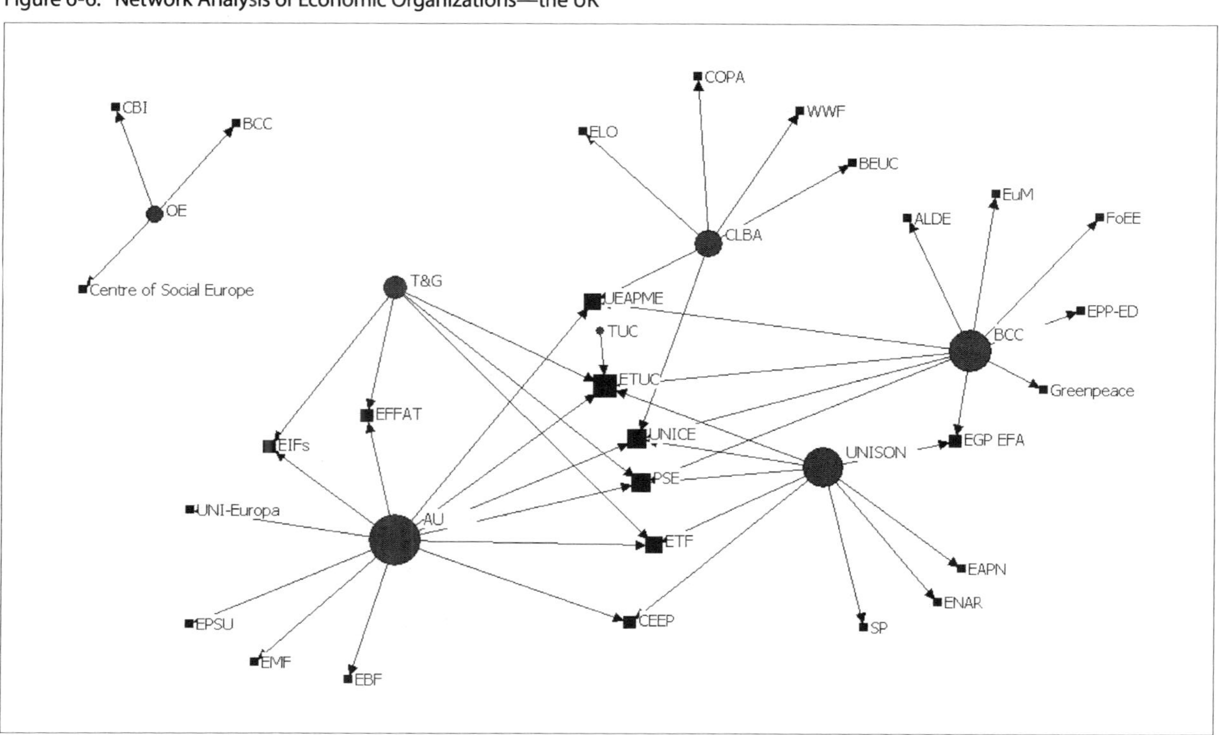

Sources: Ewelina Pawlak for ConstEPS
Note: grey circle: national organizations, black square: EU-level organizations.

                              Petra Guasti

Figure 6-7:   Involvement in Initiatives Concerning the Public, Civil Society and Citizens (%)

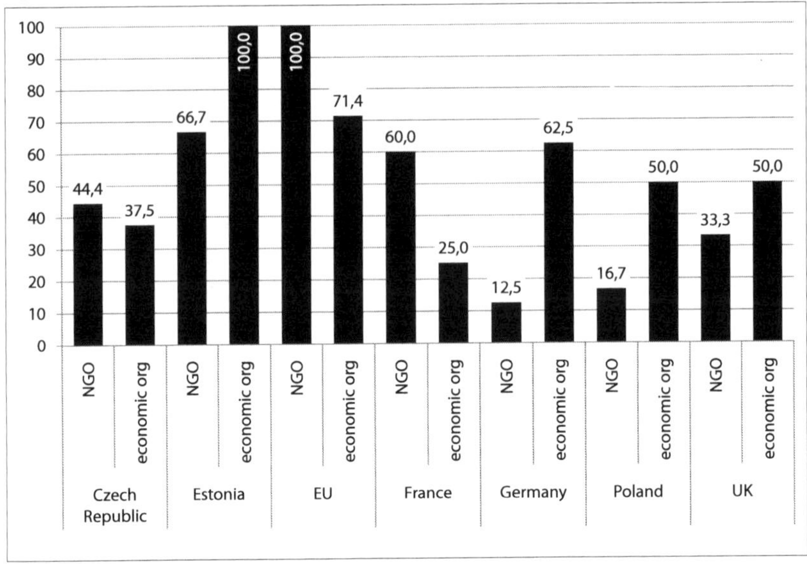

Source: ConstEPS Interviews (N=76).

Moving from the citizen-related activities to those directed at institutions (Figure 6-8 and Figure 6-9 on p. 121 and 122, respectively), it can be seen that the NGOs in the old member states, at the EU level and in Poland were more active in addressing institutions. Czech and Estonian NGOs were not very active. This finding can be related to the nature of the national debates which were rather formalized and polarized in both Estonia and the Czech Republic.

Regarding the choice of whether to address national or European institutions, there is no clear pattern among the countries under study. The EU-level organizations address all institutions at the EU and national level, although they only turn to the political parties to a much smaller degree. French organizations mainly tend to address national and European parliaments, Polish NGOs address the national government, presidency and the Commission and NGOs in the UK address the national government and national parliament. NGOs in all countries, with the exception of the Czech Republic, ascribed considerable importance (over 50%) to addressing the Constitutional Convention. NGOs in all countries paid the least attention to the political parties.

Economic organizations were very active at the EU level, in the UK, Poland and in Germany, but less so in France and the Czech Republic and passive in Estonia. As with the NGO activities, there is no clear pattern in this area. The EU-level economic

Figure 6-8:　Institutions Addressed by NGOs Regarding TCE

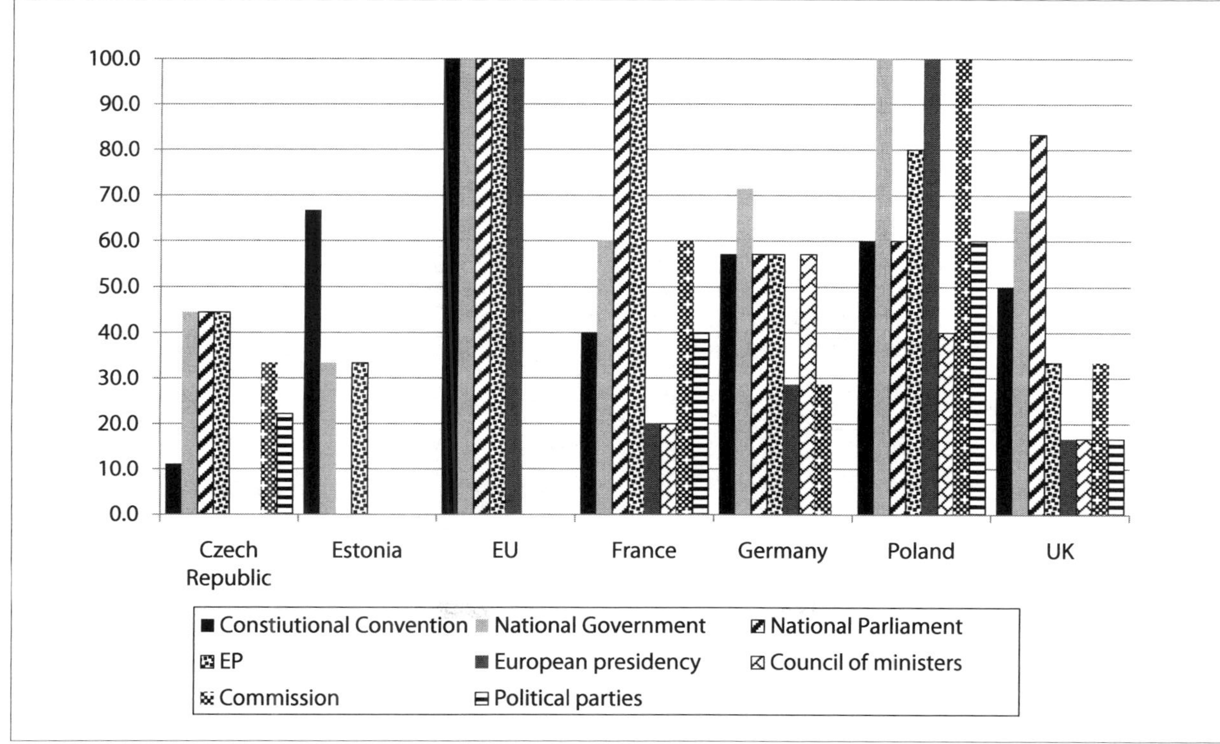

Source: ConstEPS Interviews (N=68).

Figure 6-9: Institutions Addressed by Economic Organizations Regarding TCE

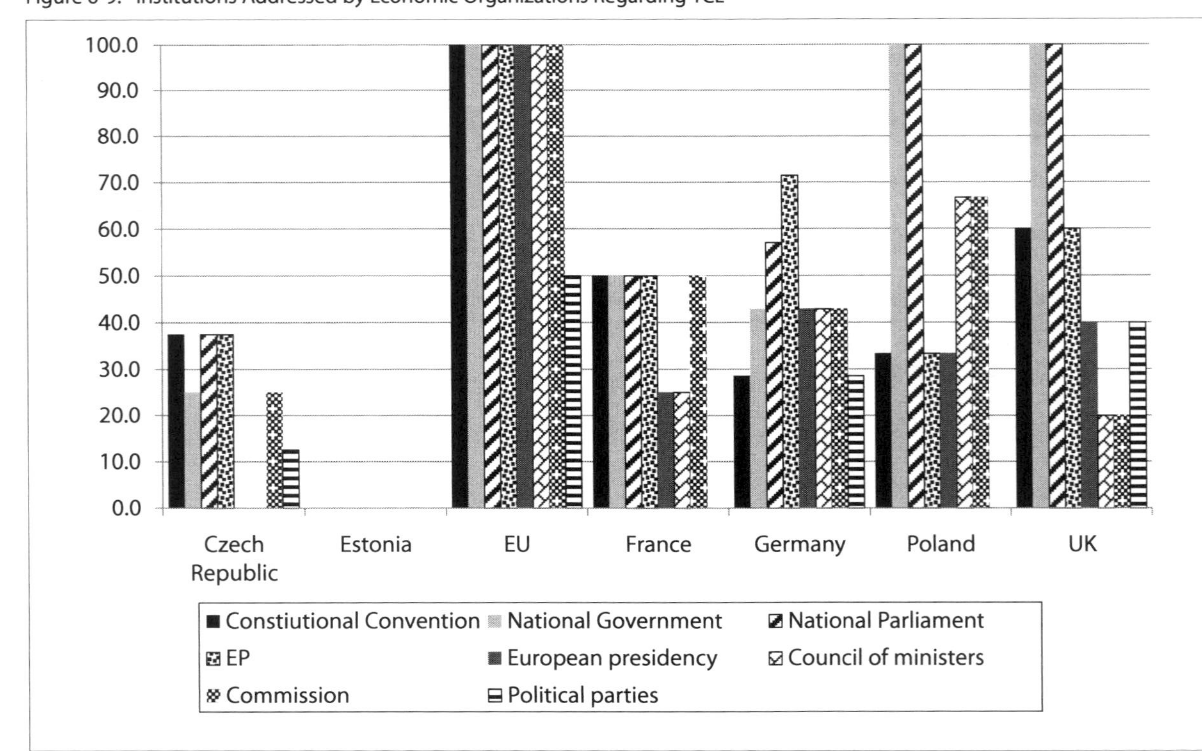

Source: ConstEPS Interview (N=68).

organizations addressed all institutions with the exception of political parties; Polish and British—and to a lesser extent German—economic organizations addressed national government and the national parliament. French and Czech economic organizations were significantly less active, addressing the Constitutional Convention, national government, the national and European parliaments and the Commission. Additionally, economic organizations addressed the constitutional convention to a much smaller degree than NGOs.

While summarizing the empirical analysis presented above, an important methodological caveat regarding network analysis has to be made. While network analysis is a very useful tool for mapping out actor constellations and connections between actors, a network analysis is unable to reveal to the researcher the strength of these connections or the importance each actor gives to these connections. Furthermore, within the public sphere, it is clear that some actors have more impact on the decision-making processes than others. Thus, in theory, actors with a single contact to the key decision-making structure is able to achieve more of their agenda than actors with multilateral linkages to the less important structures. From a methodological point of view, it is thus advisable to use network analysis as one part of explorative research and further supplement the findings based on it with other qualitative or quantitative methods of analysis.

To summarize the findings of the empirical research presented here, we can state that the cross-national comparative analysis of organized civil society actors (NGOs, think tanks and economic organizations) shows that national civil society organizations tends *to have bilateral and multilateral links to EU-level organizations and party groupings in the European Parliament.* Economic organizations are generally better connected than NGOs: both employers and trade unions are often part of multilateral transnational networks and economic organizations often have horizontal links to European political parties. If one looks at NGOs in greater detail, the analysis highlights the fact that that think tanks tend to be better connected than other NGOs.

The findings presented support the third working hypothesis—in contrast to the view of civil society among European institutions, civil society organizations do not see themselves as actors crucial to the legitimating process—instead they form contacts in order to best represent the interests of their members. In this respect, those actors involved in social dialogue defined here as economic organizations—trade unions and employers—seem to be better connected both horizontally and vertically. The results of the network analysis and the additional analysis of the interview data thus contradict working hypotheses one and two.

6.7. Preliminary Conclusions

The aim of this paper and of my project as a whole is to evaluate civil society's potential to contribute to the legitimacy of the emerging European polity. Therefore, while building on the existing literature on both civil society and legitimacy theory, the main aim of this work was not to theorize on both matters, but rather to asses existing gaps between theoretical perspectives, discourses and practices.

The empirical analysis—which goes beyond the data presented here– and includes the analysis of attitudinal data, EU documents, media and the network analysis collected by the ConstEPS research project—tries to assess the three criteria of legitimacy vis-à-vis civil society—inclusion, transparency and representation. The findings can be summarized as follows:

1. The criteria of inclusion are undermined by unequal access to decision-making processes between NGOs and economic organizations, by qualitative differences in status and the nature of civil and social dialogue, as well as the inclusion of civil society in the TCE and EU governance in general[73].
2. The criteria for transparency are weakened by the lack of formal procedures to include civil society and the absence of an assessment of civil society's democratic credentials.
3. The criteria for representation are undermined by unequal access among federalist civil society organizations to EU decision-making, as well as preferential access of transationalized civil society organizations to EU institutions.

This brings us to the question of what the primary role of European organized civil society is—according to our findings, which are supported by the report by the *Civil society contact group*, the main aim of civil society organizations at the EU level is networking and lobbying. Thus, there exists an inconsistency between the roles which EU institutions and elites expect organized civil society to play and reality.

Therefore, at the moment, civil society does not offer solutions to the democratic deficit in the European Union. Democracy in the enlarged EU is severely undermined by the fact that there is no strong commitment to changing the current level of citizen and civil society involvement in European governance and the reforms to its existing structures, channels of communications and patterns of conduct.

---

73   Kohler-Koch, Beate/ De Biévre, Dirk/ Maloney, William: Opening EU Governance to Civil Society—Gains and Challenges, CONNEX Report Series no. 5, 2008.; Kohler-Koch, Beate/ Larat, Fabrice: Efficient and Democratic Governance in the European Union. CONNEX Report series no. 9, Mannheim: MZES, 2008; Fazi, Elodie/ Smith, Jeremy: Civil dialogue: making it work better, Brussels: Civil Society Contact Group, 2006; Obradovic, Daniela: Civil Society and the Social Dialogue in European Governance, in: Yearbook on European Law, 2005 (vol. 24), pp. 261–328.

Tomasz Gabor

7. Patterns of Inter-Organizational Collaboration of Nonprofits in Central Europe

7.1. Inter-Organizational Collaboration Among Nonprofits— Why Should We Care?

In recent years, non-state actors have become increasingly active in solving public policy issues. This development is usually associated with the idea of 'governance without government', which describes a shift from hierarchical to more cooperative forms of government, a trend that has been taking place in Western Europe and the USA since the late 1970s. The main contribution of this perspective rests in introducing a new set of actors, namely private or non-state actors, who interact with public actors in networks to work on public issues. At the same time, these networks enjoy a significant degree of autonomy from the central state, which can steer them only indirectly and imperfectly.[1]

Multifold factors are responsible for the dominance of both the rhetoric and practice of 'joined up' governance. The problems that governments face, such as social exclusion, unemployment or climate change, are extremely complex. These issues bridge organizational, functional, professional and generational boundaries, but also are capable of becoming entangled in a web of other problems.[2] In the public management literature, such challenges are called 'wicked issues', and solving them requires diverse resources dispersed among a wide range of actors. Diverse organizations can, for example, pool their resources (finances, knowledge, connections) to modernize the provision of public services, particularly with respect to 'de-bureaucratized' management and accountability.[3] In light of this potential, governments, transnational organizations and private foundations are empowering non-state actors to actively participate in the public domain. Consequently, new modes of governance, e.g. various

---

1   Rhodes, Robert: The New Governance. Governing without Government, in: Political Studies, 1996 (vol. 44), no. 1, pp. 652–67; Davies, Jonathan: The Governance of Urban Regeneration. A Critique of the 'Governing without Government' Thesis, in: Public Administration, 2002 (vol. 80), no. 2, pp. 301–322.
2   Williams, Paul: The Competent Boundary Spanner, in: Public Administration, 2002 (vol. 80), no. 1, pp. 103–124.
3   Somers, John/ Bradford, David: Discourses of Partnership in Multi-agency Working in the Community and Voluntary Sectors in Ireland, in: Irish Journal of Sociology, 2006 (vol. 15), no. 2, pp. 67–85.

                               Tomasz Gabor

forms of political steering involving state and non-state actors and based primarily on a non-hierarchical interdependency,[4] are mushrooming throughout Western Europe.

In Central Europe, however, new modes of governance are still underdeveloped. This is often linked with the 'paradox of double weakness' or the so-called 'low equilibrium trap', whereby state and non-state actors mutually reinforce each other's weakness. As a result of their totalitarian past, but also due to increasing fiscal pressure, Central European governments often lack funding, expertise and administrative capacity, which impedes efficient and effective public goods delivery. One might therefore reasonably assume that the involvement of non-state actors in the design and implementation of public policies would significantly strengthen the capacity of state actors. Nevertheless, this 'win-win' situation does not seem to materialize, and it is often argued that a 'lose-lose' situation is the more likely scenario. This is because a weak state cannot offer non-state actors any rewards for resource exchange, and the weak capacities of non-state actors (insufficient finances, human capital, expertise, accountability) do not allow them to show themselves as reliable and valuable partners for the government. In addition to these weak organizational capacities, there is a lack of trust between state and non-state actors; this mutual suspicion is typical for countries with an authoritarian legacy and no tradition of institutionalized state-society relationships.[5]

Is there a way out of this double weakness paradox? How can collaboration between state and non-state actors be stimulated? Why has the European Union failed to change negative attitudes toward joint work among local actors in Central Europe? These questions have so far received little scrutiny from scholars studying institutional change in Central Europe. The noticeable exceptions either deal with one country only,[6] or comprise cross-national but small-N qualitative studies.[7] The aim of this chapter is to explore this research area using large-N, quantitative methods. The object of my inquiry is patterns of inter-organizational collaboration among nonprofits. The reasons for choosing nonprofits rather than another main category of non-state actors, e.g. business actors, are threefold. First, these organizations, which combine 'entrepreneurial spirit and the organizational effectiveness of the business firm with

---

4   Heritier, Adrienne: New Modes of Governance in Europe. Policy-making without legislation?, Lecture from 10 December 2001, University of Vienna.

5   Börzel, Tanja A./ Buzogány, Aron: Governing EU Accession in Transition Countries. The Role of Non-State Actors, in: Acta Politica, 2010 (vol. 45), nos. 1–2, pp. 158–182.

6   Bruszt, Laszlo/ Vedres, Balazs: The Politics of Civic Combinations, in: Perez Diaz, Victor (ed.): Markets and Civil Society, New York: Berghahn Books, 2006; Fric, Pavol: The Uneasy Partnership of the State And the Third Sector in the Czech Republic, in: Osborne Steven (ed.): The Third Sector in Europe: Prospects and Challenges, Abingdon, Oxon: Routledge, 2008, pp. 230–255.

7   Börzel, Tanja A./ Buzogány, Aron: Governing EU accession in transition countries. The role of non-state actors, in: Acta Politica, 2010 (vol. 45), nos. 1–2, pp. 158–182; Petrova, Tsveta/ Tarrow, Sidney: Transactional and participatory activism in the emerging European polity. The puzzle of East-Central Europe, in: Comparative Political Studies, 2007 (vol. 40), no. 1, pp. 74–94.

the common good orientation of the state and its public administration'[8], are still relatively new actors that are nonetheless playing an increasingly large role in the economy and society. In addition, they harbour the potential to become major players in service delivery and social integration as well as to significantly improve the transparency and accountability of public governance.[9] Second, one of the core characteristics of nonprofits is their orientation toward the common good: they are therefore much more likely than e.g. business actors to be involved in solving diverse social problems. Nonprofits would thus appear to be a natural ally for the state, which is the main actor responsible for public goods delivery. Third, nonprofits are more dependent on the external institutional environment for financial resources or preferential regulations than are firms; hence, according to the resource dependency[10] and institutional theories,[11] one could logically assume that 'externally induced change' is more likely to occur within the third sector.

This chapter represents a first attempt to identify the factors that shape the patterns of inter-organizational collaboration among nonprofits in Central Europe. It starts with a brief review of the literature on this subject and then proceeds to apply data reduction methods to a large-N data set collected by Bruszt and McDermott in 2007. Patterns of collaboration will then be identified and discussed. As a next step, the theoretical framework will be introduced, followed by a presentation of the main factors capable of transforming the collaborative behaviour of nonprofits. The last part of the chapter will furnish the initial results of the empirical tests.

7.2.　Inter-Organizational Collaboration of Nonprofits—Mapping Territory

The Inter-organizational collaboration of nonprofits appears to be highly important for the successful performing of their roles in service delivery, social integration, trust generation and increasing the accountability of public governance. Obviously, different types of inter-organizational relationships should have different impacts on each of

---

8　Etzioni, Amitai: The Third Sector and Domestic Missions, in: Public Administration Review, 1973 (vol. 33), no. 3, pp. 314–322, here: p. 314.

9　Zimmer, Annette/ Freise, Matthias: Bringing Society Back In. Civil Society, Social Capital, and Third Sector, in: Maloney, William A./ Deth, Jan van (ed.): Civil Society and Governance in Europe, Cheltenham: Edward Elgar, 2007, pp. 19–42; Jenei, Gyorgy/ Kuti, Eva: The Third Sector and Civil Society, in: Osborne, Steven (ed.): The Third Sector in Europe. Prospects and Challenges, Abingdon, Oxon: Routledge, 2008; Anheier, Helmuth: What Kind of Nonprofit Sector, What Kind of Society?, in: American Behavioral Scientist, 2009 (vol. 52), no. 7, pp. 1082–1094.

10　Pfeffer, Jeffrey/ Salancik, Gerald R.: The External Control of Organizations. A Resource Dependence Perspective, New York: Harper and Row Inc, 1978.

11　DiMaggio, Paul/ Powell, Walter W.: The Iron Cage Revisited. Institutional Isomorphism and Collective Rationality in Organizational Fields, in: American Sociological Review, 1983 (vol. 48), no. 2, pp. 147–160.

                                    Tomasz Gabor

the main roles of nonprofits. In general, we can distinguish between intra- and cross-sectoral collaborative patterns. Intra-sectoral collaboration refers to co-operative ties developed within the third sector. This form of cooperation usually entails organizations sharing resources, information and expertise with each other.[12] The literature on social movements highlights their unique capacity to mobilize social capital, which enables organizations to unite in common projects that surpass the achievement of individual goals. This also allows them to reduce the distance from potential allies within civil society by launching a process of wider acknowledgement of their objectives.[13] In addition, social movements appear to play a central role for the social-integrative and participatory function of nonprofits. In the Tocquevillian tradition, social integration is primarily about connections between nonprofits. NGOs, which are often strongly embedded in intra-sectoral ties, have a greater capacity to mobilize marginalized and excluded groups and to defend them from the oppressive institutions from the other sectors, the state and the market.[14] Intra-sectoral collaboration may take the form of informal ties based on personal connections, or can move beyond that and lead to the establishment of more formal coalitions for joint projects or service delivery.[15]

In contrast to the horizontal nature of intra-sectoral collaboration within the civic domain, relationships with the state are usually perceived as vertical, i.e. as consisting of unequal 'partners', with the state having the upper hand. This is particularly visible in the field of service delivery, where nonprofits deliver goods based on the funding they receive from government agencies. The state not only controls the resources in this case, but also sets up the guidelines according to which the services have to be delivered. This arrangement falls squarely under the heading of top-down, 'authoritative' or 'contracting out' relationships. In recent years, in some countries and policy fields, the relationship between nonprofits and governments has changed. State bureaucrats have learned to acknowledge the unique 'comparative advantages' held by the third sector, such as its valuable 'hands-on' experience, dedicated staff members and frequently lower personnel costs.[16] They have also realized that more equal

---

12   Mandell, Myrna/ Keast, Robert: Evaluating the effectiveness of interorganizational relations through networks, in: Public Management Review, 2008 (vol. 10), no. 6, pp. 715–731.

13   Cinalli, Manilion: Between horizontal bridging and vertical governance, in: Osborne, Steven (ed.): The Third Sector in Europe. Prospects and Challenges, Abingdon, Oxon: Routledge, 2008, pp. 88–108.

14   Skocpol, Theda: Advocates without Members. The Recent Transformation of American Civic Life, in: Skocpol, Theda (ed.): Civic Engagement in American Democracy, Washington D.C.: Brookings Inst., 1999, pp. 461–509; Diani, Mario/ McAdam, Doug (eds.): Social Movements and Networks, Oxford: Oxford University Press, 2003.

15   Brinkerhoff, Jennifer/ Brinkerhoff, Derrick: Government-nonprofit Relations in Comparative Perspective. Evolution, Themes, and New Directions, in: Public Administration and Development, 2002 (vol. 22), no. 1, pp. 3–18.

16   Struyk, Raymond J.: Nonprofit Organizations as Contracted Local Social Service Providers in Eastern Europe and the Commonwealth of Independent States, in: Public Administration and Development, 2002 (vol. 22), no. 5, pp. 429–437.

collaboration with nonprofits can help increase the range of social services, improve their quality and stimulate greater public participation and ownership of social programmes. This change of attitude toward nonprofits shifts our attention to another field that is highly relevant for exploring state-NGO relationships and one of the fastest-growing research agendas in political science: public governance. Indeed, the role of third sector organizations in the full cycle of the policy process was not analysed until recently, which is surprising when one considers the numerous studies exploring the role of nonprofits in service delivery. Public governance constitutes the focal point for exploring the role of nonprofits as agents of social (public) accountability and good governance. Policy networks are the building blocks of the concept, which recognizes that state and nonprofit organizations are collective, interconnected and interdependent policy actors. These networks can

> resist government steering, develop their own policies, mould their environments [...] and are characterized by an exchange of resources and interactions rooted in trust and regulated by rules of the game negotiated and agreed by network participants.[17]

In these 'games' nonprofits can potentially act as transmitters of norms and values to the policy process. They can also use their capacities to mobilize others and engage in advocacy and lobbying activities. In all of these ways, nonprofits can influence decision-making and help to forge new patterns of governance.[18]

7.3. Patterns Of Inter-Organizational Collaboration Among Nonprofits in Central Europe

The data used here were collected in 2007 by Laszlo Bruszt and Gerry McDermott as part of the EVOLVIN ('Evolving Regional Regimes: Challenges for Institution Building in CEE Countries') project, which explores the dynamics and variation in the modes of governance in three countries: Poland, the Czech Republic and Hungary. The aim of the survey was to identify patterns of local collaboration. In each country, two NUTS (Nomenclature of Territorial Units for Statistics) II regions, which are the official units of regional developmental programming within the EU support programmes, were established. In Poland, NUTS II are elected regions, in the Czech Republic two elected regions correspond to one NUTS II region, and in Hungary there are no elected regional governments. In each country, one region that was above average and one region that was below average with respect to economic development (three indicators were used: gross domestic product, unemployment rate and the percentage of agriculture in the

---

17   Rhodes, Robert A. W.: Policy Networks. A British Perspective, in: Journal of Theoretical Politics, 1990 (vol. 2), no. 3, pp. 292–331.
18   Zimmer, Annette/ Freise, Matthias: Bringing Society Back In. Civil Society, Social Capital, and Third Sector, in: Maloney, William A./ Deth, Jan van (eds.): Civil Society and Governance in Europe, Cheltenham: Edward Elgar, 2007, pp. 19–42.

GDP) were selected. In Poland, Malopolskie (above average) and Swietokrzyskie (below average) were selected; in Czech Republic, Jihomoravsky (above) and Moravskoslezko (below); and in Hungary, Nyugat Dunantul (above) and Del Alfold (below).

Two hundred organizations were selected in each region (for a total of 1200). Seventy percent of the interviewed organizations (841) were randomly selected from the list of EU project winners. Thirty percent of the organizations were selected randomly from the regional lists of NGOs, municipalities and universities. Nonprofits constituted the largest component (40%, i.e. 492) of all selected organizations from the third sector. This is not a representative sample of the nonprofit sector as such, but, nevertheless, the combination of the two lists should offer a good overview of the most active nonprofits in the regions covered.

Because the patterns of inter-organizational collaboration in Central Europe are mainly 'terra incognita', I did not have any *a priori* expectations of what I would find in the data. The usual strategy in such cases is data mining. Because my interest was in both project-related and stable ties, I chose the method of cluster analysis in order to organize the observed data into meaningful structures. Cluster analysis is a purely empirical, inductive and exploratory method of data analysis that aims at sorting different objects into groups in such a way that the degree of association between two objects is maximal if they belong to the same group and minimal otherwise.[19] Among the many available clustering algorithms, I chose Ward's method[20], commonly regarded as very efficient; unlike other methods, it uses an analysis of variance approach to evaluate the distances between clusters. The main challenge associated with this method is choosing the number of clusters. Here, the possibility of meaningful interpretations of results should be the applied criteria.

Since my interest is located primarily within the area of inter-organizational collaboration among nonprofits, I focused on five categories of partners: national state, regional state, local state, NGO and firm. They are the main representatives of the sectoral universe, which encompasses the state, business and civil society. These are also the most frequent partners in the projects and general activities of the nonprofits included in the sample (in the survey nonprofits were asked to identify the ten most important partners in their projects and ongoing activities). In sum, I used five variables to create the clusters.

19   Punj, Girish/ Stewart, W. David: Cluster Analysis in Marketing Research. Review and Suggestions for Application, in: Journal of Marketing Research, 1983 (vol. 20), no. 2, pp. 134–148.
20   Ward, Henry: Hierarchical Grouping to Optimize an Objective Function, in: Journal of the American Statistical Association, 1963 (vol. 58), No. 301, pp. 236–244.

Table 7-1:   Patterns of Inter-Organizational Collaboration
(Number of Project-Based and Stable Partners)

		Community (104)	Dissociated (101	Cross-sectoral (84)	Strong state (66)
National state	Mean	0.67	0.07	0.67	2.07
	Median	0	0	0	2
Regional state	Mean	0.47	0.02	0.21	0.50
	Median	0	0	0	0
Local state	Mean	1.31	0.00	1.54	0.97
	Median	1	1	1	1
Nonprofit	Mean	2.16	0.22	1.83	0.15
	Median	2	0	1	0
Business	Mean	0.03	0.11	2.11	0.21
	Median	0	0	2	0

Source: Own compilation.

The cluster analysis revealed four meaningful typical patterns of inter-organizational collaboration (Table 7-1). The largest group (22%) is composed of nonprofits belonging to the 'community' cluster. On average, these organizations have as a partner one local government and two nonprofits. Almost the same share of nonprofits under study (21%) fell under the 'dissociated' cluster. They do not have any partners in ongoing actvities or projects. 18% of all nonprofits belonged to the 'cross-sectoral cluster'. These NGOs have partners from all sectors: one from local government, on average, one from the third sector and two from business. The smallest cluster (14%), the 'strong state', consists of NGOs with ties to the state only. This is the cluster in which NGOs have the strongest ties to the national state.

As the results show, the typical partners of nonprofits are local governments, other nonprofits and national states. Collaboration with businesses and regional governments is rather underdeveloped. It is also remarkable that a large number of nonprofits still lacks any inter-organizational ties.

Data from the survey allowed exploring the relationships between the cluster type to which an organization belongs and the relationships of formal and informal accountability, and the number and type of goals that an organization pursues.

The survey included questions about informal accountability, e.g. *'When organizations make decisions, whose opinion do you take into account?'*, and formal accountability, e.g. *'To which of the following organizations does your organization formally report?'* This data allowed for testing for significant differences[21] across clusters in this respect (Table 7-2 overleaf).

---

21   The 'significance' of differences is measured using adjusted residuals (Table 2). A single plus (or minus) sign indicates the value of adjusted residuals greater (smaller) than 2.0. A double plus (double minus) sign indicates the value of adjusted residuals greater (smaller) than 4.0.

Table 7-2:   Significant Differences Among Clusters in Formal and Informal Relations of Accountability

		Community	Dissociated	Cross-sectoral	Strong state
National government	Informal				+
	Formal		-		+
Local government	Informal	+	- -	+	
	Formal	+	-		
Nonprofit	Informal	+	-		
	Formal			+	-
Business	Informal			+	
	Formal				
Broader public	Informal		-	+	
	Formal		-		
Volunteers / activists	Informal	+	-		
	Formal				

Source: Own compilation.

The 'dissociated' cluster is the least accountable towards various stakeholders. It does not take into account actors from the state and third sector when making decisions. Lack of organizational partners negatively correlates with accountability towards volunteers/activists or the broader public.

Nonprofits belonging to the 'community' cluster form a group with strong relationships towards local government and nonprofits. Moreover, only this cluster takes the opinions of volunteers/activists and donors into account when making decisions. As its name suggests, the 'cross-sectoral' cluster has strong relationships of cross-sectoral accountability (state, business and third sector). In addition, it significantly more often takes the opinions of the broader public into consideration. Members of the 'strong state' cluster are formally obligated to report to the national state, but are the weakest in terms of accountability to other nonprofits.

The survey included questions about the organizations' goals. The literature suggests that the presence of cross-sectoral ties should stimulate a greater diversity of organizational goals. Moreover, ties to particular types of organizations should affect the propensity to pursue certain types of goals, for example, ties to the national state might trigger political activism, and ties to other NGOs might stimulate activities involving the mobilization of the general public. There were fourteen types of goals listed in the survey. With the help of factor analysis, four groups of goals were identified: cohesive goals (composed of two goals), public goals (three goals), political goals (two goals) and social goals (three goals). As a next step, I created an index by adding the numbers assigned to indicate how often each goal is pursued: (never = 0, sometimes = 1, often = 2, always = 3).

Table 7-3:   Organizational Goals and Patterns of Inter-Organizational Collaboration

	Community	Dissociated	Cross-sectoral	Strong state
Number of goals (avg. = 8.2; max = 14)	8.6	7.4	8.3	8.4
Political intensity (avg. = 3.4, max = 6)	3.6	3.3	3.4	3.6
Cohesive intensity (avg. = 3.2; max = 6)	3.0	3.0	3.8	3.0
Social intensity (avg. = 5.9; max = 9)	6.5	5,4	5.6	5.9
Public intensity (avg = 6.2; max = 9)	6.2	6.2	6.3	6.0

Source: Own compilation.

The 'dissociated' cluster appears to be the worst in terms of goal intensity (Table 7-3). These nonprofits pursue a lower than average number of goals and are weaker than other nonprofits in each category of goals, except for public goals, in which the 'strong state' cluster is less active. Organizations belonging to the 'community' cluster pursue, on average, the highest number of goals. They are also by far the most active in the social area. The 'cross-sectoral' cluster is particularly strong in cohesive goals.

All in all, with respect to the relationship of accountability and the number and type of goals pursued, it is evident that there are substantial differences across the clusters. The 'dissociated' cluster is the least accountable to organizations from other sectors and pursues the fewest number of goals. This confirms the assumption about the relationship between inter-organizational collaborative ties and organizational ties. In sum, organizational ties do matter.

The 'strong state' cluster, despite its formal relationship of accountability to the national state, is not accountable to the general public, and it pursues 'public' goals to the least extent. Therefore, these organizations resemble traditional, service-oriented nonprofits and are strongly dependent on the national state, which provides them with resources and determines the categories of goods to be delivered.

Nonprofits belonging to the 'community' cluster are strongly embedded in relationships of accountability with local government and other nonprofits. They also pursue more goals (in particular in the social area) than any other cluster. These relationships, combined with a significantly higher likelihood of being accountable to volunteers and activists, suggests that these constitute Tocquevillian, 'ideal types' of nonprofits in that they stimulate social capital and primarily aim to increase participation and social integration in their local community.

The organisations in the 'cross-sectoral' are the best in terms of relationships of inter-organizational accountability. Due to their strong commitment to public and cohesive goals combined with accountability relationships to broader public they are the closest to the ideal of 'public benefit organization'.

7.4. Explaining Inter-Organizational Collaboration Among Nonprofits

The literature review delivered a convincing argument that the collaborative ties developed and maintained by nonprofits are of crucial importance for their roles in service delivery, social integration and public governance. Therefore, patterns of associating constitute a meaningful research area for many fields, including nonprofit studies, social capital, transnationalization and Europeanization, public governance, welfare states and 'new regionalism'. Students of these fields focus primarily on the outcomes of collaborative relationships in terms of increased efficiency, effectiveness or responsiveness. However, so far there have been very few attempts to identify the causal mechanisms that are responsible for collaborative behaviour in general or for the presence of co-operative ties to actors from particular domains. These studies can be divided into two groups.

The first group, predominantly located within nonprofit literatures, takes organizational characteristics (organizational capacities, collaborative culture) as explanatory factors of collaboration. Organizational capacity may encompass a multitude of dimensions; however, only a few of them were tested for their relationship with collaborative activity. Mulford and Mulford have speculated that larger organizations, measured by the size of their budgets, will be more likely to collaborate, because they have a greater ability to take advantage of their financial resources. Foster and Meinhard[22] have identified that the size of the organization does indeed matter: smaller organizations collaborate less. Additional significant factors have been added by Gazley,[23] who found that the maturity of an organization and its national affiliation increase its propensity to partner. Suarez and Hwang[24] have also looked at management degrees and conclude that managers with degrees in management are more likely to seek collaborative relationships as a legitimate and acceptable strategy for achieving the mission of their organization. Furthermore, they extend this argument to sectoral experience, and suggest that leaders might seek collaborations with organizations in the

---

22 Foster, Mary/ Meinhard, Agnes: A Regression Model Explaining Predisposition to Collaborate, in: Nonprofit and Voluntary Sector Quarterly, 2002 (vol. 31), No. 4, pp. 549–564.

23 Gazley, Beth: Intersectoral Collaboration and the Motivation to Collaborate. Toward an Integrated Theory, in: O'Leary, R./ Bingham, L.B.: Big Ideas in Collaborative Public Management, Armonk/ NY: Sharpe, M. E., 2008.

24 Suarez, David/ Hwang, Hokyu: Find a Partner. Nonprofit Organizations and the Culture of Collaboration, paper prepared for the Consortium on Collaborative Governance Mini-Conference, Santa Monica/CA, 10–12 April 2008.

sector in which they have the most experience (business with business, nonprofit with nonprofit, etc.).

The second group of studies dealing with inter-organizational collaboration comprise research projects that typically share the assumption of the neo-institutional theory, which advocates a constraining or enabling role of institutional forces on organizational behaviour.[25] Within the social capital and social movement literature, Maloney and Rossteutscher[26] studied the impact of the socio-cultural context (economic development, religion and ethnic plurality), institutional context (democratic development, federal states and institutions for direct participation) and political context (direct and indirect support, and type of welfare regime) on patterns of associating among nonprofits in several cities in Western Europe. Della Porta examined contextual factors, such as the conditions governing access to public and private funding and tax exemption or the inclusiveness of the political system, in order to explain patterns of collaboration with various categories of state actors. Baldassari and Dani[27] tried to account for differences in the networking behaviour of nonprofits in two British cities by applying the concept of political opportunity structure, understood as the formal and informal features of the political system, which enable or constrain the chances for actors to participate in the political decision-making process.[28] However, no significant impact was found since both cities are involved in the same national political, cultural and media arenas and therefore largely share the same history and culture.

The literature on Europeanization, new regionalism or governance studies has not devoted separate attention to the collaborative ties of nonprofits. However, some authors have linked certain environmental conditions with the types of networks developed by local actors. Such analyses usually focus their attention on the organization of the state (i.e. its relative power at the central, local and intermediary levels), organization of business interests, and the distance of business from the state (i.e. the role of business in the design and implementation of policies).[29] Geddes,[30] who has studied cross-national differences in the spread of local partnerships in Western Europe,

---

25   DiMaggio, Paul/ Powell, Walter W.: The Iron Cage Revisited. Institutional Isomorphism and Collective Rationality in Organizational Fields, in: American Sociological Review, 1983 (vol. 48), No. 2, pp. 147–160; Scott, Robert: Institutions and organizations, Thousand Oaks/CA: Sage, 1995.
26   Maloney, William/ Rossteutscher, Sigrid (eds.): Social Capital and Associations in European Democracies. A Comparative Analysis, London: Routledge, 2007.
27   Baldassarri, Delia/ Diani, Mario: The Integrative Power of Civic Networks, in: American Journal of Sociology, 2007 (vol. 113), no. 3, pp. 735–780.
28   Kriesi, Hans Peter: The Political Opportunity Structure of New Social Movements. Its Impact on Their Mobilization, in: Jenkins, J. C./ Klandermans, B. (eds.): The Politics of Protest Comparative Perspectives on States and Social Movements, London: UCL Press, 1995, pp. 167–199.
29   Coleman, William D.: Business and Politics. A Study of Collective Action, Kingston/ON.: McGill-Queen's University Press, 1988; Marin, Bernd: Generalized Political Exchange, Antagonistic Cooperation and Integrated Policy Circuits, Boulder/CO: Westview Press, 1990.
30   Geddes, Mike: Neoliberalism and Local Governance. Cross-National Perspectives and speculations, in: Policy Studies, 2005 (vol. 26), no. 3–4, pp. 359–375.

acknowledged the role of European Union programmes in facilitating collaborative arrangements among local actors, but also identified the impact of the type of welfare regime as significant. According to this position, the norm of local networking is particularly strong in the liberal welfare regime due to the focus on the private provision of public services and competitive mechanisms for the allocation of resources. In the continental regime, however, the partnership principle is entrenched at the national rather than the local level as part of a corporativist arrangement.

In sum, the literature review suggests that in order to account for different types of collaborative behaviour (meaning collaboration with different types of organizations), one should focus on both the organizational capacities of nonprofits and the properties of the external environment. Based on theoretical arguments and empirical evidence from a handful of research projects, several hypotheses linking a particular type of collaborative relationship with factors located within a single organization and its external environment will be presented next.

7.4.1. Organizational Capacities

The resource mobilization perspective[31] argues that the success of an organization depends on the capacity of its leadership to allocate and mobilize resources such as money, experience and information; attract grassroots membership; engage in voluntary work; and establish contact with influential individuals, top experts, etc. Due to the limited pool of available resources, if the leaders of organizations want to prevail in the competition for resources, their organizations must achieve maximum institutionalization and professionalization. Collaboration with other organizations is an optimal strategy for this purpose, given that working together can increase organizational resources and reduce competition.[32] Resource mobilization theory therefore maintains that successful organizations with more resources are strongly motivated to collaborate.

Based on what I read in the nonprofit literature, I expect that larger nonprofits (in terms of budget and number of employees) will be more likely to collaborate with organizations that can provide them with valuable resources. Organizational size should correlate with collaborative ties to the state, in particular the national state, because these ties can provide nonprofits with the most resources. Moreover, the structure of revenues can indicate the level of professionalization in nonprofits. In particular, interest from investments and income from their own activities are characteristics of the most financially stable nonprofits. In theory, they should be the most attractive

---

31   McCarthy, John D./ Zald, Mayer N.: Resource Mobilization and Social Movements: A Partial
      Theory, in: American Journal of Sociology, 1977, (vol. 82), No. 6, pp. 1212–1241.
32   Pfeffer, Jeffrey/ Gerald R. Salancik: The External Control of Organizations: A Resource Dependence
      Perspective, New York: Harper and Row Inc, 1978.

partner for the national state. Nonprofits with income from membership fees and estimated values for services should be more likely to collaborate with the local government or another nonprofit.

The literature on social movements and social capital suggests that intra-sectoral collaboration among nonprofits is not so much about financial resources (as in the case of collaboration with the state), but more about shaping a sectoral collective identity[33] and increasing the overall capacity to mobilize and represent the interests of citizens.[34] I therefore expect that size of budget will not affect an organization's propensity to partner with another nonprofit. Intra-sectoral connectivity should instead be motivated by an organization's potential to mobilize and increase participation, which can be captured by the number of volunteers that participate in its activities. Organizational age should affect the propensity to collaborate with each category of actors. Older organizations will have had more time to establish their positions in the community and develop collaborative ties.

7.4.2. Welfare State

The impact of state policies on the collaborative ties of nonprofits is traditionally associated with the concept of welfare state regimes.[35] Much in contrast to the 'paradigm of conflict'[36] assumed by the theory of state failure, the relationship between nonprofits and the state can indeed be collaborative in nature. Nonprofits are often active in a field before the government can be mobilized to respond, so they possess expertise and experience upon which the government can draw for its own activities. Nonprofits can also mobilize the political support needed to stimulate government involvement, which later can be used to guarantee a substantial role for the nonprofit providers in the fields that the government wishes to enter. Also, in many cases, support from the nonprofit sector can take on a crucial role in enhancing the role and power of the state. For all these reasons, it is generally assumed that governmental welfare spending is to a large extent transmitted to the nonprofit sector. Not surprisingly, this creates a situation of dependence[37]: the greater the welfare spending, the more heavily

---

33 Melucci, Alberto: Getting Involved: Identity and Mobilization in Social Movements, in: Kriesi, Hanspeter/ Tarrow, Sidney (eds.): From Structure to Action: Comparing Social Movements Across Cultures, International Social Movement Research I, Greenwich, CT: JAI, 1988, pp. 329–48.

34 Putnam, Robert: Making Democracy Work: Civic Traditions in Modern Italy, Princeton: Princeton University Press, 1993.

35 Salamon, Lester/ Anheier, Helmuth, The Nonprofit Sector: A New Global Force, Working Paper of the Johns Hopkins Comparative Nonprofit Sector Project, 21. Baltimore, MD: The Johns Hopkins Institute for Policy Studies, 1996.

36 Salamon, Lester M.: Partners in Public Service: Government-Nonprofit Relations in the Modern Welfare State. Baltimore: The Johns Hopkins University Press, 1995.

37 Salamon, Lester/ Anheier Helmuth: The Nonprofit Sector. A New Global Force, Working Paper of the Johns Hopkins Comparative Nonprofit Sector Project No. 21, Baltimore/MD: The Johns Hopkins Institute for Policy Studies, 1996; Fric, Pavol: The Uneasy Partnership of the State and

the nonprofits depend on government support. Therefore, financial assistance from any state agency (national, regional or local) should trigger the creation of collaborative ties between nonprofits and the various government agencies.

In the literature exploring the links between welfare states and civil society, there is an ongoing heated debate about the so-called 'crowding-out' argument.[38] This theory argues that massive amounts of welfare spending will crowd out volunteerism by pre-empting individual efforts to provide collective goods. Based on that logic, it can be assumed that greater dependence on public money will decrease the motivation for intra-sectoral networking. Similarly, it can be argued that in more donor-friendly regulatory frameworks (1%, tax exemption, etc.) NGOs will be less dependent on the state and more active in local networking.

7.4.3. Transnationalization

Foreign actors such as foundations, international organizations, and transnational NGOs can substantially alter the organizational behaviour of nonprofits, including their patterns of associating, through financial or non-monetary support (e.g. skills and knowledge). This might be particularly valid for CEE countries, in which inter-organizational collaboration was not a common practice at the local level at the beginning of the 1990s. This was mostly due to the fact that the new set of actors who emerged after the fall of communism found themselves disconnected from pre-existing networks (nonprofits, SMEs, local governments). Foreign actors were convinced about the advantage of the collaborative approach and tried to promote this organizational practice in CEE. For the purposes of this analysis, it will be assumed that foreign ties (e.g. donor–funder relations), but also relations of accountability (i.e. reporting to others or taking others into account when making decisions), increase innovative, horizontal, intra-sectoral and cross-sectoral collaborative practices.

The European Union is a unique transnational actor whose huge political and economic power enables it to significantly transform patterns of collaboration between local actors, including nonprofits. Therefore, it is not surprising that the EU is commonly considered to be one of the main driving forces in the development of local networks.[39] There are two primary reasons explaining the Commission's 'commitment' to partner-

---

the Third Sector in the Czech Republic, in: Osborne, Steven (ed.): The Third Sector in Europe. Prospects and Challenges, Abingdon, Oxon: Routledge, 2008, pp. 230–255.

38 van Oorschot, Wim/ Arts, William: The Social Capital of European Welfare States. The Crowding Out Hypothesis Revisited, in: Journal of European Social Policy, 2005 (vol. 15), no. 1, pp. 5–26.

39 Bennett, Robert/ Krebs Günter: Local Economic Developments Partnerships. An Analysis of policy networks in EC-LEDA Local Employment Development Strategies, in: Regional Studies, 1994 (vol. 28), No 2, pp. 119–140; Bachtler, John/ McMaster, Irene: EU Cohesion Policy and the Role of the Regions. Investigating the Influence of Structural Funds in the New Member States, in: Government and Policy, 2008 (vol. 26), no. 2, pp. 398–428.

ship working. The first reason concerns the EU-driven notion of a 'Europe of Regions', with the underlying principle of distributing authoritative decision-making among multiple territorial levels in order to strengthen regional administrations.[40] Although mainly associated with creating and strengthening 'regional governance', 'new region-alism' also advocated social co-operation for more socially inclusive and economically efficient development on the ground.[41] Directly connected to the 'regional shift' in the EU's priorities is the idea of 'networked governance'. It broadens the discussion about EU governance by introducing a 'system of governance', whereas the 'Europe of Regions' was primarily aimed at introducing a new, regional 'level of government'. 'Network governance' can be understood as an organizing principle for the rela-tions between actors within the EU's political system. This system, as any other sys-tem, strongly depends on well-developed channels of communication. Because of its polycentric character, governance cannot take place in an authoritative manner, but has to be anchored in consensual decision-making, and the hierarchical system has to be replaced by functional networks.[42] Such a system gives priority to problem-solving strategies rather than bargaining.[43] The primary role of 'network governance' is to co-ordinate a diverse range of actors and to approximate their various interests. Inter-organizational collaboration appears to be a perfect tool for achieving this goal at the local level. Having acknowledged the advantage of the 'partnership approach' with regard to economic efficiency, social inclusiveness, or consensual decision-mak-ing, the EU made it a key principle of the Structural Funds. And, like any other actor, the EU bears responsibility for partnership becoming a 'way of doing things'.[44]

Obviously, this collaborative approach to project delivery was not necessarily 'com-patible' with the domestic practices in Central European countries. There were numer-ous attempts to introduce institutional experiments based largely on cross-sectoral partnerships and initiated mostly by international organizations (e.g. the OECD, the World Bank, etc.), foreign nonprofits or national or regional authorities.[45] Partnership, however, especially of a cross-sectoral nature, was still 'terra incognita' for most of the

40 Hooghe, Liesbet/ Marks, Gary: Multi-Level Governance and European Integration, Lanham/MD: Rowman and Littlefield, 2001.
41 Amin, Ash: An Institutionalist Perspective on Regional Economic Development, in: International Journal of Urban and Regional Research, 1999 (vol. 23), No. 2, pp. 365–78.
42 Kohler-Koch, Beate: European Networks and Ideas. Changing National Policies?, in: European Integration Online Papers, 2002 (vol. 6), no. 6, http//eiop.or.at/eiop/texte/2002–006a.htm
43 Scharpf, Fritz: Governing in Europe. Effective and Democratic?, Oxford: Oxford University Press, 2002.
44 Roberts, Peter: Partnerships, programmes and the promotion of regional development. An eval-uation of the operation of the structural funds regional programmes, in: Programme Planning, 2003 (vol. 59), pp. 1–69.
45 Stark, David/ Vedres, Balazs/ Bruszt, Laszlo: Rooted Transnational Publics. Integrating Foreign Ties and Civic Activism, in: Theory and Society, 1996 (vol. 35), No. 3, pp. 323–349; Bruszt, Laszlo: Multi-level governance. The Eastern Version. Emerging Patterns of Regional Development Patterns in the New Member States, EUI Working Papers, 2007/13.

organizations in CEE. Prior to the accession, local level actors like municipalities, NGOs and firms (mostly SMEs), despite their generally weak organizational capacities (most of them were founded only a few years earlier), lacked collaborative resources (ties, know-how, etc.).[46] Empowering and upgrading their capacities, including for collaboration, has become one of the primary goals of the European Union.

However, one has to distinguish between the transformatory power of EU pre-accession programmes, which were introduced at the beginning of the 1990s, and EU Structural Funds, the main developmental instrument available only to member states. The EU pre-accession programmes (e.g. PHARE, ISPA) were primarily intended to strengthen the position of sub-national actors so that they could become players in developmental governance. It was hoped that the programmes would allow for the representation of a greater variety of local interests and accommodate more diverse developmental goals. Moreover, promoting inter-organizational cooperation was supposed to contribute to the growth of endogenous growth capacities, which would presumably decrease the need for external aid and prevent the problem of 'self-learned helplessness'.[47] Participation in trainings and exchange programmes provided actors with cultural capital (e.g. know-how and skills) and enabled them to participate in projects that for the most part promoted the cross-sectoral approach (most of all PHARE). This served to equip the organizations with social capital in the form of new or much stronger personal and inter-organizational ties.[48] The beneficiaries of these programmes included various NGOs, municipalities, and small and medium-sized enterprises. Although the scale of the aid targeting non-state actors was not particularly impressive (e.g. annual support for NGO capacity building amounted to around 1–2 million euros per country), especially in comparison to the resources provided to strengthening central governments, the effect of the support on their abilities to influence the making and implementation of developmental policies can hardly be overestimated.[49] The implementation of the Structural Funds in CEE countries took place within the centralized, state-dominated framework. Moreover, massive inflows of money, weak administrative capacities, time pressure, and political conflicts about 'key projects' impeded the learning process on the ground.[50] Pressure to spend EU money as fast as possible in order to pump up 'absorption capacity'—an ill-defined

---

46   Boerzel, Tania: Paradox of Double Weakness, Research Report for the Project New Modes of Governance, 2007.
47   Bruszt, Laszlo/ Vedres, Balazs: Fostering Developmental Agency from without, paper prepared for the EUSA Eleventh Biennial International Conference Los Angeles/CA, 23–25 April 2009.
48   Börzel, Tanja A./ Buzogány, Aron: Governing EU Accession in Transition Countries. The Role of Non-state Actors, in: Acta Politica, 2010 (vol. 45), Nos. 1–2, pp. 158–182.
49   Bailey, David/ Lisa de Propris: A Bridge to Phare? EU Pre-Accession Aid and Capacity-Building in the Candidate Countries, in: Journal of Common Market Studies 2004 (vol. 42), no. 1, pp. 77–98.
50   Bruszt, Laszlo: Multi-level governance. The eastern version. Emerging Patterns of Regional Development Patterns in the New Member States, EUI Working Papers, 2007/13.

indicator of a state's effectiveness—resulted in a greater role for state agencies in the implementation of various EU-financed projects.

All in all, I expect that the pre-accession projects and trainings stimulated horizontal collaborative relationships, in particular with local government, other nonprofits and business. In contrast, I expect that projects received within the EU Structural Funds framework mostly stimulated ties to national and regional states.

7.4.4. Regional Governance

This perspective builds upon political opportunity theory[51] and is particularly useful for explaining co-operative relationships with the state. According to this theory, the success of organizations in their attempts to penetrate the political system depends on the degree of the system's openness, the character of the authorities' reaction, and the existence and status of allies in the political power configuration. It argues that the more open the political system is, the more amenable the officials' response will be; and the more powerful the organizations' allies are, the greater the likelihood that relationships between the state and nonprofits will tend toward collaboration rather than conflict. The main challenge connected with this perspective is the operationalization of the 'openness' of the political system. Tarrow has suggested focusing attention on legal arrangements, configurations of alliances in the party system, and the prevailing strategies of the ruling elites. Della Porta[52] has cited the 'openness' of a political system as an indicator for the amount of resources offered to civil society organizations. In this Ph.D. project, I will focus on the properties of regional governance in terms of the opportunities for nonprofits to participate.

Why should we study the regional state? The importance of the role that the state plays in the process of arriving at different non-hierarchical modes of socio-economic governance is well established in the literature on developmental state or embedded politics.[53] This theory claims that the state has several unique features, including the capability to change the distribution of power among sub-national actors, alter their incentives, and set the rules of co-operation for as well as monitor collective action. The state should therefore be able to facilitate the emergence of developmental alliances even when the conditions do not favour institutional experimentation (e.g. lack

---

51 Tilly, Charles: From Mobilization to Revolution, Reading/MA: Addison-Wesley, 1978.
52 Donatella, Della Porta: Democracy in Social Movements, New York: Palgrave Macmillan, 2009.
53 Evans, Peter: Development as Institutional Change: The Pitfalls of Monocropping and the Potentials of Deliberation, in: Studies in Comparative International Development, 2004 (vol. 38), pp. 30–52. McDermott, Gerry: Institutional Change and Firm Creation in East-Central Europe. An Embedded Politics Approach, in: Comparative Political Studies, 2004 (vol. 37), No.2, pp. 188–217.

of trust, fear of hold-up, etc.).[54] By providing resources to these actors, the state might induce learning on the ground, and by providing channels for mediation between various local experiments, it might induce knowledge transfer across the various domains and levels.[55]

Since this research project aims to explain different sub-national patterns of partnering, it will focus primarily on the regional state, which is the 'meso-level' of state administration. This choice was dictated by the fact that the state's capacity to foster and monitor institutional experimentation on the local level depends on the way that political power is distributed within regional policy-making as well as on the way economic and societal actors are included in decision-making on the regional level. Consequently, the mode of regional governance represents 'higher-order governance'[56] or 'meta-governance'[57] in relation to local experimentation on the ground, and can be defined as the way that relationships are organized among different levels of the state and among different categories of stakeholders. Here, the regional level of the state operates as a liaison or broker in creating networks and empowering non-state actors[58].

In order to establish links of causality between regional governance and patterns of associating, and consequently come up with a testable hypothesis, one has to identify the relevant institutions of regional governance. This task is particularly challenging because the concept of governance (and its many variations, e.g. multi-level governance, corporate governance, etc.) has become one of the 'buzz words' increasingly used to address various issues in different contexts.

Following Bruszt's[59] argument that 'developmental governance is primarily about the power to decide who has a say and what counts in planning development', it will be analysed, on one side, how much room for making developmental decisions is devolved to regions, and on the other, the extent to which various nonprofits are involved in decision-making on the regional level.

With respect to the first dimension, regions that have greater autonomy in setting their goals and defining the means of development cast a 'more credible shadow of

---

54   Scharpf, Fritz: Games Real Actors Play, Boulder/CO: Westview Press, 1997; Benz, Arthur/ Fürst, Dietrich: Policy learning in regional networks, in: European Urban and Regional Studies, 2002 (vol. 9), No. 1, pp. 21–36.

55   Bruszt, Laszlo/ Stark, David: Who Counts? Supranational Norms and Societal Needs, in: East European Politics and Societies, 2002 (vol. 17), no. 1, pp. 74–82.

56   Herrigel, Gary: Emerging Strategies and Forms of Governance in High-wage Component Manufacturing Regions, in: Industry and Innovation, 2004 (vol. 11), Nos. 1 and 2, pp. 45–79.

57   Jessop, Bob: The Rise of Governance and the Risks of Failure. The Case of Economic Development, in: International Social Science Journal, 1998 (vol. 50), No. 155, pp. 29–46.

58   Ansell, Chris: The Networked Polity. Regional Development in Western Europe, in: Governance. An International Journal of Policy and Administration, 2000 (vol. 13), no. 3, pp. 303–333.

59   Bruszt, Laszlo: Multi-level Governance. The Eastern Version. Emerging Patterns of Regional Development Patterns in the New Member States, EUI Working Papers, 2007/13, p. 610.

hierarchy'. They can therefore more easily enforce the 'rules of the game' and, consequently, stimulate innovative institutional experiments (e.g. innovative project partnerships involving NGOs and the state). The presence of formal rules that force the central state to take into account the interests of the regions will be an indicator of the first dimension.

The involvement of sub-national actors in developmental decision-making on the regional level will be identified by the presence of a political representative body that is accountable to a sub-national actors' body (which means that an institution consisting of actors hand-picked by the national government does not fulfil these criteria) and responsible for final decisions on fundamental issues (developmental goals, allocation of resources, planning schemes, etc.). The diverse organizational background of the actors involved in the work of this institution should facilitate more innovative developmental action on the ground. Additionally, one could assume that the prevalence of interactions between two types of actors (e.g. NGOs and the state) could lead to similar patterns of interaction at the local level.

For the purpose of this project, I will assume that the more room the regional state grants nonprofits in defining their goals and means of development, the more collaborative ties the organizations will develop to the state and within the sector. This will be tested by measuring the extent to which nonprofits participate in the committees that set the priorities for national, regional and EU programmes, which are all discussed and agreed upon on the regional level. Moreover, I expect that a rich institutional setting that supports nonprofits' activities within the public domain should positively correlate with patterns of inter-organizational collaboration.

7.5. Conclusion

The results of first data analyses (not shown here) only partially confirm expactations from the theoretical framework. As expected, the size of an organisation's budget affects the type of inter-organizational ties with the state. Organizations with bigger budgets maintain collaborative ties with higher tiers of government ('strong state' cluster), whereas those with smaller budgets collaborate mostly with municipalities ('community' cluster). Size of budget does not affect collaboration with other nonprofits. Here, social rather than economic capacity is the explanatory factor. Organizations that rely on volunteers in their activities tend to be highly embedded in intra-sectoral ties ('community' cluster). With respect to the welfare state argument, receiving money from the state has a diverging impact on the nonprofits. On the one hand, organizations that receive money from national government do not maintain any collaborative ties with non-state actors ('strong state'). On the other hand, money from municipalities is correlated with rich inter-organizational ties ('community' and 'cross-sectoral' cluster). Moreover, nonprofits without state funding are not collaborating at all. Similarly to the state funding, financial support from the European Union has also affected patterns of inter-organizational collaboration in a diverging manner. Pre-accession pojects and trainings have led to an increase of cross-sectoral ties ('cross-sectoral' cluster). On the contrary, organizations that received the most support from EU Structural Funds projects collaborate only with the state, in particular at the national and regional level ('strong state'). Nevertheless, data show that Europeanization led to an increae of collaborative ties, since nonprofits without any pre-accession or EU SF projects belong to the 'dissociated' cluster. It is also remarkable, that participation in regional governance stimulates ties only to the national and regional state.

In sum, results of first data analyses allow to conclude that the biggest impact towards diversity of inter-organizational collaboration came from funding by the local state and participation in the EU pre-accession programmes. Surprisingly, large, professionalized organizations that have received the biggest share of EU Structural Funds tend to maintain collaborative ties exclusively with higher tiers of government. Since these oganizations are not accountable to other nonprofits, their intensive involvement in regional governance bears the risk of clientelism. All in all, it can be argued that decentralized funding schemes lead to diverse and beneficial constellations of partners, whereas centralized (both domestic and EU) financial support stimulates ties only to the government. The data to a large extent confirm the expectation that in countries where funding for nonprofits is distributed mostly in a centralized manner, as in the Czech Republic, there is a bigger 'strong state' cluster, whereas in those, where decentralized funding is the dominant way of financing nonprofits (e.g. Poland) 'cross-sectoral', and 'community' clusters are prevailing.

Veronika Pasynkova

8. Successor Parties and Trade Unions in the Post-Communist States. Institutionalizing Informal Relationships

8.1. Introduction

The specific character of post-communist democracies greatly depends on the transformation of the informal relationships and networks that were typical for the late communist period. The institutional basis of post-communist states was the former communist regimes; likewise, civil society institutions were formed on the basis of their communist predecessors, such as successor parties and trade unions.

Today, the successor parties are legitimate actors in the political processes of post-communist democracies. In Poland, Hungary, Bulgaria and Romania, they have been state-level policy-makers for a long time. In other countries, such as the Czech Republic and Russia, the successor parties acted as a strong and constant opposition to the government. The civil society institutions inherited by the post-communist regimes include not only the former communist parties themselves but also structures that were ideologically and organisationally subordinated to them. These institutions, such as trade unions, youth groups and women's organizations, are known as civil society institutions in traditional democracies. However, their communist counterparts were controlled by the regime and thus possessed various functions. This legacy may undermine popularity of civil society organizations descended from the former communist regimes in post-communist democracies. However, these organizations, particularly trade unions, nevertheless participate in democratic processes and influence them both in formal and informal ways.

As the experience of Russia and East Central Europe shows, successor parties, trade unions and the state conform to different models of relationships depending on their degree of institutionalization and role in the post-communist period. In this research, I will describe the formation of relationships between these three groups in post-communist democracies on the basis of informal relations inherited from communist regimes.

My research covers the period between 1989 and 2004, from the beginning of the post-communist era to the accession of most East Central European countries to the European Union. The specific features of the various communist parties and trade unions that were in place in the late communist period are also taken into consideration. The relationships between successor parties, trade unions and the state are investigated in terms of the institutional design of the post-communist regimes, the level of the successor parties' and trade unions' electoral participation, and the process of social dialogue regulating the labour relations between trade unions and the state.

8.2. Successor Parties and Trade Unions as Post-Communist Actors

The former communist parties of East Central Europe are known as 'successor parties'. The term 'successor parties' refers to political organizations (parties), which grew out of ruling communist parties and inherited their main resources, personnel and membership.[1] At the same time, successor parties are recognized by a public that legitimates them as the legal heirs of ruling communist parties.[2] Another criterion for successor parties is their electoral success in free parliamentary elections to confirm their status as parties that have adjusted to the conditions of post-communist regimes due to or despite their inherited resources.[3] In general, the criteria for successor parties include: a) material resources (properties, funds), membership, personnel inherited from the former communist parties; b) legal and legitimate status as the ruling parties' heirs.[4]

In my research, I am focusing on a number of successor parties including Social Democracy of the Polish Republic (SDPR) (known as the Democratic Left Alliance (DLA) after 1999), the Communist Party of the Russian Federation (CPRF), the Hungarian Socialist Party (HSP), the Bulgarian Socialist Party (BSP), the Social Democratic Party of Romania (SDPR), the Communist Party of Bohemia and Moravia (CPBM) and the Party of Left Democrats in Slovakia (PLD).

Successor parties demonstrate different ideological trajectories in the post-communist period.[5] At the beginning of the post-communist transformations, some

---

1 Ishiyama, John T.: The Communist Successor Parties and Party Organizational Development in Post-Communist Politics, in: Political Research Quarterly, 1999 (vol. 52), no. 1, pp. 87–112, here p. 88; Golosov, Grigorii V.: Partiinye sistemy Rossii i stran Vostochnoi Evropy, Moscow: Ves' mir, 1999, here p. 51.
2 Mahr, Allison/ Nagle, John D.: Resurrection of the Successor Parties and Democratization in East Central Europe, in: Communist and Post Communist Studies, 1995 (vol. 28), no. 4, pp. 393–409.
3 Lubecki, Jacek: Echoes of Latifundism? Electoral Constituencies of Successor Parties in Post-Communist Countries, in: East European Politics and Societies, 2004 (vol. 18), no. 1, pp. 10–44, here p. 10.
4 Ishiyama, John T./ Shafqat, Sahar: Party Identity Change in Post-Communist Politics: The Cases of the Successor Parties in Hungary, Poland, and Russia, in: Communist and Post Communist Studies, 2000 (vol. 33), no. 4, pp. 439–455, here p. 440.
5 Cotta, Maurizio: Building Party Systems After the Dictatorship. The East European Cases in a Comparative Perspective, in: Pridham, Geoffrey/ Vanhanen, Tatu (eds.): Democratization in Eastern Europe. Domestic and International Perspectives, London, New York: Routledge, 1994, pp. 99–127; Ishiyama, John T./ Bozóki, Andraś: Adaptation and Change. Characterizing the Survival Strategies of the Communist Successor Parties, in: Journal of Communist Studies and Transition Politics, 2001 (vol. 17), no. 3, pp. 32–51.

researchers claimed that the successful adaptation of successor parties was a result of their social democratization, as the cases of SDPR and HSP confirmed.[6] However, successor parties such as CPRF and particularly CPBM did not follow the social democratic ideology but survived and adapted effectively to the post-communist regimes.

Following the typology developed by J. Ishiyama and A. Bozóki, the successor parties can be divided into four basic ideological types along the dimensions of modernization and nationalization. Firstly, the orthodox communist type describes the Communist Party of Bohemia and Moravia in the Czech Republic, which is a non-reformed and non-nationalized successor party. Secondly, the Communist Party of the Russian Federation is a non-reformed but nationalized successor party of the national communist type. The third type is reformed, non-nationalized successor parties, which include the modernized social democratic Hungarian Socialist Party and Social Democracy of the Polish Republic. Finally, the Bulgarian Socialist Party and the Social Democratic Party of Romania are categorized as national socialist and populist; they are labelled as the reformed nationalized type of successor party[7].

According to H. Kitschelt, the successor parties' development depends on the earlier types of communist regimes: patrimonial, bureaucratic authoritarian and national consensus. The national consensus regime of Poland and Hungary led to the formation of the social democratic successor parties, the bureaucratic authoritarian regime of Czechoslovakia produced the orthodox communist successor party, and the patrimonial regime of the USSR and Romania resulted in the creation of the national communist and national socialist parties based on clientelistic relations[8].

Most trade unions in East Central Europe also have communist origins[9] that justify considering them to be 'successor' or 'former official' trade unions. There are at least four development trajectories in the trade union movement at the beginning of post-communist transition. The first trajectory is illustrated by the case of Poland,

---

6   Mahr, Allison/ Nagle, John D.: Resurrection of the Successor Parties and Democratization in East Central Europe, in: Communist and Post Communist Studies, 1995 (vol. 28), no. 4, pp. 393–409; Waller, Michael: Starting-up Problems: Communists, Social-Democrats and Greens, in: Wightman, Gordon (ed.): Party Formation in East Central Europe. Post-Communist Politics in Czechoslovakia, Hungary, Poland, and Bulgaria, Aldershot: Edward Elgar, 1995, pp. 218–237.

7   Ishiyama, John.T./ Bozóki, Andraś: Adaptation and Change. Characterizing the Survival Strategies of the Communist Successor Parties, in: Journal of Communist Studies and Transition Politics, 2001 (vol. 17), no. 3, pp. 32–51, here p. 36; Bozóki, Andraś/ Ishiyama, John T. (eds.): The Communist Successor Parties of Central and Eastern Europe, Armonk/NY, London: M.E. Sharpe, 2002, here p. 7.

8   Kitschelt, Herbert: Constraints and Opportunities in the Strategic Conduct of Post-Communist Successor Parties. Regime Legacies as Causal Argument, in: Bozóki, Andraś/ Ishiyama, John T. (eds.): The Communist Successor Parties of Central and Eastern Europe, Armonk/NY, London: M.E. Sharpe, 2002, pp. 14–40.

9   Kubicek, Paul: Organized Labor in Postcommunist States. From Solidarity to Infirmity, Pittsburgh: University of Pittsburgh Press, 2004; Ost, David: The Defeat of Solidarity. Anger and Politics in Postcommunist Europe, Ithaca/NY: Cornell University Press, 2005, here p. 17.

where the independent trade union 'Solidarity' shaped the political landscape and forced the official All-Poland Alliance of Trade Unions (OPZZ) to compete actively for their resources and membership.[10] The second path is characterized by the almost complete disappearance of communist trade unions in Czechoslovakia due to the unification of the powerful striking committees into the Confederation of Trade unions of Bohemia and Moravia (CTUBM). CTUBM acted as a partner of the first post-communist governments in the Czech Republic, supporting the liberal economic policy.[11] The third tendency is the case of Hungary, which has strong competition between former official and independent trade unions within the National Trade Union Council. The National Confederation of Hungarian Trade Unions (NCTU) became a successor trade union. Finally, the case of Russia demonstrates the formation of a number of formally independent trade unions as part of interest group and corporation structures in their fight for the distribution of political and economic resources.[12] The Federation of Independent Trade Unions of Russia (FITUR), however, was forced to demonstrate loyalty to President and kept a monopolistic position in exchange for political subordination.

I believe that the case of Bulgaria can be located between the first and the second types due to the strong independent trade union 'Podkrepa' that opposed the former official Confederation of Independent Trade Unions of Bulgaria (CITU). At the same time, CITU was recognized as and performed as a government partner. As for the case of Romania, it is close to that of Hungary in terms of trade union pluralism with its National Confederation of Free Romanian Trade Unions (NCFTU) as the successor trade union.[13]

Both successor and independent trade unions in East Central Europe stand out due to their strong political functions in addition to their traditional activity of social protection.[14] D. Ost explains their shift to the political sphere by referring to the consequences of the transition to the liberal economy. The institutionalization of trade unions and the realization of the goals of social protection are possible only due to direct or

---

10   Hausner, Jerzy: Organizacje interesu i stosunki przemysłowe w krajach postsocjalistycznych, in: Przegląd Socjologiczny, 1994, no. 43, pp. 9–26.
11   Hausner, Jerzy/ Pedersen, Ove/ Ronit, Karsten (eds.): Evolution of Interest Representation and Development of the Labour Market in Post-Socialist Countries, Cracow: Cracow Academy of Economics, 1994, here p. 402.
12   Ibid., pp. 403–404.
13   See, Kideckel, David A.: Winning the Battles, Losing the War: Contradictions of Romanian Labor in the Postcommunist Transformation, in: Crowley, Stephen/ Ost, David (eds.): Workers After Workers' States. Labor and Politics in Postcommunist Eastern Europe, Lanham et al.: Rowman and Littlefield Publishers, 2001, pp. 102–132.
14   See, for example: Ost, David: Labour, Class, and Democracy; Shaping Political Antagonisms in Post-Communist Society, in: Crawford, Beverly: Markets, States, and Democracy: The Political Economy of Post-Communist Transformation, Boulder: Westview, 1995, pp. 177–203.

indirect political participation.[15] To achieve political representation, trade unions not only have to take part in social dialogue, but also enter the electoral field. As a result, trade unions try to find appropriate allies to take part in parliamentary elections.

After the ruling communist parties collapsed, their formal connections with official trade unions disappeared as well. Both successor and independent trade unions immediately claimed to reject the leading role of communist party. However, the foundation of successor parties revealed that the parties maintained informal relations with former official trade unions in order to initiate political cooperation for effective electoral participation and lobbying common interests in the process of social dialogue.

Cooperation with trade unions is considered to be a factor contributing to the successful development of successor parties. For example, M. Waller attributed the electoral successes of the Polish and Hungarian communist parties to their close cooperation with the former official trade unions, which remained quite powerful during the transition process.[16] J. Ishiyama tested this hypothesis and verified that both Poland and Hungary had large trade unions that enjoyed a relatively low level of distrust among the population.[17] However, electoral success is not always contingent upon cooperation with trade unions. For example, L. Cook and L. March discovered that there was no formal cooperation between Russian trade unions and the CPRF because the Federation of Independent Trade Unions of Russia refused to work with the communists, preferring to collaborate with the 'party of power' instead.[18]

M. Orenstein developed the explanatory model of relations between successor parties and trade unions in East Central Europe. He hypothesized that the determining factor in this cooperation is the direction of the successor parties' ideological evolution. He identified two stages in the transformation of the most successful Polish and Hungarian successor parties. In the first, there was an intra-party division into conservative and reformist wings. After their victory, the reformers initiated cooperation with trade unions in the second stage and consequently gained mass electoral support. The Polish successor party made electoral coalitions with trade unions and encouraged trade union leaders to take part in the party's activities.[19] Orenstein's model con-

---

15   Herod, Andrew: Theorizing Trade Unions in Transition, in: Pickles, John/ Smith, Adrian: Theorizing Transition: The Political Economy of Post-Communist Transformations, New York, London: Routledge, 1998, pp. 197–217.

16   Waller, Michael: Adaptation of the Former Communist Parties of East Central Europe. A Case of Democratization?, in: Party Politics, 1995 (vol. 1), no. 3, pp. 373–390.

17   Ishiyama, John T.: The Communist Successor Parties and Party Organizational Development in Post-Communist Politics, in: Political Research Quarterly, 1999 (vol. 52), no. 1, pp. 87–112.

18   Cook, Linda J.: Trade Unions, Management, and State in Contemporary Russia, in: Rutland, Peter (ed.): Business and State in Contemporary Russia, Boulder/CO: Westview Press, 2001, pp. 151–172; March, Luke: For Victory? The Crises and Dilemmas of the Communist Party of the Russian Federation, in: Europe-Asia Studies, 2001 (vol. 53), no. 2, pp. 263–290.

19   Orenstein, Mitchell A.: A Genealogy of Communist Successor Parties in East-Central Europe and the Determinants of Their Success, in: East European Politics and Societies, 1998 (vol. 12), no. 3,

firms the significance of trade unions in the transformation of successor parties, but it does not explain the institutional success of the successor parties that did not cooperate with trade unions.

8.3. Developments of Communist Legacies

The disintegration of communist regimes and the institutional model of 'party—state' was the starting point for building post-communist relations between former communist parties, trade unions and the state in Russia and East Central Europe. The party state model was based on hierarchal rule of the ruling party and its subordinated satellites, including komsomol organizations and trade unions. Communist party authorities ruled ministries, which acted as the formal governing bodies of the communist state.[20]

In the late communist period, the role of ministries was not limited to fulfilling the ruling party's tasks.Ministries were also influential actors with their own particular interests. In addition to the communist party hierarchy, there was a specific system of interest lobbying to defend the interests of ministries and official trade unions.[21] The communist process of state government incorporated a complicated system of formal and informal negotiations between the ruling party and its formally subordinated partners. This system can be characterized as 'corporatism', but one that differs from the corporate relations in Western democracies, where the state is separated from interest groups on the principle of equal opportunity.[22] In communist corporatism, actors were integrated into the state structures through the organizational pivot of the ruling party. The subordination of state institutions and interest groups to the communist party was eliminated following the structural changes to the communist regimes.[23]

The collapse of communism brought about institutional weakness and the disintegration of systemic links with ruling communist parties in East Central Europe. In Poland, Hungary, Czechoslovakia, and Russia, laws were passed prohibiting communist party organizations' activity in state governing bodies and public institutions.[24] In Bulgaria and Romania, the communist parties remained in power, so the process of ousting party organizations was postponed, and there was a slower transforma-

---

pp. 472–499.

20   Csanádi, Maria: Party-States and Their Legacies in Post-Communist Transformation, Cheltenham, Northampton/MA: Edward Elgar, 1997.

21   Gregory, Paul R.: Restructuring the Soviet Economic Bureaucracy, Cambridge: Cambridge University Press, 1990, here p. 12.

22   Kubicek, Paul: Organized Labor in Postcommunist States. From Solidarity to Infirmity, Pittsburgh: University of Pittsburgh Press, 2004.

23   Csanádi, Maria: Party-States and Their Legacies in Post-Communist Transformation, Cheltenham, Northampton/MA: Edward Elgar, 1997, here pp. 312–313.

24   Kostelecký, Tomas: Political Parties After Communism. Developments in East-Central Europe, Washington, D.C.: Woodrow Wilson Center Press, 2002.

tion of party bodies into the institutional structures of the post-communist state.[25] To a greater or lesser extent, party structures served as a foundation for institutional building in all post-communist countries, but the process was corrected by the initiatives of post-communist governments including lustration and the redistribution of ruling parties' properties.[26]

The redistribution of the property of communist parties and their satellites was typical for post-communist regimes, but the mechanisms of redistribution varied depending on the authority of the former communist organization and the efficiency of post-communist institutions, particularly constitutional courts. Successor parties and former official trade unions applied to constitutional courts in an attempt to avoid the confiscation of their property. For example, SDPR and OPZZ in Poland were able to keep a large part of their institutional predecessors' property due to the loyal decisions of the Constitutional Court.[27] However, the threat of confiscating property by the president forced FITUR in Russia to capitulate in their fight to occupy an independent political position and compelled them to support Boris Yeltsin in the armed conflict between the parliament and the president in 1993.[28]

In the cases of Bulgaria and Romania, the redistribution of communist parties' property was not so obvious, but both BSP and SDPR used fictional owners to keep most of their resources and their satellites' property.[29] Due to these manoeuvres, the non-communist governments that followed communist reformers were unable to take effective steps to redistribute communist property because their new owners were not formally related to the communist successors. As a result, the distribution of communist property greatly affected the relationships of successor parties with the post-communist state.

The post-communist transformations destroyed the institutional link of 'party—state' typical for communist regimes. Party organizations in state bodies and pub-

---

25   Gallagher, Tom: A Feeble Embrace: Romania's Engagement with Democracy, 1989–1994, in: Journal of Communist Studies and Transition Politics, 1996 (vol. 12), no. 2, pp. 145–172; Karasimeonov, Georgi: Differentiation Postponed: Party Pluralism in Bulgaria, in: Wightman, Gordon (ed.): Party Formation in East Central Europe. Post-Communist Politics in Czechoslovakia, Hungary, Poland, and Bulgaria, Aldershot: Edward Elgar, 1995, pp. 154–179.
26   Calhoun, Noel: The Ideological Dilemma of Lustration in Poland, in: East European Politics and Societies, 2002 (vol. 16), no. 2, pp. 494–520.
27   Zubek, Voytek: The Reassertion of the Left in Post-Communist Poland, in: Europe-Asia Studies, 1994 (vol. 46), no. 5, pp. 801–837.
28   Crowley, Stephen: The Social Explosion That Wasn't: Labor Quiscence in Postcommunist Russia, in Crowley, Stephen/ Ost, David (eds.): Workers After Workers' States. Labor and Politics in Postcommunist Eastern Europe, Lanham et al.: Rowman and Littlefield Publishers, 2001, pp. 199–218, here p. 208.
29   Murer, Jeffrey S.: Mainstreaming Extremism. The Romanian PDSR and the Bulgarian Socialists in Comparative Perspective, in: Bozóki, Andraś/ Ishiyama, John T. (eds.): The Communist Successor Parties of Central and Eastern Europe, Armonk/NY, London: M.E. Sharpe, 2002, pp. 367–396.

lic institutions were liquidated.[30] Former communist parties transformed themselves organizationally and ideologically and acquired the status of successor parties by accepting the new rules of post-communist regimes. Successor parties started seeking the typical goal of traditional parties of participating in parliamentary elections in order to take part in government and decision-making processes. However, in the parliamentary elections, successor parties faced political isolation from the other parties, which did not want to work with former communist parties.[31] Ignored by most post-communist actors, the successor parties had to consider the former satellites of the ruling communist parties that survived and had retained some public support as potential allies. According to these criteria, it was an obvious choice for the successor parties to focus their attention on the former official trade unions. As for trade unions, at first they were not enthusiastic about the former communist parties as political partners since they were afraid of keeping the reputation of being communist-oriented organizations.

After the formal dissolution of the ruling communist parties, former official trade unions strived for the status of independent institutions. To survive in the post-communist regimes, they needed to realize their mobilization potential and be recognized by the state as a social dialogue partner. The social dialogue became institutionalized as the main form taken by the relationships between trade unions and the state in the post-communist period,[32] but in order to become legitimate representatives of the workers, former official trade unions had to compete fiercely against independent trade unions for their members.[33] In most East Central European countries, the first post-communist governments tried to suspend the activities of successor trade unions, seeing in them a potential source of support for communist forces. In some cases, the governments passed laws on the redistribution of communist trade unions' properties between successor and independent trade unions. Former official

---

30   Gregory, Paul R.: Restructuring the Soviet Economic Bureaucracy, Cambridge: Cambridge University Press, 1990; Csanádi, Maria: Party-States and Their Legacies in Post-Communist Transformation, Cheltenham, Northampton/MA: Edward Elgar, 1997, here p. 223.
31   Bukowski, Charles/ Racz, Barnabas (eds.): The Return of the Left in Post-Communist States. Current Trends and Future Prospects, Cheltenham, Northampton/MA: Edward Elgar, 1999; Curry, Jane L./ Urban Joan B. (eds.): The Left Transformed in Post-Communist Societies. The Cases of East Central Europe, Russia and Ukraine, Lanham et al.: Rowman and Littlefield Publishers, 2003.
32   Casale, Giuseppe: Evolution and Trends in Industrial Relations in Central and Eastern European Countries, in: International Journal of Comparative Labour Law and Industrial Relations, 2003 (vol. 19), no. 1, pp. 5–32; Candland, Christopher/ Sil, Rudra (eds.): The Politics of Labour in a Global Age. Continuity and Change in Late-Industrializing and Post-Socialist Economies, Oxford, New York: Oxford University Press, 2001, here p. 285.
33   Hausner, Jerzy/ Pedersen, Ove/ Ronit, Karsten (eds.): Evolution of Interest Representation and Development of the Labour Market in Post-Socialist Countries, Cracow: Cracow Academy of Economics, 1994, here p. 394.

trade unions opposed the attempts with more or less success.[34] To keep properties and acquire the status of a social dialogue partner, successor trade unions claimed to reject their communist past and recognize e the post-communist regimes. However, this did not mean that they were loyal to the new governments. Trade unions actively used mass strikes and the workers' movement to strengthen their political positions, forcing post-communist governments to recognize them and start negotiations with them.[35]

Regardless of the active participation of the trade unions, the efficiency of social dialogue institutions was quite low from the beginning of the post-communist transformations. Social partners such as the trade unions and entrepreneurs' associations were weak due to state pressure.[36] The first post-communist governments provided a policy of shock therapy dictated by the requirements of democratic transformation, so the interests of trade unions and entrepreneurs were seen as being of secondary importance. Since social dialogue was not an effective means for trade unions to lobby for their interests, their activity shifted to the political field, which provided trade unions with an additional lobbying channel.[37]

In their search for political partners, the former official trade unions faced similar problems to the successor parties. Trade unions found themselves isolated because most political actors did not want to cooperate with potentially communist partners. In spite of the formal dissolution of institutional links with former communist parties, some regional party and trade unions organizations continued informal cooperation. In Poland and Hungary, the choice of regional organizations was crucial for both successor parties and trade unions when choosing a political partner at the national level. There, the electoral coalitions of successor parties and former official trade unions were established as a result of informal interactions at the regional level.[38]

---

34 Crowley, Stephen/ Ost, David (eds.): Workers After Workers' States. Labor and Politics in Postcommunist Eastern Europe, Lanham et al.: Rowman and Littlefield Publishers, 2001.

35 Orenstein, Mitchell A., Hale, Lisa E. Corporatist Renaissance in Postcommunist Central Europe?, in: Candland, Christopher/ Sil, Rudra (eds.): The Politics of Labour in a Global Age. Continuity and Change in Late-Industrializing and Post-Socialist Economies, Oxford, New York: Oxford University Press, 2001, pp. 258–283; Ost, David: The Weakness of Strong Social Movements: Models of Unionism in the East European Context, in: European Journal of Industrial Relations, 2002 (vol. 8), no. 1, pp. 79–96.

36 Peregudov, Sergei P.: Korporacii, obschestvo, gosudarstvo: evoluciya otnoshenii, Moscow: Nauka, 2003.

37 Ost, David: Labour, Class, and Democracy; Shaping Political Antagonisms in Post-Communist Society, in: Crawford, Beverly: Markets, States, and Democracy: The Political Economy of Post-Communist Transformation, Boulder: Westview, 1995, pp. 177–203.

38 See, for example: Orenstein, Mitchell A.: A Genealogy of Communist Successor Parties in East-Central Europe and the Determinants of Their Success, in: East European Politics and Societies, 1998 (vol. 12), no. 3, pp. 472–499.

8.4. Arenas and Models of Relationships

To develop theoretical models for the analysis, I borrow the term 'arena' from G. Tsebelis,[39] who describes the relations between actors and institutions as nested games on different levels called arenas. Arenas can be independent but can also overlap in some places, and they are limited by the existing institutional conditions that govern the simultaneous participation of actors and institutions in the different arenas.

I have defined three arenas in which the relationships between successor parties, trade unions and the state take place depending on the institutional links between them: 1) the institutional design arena, 2) the electoral arena and 3) the social dialogue arena.

The institutional design arena determines relationships between political parties (successor parties) and the state (government and/or president). After parliamentary elections, parties win seats in parliament, allowing them to determine state policies either directly (if the government is formed by parliament) or indirectly (if government is the formed by the president). Due to the institutional design of the political system, successor parties more or less have the opportunity to integrate into the system of state government. The institutional design of post-communist regimes is constructed during the post-communist transformation period under the influence of the institutional legacy of communism and transition.

The electoral arena can contain electoral coalitions between successor parties and former official trade unions during parliamentary elections. This political cooperation based on informal relations can be initiated because of successor parties' ideology. It is more likely that trade unions would prefer to cooperate with social democratic parties, while social democrats regard trade unions as their traditional pillar.

The social dialogue arena is a place where the state and trade unions interact in tripartite negotiations. The character of the relationships between the state and trade unions can be affected by clientilistic relations inherited from communist regimes. In post-communist regimes, clientilistic links can be a more efficient means of lobbying in favour of trade unions' interests than formal social dialogue institutions with their complicated and unpredictable negotiation procedures that involve a third partner—entrepreneurs' associations—whose interests oppose those of the trade unions.

Accordingly, the models of relationships between the three groups assume the following working or non-working institutional links: 'successor parties—state' in the institutional arena, 'successor parties—trade unions' in the electoral arena and 'trade unions—state' in the social dialogue arena.

---

39 Tsebelis, George: Nested Games. Rational Choice in Comparative Politics, Berkley, Los Angeles, London: University of California Press, 1990.

I have developed three models of relationships for the interactions between successor parties, trade unions and the state.

Model 1. This model is characterized by working institutional links extending in all directions of the hypothetical triangle 'successor party—trade unions—state'. The institutional design of the political system in Model 1 allows the successor party to form the government and set state policy after the successor party wins the parliamentary election. During the parliamentary election, the successor party and former official trade unions create an electoral coalition using their informal links inherited from the communist regime. The interactions between the trade unions and the state occur in the social dialogue process with clientelistic relations having a minimal role in trade union lobbying. In this model, formal relations between the successor parties, trade unions and the state prevail.

Model 2. In this model, the institutional links in the triangle 'successor party—trade unions—state' do not work. The institutional design of the political system that is typical for Model 2 does not allow the successor party to form the government or state policy regardless of the election results. Even if the successor party receives the majority of votes and seats in the parliament and the party acts in opposition to the current government, the decision-making process concentrates among informal groups. The successor party and former official trade unions do not form an electoral coalition after the parliamentary election, even in the presence of informal links that can contribute to the formalization of political cooperation. The formal interactions between the trade unions and the state take place in the tripartite negotiation process, but trade union lobbying is more efficient via informal clientelistic relations. Therefore, for this model, informal relations are not formalized but institutionalized in a new way.

In addition, a third model (Model 3) can be defined that represents the middle ground between Model 1 and Model 2. The combinations of working institutional links in the triangle 'successor party—trade unions—state' may hypothetically vary, but the typical mixed model includes working links within the institutional and social dialogue arenas and a non-working link in the electoral arena.

In order to test these models of relationships, I conducted a comparative analysis of some of the available cases in the East Central European region, with an emphasis on Poland and Russia. Hungary, the Czech Republic, Slovakia, Romania and Bulgaria were also analysed. The former Yugoslav states were not included in the analysis because of the specific character of their nation-building and long-lasting military conflicts. The results of the analysis are summed up in Table 8-1 overleaf.

Table 8-1:   Models of Relationships of Successor Parties, Trade Unions and the State

Country	Relationship 'successor party—state'	Relationship 'successor party—trade unions'	Relationship 'trade unions—state'	Model
Poland	+	+	+	1
Russia	-	-	-	2
Hungary	+	+	+	1
Bulgaria	+	-	+/-	3
Romania	-	-	-	2
Czech Republic	+	-	+/-	3
Slovakia	+	-	+/-	3

The cases of Poland and Hungary conform to Model 1, the cases of Russia and Romania conform to Model 2, and the cases of Bulgaria, the Czech Republic and Slovakia fall somewhere in between (Model 3). A brief description of the cases in a comparative perspective is given below.

8.5. Successor Parties, Trade Unions and the State in the Institutional, Electoral and Social Dialogue Arenas

The analysis of the institutional changes in Russia, Poland, Hungary, Bulgaria, Romania, the Czech Republic and Slovakia during the post-communist period revealed a correlation between the legacy of the communist regime and the post-communist institutional design. The communist regime in Poland—characterized by H. Kitschelt as being 'national consensus'—produced post-communist transformations in the form of negotiations or 'pacted transition'.[40] The institutional post-communist design in Poland was constitutionally established in the 1993 Small Constitution and was consolidated after the 1997 constitution. Despite the intention of the first president, Lech Wałęsa, to assume full executive powers, Poland instead ended up with the so-called premier–presidential system. The government in Poland is formed based on election results, and the prime minister is elected by the parliament and confirmed by the president. As a result, the post-communist regime in Poland contributed to the integration of parties that win parliamentary elections into the governance system. This

---

40   Kitschelt, Herbert et al.: Post-Communist Party Systems. Competition, Representation, and Inter-Party Cooperation, Cambridge, New York: Cambridge University Press, 1999, here p. 24.

allows parties to form government and state policy, and also to nominate their candidate for the position of prime minister.[41]

The communist regime in Russia, which Kitschelt described as patrimonial, produced coercive post-communist transformations.[42] The post-communist institutional design was established by the 1993 constitution. Following Boris Yeltsin's efforts to assume full executive powers, Russia became a so-called president–parliamentary system.[43] In this arrangement, the president forms the government and nominates the prime minister, who must be confirmed by the parliament. As a result, the post-communist regime in Russia contributed to the isolation of the governance system, including the presidential administration and government, from the parties. Parties that win parliamentary elections are therefore not able to influence state policy directly.[44]

The national consensus communist regime in Hungary resulted in the post-communist negotiated transformations in the form of a pact that was similar to that in Poland. In Hungary, the pact established a parliamentary political system. The post-communist changes to the patrimonial communist regime in Bulgaria also had a negotiated character; the political system there can also be described as parliamentary in nature. Coercive transformations in the communist regime took place in Romania that included military conflicts and the execution of the Ceausescu family. The country's post-communist transformation can be characterized as an imposed transition; it finally ended in a premier—presidential political system. In the case of Czechoslovakia, the bureaucratic authoritarian communist regime became a parliamentary type system in both the Czech Republic and Slovakia as a result of the negotiated transformation process.

In each case analysed, the successor parties maintained their organizational structures at the regional level. However, in Poland, Hungary and Slovakia, the communist ruling parties were formally dissolved following the foundation of new successor parties in 1989–1990. In Russia, the communist party was suspended until the 1993 constitutional court decision that legalized the party's regional organizations. In Bulgaria and the Czech Republic, the former communist leadership simply changed their parties' names. In Romania, the former communist party was transformed into the interim

---

41   Shugart, Matthew S./ Carey, John T.: Presidents and Assemblies. Constitutional Design and Electoral Dynamics, Cambridge: Cambridge University Press, 1992; Millard, Frances: Polish Politics and Society, London, New York: Routledge, 1999; Szczerbiak, Aleks: Poles Together? Emergence and Development of Political Parties in Post-Communist Poland, Budapest: Central University Press, 2001.
42   Kitschelt, Herbert et al.: Post-Communist Party Systems. Competition, Representation, and Inter-Party Cooperation, Cambridge, New York: Cambridge University Press, 1999, here p. 23.
43   Shugart, Matthew S./ Carey, John T.: Presidents and Assemblies. Constitutional Design and Electoral Dynamics, Cambridge: Cambridge University Press, 1992.
44   Sakwa, Richard: Russian Politics and Society, London, New York: Routledge, 2002.

umbrella structure that later became the source of the successor party and other political parties.[45]

The transformations of the former official trade unions in these countries were founded on the resurrection of informal links between the regional organizations and the leaderships of the official trade unions. This occurred in all cases except for the Czech Republic. In Russia, Poland, Hungary, Romania, Bulgaria and Slovakia, the successor trade unions were established with communist resources. In contrast, in the Czech Republic, various trade unions appropriated the old communist trade union structures.[46]

The transformation of the Polish successor party, Social Democracy of the Polish Republic / Democratic Left Alliance, underwent processes of modernization and social democratization. The party kept its organisational infrastructure and elaborated an ideology around a social democratic platform. Consequently, the party preferred to cooperate with the trade unions. The former official trade union federation, the All-Poland Alliance of Trade Unions, tried to gain independence from the government after the constitutional court's decision to grant the communist trade unions' properties to OPZZ. Despite the resistance of the OPZZ leadership, the regional OPZZ trade unions rehabilitated the partnership agreement with SDPR and contributed to the formation of their electoral and parliamentary coalitions under the leadership of SDPR and OPZZ.[47]

The transformation of the Russian successor party, the Communist Party of the Russian Federation, took the form of nationalization. A. Bozóki and J. Ishiyama

---

45   For details, see: Szajkowski, Bogdan (ed.): Political Parties of Eastern Europe, Russia and Successor States, London: Longman,1994; Linz, Juan J./ Stepan, Alfred C.: Problems of Democratic Transition and Consolidation. Southern Europe, South America and Post-Communist Europe, Baltimore, London: Johns Hopkins University Press, 1996; Lewis, Paul G.: Political Parties in Post-Communist Eastern Europe, London, New York: Routledge, 2000.

46   Crowley, Stephen/ Ost, David (eds.): Workers After Workers' States. Labor and Politics in Postcommunist Eastern Europe, Lanham et al.: Rowman and Littlefield Publishers, 2001; Candland, Christopher/ Sil, Rudra (eds.): The Politics of Labour in a Global Age. Continuity and Change in Late-Industrializing and Post-Socialist Economies, Oxford, New York: Oxford University Press, 2001.

47   For details, see: Millard, Frances: Polish Politics and Society, London, New York: Routledge, 1999; Szczerbiak, Aleks: Poles Together? Emergence and Development of Political Parties in Post-Communist Poland, Budapest: Central University Press, 2001; Szczerbiak, Aleks: Old and New Divisions in Polish Politics. Polish Parties Electoral Strategies and Bases of Support, in: Europe-Asia Studies, 2003 (vol. 55), no. 5, pp. 729–746; Grzymala-Busse, Anna: The Programmatic Turnaround of Communist Successor Parties in East Central Europe, 1989–1998, in: Communist and Post-Communist Studies, 2002 (vol. 35), no. 1, pp. 51–66; Markowski, Radoslaw: The Polish SLD in the 1990s. From Opposition to Incumbents and Back, in: Bozóki, Andraś/ Ishiyama, John T. (eds.): The Communist Successor Parties of Central and Eastern Europe, Armonk/NY, London: M.E. Sharpe, 2002, pp. 51–88; Curry, Jane L.: Poland's Ex-Communists. From Pariahs to Establishment Players, in: Curry Jane L./ Urban, Joan B. (eds.): The Left Transformed in Post-Communist Societies. The Cases of East Central Europe, Russia and Ukraine, Lanham et al.: Rowman and Littlefield Publishers, 2003, pp. 19–60.

characterize the CPRF as a national communist party. The party kept its organizational infrastructure and elaborated an ideology on the national patriotic platform. Originally, the CPRF's ideology included social democratic elements, but its attempts to establish political cooperation with the former official trade unions failed. However, there were isolated cases of informal cooperation between the CPRF and trade unions at the regional level.[48]

The relationships of successor parties and trade unions in the electoral arena in Hungary, Bulgaria, Romania, the Czech Republic and Slovakia followed the ideological evolution of the successor parties. This analysis considered the parliamentary elections of 1990, 1994, 1998, 2002 in Hungary; 1991, 1994, 1997, 2001 in Bulgaria; 1990, 1992, 1996, 2000 in Romania; 1992, 1996, 1998, 2002 in the Czech Republic; and those of 1992, 1994, 1998, 2002 in Slovakia. The electoral cooperation based on the inherited communist institutional links depends on the direction of the successor party's ideological evolution.

The case of Hungary is rather similar to that of Poland: the ideological evolution of HSP was accompanied by modernization and social democratization. The new ideological platform led to electoral cooperation between HSP and NCTU. In Bulgaria, the national socialist ideology of the successor party, BSP, was not acceptable to the former official trade unions, despite the successor party's long period in power. On the opposite end of the spectrum, Romania's former official trade unions adopted a very different strategy: they agreed to a political partnership with the ruling SDPR, despite the national socialist character of the latter. Here, trade unions obtained pro-government status due to the personal (clientelistic) relations with the leadership of the successor party; the electoral cooperation proved to be unnecessary. In the Czech Republic, CPBM adopted an orthodox communist ideology that resulted in the long-term political isolation and non-participation of the successor party in the government. The Czech trade unions refused to engage in electoral cooperation, not only with CPBM, but also with the other parties. Finally, in Slovakia, PLD came to embody a modernized, social democratic ideology, similar to the Hungarian and Polish cases. However, there was no electoral partnership between PLD and CTUS due to the refusal

---

48   For details, see: Urban, Joan B./ Solovej, Valerij D.: Russia's Communists at the Crossroads, Boulder/CO: Westview Press, 1997; Sakwa, Richard: Russia's 'Permanent' (Uninterrupted) Elections of 1999–2000, in: Journal of Communist Studies and Transition Politics, 2000 (vol. 16), no. 3, pp. 85–112; Sakwa, Richard: Russian Politics and Society, London, New York: Routledge, 2002; Sakwa, Richard: The 2003–2004 Russian Elections and Prospects for Democracy, in: Europe-Asia Studies, 2005 (vol. 57), no. 3, pp. 369–398; Simon, Rick: Labour and Political Transformation in Russia and Ukraine, Aldershot: Ashgate, 2000; March, Luke: The Communist Party in Post-Soviet Russia, Manchester, New York: Manchester University Press, 2002.

of the CTUS leadership, despite the periodic inclusion of trade union candidates on the PLD's electoral lists.[49]

In Poland, the powerful trade union actor, Solidarity, has a significant impact on the relations between OPZZ and the Polish government. The Solidarity trade unions did not find the tripartite negotiations necessary since they were active political participants in their own right and directly involved in the first post-communist governments. The institutional establishment of the social dialogue in Poland was possible due to OPZZ's initiative in 1994 after the SDPR government came to power. Afterwards, the tripartite negotiations between the government, OPZZ, Solidarity and employers' associations occurred regularly and their decisions acquired legal status.[50]

The Federation of Independent Trade Unions of Russia found themselves at the mercy of the president and presidential administration after they nearly lost their properties in the 1993 conflict between the president and the supreme council. Afterwards, FITUR dutifully played the role of a pro-government trade union and refused to partner the opposition parties, including CPRF. FITUR's independent political foray into a paradoxical coalition with the Union of Industrialists and Entrepreneurs failed in 1995. The relations between FITUR and the Russian government were largely determined by the president's influence. Despite the presidential decree establishing social dialogue institutions, they did not play a substantial role in the policy-making process in either the social or economic spheres.[51] To lobby their own interests, the trade unions had to use other, mostly informal, channels, such as personal and clientelistic relations.[52]

The analysis of the relationships between the trade unions and state (government) in the social dialogue process in Hungary, Bulgaria, Romania, the Czech Republic and Slovakia also considered the indirect participation of successor parties. The efficiency of the social dialogue was analysed in each case by referring to the role of clientelistic relations in the interactions between the trade unions and the state.

---

49   Bukowski, Charles/ Racz, Barnabas (eds.): The Return of the Left in Post-Communist States. Current Trends and Future Prospects, Cheltenham, Northampton/MA: Edward Elgar, 1999; Curry Jane L./ Urban, Joan B. (eds.): The Left Transformed in Post-Communist Societies. The Cases of East Central Europe, Russia and Ukraine, Lanham et al.: Rowman and Littlefield Publishers, 2003; Grzymala-Busse, Anna: Redeeming the Past. The Regeneration of Communist Parties in East Central Europe, Cambridge: Cambridge University Press, 2002.

50   Crowley, Stephen/ Ost, David (eds.): Workers After Workers' States. Labor and Politics in Postcommunist Eastern Europe, Lanham et al.: Rowman and Littlefield Publishers, 2001; Kubicek, Paul: Organized Labor in Postcommunist States. From Solidarity to Infirmity, Pittsburgh: University of Pittsburgh Press, 2004.

51   Peregudov, Sergei P.: Korporatsii, obshchestvo, gosudarstvo. Evolutsiya otnoshenii, Moscow: Nauka, 2003.

52   Afanasiev, Mikhail N: Klientelizm i rossiiskaya gosudarstvennost', Moscow: MONF, 2000; Simon, Rick: Labour and Political Transformation in Russia and Ukraine, Aldershot: Ashgate, 2000; Cook, Linda J.: Labor and Liberalization. Trade Unions in the New Russia, New York: Twentieth Century Fund Press,1997; Clarke, Simon: Russian Trade Unions in the 1999 Duma Election, in: The Journal of Communist Studies and Transition Politics, 2001 (vol. 17), no. 2, pp. 43–69.

The institutionalization of the social dialogue occurred according to different scenarios. In Hungary, Bulgaria, the Czech Republic and Slovakia, the trade unions initiated the establishment of the social dialogue institutions in 1990–1991. In contrast, in Romania, the government and president (i.e. the state) regulated the trade unions' activity. These tripartite negotiations and the resulting social dialogue can be judged to have been successful in Hungary, where trade unions became influential participants in the social dialogue, as in Poland. In the Czech Republic, Slovakia and Bulgaria, the efficiency of the social dialogue seemed to be average, since the initial active participation of trade unions in the social dialogue evolved into governmental regulation of labour relations. In Romania, similar to the case of Russia, the social dialogue exhibited a low degree of efficiency. Despite the formal existence of the social dialogue in Romania, the relationships between the trade unions and the government were based on clientelism and thus became subordinated.[53]

8.6. Conclusions

I have defined three models of relationships between successor parties, trade unions and the state in East Central Europe. According to Model 1, which specifies prevailing formal relations, the institutional design of the political system allows the successor party to form the government and state policy after the successor party wins the parliamentary election; during the parliamentary elections, the successor party and former official trade unions form an electoral coalition, and the interactions between trade unions and the state take place in the social dialogue. This model can be labelled as 'formal'. According to Model 2, in which informal relations prevail, the above-mentioned institutional links do not work. Finally, the 'mixed' Model 3 is the intermediate option between Model 1 and Model 2.

After a consideration of the factors determining the relationships between successor parties, trade unions and the state, the role of the communist legacy should be emphasised as being central. The types of past communist regime and post-communist transition seem to affect the post-communist institutional design and the relationships of successor parties and the state. In Poland, Hungary, Bulgaria, the Czech Republic and Slovakia, the national consensus and bureaucratic types of communist regime contributed to the formation of the premier–presidential and parliamentary

---

53 Hausner, Jerzy (ed.): Evolution of Interest Representation and Development of the Labour Market in Post-Socialist Countries, Cracow: Cracow Academy of Economics, 1994; Crowley, Stephen/ Ost, David (eds.): Workers After Workers' States. Labor and Politics in Postcommunist Eastern Europe, Lanham et al.: Rowman and Littlefield Publishers, 2001; Candland, Christopher/ Sil, Rudra (eds.): The Politics of Labour in a Global Age. Continuity and Change in Late-Industrializing and Post-Socialist Economies, Oxford, New York: Oxford University Press, 2001; Kubicek, Paul: Organized Labor in Postcommunist States. From Solidarity to Infirmity, Pittsburgh: University of Pittsburgh Press, 2004.

systems respectively. Under these systems, political parties are able to form the government and state policy after they win a parliamentary election. In Romania and Russia, the patrimonial communist regime was the institutional reason underlying the exclusion of political parties from the formal channels for shaping state policy as a result of the powerful influence of informal groups in the decision-making processes.

The successor parties and former official trade unions should be considered to be the institutional heirs of the former communist regimes; the move by trade unions to the political field has led to electoral cooperation between trade unions and successor parties. Cooperation based on the inherited communist institutional links depends on the direction of the successor party's ideological evolution. In Poland and Hungary, the successor parties' adoption of a social democratic ideology and modernization contributed to their electoral cooperation with trade unions.

The efficiency of the interactions between trade unions and the state in the social dialogue institutions depends on the extent to which informal clientelistic links were used. The efficiency of tripartite negotiations with influential trade unions was high in Poland and Hungary. Medium efficiency, characterized by the initial active participation of trade unions in the social dialogue and followed by state regulation of labour relations, was typical for the Czech Republic, Slovakia and Bulgaria. Finally, low efficiency, along with the formal existence of social dialogue institutions and the regular use of clientelistic links by trade unions and the government, made the social dialogue subordinate to the state in Russia and Romania.

Andreea Carstocea

9. 'Ethno-Business'. The Unexpected Consequence of National Minority Policies in Romania

9.1. Introduction

This research concerns a series of unintended consequences of the post-1990 policies for the protection of national minorities in Romania.[1] The media and the public at large dubbed these unexpected developments as 'ethno-business', a term originally coined in Hungary in the 1990s to denote the strategies of political entrepreneurs who exploited the existing legal framework for the protection of national minorities to obtain material, financial or political gains.[2] Later, this label was used for similar phenomena occurring in Romania.

Utilizing available information (mainly media reports), a series of background interviews with minority stakeholders, and my work experience, I was able to classify the strategies that have come to be known as 'ethno-business' under three headings:

1. entrepreneurship of non-minority leaders, whereby ethnic Romanian political entrepreneurs run for elections on a national minority mandate by claiming to belong to that respective minority (e.g. the cases of the leaders of the Italian, Ruthenian and Macedonian minorities);

---

1   The Romanian state currently recognizes twenty ethnic groups as 'national minorities'. According to the latest census (2002), national minorities constitute the following percentages of the total population: Hungarians 6.6%, Roma 2.5%; all other eighteen minorities are below 0.5% of the total population, as follows: the Ukrainian and German minorities each amount to 0.3% of the total population; the Lippovan Russian and Turkish minorities amount to 0.2%; the Tartar, Slovak and Serb minorities 0.1%; while the remaining minorities fall below 0.1% of the total population (Bulgarians, Croats, Greeks, Jews, Czechs, Polish, Italians, Armenians, Macedonians, Albanians and Ruthenians).

2   In a study concerning minority rights in Hungary, Andras L. Pap describes several ‚ethno-business' instances, such as repeated cases of candidates running for office as Roma in one election and later as Germans in the following term. Also, he mentions cases where in several municipalities where according to the census results there was no person belonging to a national minority, numerous minority candidates were registered for election to a minority self-government. Maybe the most absurd example of misuse of minority policies is the case of a small village's football team which registered as German minority candidates for the elections to express their admiration of German football. The matter of concern for Pap are the ill-designed policies for the protection of national minorities; he also stresses that the fact that voters not belonging to a minority can vote in the elections for minority self-governments undermines the whole idea of minority rights. See Pap, András L.:Human Rights and Ethnic Data Collection in Hungary, in: Human Rights Review, 2008 (vol. 9), no. 1, pp. 109–122.

2. attempts by political entrepreneurs to re-create ethnic identities long assimilated under communism in order to enable them to claim benefits for these 'new' ethnic groups (e.g. the Ruthenian and Macedonian minorities); and

3. the extreme fragmentation of the socio-political organizations representing national minorities (e.g. the Bulgarian and Italian minorities).

To date, this phenomenon—whether taking place in Romania or elsewhere—remains largely unresearched. The existing literature on 'ethno-business' in Romania consists of a handful of studies (some of which fall short of academic standards), along with numerous media reports. They all describe the strategies included under the label of 'ethno-business' in negative terms, associating them with the perceived generalized corruption of the Romanian political environment.

My study seeks to answer two principal questions. First, after presenting an analysis of the post-1990 opportunity structures for national minorities in Romania and outlining the legal, institutional and political circumstances that paved the way for the emergence and development of 'ethno-business', the study clarifies and delineates this phenomenon from the perspective of clientelism theories. Following Simona Piattoni, this research will refrain from labelling political clientelism as simply an unavoidable cultural or developmental factor (i.e. stating that clientelism and corruption are inherent traits in Romanian political culture, and that therefore its recent democracy cannot escape these strategies) and will instead regard them as "strategies for the acquisition, maintenance, and aggrandizement of political power, on the part of the patrons, and strategies for the protection and promotion of their interests, on the part of the clients".[3] The second line of inquiry pertains to the effects of 'ethno-business' as a clientelistic form of democratic representation. The effects of clientelistic strategies of the 'ethno-business' type on the democratic representation of persons belonging to minority communities will be assessed using Hanna Pitkin's understanding of four different types of 'representation', i.e. formalistic, descriptive, symbolic, and substantive representation.[4] This will be carried out by examining the implications for representation presented by each of the three types of 'ethno-business' strategies identified.

9.2. The Evolution of Opportunity Structures for Organizations of National Minorities after 1989

Most studies and reports focusing on 'ethno-business' identify the post-1990 legal and institutional arrangements for national minorities as the main catalysts for this phenomenon. An analysis of the strategies that fall under the label of 'ethno-business'

---

3   Piattoni, Simona: Clientelism, Interests and Democratic Representation, Cambridge and New York: Cambridge University Press, 2001, p. 2.

4   Pitkin, Hanna F.: The Concept of Representation, Berkeley, Los Angeles, London: University of California Press, 1972.

from the perspective of clientelism should therefore commence with an examination of the opportunity structures created after 1989 for national minorities in Romania.

After the fall of communism, Romania displayed a general lack of human rights policies and institutions, as well as the absence of a strong civil society. Upon the start of the negotiations to join the Council of Europe and later the European Union, the country found that it needed to set up new institutions, laws and policies for the protection of human rights in general, and minority rights in particular, to meet the conditions for accession.[5] The power asymmetry in the negotiations between Romania and the various European organizations led to a rushed adoption of many European and international norms. Arguably, Romania (as well as other candidate states) accepted these norms not as ends in themselves, but simply as binding conditions for membership, which has led many researchers to conclude that the state's attitude towards minority rights was purely instrumental.[6]

The new Romanian constitution of 1991[7] stipulates a fairly extensive set of political, educational and cultural rights for national minorities. Thus, Art. 59 guarantees the political representation of national minorities, stating that 'organizations of citizens belonging to national minorities, which fail to obtain the number of votes for representation in Parliament, have the right to one Deputy seat each, under the terms of the electoral law.' Discrimination on the basis of race, nationality, ethnic origin, language, religion, sex, opinion, political affiliation, property or social origin is forbidden (Art. 4), and freedom of religion is guaranteed (Art. 29). Concerning education, Art. 32 provides the right of persons belonging to national minorities to both learn and be educated in their mother tongue.[8]

The principle at the core of minority provisions in Romania is the freedom to choose one's national identity; the state guarantees the right to the preservation, development and expression of the ethnic, cultural, linguistic and religious identity of persons belonging to national minorities (Art. 6 of the 1991 Constitution). An important feature of the Romanian legal system is that neither the Constitution nor any subsequent law offers a list of the national minorities recognized by the state; also, there is

---

5   For instance, the criteria for EU membership included a provision whereby candidate countries were required to ensure the stability of institutions guaranteeing democracy, the rule of law, human rights and respect for and protection of minorities. See Accession Criteria, Copenhagen European Council, http://ec.europa.eu/enlargement/enlargement_process/accession_process/criteria/index_en.htm, accessed 22 January 2009.
6   Tesser, Lynn M.: The Geopolitics of Tolerance. Minority Rights under EU Expansion in East-Central Europe, in: East European Politics and Societies, 2003 (vol. 17), no. 3, pp. 483–532, here p. 493.
7   The Constitution was revised in 2003; however, the revisions did not touch upon the legislation regarding the status of national minorities and their rights.
8   See the 1991 Constitution of Romania, http://www.parlament.ro/pls/dic/site.page?den=act1_2

no definition outlining the set of characteristics that qualifies an ethno-cultural community for recognition as a national minority.[9]

The Romanian Constitution provides for the parliamentary representation of minorities by allowing each minority to send one representative to the Chamber of Deputies (the lower chamber of Parliament) regardless of the normal electoral threshold.[10] The first post-1989 law regulating Romanian parliamentary and presidential elections[11] considered organizations of national minorities who wished to contest the elections as similar to political parties (Art. 96). This meant that they were allowed to participate in the elections by behaving as political parties, even if their legal status was that of non-governmental organizations. This exception to the general rule of elections remains in force.

The 1992 Electoral Law laid out clearer rules for the parliamentary representation of national minorities. It continued to allow organizations representing national minorities to participate in the national elections as parties,[12] but it also specified an electoral threshold of 5% of the average number of votes received by an elected deputy as a prerequisite for entering Parliament.[13] In cases where multiple organizations representing the same national minority competed for entry into Parliament, the organization receiving the highest number of votes would prevail (provided that the number of votes it received passed the aforementioned 5% threshold).[14] These arrangements proved to offer a very flexible and accessible path for parliamentary representation for national minorities. This is witnessed by the steady increase in the number of minority

---

9   This is the solution that Hungary chose for regulating the issue of its national minorities. Hungarian law also provides a list of the thirteen ethnic groups that qualify as national minorities, but this list is not finite: any other ethnic group can claim the status of ethnic or national minority once it has fulfilled a number of prerequisites. Thus, Hungarian legal arrangements describe national minorities as any 'ethnic group which has been living on the territory of the Republic of Hungary for at least one century, which represents a numerical minority among the citizens of the state, the members of which are Hungarian citizens, and are distinguished from the rest of the citizens by their own language, culture and traditions, and at the same time demonstrate a sense of belonging together, which is aimed at the preservation of all these, and at the expression and the protection of the interests of their historical communities.' Art. 1 (2) of Act LXXVII on the Rights of National and Ethnic Minorities (1993).

10   There are no similar provisions for accession to the Senate (the upper chamber of Parliament); however, the Democratic Union of Hungarians in Romania (DUHR), having consistently passed the general electoral threshold, has been permanently present in this chamber as well.

11   Art. 96 of the Decree—Law 92 of 14 March 1990 regulating the Election of Parliament and of the President of Romania.

12   Art. 4 (2) of Law 68 of 15 July 1992 concerning the Election of the Chamber of Deputies and the Senate.

13   Art. 4 (1) of Law 68 of 15 July 1992 concerning the Election of the Chamber of Deputies and the Senate.

14   Art. 68 (1g) of Law 68 of 15 July 1992 concerning the Election of the Chamber of Deputies and the Senate. For the 2000 elections, a deputy elected to the Chamber of Deputies received an average of 25,419 votes. This means that to be elected on a minority mandate, a minority leader had to obtain a minimum of 1270 votes nationally.

organizations entering Parliament over the years, from twelve organizations in 1990 to thirteen in 1992, fifteen in 1996 and eighteen in 2000 and 2004.[15]

The Electoral Law was substantially amended in March 2008, with important consequences for both mainstream parties and minority organizations competing for entry into Parliament.[16] By introducing a mixed member proportional representation system, the law reformed the old electoral system, which until then had been based on single-vote proportional representation. In terms of the effects it produced on the representation of national minorities, several features should be pointed out. First, for the first time in post-1989 legislation, the law introduced a definition of 'national minority' as 'that ethnic group which is represented in the Council of National Minorities' (Art. 2 (cc))[17]. Second, the threshold for entering Parliament was raised to 10% of the average number of votes received by a deputy (Art. 9 (1)). Third, contesting elections became restricted to those organizations of citizens belonging to national minorities 'who are represented in Parliament'. (Art. 9 (2)); the conditions for organizations not represented in Parliament to enter the electoral competition now required them to have the status of 'public utility organizations' as well as a list of members comprising at least 15% of the total number of citizens who in the latest census declared themselves as belonging to that ethnicity (Art. 9 (3)).

The consequences for minority representation were twofold. First, the law brought about an exclusion from recognition as a national minority for any ethnic group presently outside Parliament. This is due to a legal circularity arising from linking the definition of a national minority to the presence of that ethnic group in the Council of National Minorities. Any ethnic group not represented in the Council which now wishes to be granted the status of national minority can only do so if it becomes a member of the Council of National Minorities. However, Art. 2 of Government's Decision 589 /

---

15   The information is available on the website of the Romanian Chamber of Deputies, www.cdep.ro

16   See Law 35 of 13 March 2008, concerning the election of the Chamber of Deputies and the Senate and the amending and completing of Law 67 / 2004 concerning the election of local public administration, of Law 215 / 2001 on local public administration, and of Law 393 / 2004 concerning the Statute on locally elected officials.

17   In addition to their guaranteed parliamentary participation, in 1993 national minorities were invited to join the newly created Council for National Minorities, as a consultative body of the Romanian government, which initially comprised all organizations representing national minorities, as provided in Art. 1 of Government's Decision 137 / 6 April 1993, concerning the organization and functioning of the Council for National Minorities. In 2001 the Council (renamed the Council of National Minorities) was re-organized and stipulated that only those organizations that obtained a seat in Parliament could become members of this body, as provided in Art. 2 of Government's Decision 589 / 21 June 2001, on the setting up of the Council of National Minorities. According to the new regulations, each minority, regardless of its size or socio-economic characteristics, was allowed to send only one representative association to the Council, namely the organization that succeeded in passing the electoral threshold for parliamentary representation.

21 June 2001 on the setting up of the Council of National Minorities clearly states that only those organizations already present in Parliament may become members of this body. In practical terms, this means that no ethnic group which is not currently represented in Parliament can obtain the status of national minority. A second consequence concerns electoral participation by organizations representing a national minority (that is, an ethnic group already represented in the Council of National Minorities by an organization) that are presently outside Parliament. In effect, the conditions for participation in the elections ('public utility' status, list of members including 15% of the respective ethnic group) are nearly impossible to fulfil. This is because the status of 'public utility' can only be obtained through a Government Decision;[18] of the three applications submitted since 2008 by organizations claiming to represent various national minorities, none has been successful.[19]

9.3.   Strategies included under the label of 'ethno-business'

On the basis of available information (mostly media and NGO reports), a series of background interviews with minority stakeholders, and my professional experience,[20] I was able to classify the strategies that have come to be known as 'ethno-business' under three headings:

(a) Attempts by political entrepreneurs to re-create ethnic identities long assimilated under communism in order to claim benefits for these 'new' national minorities
In the communist era, the official discourse maintained that national minorities enjoyed extensive rights, but there was a significant difference between the *pays légal* and *pays réel*. When the regime undertook strong measures to Romanianize the population, many small (or dispersed) ethnic groups were essentially coerced to abandon their culture and language, and thus became assimilated into the majority population. Following the adoption of a new protection system for national minorities in 1989, however, several entrepreneurs saw an opportunity for material, political and financial gain. Accordingly, they actively began to revive the identities of the assimilated ethnic groups. Christopher Decker argues that in this case, 'ethno-business' is entirely generated by elites seeking to access political power: they begin by creating a 'new' minority, obtaining a seat in Parliament, and finally enjoying the spoils of office.[21] His

---

18   See Art. 38 and 39 of Law 246 of 18 July 2005 for the Approval of Government's Ordinance 26 / 2000 concerning Associations and Foundations.
19   Interview with Ms Adriana Petraru, Head of the Legal Office of the Department for Interethnic Relations, Government of Romania, May 2010.
20   I have been working as a civil officer for the Department for Interethnic Relations, the main governmental body dealing with national minority issues, since 2001.
21   Decker, Christopher D.: The Use of Cultural Autonomy to Prevent Conflict and Meet the Copenhagen Criteria. The Case of Romania, in: Ethnopolitics, 2007 (vol. 6), no. 3, pp. 437–450.

assertion is however not backed by empirical evidence, and therefore the extent to which political entrepreneurs engaged in 'inventing' minorities from scratch remains an open question. However, their role in re-constructing identities that became assimilated during communism is obvious.

The Cultural Union of Ruthenians and the Association of Slav-Macedonians (later renamed the Association of Macedonians) were both set up in 2000. At the time, the provisions in the electoral law concerning the parliamentary representation of national minorities did not require organizations claiming to represent a national minority to demonstrate the existence of that particular ethnic group on Romanian territory (through census results or otherwise). Thus, the fact that the 1992 census (the most recent at the time) did not include the categories of 'Ruthenian' and 'Macedonian' nationalities (and therefore no person with these particular ethnic backgrounds was registered) did not constitute a legal impediment for these two organizations to run in the 2000 elections and each win a seat in the Chamber of Deputies. Once they entered Parliament, the organizations received automatic access to the Council of National Minorities, and the ethnic group they claimed to represent received the status of national minority.

A number of common traits can be identified in the communities in which this type of strategy occurs. The first one concerns the high discrepancy between the number of persons of a certain ethnic background (as indicated by census results) and the number of votes received by organizations purporting to represent them in the general elections; the latter often exceeds the former. The second indicator shows a gradual increase in the number of schools offering instruction in a particular minority language, of newspapers in a minority language and of cultural events reflecting the heritage of a certain minorities—without any significant demographic change (such as an increase in the respective minority population) to warrant these developments.

(b) Entrepreneurship of non-minority leaders, whereby ethnic Romanian political entrepreneurs run for elections on a national minority mandate by claiming to belong to that respective minority. However, their ethnic background and their legitimacy as leaders is contested by other members of the community.
There have been several such cases in the recent history of minority representation in Romania. Examples include Vasile Ioan Savu, deputy for the Slav-Macedonian minority between 2000 and 2004; Oana Manolescu, deputy for the Albanian minority since 1996; and Mircea Grosaru, deputy for the Italian community since 2000.

Vasile Savu, the leader of the Macedonian organization, initially made a career as a union leader for workers in the coal industry. In 1999, a few months before the national elections, he set up the Association of Slav Macedonians and later stood as a candidate in elections to represent this ethnic group. An ethnic Romanian who does not speak Macedonian, Savu was ultimately repudiated by the Macedonian community and removed from leadership in the 2004 elections.[22] Another interesting case is that of Gheorghe Firczak; unlike the other candidates mentioned above, his ethnic background is unclear. He participated in the 1996 elections as a Hungarian candidate for Parliament on behalf of the Free-Democrat Hungarian Party of Romania, but neither he nor the party received enough votes. He then became a member of the Social-Democrat Party, one of the most prominent mainstream parties in Romania, but soon left. He finally founded the Cultural Union of Ruthenians in Romania, became its first president, ran in the 2000 elections and managed to enter Parliament as a deputy for the Ruthenian minority.[23] He has remained in office to this day.

(c) The extreme fragmentation of the socio-political organizations representing national minorities

As mentioned above, with the new legal and institutional opportunities created after 1989, there was a flurry of non-governmental organizations jockeying to enter parliament (and reap the subsequent financial and political advantages) on a minority mandate. Some minorities were particularly affected by this phenomenon, such as the Italian minority (there are 3,288 Italians living in Romania, according to the latest census). Over time, 18–19 organizations have attempted to gain parliamentary representation,[24] but the vast majority of them have been unsuccessful. Other minorities, such as Bulgarians and Poles, have also been confronted with the problem of fragmentation.

9.4. Relevant Theoretical Aspects of Clientelism

According to recent definitions, clientelism fundamentally represents an asymmetrical power relationship between two (or more) actors, both of whom have an interest in initiating and/or continuing it.[25] Robert Gay, for instance, defines clientelism as 'the distribution of resources (or promise of) by political office holders or political candidates in exchange for political support, primarily—but not exclusively—in the form of the vote'.[26] Luis Roniger offers a broad definition of clientelism, describing it as an

> asymmetric but mutually beneficial relationship of power and exchange, a non-universalistic quid pro quo between individuals or groups of unequal standing. It implies mediated

---

22 Alionescu, Ciprian: Parliamentary Representation of National Minorities in Romania, in: Southeast European Politics, 2004 (vol. 5), no. 1, pp. 60–75, here p. 69.
23 Ibid, p. 68.
24 Interview with Dan Oprescu, former head of the National Agency for the Roma, May 2010.
25 See Roniger, Luis: Political Clientelism, Democracy, and Market Economy, in: Comparative Politics, 2004 (vol. 36), no. 3, pp. 353–375, here pp. 355–356, for an analysis of the historical evolution of research on clientelism.
26 Gay, Robert: Community Organization and Clientelist Politics in Contemporary Brazil. A Case Study from Suburban Rio de Janeiro, in: International Journal of Urban and Regional Research, 1990 (Vol. 14), no. 4, pp. 648–665, here p. 648.

and selective access to resources and markets from which others are normally excluded. This access is conditioned on subordination, compliance or dependence on the good-will of others.[27]

Some scholars note that a patron-client relationship sometimes involves the presence of a broker; in these situations, the dyadic relationship described above becomes a

> three-party transaction in which a broker acts as a middleman to arrange an exchange of resources between two parties separated by geographic or personal distance such as differences in rank or office.[28]

The causes and persistence of clientelistic strategies have been explained in various ways; two of the most frequently cited root causes are cultural determination and structural opportunism. A different historically-oriented approach associates (the emergence of) clientelism with democratization and democracy. In this sense, Martin Shefter argues that the emergence of patronage is linked to the way in which a party acquires its initial popular base; he also distinguishes between two types of parties. 'Externally mobilized' parties are those established by elites not holding positions in the prevailing regime and who thus mobilize support in order to either enter that polit-ical system or to overthrow it. As these parties do not have access to state resources, they have to rely on other means to acquire a following; these origins make it less likely that the party will recourse to patronage once it reaches a position of power.[29] On the contrary, 'internally mobilized' parties are those founded by elites who hold positions within the prevailing regimes and who mobilize popular support to secure their hold over government. They are in a position to use the resources of the state to acquire a following and they have every incentive to use them; they are therefore more likely to use patronage, unless a coalition seeking to abolish patronage and to defend the integrity of the civil service was already formed before the masses became mobilized into politics.[30]

Assessments of the effects of clientelism on democracy and the functioning of democratic institutions can be seen from very different perspectives. One point of view is that clientelism is detrimental to democracy because it undermines accountability and leads to poor quality governance (by promoting overemployment and underqualified personnel in public administration), distorted bidding for public works, and overpric-ing.[31] A different perspective emphasizes the pragmatic aspects of clientelism, seeing

---

27   Roniger, Luis: Political Clientelism, Democracy, and Market Economy, in: Comparative Politics, 2004 (vol. 36), no. 3, pp. 353–375, here p. 353.

28   Kettering, Sharon: The Historical Development of Political Clientelism, in: Journal of Interdisciplinary History, 1988 (vol. 18), no. 3, pp. 419–447, here p. 425.

29   Shefter, Martin: Party and Patronage. Germany, England, and Italy, in: Politics & Society, 1977 (vol. 7), no. 4, pp. 403–451, here p. 416–417.

30   Ibid., p. 417.

31   Roniger, Luis: Political Clientelism, Democracy, and Market Economy, in: Comparative Politics, 2004 (vol. 36), no. 3, pp. 353–375, here p. 354.

it as an important problem-solving tool for obtaining benefits, access to resources, and articulating local-regional-national relations.[32]

In the present analysis of Romanian 'ethno-business' strategies, clientelism will be considered according to the work of researchers such as Robert Gay, as a relationship between two actors (the local constituency and the state resources). In addition, the local political entrepreneur (the minority leader) will be considered as a broker between the two. In terms of the root causes of this type of clientelistic strategy, this analysis will also consider Luís de Sousa's view that cultural explanations of clientelism are relevant because cultural factors shape the expectations of those involved in the exchange.[33] In this respect, the analysis will particularly emphasize the role of opportunity structures in the emergence of 'ethno-business'. Therefore, I will endeavour to conduct my assessment of the effects of 'ethno-business' on democracy and democratic representation by evaluating the phenomenon's potentially positive aspects along with its more publicized negative effects. To this end, Alena Ledeneva's understanding of such informal strategies as potentially able to 'compensate for defects in the formal order while simultaneously undermining it' will figure into the analysis.[34]

9.5. 'Ethno-Business' and Clientelism

As outlined above, the system for the protection of national minorities contains important provisions promoting their participation in political life. These institutional and legal arrangements have unintentionally sparked a large number of non-governmental associations claiming to represent the interests of various ethnic groups as a vehicle for entering parliament on a minority mandate.

An organization successful in sending a representative to Parliament benefits from a series of advantages: it is henceforth the only organization representing the interests of that particular minority in the Council for National Minorities, and therefore the sole recipient of the state budget allocations for that minority. This means that all other organizations claiming to represent the same minority are excluded from participating in the Council of National Minorities and, crucially, they are also excluded from receiving any financial support from the state.

The total budgetary allocations for the organizations in the CNM have increased gradually, from 90 mln Romanian Lei (about 4 mln Euros at the time) in 2001 to 240

---

32 Ibid., p. 355.
33 de Sousa, Luís: Clientelism and the Quality(ies) of Democracy. Public and Policy Aspects, in: DISC Working Paper Series, DISC WP/2008/2, Central European University, Center for the Study of Imperfections in Democracy, pp. 1–19, here p. 7, http://pdc.ceu.hu/archive/00004462/01/dis cwp-2008-02.pdf
34 Ledeneva, Alena: How Russia Really Works, Ithaca/NY, London: Cornell University Press, 2006, p. 11.

mln Lei (6 mln Euros) in 2004, reaching 70 mln RON (17 mln Euros) in 2010. With that they receive considerably more funding than political parties, as Table 9-1 indicates.

Table 9-1:   Total Budgetary Allocations to National Minorities and Parliamentary Parties

	Amount of public funding allocated to the organizations of national minorities	Amount of public funding allocated to all parliamentary parties, excluding the organizations of national minorities
2008	65.7 mln RON (16 mln Euros)	8.1 mln RON (2 mln Euros)
2009	70.0 mln RON (17 mln Euros)	7.0 mln RON (1.7 mln Euros)

Sources: Annex to the Governement's Decision 103/2008 concerning the distribution and usage of the amounts provided under para. a) and b) of the Annex 3/ 13/02a of the 2008 State Budget Law 388/2007; Summary of the Subsidies for Political Parties in 2008 drafted by the Permanent Electoral Authority, http:// www.roaep.ro/ro/section.php?id=28&l2=39; Annex to the Government's Decision 396/2009 concerning the distribution and usage of the amounts provided under para. a) and b) of the Annex 3/13/02a of the 2009 State Budget Law 18/2009; Summary of the Subsidies for Political Parties in 2009 drafted by the Permanent Electoral Authority, http://www.roaep.ro/ro/section.php?id=28&l2=39

One important aspect is the provision of the 2008 Electoral Law, which, as argued above, in practice presently prevents organizations outside the Council of National Minorities from running in future elections. Multiple interviews with stakeholders in minority issues indicate that this provision, rather than being a measure taken by the state to counteract ethno-business strategies, was introduced following pressure from the organizations' members in the CNM at the time, with the intention to exclude potential challengers to public funding for national minorities.[35]

In the case of 'ethno-business', there are two levels of analysis to consider with a view to clientelistic strategies: 1) the interaction between the state and the representative minority organization, as represented by its leaders, and 2) the relationship between the minority leader and his or her constituency.

9.5.1.   The Relationship Between the State and Minority Leaders

As mentioned above, external conditionality was a determining factor in the setup of minority policies in Romania in the early 1990s; accordingly, politicians created a set of institutional and legal arrangements that were more favourable to national minorities. To this external catalyst, domestic pressures were added from the powerful organizations representing the interests of the Hungarian minority, which constitutes 6.6% of Romania's total population. According to Gabriel Andreescu[36] and Istvan Horvath[37],

---

35   Interview with Dan Oprescu, former head of the National Agency for the Roma, May 2010; Interview with Ms Adriana Petraru, Head of the Legal Office of the Department for Interethnic Relations, Government of Romania, May 2010.

36   Andreescu, Gabriel: Ruleta. Romani si maghiari, 1990–2000 (The Roulette. Romanians and Hungarians. 1990–2000), in: Editura Polirom, 2001, p. 150.

37   Horvath, Istvan/ Scacco, Alexandra: From the Unitary to the Pluralistic. Fine-Tuning Minority Policy in Romania, in: Biro, Anna-Maria/ Kovacs, Petra (eds.): Diversity in Action. Local public

this institutional configuration served an additional political purpose for all subsequent governments, which was to promote many smaller minorities as a counterbalance to the dominant Hungarian minority. By granting these small minorities parliamentary seats and significant financial support, the various governments hoped to attract their support (in the form of votes and lobbying) against Hungarian minority demands. Over time, however, it became evident that small minorities tended to align their positions with that of the Democratic Union of Hungarians, thus maximizing their negotiation potential in dealing with the government.

The reluctance of successive governments to take any corrective measures to counteract 'ethno-business' is easily clarified when the long-term positioning of the Parliamentary Group of National Minorities is taken into consideration.[38] Many interviewees remarked upon the constant stream of support the minority deputies have offered to the government of the day, regardless of its political colour.[39] Given the total size of the Chamber of Deputies (333 deputies), the bargaining power of the minority deputies is generally low. However, two recurring phenomena point to an (intermittent) increase in the relative political relevance of the Parliamentary Group of National Minorities. First, the voting pattern of the Group shows that it generally follows the vote of the deputies of the Democratic Union of Hungarians in Romania (DUHR); the combined number of votes of the two groups is thus forty, which bolsters its bargaining power. Second, the DUHR has traditionally (although not exclusively) either entered into a coalition with the ruling party or supported it without actually entering the government.[40] This, combined with the above-mentioned support DUHR receives from smaller minorities, boosts the relevance of the two parliamentary groups (the DUHR and the Parliamentary Group of National Minorities) in decision-making. The support they in turn give to the ruling party is by and large contingent on receiving improved conditions for the communities they represent.[41]

---

management of multi-ethnic communities in Central and Eastern Europe, Budapest: Open Society Institute, 2001, pp. 241–272, here p. 254.

38   The Parliamentary Group of National Minorities comprises all eighteen deputies entering parliament on a national minority mandate. The Democratic Union of Hungarians in Romania forms a separate parliamentary group.

39   Interview with Rodica Precupetu, Head of Unit at the Department for Inter-Ethnic Relations, May 2010; interview with Dan Oprescu, former head of the National Agency for the Roma, May 2010.

40   The DUHR was part of the government coalition between 1996–2000 (along the Democratic Convention), also between 2004–2008 (first with the DA Alliance, then with the Liberal Party). Between 2000–2004, DUHR supported the governmental coalition (formed by the Social Democratic Party and the Humanist Party) without entering it. Since 2009 it has been part of a government coalition with the Liberal Democratic Party.

41   Such as improved educational facilities, increases in funding, or sometimes political appointments for representatives of DUHR or, less frequently, for those of smaller minorities. Interview with Dan Oprescu, former head of the National Agency for the Roma, May 2010.

9.5.2. The Relationship Between the Minority Leader and His or Her Constituency

The minority leader (the broker) is the one offering his or her constituency access to (mainly financial) resources, which will ultimately be translated into investments in infrastructure, schools and jobs as well as cultural, educational, and minority media opportunities.

The success of 'ethno-business' strategies essentially depends on the number of votes minority entrepreneurs can generate in the general elections. Regardless of the type of strategy under consideration, the researchers and various governmental experts interviewed for this analysis described minority entrepreneurs as resourceful local managers who were quick to seize the opportunity to access Parliament and state finances on a minority mandate (because prior to the 2008 Electoral Law, this was a much easier route than the 'normal' one). In addition, a governmental officer in the field of national minorities[42] offered some insights into the workings of the electoral process at the local level by stating that entrepreneurs are known to offer material incentives in the form of money and presents. These incentives are offered to the members of the respective ethnic group, but not exclusively; as the need for votes increases (especially in cases where many organizations are competing for entry into Parliament), the entrepreneurs also target non-minority populations. This is fairly easy, since minority communities are far from homogeneous, having mixed over time with the Romanian majority.

9.6. Effects of Ethno-Business on Democratic Representation

The classic theoretical analysis of the concept of representation is that of Hanna Fenichel Pitkin. She begins with the etymology of the term and derives its basic meaning, 'to make present something that is *not* in fact present', from the Latin root (*repraesentare*) of the word.[43] Having studied the modern uses of the concept, she distinguishes among the formalistic, descriptive, symbolic and substantive understandings of 'representation'.

9.6.1. Types of Representation

In Pitkin's view, *formalistic* representation refers to the institutional setting that allows representation to be initiated and performed. Since ancient times, this kind of representation has been approached from two different angles—authorization

---

42   Interview with a government officer who requested that her name remained anonymous, May 2010.

43   Pitkin, Hanna F.: The Concept of Representation, Berkeley, Los Angeles, London: University of California Press, 1972, p. 92.

and accountability. Authorization theorists define a representative as someone who has been elected (authorized), thereby focusing on the initiation of representation. Conversely, accountability theorists focus on the termination of representation, defining a representative as someone who will be subject to election (held to account).[44]

Pitkin's other three interpretations of the concept of representation (descriptive, symbolic and substantive) are not related to its formal aspects, but to its descriptive (i.e. what a representative stands for, or what he or she must be like in order to represent others) and substantive (i.e. what a representative does) elements.[45]

In this sense, *descriptive* representation refers to the representative's resemblance to those he or she represents. The focus is therefore not on the representative's actions or behaviour, but rather 'on what he *is* or is *like*, on being something rather than doing something'.[46] Likewise, *symbolic* representation does not refer to anything that a representative does for his or her constituency; instead, the focus is on the representative's symbolic 'standing for' someone or something (a people, their opinion, etc.). Symbolic representation rests on people's beliefs, however engendered, involving no rational or objective connection between who or what represents and who or what is represented.[47]

Finally, *substantive* representation departs from the passive, descriptive and symbolic meanings of the concept and focuses instead on what the representative does for his or her constituents. Here, Pitkin distinguishes among three types of 'acting for' the represented: 'the idea of substitution or acting instead of, the idea of taking care of or acting in the interest of, and the idea of acting as a subordinate, on instructions, in accord with the wishes of another'.[48]

9.6.2.   Practical Applications of Pitkin's Theory

In practical terms, her contribution helps clarify what the act of representation entails—whether we speak of representation of a minority group, of a local constituency, or of an interest group generally.

In terms of *formalistic representation*, whether we agree with Pitkin that accountability is a corrective to the authorization view, or whether we consider these two perspectives as opposed to and independent from one another, this understanding of representation can be used to analyse the representativity of a political system. In a

---

44   Ibid., p. 58.
45   These two aspects are reflected in the distinction between two German words, both translatable through 'represent': *darstellen* (descriptive and symbolic standing for someone or something) and *vertreten* (act for another). Pitkin, Hanna F.: The Concept of Representation, Berkeley, Los Angeles, London: University of California Press, 1972, p. 59.
46   Ibid., p. 61.
47   Ibid., p. 110.
48   Ibid., p. 139.

totalitarian system, for instance, such as communist Romania, where elections were held periodically but results were rigged, one cannot speak of an authorization being conferred upon the 'winners' by the voters. By the same token, the notion of accountability is rendered meaningless, since the usual mechanism for 'punishing' representatives, i.e. not re-electing them, has no teeth in a totalitarian state.

Descriptive representation seems to be particularly relevant for systems of proportional representation; its advocates emphasize, among other things, the importance of having representatives who resemble and reflect their constituency. Proportionalists, on the other hand, are particularly interested in the degree to which a representative body resembles its constituents, as they link its composition to the types of activities it undertakes.[49] In other words, they expect a representative to reflect the popular opinion—and act accordingly—and this can be done only if representatives resemble their constituencies. A 2008 study seeking to understand how descriptive representation changes patterns of civic engagement in the case of women and young people empirically confirmed the importance of representatives mirroring their constituents.[50] Drawing on a set of data collected in ninety countries from 1981 to 2007, the researchers concluded that in societies where women or young people are more fully represented—for instance through a quota system—in national parliaments, the gap in political interest and civic engagement is reduced and, in the case of women, even reversed. A conclusion of the study is that descriptive representation among visible political minorities can function as a cognitive shortcut, guiding voters' decisions at the ballot box.[51]

Concerning the importance of *symbolic representation*, it probably becomes the most obvious in the case of nationalist leaders who stand for the ideals of their nation and are thus able to mobilize wide support for their cause (Lajos Kossuth, Kemal Ataturk and Tudor Vladimirescu being just a few examples).

The underlying idea in the case of *substantive representation*, whether meaning to act instead of someone, in the interest of someone, or on instructions from someone, is that representatives act in the best interest of their constituency. Who determines what the 'best interest' is and how it can be achieved are important questions that many scholars have attempted to answer, giving rise to the 'mandate vs. independence' debate.

---

49 Ibid., pp. 62–63.
50 Norris, Pippa/ Krook, Mona L.: One of Us. Multilevel Models Examining the Impact of Descriptive Representation on Civic Engagement, paper presented at the APSA 2009 Toronto Meeting, http://papers.ssrn.com/sol3/papers.cfm?abstract_id=1451149, accessed 21 May 2010.
51 Ibid., p. 4.

9.6.3. Democratic Representation and the Case of 'Ethno-Business' in Romania

Regardless of the form under discussion, it is generally agreed that 'ethno-business' shapes the link between citizens and their elected representatives. Importantly, Hanna Pitkin challenges the common assumption that representation equals democracy, stressing that the two concepts are in fact very different and have a 'problematic' relationship.[52]

The quality of a democracy may be assessed by referring to a series of indicators, including representativity. Starting from a definition of democracy as a form of government that institutionalizes the link between the preferences of citizens and the actions of politicians, Andrew Roberts finds that the responsiveness of elected officials to the constituency's policy preferences, their accountability (by which he understands the capacity of the public to remove an unsuccessful policymaker from office during elections) and their representativeness (policy-makers and their policy directions as reflecting the citizens' preferences) are all factors that determine the quality of a democracy.[53] Roberts' analysis is more empirically oriented than Pitkin's, whose approach is more theoretical and conceptual, but both see democracy as made up of different and sometimes contradictory elements of which (forms of) representation is one.

Hanna Pitkin's categories of representation	Symbolic	Descriptive	Substantive	Formal
Andrew Roberts' factors determining the quality of democracy				Accountability Representativity
			Responsiveness	

Roberts' theoretical categories refer mainly to the relationship between voters and their elected representatives. The factors he sees as determining the quality of a democracy by and large coincide with Pitkin's formal category of representation, and the policy maker's responsiveness to his or her electorate appears to be linked both to Pitkin's formal and substantive aspects of representation.

Also, as Pitkin approaches representation from a very theoretical and broad perspective (her research is not confined to representation as related to the electoral process), she is not concerned with clientelism and its effects on representation. Roberts's

---

52   Pitkin, Hanna F.: Representation and Democracy. An Uneasy Alliance, in: Scandinavian Political Studies, 2004 (vol. 27), no. 3, pp. 335–342.
53   Roberts, Andrew: The Quality of Democracy, in: Comparative Politics, 2005 (vol. 37), no. 3, pp. 357–376, here p. 358.

approach to democratic representation, both generally and with respect to the electoral process specifically, considers it to be based on ideology and not on clientelistic purposes. Considering that organizations of national minorities behave to a large extent as interest parties, and less as programmatic parties, applying Roberts' categories to their case will have to take this aspect into account.

Before embarking on an analysis of the effects of ethno-business on the democratic representation of national minorities, we first need to explore the general effects of ethno-business on democratic representation in Romania. In terms of *accountability*, minority deputies play by the same rules as any deputy elected on a 'normal' ballot—that is, they can be voted out of office if their constituencies deem their performance to be unsatisfactory. Before 2008, the Electoral Law allowed multiple organizations representing the interests of the same national minority to contest the elections freely—and indeed there were many cases where the incumbent was replaced.[54] The 2008 changes to the electoral legislation make it almost impossible for any 'outsider' organization to challenge the incumbent deputy. From this perspective, the degree of accountability of the incumbent deputy—and the organization he or she represents—is relatively low, as voters wishing to elect a minority leader are faced with a single option; their alternative in this case is to cast their vote for a non-ethnic party.

As the parliamentary seats obtained by national minorities are the result of special arrangements, *representativity*, if understood as proportional representation, is indeed distorted at the national level, albeit intentionally; the purpose of these arrangements was to allow national minorities to participate more effectively in public and political life. This distortion is not unusual, however, as most positive discrimination measures imply the over-representation of certain groups. Concerning the representativity of the elected minority deputy in relation to the community he or she represents, this may depend on various geographical, cultural or religious factors. A good example of a case where the representativity of a deputy is difficult to achieve is the Bulgarian minority, which is geographically divided into two separate areas, and which is further divided in terms of religion and culture. As the Bulgarian minority is entitled to just one seat in Parliament, the elected deputy will face the challenge of representing the whole minority, and not just the one from his or her area of origin.

Finally, the 2008 changes to the electoral legislation have some bearing on the *responsiveness* of minority deputies to the policy preferences of their constituencies. Until 2008 the potential competition from other organizations challenging the incumbent meant that there was at least some pressure on the respective deputy to comply

---

54   A few examples: Dumitru Rotaru, the representative of the 'Bratstvo' Community of Bulgarians in Romania, elected in 2000, was replaced in 2004 with Niculae Mircovici, representative of the Bulgarian Union of Banat, Romania. Similarly, Ileana Stana-Ionescu, representative of the Italian Community in Romania, elected in 2000, was replaced in 2004 by Mircea Grosaru, representative of the RO.AS.IT, the Association of Italians in Romania.

with the preferences of his or her voters. After 2008, the virtual elimination of the competition from other organizations representing the interests of the same minority means that there is less pressure to satisfy one's constituency. The only 'danger' the incumbent organizations face is that should they alienate their voters, these could choose to cast their vote in favour of non-ethnic parties and thus cause the minority organization to fail to meet the electoral threshold. However, given the relatively small number of votes these organizations have to gather nationally in order to enter Parliament (10% of the average number of votes cast in favour of a deputy), the pressure is not particularly high.

An assessment of the effects of ethno-business on democratic representation in Romania should include the categories described by Pitkin and Roberts, and is best structured along the three main types of such strategies.

9.6.4.   Entrepreneurship of Non-Minority Leaders

An analysis of election results over the years shows that the number of votes a minority leader receives sometimes greatly exceeds the number of persons belonging to that respective minority.[55] This suggests that persons of other ethnic backgrounds have crossed over to vote for a non-minority entrepreneur, which influences the outcome. In the event that the members of the minority community disagree with the election results (i.e. oppose the election of a non-minority candidate running on a minority mandate), they may have difficulty removing the representative from office in the next round of elections due to the high number of 'external' votes. This has a bearing on the leader's accountability and representativity (in Roberts' terminology) in front of the community he or she represents on an ethnic mandate.

At this point, Pitkin's categorization is particularly useful with respect to representativity: because the leader is not a member of the community he or she represents, the descriptive component of representation may be particularly problematic. Symbolic representation may also be an issue, for even when the leader employs symbolic cues, he or she may have difficulty establishing credibility in the constituency. Finally, one important aspect of a non-minority leader's viability pertains to the substantive category of representation: the question then is under what circumstances the constituency is willing to prioritize a candidate's managerial skills over his or her ethnic non-belonging.

9.6.5.   (Re)construction of Assimilated Ethnic Communities

This type of strategy raises some interesting questions related to representativity. In terms of descriptive and symbolic representation, the entrepreneur fulfils a problematic

---

55   Based on consecutive election results as compared to the 1992 and 2002 census results.

role: the community whose interests he or she claims to represent on an ethnic mandate has usually already been assimilated into the majority.[56] The question is then how such leaders manage to fulfil their role as a representative of the community; simply put, who do they represent and how? One possible answer to this question may relate to the substantive category of representation. As in the other types of ethno-business strategies, the leader's electorate may prioritize his or her managerial skills, and may choose to take advantage of the minority policies that allow them to send a representative to Parliament. A good example in this sense is the case of the Macedonian minority. As mentioned above, there was no mention of a Macedonian population in the 1992 census; however, 2000 saw the emergence of the Association of Slav Macedonians[57], who in the same year ran in the elections and managed to gather 8,809 votes. The following census (2002) recorded 731 ethnic Macedonians living in Romania. Since 2004 the Association of Macedonians has been represented in Parliament by the same deputy (Liana Dumitrescu), who is regarded as one of the most active minority entrepreneurs. She has contributed significantly to the local community, establishing schools with instruction in Macedonian and organizing cultural events reflecting Macedonian traditions. In addition, she has tirelessly encouraged the Romanian population to join the ranks of her organization by emphasizing that her endeavours benefit the whole community and not just the Macedonian ethnic group.[58] Another hypothesis is that this arrangement constitutes a case of political clientelism, in which the entrepreneur manages to gather the necessary votes by promising material benefits to the individual voters.

9.6.6. Organizational Fragmentation and Its Effects on Democratic Representation of National Minorities

The legislative arrangement introduced in Romania to improve minority representation prior to 2008 produced a flurry of organizations competing for access to Parliament, which in the case of several minorities greatly fragmented their political environment. The effects on democratic representation vary with the type of fragmentation of the political environment that is characteristic of each minority.

In the case of the Italian minority,[59] around eighteen organizations have sought to enter the electoral competition on a minority mandate over the years. Paradoxically, such a surge in competition can actually endanger a minority from sending a deputy

---

56 This scenario is compounded by the fact that in practical terms, it often overlaps with another type of ethno-business, in which the leader does not share the ethnic background of the community he or she represents.

57 Later re-named the 'Association of Macedonians'.

58 Interview with Ms Rodica Precupetu, Head of Unit, Department for Inter-Ethnic Relations, May 2010.

59 According to the 2002 census, the Italian minority consisted of 3,331 persons.

to Parliament. Considering the relatively small pool of potential voters, the proliferation of groups vying for a seat could theoretically scatter the votes so thinly that none of the organizations would end up receiving enough votes to obtain a seat. With the 2008 changes to the Electoral Law, this type of competition was blocked, so that potential voters for the Italian minority could only vote for the incumbent Italian organization.

In the case of the Bulgarian minority, the fragmentation of the political environment reflects a geographical, cultural and religious divide, rather than being the product of institutional incentives. The Bulgarian minority is divided geographically into two areas, corresponding to two Bulgarian communities of unequal size, with different religious (one Roman Catholic, the other Orthodox), cultural and historical backgrounds. Democratic representation is more nuanced here and raises multiple issues. Because only one organization per minority group could enter Parliament, until 2008 the prevailing organization tended to favour its own constituency and neglect the interests of the other one once in power. The *accountability* of the elected representative depended on the relative size of the two communities and on the number of votes each was able to generate during elections. In terms of an analysis of the leader's *representativeness*, Hanna Pitkin's categorization is especially useful. For this specific case, the issue of descriptive representation is particularly problematic, given the difference in religious and cultural backgrounds of the two communities. Symbolic representation is equally complex, in that at any given time one or the other of the two communities did not find itself reflected in the representative's use of cultural, historical or religious symbols. Finally, the *substantive* aspect of representation is essential; the quality of democracy is determined to a great extent by the capacity of the leader to act according to the policy preferences of such a culturally and geographically divided minority. These issues were aggravated by the 2008 changes in legislation, which virtually excluded one part of the ethnic group from the electoral competition.

9.7. Conclusion

This study has tackled the issue of minority representation from an angle which departs from the standard academic approach to minority rights. Most of the studies addressing the rights of national minorities aim to assess the state's (non)fulfilment of its international and domestic commitments, leaving aside the second component of the nexus of rights and duties represented by law. In contrast to these approaches, by focusing on the strategies contained under the title of 'ethno-business' in Romania, this research has analysed the ways in which the recipients of minority policies—here, the organizations representing national minorities—sometimes choose to make use of these rights. It is important to mention that these strategies are not common to all twenty minorities recognized by the Romanian state. They tend to occur in the case of small minorities who are either geographically dispersed, or went through an intense process of assimilation before 1989.

In addition to the analysis of the strategies employed by political entrepreneurs in order to benefit from the provisions related to the legal and institutional settings for national minorities, this chapter also looked at the ways in which these 'ethno-business' strategies shape the political representation of national minorities. Based on Hanna Pitkin's theory of representation, which distinguishes between the formalistic, descriptive, symbolic, and substantive categories of representation, this analysis assessed how each of the three 'ethno-business' strategies under discussion shapes one or several of Pitkin's categories. The analysis reveals that each of the three 'ethno-business' strategies has an important effect on the representation of national minorities, as they influence substantially all or most of Pitkin's categories of representation.

Maja Nenadović

10. If You Ignore It, It Will (Not) Go Away. Exploring How and Why the International Community Turned a Blind Eye to Corruption in Bosnia-Herzegovina and Kosovo

10.1. Introduction

Billions of euros have thus far been poured into the post-conflict reconstruction of Bosnia-Herzegovina (BiH) and Kosovo.[1] As unique cases of intervention and statebuilding under the aegis of international administration, they exemplify a multitude of lessons learned for other types of international interventions. Democracy was identified as the desired end goal of post-conflict reconstruction efforts in the Balkans,[2] and aiding the spread of democracy became one of the main pillars of the international administrations mandated with this task. One of the ways in which international organizations tried to install democracy in Bosnia-Herzegovina and Kosovo was by assisting the development of their political parties. As a specific type of democracy assistance, party aid sought to strengthen, internally democratize and in general organizationally develop political parties to serve as catalysts, rather than inhibitors, of the internal democratization processes.

Meanwhile, political elites in both countries have been roundly criticized for their behaviour and functioning in the course of Bosnia-Herzegovina's and Kosovo's problem-ridden paths to democracy. Fifteen and eleven years into the international administration of BiH and Kosovo, respectively, these major actors are plagued with corruption scandals as they continue to demonstrate political immaturity and a lack of capacity. Their ineptitude has not only served as a warrant for extension of international administration mandates there but also underscores the importance of studying political party assistance as a tool of democracy promotion. The potential as well

---

1   Various sources offer conflicting information on the total sums that financed post-conflict reconstruction and statebuilding projects in both countries. The World Bank estimates that in BiH alone, the international community provided $5.1 billion from 1996–2004. (Source: Author's e-mail communication with a local senior official from the Sarajevo World Bank office, BiH, 27 May 2010.) For Kosovo, the figure most often cited is $3 billion for the decade of international assistance (1999–2009), for e.g. Bytyci, Fatos: After billions in aid, Kosovo still poor and idle, in: Reuters, 19 November 2009.

2   The Dayton Agreement in Bosnia-Herzegovina prescribed, 'that democratic governmental institutions and fair procedures best produce peaceful relations within a pluralist society'. (General Framework Agreement for Peace 1995, Annex 4, preamble.) In Kosovo, the UNSCR 1244 instituted, 'transitional administration while establishing and overseeing the development of provisional democratic self-governing institutions to ensure conditions for a peaceful and normal life for all inhabitants of Kosovo'. (Security Council Resolution 1244, S/Res/1244, 10 June 1999.)

as the limits of this form of aid urgently need to be re-evaluated with respect to its efficacy vis-à-vis the empowerment, capacity-building and democratic socialization of political parties in post-conflict areas.

Building on existing research on the effects of party assistance in BiH and Kosovo within the wider framework of statebuilding and democracy promotion,[3] this research paper analyses the issue of corruption and patronage in BiH and Kosovo and the international community's inability and unwillingness to engage with it. It explores the reasons behind this omission as well as the dire consequences that corruption, organized crime and clientelism have had on the transition processes in these two countries. Both countries seem to have sunken into a state of institutionalized kleptocracy, despite the extensive, sustained international effort to institute democratic rule.

The next section will set forth some definitions as well as provide facts on the two case studies under analysis, with particular emphasis on data on corruption. The third section briefly looks at some theoretical underpinnings on democratic representation. The fourth section focuses exclusively on the international administrations, their officials, and the way they have engaged with corruption among local political elites in BiH and Kosovo to date. The next section analyses the work of political party assistance organizations and evaluates how this external assistance has impacted corruption in these two countries. Finally, this research concludes that in post-conflict countries such as Bosnia-Herzegovina and Kosovo, building political parties with the aim of supporting democratic development comes with more challenges and risks than opportunities. The lesson to take home is that not even international administrations with extensive mandates can serve as a sufficient impetus for democratization if the international community chooses to ignore or is unable to tackle corruption at the very outset of post-conflict reconstruction and statebuilding programmes. Similarly, in post-conflict contexts, political party assistance may prove ineffectual at best and potentially aggravating to democracy's development at worst.

10.2. Definitions

Before delving into a description and evaluation of how the international community tackled the problem of post-conflict corruption in BiH and Kosovo, this section will define some key terms. 'International community', a vague term that defies clear definition, stands for international administrations and international political party assistance

---

3   A Ph.D. project entitled 'Installing Democracy in the Balkans. Analysis of Political Party Assistance in Bosnia-Herzegovina and Kosovo' inspired this particular paper. Conducted between 2007–2010, combining qualitative (166 interviews, participant observation, primary documents analysis) and quantitative (131 survey questionnaires) methodologies and based on extensive field research in Bosnia-Herzegovina, Kosovo, the United States, Germany and the UK, this Ph.D. research uncovers the as-yet untold story of foreign aid provided to political parties and its dubious impact on local democratization processes.

organizations in this text. 'International administration' denotes the most extensive type of international intervention in post-conflict territories, in which international actors are 'literally taking over the governance function from local actors'.[4] The chief international administration institution in BiH is the Office of the High Representative (OHR); its counterpart in Kosovo is the United Nations Mission in Kosovo[5] (UNMIK), headed by the Special Representative of the Secretary General (SRSG). In both countries, the work of international administrations in the democratization field was supplemented by the Organization for Security and Cooperation in Europe (OSCE). Finally, 'party assistance' refers to the set of programmes and activities implemented by various democracy promotion organizations active in BiH and Kosovo, starting with the National Democratic Institute (NDI) and the International Republican Institute (IRI) from the US, various German political foundations (Konrad Adenauer Stiftung—KAS, Friedrich Ebert Stiftung—FES, Friedrich Naumann Stiftung—FNS) and also involving some smaller assistance programmes, such as those of Dutch political parties (Alfred Mozer Stichting—AMS of the Dutch Labour Party, and programmes hosted by the liberal parties VVD and D66). The goal of party aid is to bolster political party development and to democratize and strengthen party systems in new democracies. Meant to empower political parties in transition countries with a set of tools and know-how, party aid trainings and seminars concentrate on issues such as internal party organization, campaigning, media relations, platform creation, message development, membership strategy and the like, all in the hopes of making parties more transparent and democratic, and hence more accountable to the electorate.[6] Party assistance organizations have been active in BiH since the very beginning of international administration

---

4　Fukuyama, Francis: State Building. Governance and World Order in the 21st Century, New York: Cornell University Press, 2004, p. 93.

5　While OHR in BiH is still active despite the continuing discussions on dismantling it, leaving only the European Union Special Representative (EUSR) office in its place, the status of the UNMIK has come under question since Kosovo's proclamation of independence in February 2008. The UNMIK's administration of Kosovo was based on UNSCR 1244, which forbade Kosovo from proclaiming independence and which considered Kosovo to be part of Serbian territory. Following the proclamation of independence, it was negotiated that the European Union Special Representative (EUSR), the International Civilian Office (ICO) and the European Union Rule of Law Mission in Kosovo (EULEX) would take over most of the UNMIK's tasks in the country, thus reflecting Kosovo's new, independent status. However, this takeover has failed to materialize, and all organizations continue to exist side by side—their mandates unclear, work stalled. For more on this, read Bieber, Florian: Kosovo. One year on, in: Open Democracy News Analysis, 17 February 2009, http://www.opendemocracy.net/article/kosovo-one-year-on

6　More information about political party assistance, its main tenets, activities and strategies can be found in Carothers, Thomas: Confronting the Weakest Link. Aiding Political Parties in New Democracies, Washington D.C.: Carnegie Endowment for International Peace, 2006. Also, Kumar, Krishna: Reflections on international political party assistance, in: Democratization, 2005 (vol. 12), no. 4, pp. 505–527.

(1996), and in Kosovo they began operating soon after the end of NATO's Operation Allied Force[7] (1999).

10.3. Considering Democratic Representation

More than half a century ago, Schattschneider claimed that 'modern democracy is unthinkable save in terms of political parties'.[8] This belief still holds true today. What functions do parties fulfill that makes them essential constituent parts of modern democracies? Diamond and Gunther identify several roles for political parties.[9] A core function is elite recruitment, which ties in with candidate nomination and electoral mobilization. Parties also facilitate the process of structuring the choices and alternatives on different policy issues and they act as organizations of social representation by advancing different groups' specific interests. Furthermore, they form coalitions, negotiate joint policies through inter-party cooperation, which in turn constitutes their interest aggregation function. Once elected, they take part in forming and sustaining governments in office by performing different roles and holding power positions. Finally, they also play a role in social integration by enabling citizens to participate in political processes. In other words, their functions as articulators, aggregators and representatives of social interests and demands place political parties in the position to shape public opinion and the perceptions of the society they inhabit. At least, this is the theory.

Central to the notion of representation is the relationship between the principal, the one doing the representing, i.e. political parties and representatives elected from their ranks to serve as public officials, and the agent, or the represented party, i.e. the people or voters. However, Hanna Pitkin points out the paradox inherent in this concept: the people are not present in decision-making processes, but are yet somehow still (re)present(ed).[10] As democracy emerged as the dominant and preferred mode of governance in Western countries, representation as its main mechanism received increasing attention. The critics, starting with Rousseau, pointed out how active partic-

---

7   The military combat sorties and air strikes that were at the heart of NATO's Operation Allied Force were carried out against Serbia from March till June of 1999. This unprecedented intervention—conducted without a United Nations Security Council resolution, on humanitarian grounds—targeted Serbian president Slobodan Milošević and his policy of human rights violations carried out against the ethnic Albanian majority living in Kosovo.
8   E.E. Schattschneider: Party Government, New York: Rhinehart & Co., 1942, p. 1.
9   Diamond, Larry/Gunther, Richard: Types and Functions of Parties, in: Larry Diamond/Richard Gunther (eds.): Political Parties and Democracy, Baltimore/London: The Johns Hopkins University Press, 2001, p. 7–8.
10   Pitkin, Hanna: Representation and Democracy: Uneasy Alliance, in: Scandinavian Political Studies, 2004 (vol. 27), p. 336.

ipation of the people was the only way of realizing true democracy.[11] They view representation in democratic systems as effectively reduced to only one genuine moment of participation—the casting of the vote—after which people once again become the nameless, voiceless masses whose interests are supposedly represented by the elected political elites. As Pitkin puts it, the problem with representation is that 'the representatives act not as agents of the people but simply instead of them'.[12] What effect does this have on democracy?

One of the side effects is that people feel alienated 'from what is done in their name and from those who do it'.[13] Related to this is the growing number of those disenchanted with the democratic system of government who fail to show up to elections and cast their votes. This democratic deficit evident in low voter turnouts threatens one of the basic pillars of democratic representation, which is participation in elections. If fewer and fewer people vote, can some countries still be considered 'democratic'? An additional issue that problematicizes the paradoxical link between democracy and representation is the difficulty of holding the elected officials accountable. Short of 'punishing' an elected official by withdrawing one's vote at the next elections, the people have little control over what their representatives do once in office.

Finally, what happens to democracies in which accountability of public officials is low, or non-existent? Corruption can take many shapes and forms, from bribery of public officials to the mismanagement of public funds, while the overall effect of such misconduct is 'distortion of the workings of the political system'.[14] When coupled with the already discussed uneasy relationship between democracy and representation, the result in corrupted countries that are undergoing the democratization process is democracy with adjectives.[15] Researchers have thus identified different types of democracy, labelled as illiberal, phantom, façade, electoral, etc.

This section has identified the tensions between representation, democracy and problems stemming from corruption for the development and functioning of states. The next sections will illustrate these tensions through the examples of Bosnia-Herzegovina and Kosovo, showing how unrestrained corruption hampers (post-conflict) countries' chances for democratization.

---

11   Rousseau, Jean-Jacques: The Social Contract, Harmondsworth, England: Penguin, 1968, p. 101–2, 110, 141, in: Pitkin, Hanna: Representation and Democracy: Uneasy Alliance, in: Scandinavian Political Studies, 2004 (vol. 27), p. 339.
12   Pitkin, Hanna: Representation and Democracy: Uneasy Alliance, in: Scandinavian Political Studies, 2004, (vol. 27), p. 339.
13   Ibid.
14   Karklins, Rasma: Typology of Post-Communist Corruption, in: Problems of Post-Communism, July/August 2002 (vol. 49), no. 4, pp. 22–32.
15   For more discussion on the concept of 'democracy with adjectives', see: Collier, David/ Steven Levitsky: Democracy 'With Adjectives': Conceptual Innovation in Comparative Research, in: World Politics, April 1997 (vol. 49), no. 3, pp. 430–451.

10.4. Facts on Corruption

'Corruption' is a complex and culturally relative term. The leading international organization addressing this problem, Transparency International (TI), defines corruption as 'the abuse of entrusted power for private gain'.[16] This research will rely on this definition to study the question of corruption in BiH and Kosovo. It is important to note that it is impossible to measure actual corruption in a given country directly; Transparency International has therefore developed a 'Corruption Perceptions Index', which accordingly documents the perceived level of public sector corruption through various surveys. In this sense, the principle 'esse est percipi' (to be is to be perceived) is in force here, as people's perception of corruption has a real impact on their trust in their public officials as well as on the overall quality of democracy in their country.

Why is corruption an especially prominent problem in post-conflict areas? According to TI, corruption thrives in certain types of environments:

> [...] corruption thrives where temptation coexists with permissiveness. Where institutional checks on power are missing, where decision making remains obscure, where civil society is thin on the ground, where great inequalities in the distribution of wealth condemn people to live in poverty [...].[17]

Post-conflict environments fit the above description perfectly. Another element playing a role in corruption in post-conflict areas is the large sums of money disbursed by the international community. While geared toward reconstruction, humanitarian aid and statebuilding, the aid often falls into the wrong hands thanks to the lack of rule of law and institutional checks on power. Furthermore, because war economies are dependent on organized crime channels, peace agreements often result in placing 'the same traffickers and warlords who used the conflict as a profit-generating event' into power.[18] Similarly, peace agreements almost invariably tend to impose some sort of power-sharing in post-conflict governments, because this arrangement is thought to facilitate democratization. However, corruption often 'provides the glue to hold formerly warring parties together'[19] in their joint project of extracting profit and wealth from the state and from the post-conflict reconstruction process in general. Finally, it is an understatement to assert that 'warlords are not typically the best qualified individuals to assume the challenging role of statebuilding'[20]—and yet they are precisely

---

16   Transparency International web site: Frequently Asked Questions About Corruption, at: http://www.transparency.org/news_room/faq/corruption_faq, accessed 22 May 2010.

17   Ibid.

18   Scharbatke-Church, Cheyanne/ Kirby Reilin: Lilies that fester. Seeds of corruption and peacebuilding, in: New Routes, Pilfering the Peace. The nexus between corruption and peacebuilding, 2009 (vol. 14), no. 3–4, p. 4.

19   Ibid., p. 5.

20   Dininio, Phyllis: Warlords and corruption in post-conflict governments, in: New Routes, Pilfering the Peace. The nexus between corruption and peacebuilding, 2009 (vol. 14), no. 3–4, p. 28.

the ones who are often left in power once the conflict ends. As creating functional and democratic states is the final goal of the international community's post-conflict reconstruction and statebuilding interventions, corruption—which is 'inherently contradictory and irreconcilable with democracy'[21]—makes the success of such interventions less likely.

TI's Corruption Perception Index (CPI) for 2009 placed Bosnia-Herzegovina in 99th place, with a score of 3.00/10.00. It is interesting to note that in 2003, BiH scored 3.3 and was in 70th position on the CPI countries list. What accounts for this precipitous drop in ranking? Despite the unprecedented scope of international intervention in the country, including the presence of an international administration with an extensive governance mandate, the country was felled by corruption. The paradox behind this deterioration is evident:

> Bosnia has received, since the end of the war, more financial donations from foreign donors for reconstruction than was pumped into 18 Western European countries under the post-World War II Marshall Plan. But in the case of Bosnia, the results of that major infusion of cash are less than clear. The misuse of foreign donations indirectly led to creation of some 50 wealthy businessmen, who before the war worked as fruit sellers in the outdoors markets, preachers, police officers, journalists, gas station workers and the like.[22]

Three different state commissions have been formed since 1996 to try to determine how the foreign donations were used and what exactly the money was spent on. Members of one of those commissions, 'after finding and publishing their first evidence of the unauthorized use of donations, were pressured, blackmailed, fired and, in some cases, victims of massive nervous breakdowns'.[23] One of the conclusions of the report was that

> [...] the country had received €7.5 billion in donations from foreign countries and organizations, but only €3.7 billion had been accounted for—meaning that the Bosnian government had proper paperwork for that amount only. The commission concluded that billions of euros intended for economic development and refugee returns ended up in [...] the pockets of government officials, mobsters and criminals.[24]

Precisely because of the widespread nature of the corruption involved and the damage that it has wrought on the post-conflict statebuilding and democratization processes in Kosovo and BiH, the present research investigates how and why this thievery was allowed to flourish under the international community's watch.

21　Transparency International web site: Frequently Asked Questions About Corruption, accessed 22 May 2010.

22　Alić, Anes: Bosnia. The donation sieve, in: ISN Security Watch, 19 February 2009.

23　Ibid.

24　Ibid.

In Kosovo, the general perception holds that most—if not all—political parties in Kosovo are in one way or another linked to organized crime networks.[25] If one adds to this the fact that several leaders and prominent members of the main political parties in Kosovo have declared incomes exceeding one million euros in a country with a virtually non-existent economy, the allegation becomes hard to ignore.[26] One local report challenges this dominant perception, arguing that Kosovo has more of an image problem than an actual corruption issue, and goes on to provide evidence of the discrepancy between perception and actual instances of corruption documented on the ground.[27] This same local report also takes offence at the TI International Global Corruption Barometer Survey of 2007, which placed Kosovo in the unenviable position of world's 4th most corrupt country. At the same time, however, Kosovo's proclamation of independence did little to exonerate its problematic image. In November of 2008, a high-profile political scandal erupted after Kosovar police apprehended three German citizens accused of planting an incendiary device in the European Union offices. It was later revealed that they were in fact German Federal Intelligence Service (BND) officers who were investigating links between organized crime and local politicians. One report by the BND concluded that 'The key players (including Haliti, Haradinaj, and Thaçi) are intimately involved in inter-linkages between politics, business, and organized crime structures in Kosovo.'[28] The same report also concluded that at the end of the 1990s, Prime Minister Hashim Thaçi was 'leading a criminal network operating throughout Kosovo'.[29] In response to the scandal, a high-ranking BND official spoke out sharply against Kosovo: 'The German government [has] allowed itself to be dragged by the nose [...] by a country in which organized crime is the form of government.'[30] Given that an international administration has run Kosovo since 1999, it is imperative to ask

---

25   Strazzari, Francesco: The Decade Horribilis. Organized violence and Organized Crime along the Balkan Peripheries, 1991–2001, in: Meditteranean Politics, July 2007 (vol. 12), pp. 185–209; Rosenthal, John: Corruption and Organized Crime in Kosovo. An Interview with Avni Zogiani, in: World Politics Review, 2 February 2008; Mayr, Walter: Confusion and Corruption in Kosovo. Part 2: More Greed than Pioneer Spirit, in: Der Spiegel, translated from German by Christopher Sultan, 24 April 2008, http://www.spiegel.de/international/world/0,1518,549441-2,00.html; Collaku, Petrit: Corruption Wide Spread in Kosovo, in: Balkan Insight, 9 December 2009.

26   For the 2007 general elections, all candidates running for office had to declare their incomes. The database in which one could look up the candidates' financial records could be accessed from the OSCE Mission in Kosovo Elections website at: http://kosovoelections.org/, accessed 28 November 2007. In the meantime, this public database was taken offline.

27   Image Matters! Deconstructing Kosovo's Image Problem, in: Kosovar Stability Initiative report, November 2008, p. 25–26. This report draws on: MSI Corruption Survey. USAID, May 2003, and UNDP, Combating Corruption in Kosovo. A citizen's perception survey in support of Kosovo's Anti-corruption Strategy, April 2004.

28   BND Kosovo affair. German spy affair might have been revenge, in: Welt Online, translated by Jacob Comenetz, 30 November 2008.

29   Ibid.

30   Ibid.

the same question that was posed in Bosnia's case: How and why did the international community fail to prevent the entrenchment of corruption in Kosovo under its watch?

10.5. International Administrations

This section explores how international administrations—the highest governance bodies in both BiH and Kosovo—interacted with local political elites. The first part describes the interaction patterns in terms of their implications for corruption in the two countries; the second part hypothesizes about possible reasons behind the international administrations' inability or unwillingness to tackle the corruption problem among local political elites.

10.5.1. The Relationship between International Administrations and Local Political Elites

Although the OHR in BiH and the UNMIK in Kosovo had very similar mandates in that both international administrations were able to impose legislation and remove obstructive politicians from power, the way in which these administrations exercised these mandates is strikingly different. One of the goals of the OHR in BiH was to remove nationalists from power, and in their effort to accomplish this goal, different High Representatives dismissed popularly elected representatives from their posts on a fairly regular basis in the 1997–2006 period. One of the most prominent dismissals was that of Croat member of the Presidency[31] Dragan Čović, who was under investigation for corruption and fraud, in 2005.[32] However, even though he was removed from power, Čović returned to Mostar, where he was re-elected as the President of the Croat Democratic Union (HDZ) nationalist political party. In 2006 the HDZ party suffered a split, and its radical breakaway faction HDZ1990 argued that the party under Čović's leadership had become too moderate and no longer advocated for the interests of the Croats living in BiH. The international administration once again allowed Čović to compete in elections, because he was now cooperating with them and was indeed seen as 'moderate'. While the active removal of nationalists from power made the nationalist political parties sensitive to their candidate selection,[33] it nevertheless failed to deplete the nationalist ranks: whenever their elected representatives were removed from power, there were plenty of new party members eager to take their place. In other words, even though the international administration in BiH had the

---

31　The peace agreement stipulated a three-member presidency, with each ethnic group (Bosniak, Croat, Serb) having a representative in the executive function, with a rotating chairmanship.

32　The large majority of other representatives were removed due to their obstruction of the peace agreement implementation process, rather than for corruption and fraud investigations.

33　Manning, Carrie: The Making of Democrats. Elections and Party Development in Postwar Bosnia, El Salvador and Mozambique, New York: Palgrave MacMillan, 2008, pp. 79–81.

power to remove nationalists from office, it still failed to achieve its goal of putting moderates in power. Moreover, it sent a very mixed message to the population of BiH: the politicians who cooperated with the international administration were immune to prosecution and investigation on corruption, while those who were obstructive and uncooperative risked investigation.

In Kosovo, the international administration never dismissed any local officials, even those alleged for involvement in corruption and fraudulent activities. Learning from the way the enforcement of this mandate backfired on the OHR in Bosnia-Herzegovina, the UNMIK 'hoped that the electorate, opposition, civil society and the media would hold Kosovar politicians to account'.[34] While in BiH, the OHR tried to remove nationalists from power, in Kosovo the international administration actively cooperated with all of the Kosovar Albanian political parties, including those whose leaders were allegedly heavily involved with organized crime. This cooperation went even further in 2005, when Prime Minister Ramush Haradinaj was indicted by the ICTY for war crimes: he resigned from his post and went voluntarily to The Hague to stand trial. Astonishingly, the SRSG at the time, Soren Jessen-Petersen, openly lamented Haradinaj's departure, advocating for his release on bail while offering guarantees for 'his good friend'.[35] The UNMIK's public support of an indicted war criminal shocked the Tribunal's prosecution team, who 'felt [the support] gave Haradinaj international legitimacy and fostered a chilling effect that discouraged prosecution witnesses from testifying against him'.[36] Haradinaj was subsequently exonerated by the ICTY and released back to Kosovo in 2008. The international administration's support for Kosovo's political elite extended to protecting them from investigation and looking the other way when allegations of wrongdoing surfaced. This indulgent treatment only served to reinforce the elite's aura of untouchability.[37]

Despite the abundance of allegations for corruption, fraud and abuse of position, international administrations never prosecuted or investigated politicians consistently. Several individuals were put under the magnifying glass by the international prosecutor's office in BiH, but only as a means of scaring them into submission.[38] The same method was attempted on SNSD leader Milorad Dodik[39] in BiH, and more recently on

---

34	King, Iain/ Whit Mason: Peace At Any Price. How the World Failed Kosovo, New York: Cornell University Press, 2006, pp. 163–164.
35	Terdevci, Fatmire: Kosovo. Haradinaj's Departure, in: Transitions Online, 14 March 2005.
36	Haradinaj, a forced marriage between politics and justice, in: International Justice Tribune, 17 March 2008.
37	Strazzari, Francesco: L'Oeuvre au Noir. The Shadow Economy of Kosovo's Independence, in: International Peacekeeping, 2008 (vol. 15), no. 2, pp. 155–170, p. 161.
38	A case in point is Dragan Čović of the Croat nationalist HDZ party. It is rumoured that he struck a deal with the international community to uphold and push the reforms that they initiated, and that in exchange they allowed him to continue his engagement in politics.
39	The saga of investigating Milorad Dodik for corruption and organized crime has been going on since 2009, when the international administration first authorized the launch of the investigation.

the PDK's Fatmir Limaj[40] in Kosovo. This selective and strategic approach to eradicating corruption among politicians sent a strong message to the people: that accountability was not a highly appreciated value in the budding democracies of BiH and Kosovo.

Previous research has determined that despite their overarching governance powers, international administrations have failed to come up with political party regulations and laws that would significantly rein in the local political elites' behaviour.[41] Regarding party financing, an extensive investigation has revealed that state budget funds are by far the biggest source of financing for political parties in BiH:

> The funds put aside for some political parties were up to as high as a million EUR per year [...] these funds are progressively increasing, and the estimate is that public budgets on all levels of governance yearly distribute as much as 10 million Euros to political parties.[42]

This goes to show that the laws on party financing in BiH have not prevented 'the dominant predatory elite project in post-communism—extraction from the state'.[43] Finally, in Kosovo, even though there are several domestic and international anti-corruption agencies currently active on the ground, none of these has investigated politicians despite the reports of investigatory journalists alleging fraudulent activities.[44]

10.5.2. Exploring Why International Administrations Failed to Tackle Corruption

Why were the approaches used by international administrations in BiH and Kosovo so strikingly different? Several authors have pointed out the detriments of the international administration's cooperation with and endorsement of the Kosovar political elites in the immediate aftermath of Operation Allied Force.[45] Since the NATO

No concrete steps have been taken in the meantime, and Dodik has rejected all of the allegations as unfounded, claiming that the international community and the Federation BiH are out to dissolve the RS entity.

40 The first prominent case of a high-level politician being investigated for corruption in Kosovo is that of Fatmir Limaj of the ruling PDK party. The current Minister of Transport is under investigation by the EULEX, and his offices as well as his private property were raided for evidence of fraudulent road tenders in May 2010. See: Marzouk, Lawrence: Fatmir Limaj: Kosovo's Road Builder, in: Balkan Insight, 5 May 2010.

41 Nenadović, Maja: An Uneasy Symbiosis. The Impact of International Administrations on Political Parties in Post-Conflict Countries, in: Democratization, 2010 (vol. 17), no. 6, pp. 1153–1175.

42 Martinović, Aleksandra: Strogo Kontrolisana Anarhija. Financiranje političkih stranaka u BiH [Strictly Controlled Anarchy. The Financing of Political Parties in BiH], in: Pulse of Democracy, October 3, 2008, available at: http://www.pulsdemokratije.ba/index.php?l=bs&id=1084 (accessed 5 October 2008). Note: the sums were converted from BAM/KM to EUR currency.

43 'In Search of Responsive Government: State Building and Economic Growth in the Balkans,' in: Policy Studies Series, Central European University, 2003, p. 44.

44 Author interviews with representatives of five local and international anti-corruption agencies, in Prishtina, Kosovo, May 2008.

45 King, Iain/ Whit Mason: Peace At Any Price. How the World Failed Kosovo, New York: Cornell University Press, 2006, pp. 163–164; O'Neill, William G.: Kosovo. An Unfinished Peace, London: Lyne Rienner Publishers, 2002; Wolfgram, Mark A.: When the Men with Guns Rule. Explaining

operation was carried out jointly with KLA ground forces, the international administration entered Kosovo to find that KLA commanders had effectively occupied municipal town hall centres and proclaimed themselves to be in charge. The demilitariza-
tion of the KLA and the transformation of its political factions, the AAK and the PDK,
into legitimate political parties would ultimately take years. Because the international
administrations found that removing 'undemocratic' politicians from power did not
yield the desired results in BiH, they decided they would save themselves the trou-
ble in Kosovo, and instead attempted to reform the local elites through cooperation.
Provisional Institutions of Self-Government (PISG) came into being, and the international administration assisted the work of these institutions by providing a host of
international advisers to shadow and accompany the local political elites.

In time, the problem of corruption became more of a sound bite or lip service
that international officials paid in their public talks addressing the local political elites
than something that the international administrations seriously intended to eradi-
cate in BiH and Kosovo. As one high-level international administration official admits,

> Fighting corruption in Bosnia was beyond complex. It was like fighting the Hydra: you cut
> off one head, and in its place two heads would appear. Corruption permeated all sectors of
> society, and even though international administrations were equipped with extensive gov-
> ernance mandates—we did not have the capacity to address corruption systematically.[46]

On the one side lies the definite complexity of the problem of deeply ingrained corruption and the symbiotic relationship between organized crime networks and local
political elites. On the other side, however, is the international administrations' attitude toward the issue. The next section looks at how they treated corruption within
their own ranks.

One grave problem is that the international administrations in BiH and Kosovo
never led by example; they failed to enforce accountability in their own backyard. While
preaching rule of law, they themselves repeatedly succumbed to corruption scandals
perpetrated by their own officials. In one of his reports on Kosovo, investigatory journalist Maciej Zaremba revealed how one of the SRSGs refused to investigate corruption allegations in his own administration.[47] In the most prominent corruption scandal, the international official in charge of managing the KEK, Joe Truschler, embezzled
$4.3 million; the UN auditors who investigated the case concluded that he had been
given a 'licence to steal'.[48] This and other cases, as well as the general sense that inter-

---

Human Rights Failures in Kosovo since 1999, in: Political Science Quarterly, Fall 2008 (vol. 123),
no. 3, pp. 461–484.

46   Author interview with a former high-level international administration official, Washington D.C.,
     USA, 4 April 2008.
47   Zaremba, Maciej: Izvještaj iz Unmikistana. Autonomna Korupcija [Report from Unmikistan:
     Autonomous Corruption], in: Feral Tribune, 25 January 2008.
48   Zaremba, Maciej: Report from Unmikistan: Autonomous Corruption, in: Feral Tribune, 25 January
     2008.

national officials were 'above the law', has damaged both the local population's trust in their administrators and the international community's efforts to democratize their protectorates. Finally, the Ombudsperson reports in Kosovo have long been critical of the international role there, accusing international administrations of turning a blind eye to human rights violations, operating in the least transparent manner and demonstrating an apparent lack of accountability.[49] That post-conflict environments constitute a particularly rich ground for corruption lies in the fact that international community representatives themselves are not immune to it.[50]

10.6. Political Party Assistance Organizations

This section explores how party assistance organizations, i.e. the international democracy promotion institutions active in BiH and Kosovo, interacted with local political elites. The first part describes the impact of their work, especially in relation to corruption. The second part explores the reasons behind the party assistance organizations' inability or unwillingness to engage with corruption issues among local political elites.

10.6.1. The Impact of Party Aid on Local Political Elites

The main difference in the approaches between the German and American party aid organizations is that while the former tend to provide bilateral assistance to their ideologically close sister parties in new democracies, the latter provide multilateral assistance to all parties deemed to be democratic, viable and capable of absorbing assistance.[51] In keeping with this policy, American party assistance organizations were barred from working with nationalist parties in BiH. In Kosovo, however, there were no restrictions placed on party assistance organizations, and the American party aid organizations thus assisted all the parties that had successfully registered with the OSCE. The American party organizations in BiH and Kosovo concentrated on internal organization and electoral campaigning skills. Their German counterparts, on the other hand, focused more on helping parties to sharpen their ideological profile along the lines of European ideological party families (Social Democrats, Christian Democrats /

---

49   For more information, please refer to all the reports listed on the Ombudsperson official website: www.ombudspersonkosovo.org
50   TIRI is one of the only international organizations dedicated solely to promoting integrity, with a special section for integrity in the reconstruction of post-conflict areas. Having recognized this context as especially susceptible to widespread corruption, TIRI advocates for better transparency, coordination and accountability for beneficiaries and donors alike. As TIRI explains, 'If peace and aid are seen to bring inequality and corruption rather than fairness and integrity, the risk of instability increases.' www.tiri.org
51   Political Party Development Assistance, policy brief published by the Center for Democracy and Governance, United States Agency for International Development, April 1999.

Conservatives and Liberals). Party assistance organizations from both Germany and US helped local partner party leaders to polish and improve their image.

Extensive research on party aid in both countries has revealed that party assistance, despite the highly unusual context in which it took place, did not differ much from the standard template.[52] The fact that both BiH and Kosovo are post-conflict, internationally administered countries did not seem to bear much relevance for the planning and programming of party aid. Similarly, party assistance organizations in BiH did not to cooperate with the OHR nor have they attempted to affect the international administration's attitude and influence on political elites. In Kosovo, on the other hand, the NDI has made active efforts to participate in electoral law reform and other aspects of party politics that were influenced by international administration officials.

What was the impact of party assistance on parties in BiH and Kosovo since the beginning of international administrations (1996 and 1999, respectively) until 2009? The results of four years of research point to substantial omissions in party assistance programming and provision in both BiH and Kosovo. In BiH, the assistance was geared heavily toward removing the nationalist parties from power and installing moderates in the hopes of supporting democratization. The result exemplifies the law of unintended consequences: party assistance led to the empowerment of a moderate-party-turned-nationalist-party and ultimately proved obstructive to the democratization and peacekeeping processes. The Alliance of Independent Social Democrats (SNSD), under the leadership of Milorad Dodik, was the biggest party aid recipient in BiH. Before its rise to power in 2006, it was the international party assistance organizations' most eager local partner and the party most open to the various trainings, seminars, consultations and advice provided by international experts. Following the SNSD's rise to power, however, Dodik began railing against the Bosniak member of the presidency, Haris Silajdžić, using nationalist rhetoric and alarming the international community in the process. When a few cautious voices from the international community asked for some 'insider info' on Dodik's increasingly nationalist rhetoric, the NDI confidently responded, 'Don't worry, we have Dodik under control.'[53] However, the antagonism between the two politicians grew progressively more heated over the course of 2007, climaxing with Dodik's threats to hold a referendum in the Republika Srpska following Kosovo's proclamation of independence in February of 2008. At this point, a fellow American OSCE staff member inquired what was going on with the SNSD. This time, the NDI's response was one of alarm, i.e.: 'We no longer have any control over

---

52   The standard template or 'toolbox' is documented in Carothers, Thomas: Confronting the Weakest Link. Aiding Political Parties in New Democracies, Washington D.C.: Carnegie Endowment for International Peace, 2006.

53   Author interview with a high-positioned OSCE official in New York City, USA, 25 April 2009. This NDI attitude of 'having Dodik under control' was confirmed in further interviews with NDI officials in Sarajevo, BiH on 24 June 2007 and in Banja Luka on 18 June 2008.

him. He's gone rogue!'[54] Soon thereafter, the US State Department publically prohibited US organizations to cooperate with the SNSD, thus ending US party assistance to Dodik's party on a very sour note.

In Kosovo, the party assistance organizations effectively helped build parties from scratch, as Kosovo did not have functioning political parties prior to international intervention. Accordingly, they had a tremendous influence in shaping these parties: they not only helped to build the parties' internal organization but also taught the parties how to compete in elections and run professional campaigns. In addition, the organizations helped leaders to polish their public image:

> Comparing Thaçi in 2000, and the one who is aspiring to Prime Minister post now—one cannot help but conclude that he's had consultants helping him with his image. Whether they were NDI and German political foundations, or foreign paid consultants that he has hired himself, it's not clear—but it is obvious that they have taught him to tone down his ex-guerrilla fighter behaviour, and assume a more professional, moderate and modern politician role. His fashion changed, his speaking—even his hand gestures.[55]

When confronted with the widely held perception in Kosovo that political party leaders are linked to organized crime networks, international party assisters either shrugged off the issue ('Those are just allegations; there is no proof. Everyone is innocent until proven guilty.'[56]) or acknowledged it, but distanced themselves ('We do not support individuals, we only support political parties as organizations!'[57]). This convenient denial shielded them from the glaring irony of democracy-promotion organizations empowering and professionalizing former warlords, who in turn legitimized their grip on power by reorganizing themselves into political parties.

10.6.2. Exploring Why Party Aid Failed to Address Corruption

It is difficult to determine why exactly party assistance organizations turned a blind eye to corruption in BiH and Kosovo in the period under study. One of the major flaws in their approach was the focus on form over content: while the organizations worked hard on reforming the parties' internal organization and strengthening their election campaigning capacity, they nevertheless failed to address the underlying norms and values that informed the behaviour and attitudes of local political elites. When probed about the need to address the issues of nationalism and corruption in their work with political parties, one NDI official simply stated,

---

54 Author interview with a high-positioned OSCE official in New York City, USA, 25 April 2009.
55 Author interview with local political analyst / journalist in Prishtina, Kosovo, 15 November 2007.
56 Author interview with NDI staff member in Prishtina, Kosovo, 31 January 2007.
57 Author interview with NDI staff member in Prishtina, Kosovo, 20 November 2007.

                                     Maja Nenadović

> All we can do is talk about why corruption is bad and how it damages a society's chances for democratic development. But the bottom line is—you can't teach someone not to be corrupt.[58]

Perhaps he is right: perhaps norms cannot be transferred by the mere act of talking about them, nor can political elites be socialized to adopt a different form of behaviour via various workshops and trainings. But all the same, there is no excuse for the party assistance organizations' failure to address the content of the parties' politics and the deep-rooted corruption among political elites.

One possible cause behind this failure may lie in the timing. When the party assistance organizations first became engaged in BiH and Kosovo, donor support and investment in these areas were very high, and securing funding for party aid programmes was not very difficult. Prior to their arrival, however, the organizations had not had sufficient time to assess the local situations and their local partner parties in detail, so they tended to provide assistance without much specific background knowledge. As the party assistance organizations rode high on the wave of international goodwill, cash and a mixture of naïveté and hubris, political parties in BiH and Kosovo welcomed them with open arms, eager to obtain their advice and learn about the workings of Western democracies. In time, however, as funding for party aid work decreased and parties grew stronger with each passing election, their enthusiasm for assistance withered, and the party aid organizations suddenly found that the tables had turned: now *they* were the ones depending on local parties for cooperation. With this reversal of the balance of power between assisters and aid recipients, the party assistance organizations felt less able to dictate the terms of cooperation.

Finally, this brings us to the last potential cause behind the party assistance organizations' inability or unwillingness to tackle the issue of corruption associated with their local partner parties: the aid was unconditional. It was distributed indiscriminately (except to BiH nationalist parties, which received no aid); the political parties never had to 'earn' it. From the outset, party aid served its own purpose, and party assistance organizations depended on their local partner parties to continue providing the raison d'être for the continued funding of aid programmes. During our interviews, several staff members of party aid organizations tried to explain to me that building trust with their partners was of the utmost importance, arguing that it was a long-term and delicate process.[59] For this reason, the assisters felt that 'it was not their business to preach to parties against corruption'[60] because this would alienate their partners and make cooperation impossible.

---

58   Author interview with NDI staff member, Sarajevo, BiH, 18 June 2007.
59   Author interview with party aid organization staff members (KAS, NDI, IRI, FES) in Sarajevo, BiH and Prishtina, Kosovo, November 2007, May 2008, June 2009.
60   Author interview with NDI staff member in Prishtina, Kosovo, 26 November 2007.

10.7. Conclusion

Political corruption and clientelism are two of the key issues in BiH's and Kosovo's problematic post-conflict transitions. Permeating deep into state administration, the private sector and society at large, the political parties' patronage networks and unprosecuted corruption scandals have led to a widespread perception among citizens of BiH and Kosovo that their political elites are untouchable, i.e. immune to punishment and exempt from the rule of law. Because party development in both countries is heavily influenced by post-communist and post-conflict legacies, corruption is even more deeply entrenched in these societies. In Bosnia-Herzegovina, those willing to cooperate with the international community could do as they pleased, while those opposing the international administration's policies invited investigation. In Kosovo, the entire international community closed its eyes to the pervasiveness of organized crime infiltration into society and the sector's symbiotic relationship with political elites.

International administrations are found to have approached corruption in a half-hearted manner, never truly committing to fighting it. While they tried to remove nationalists from power in BiH, their activities failed to achieve the desired results. In their desire to keep the peace process going at any cost, they only prosecuted politicians who were obstructive to the reform process, leaving those who cooperated with the international efforts free to engage in corrupt activities. This sent the message to the people that some people were above the law. The situation was even worse in Kosovo, where international administrations coddled local warlords-turned-politicians and shielded them from investigation on corruption allegations. Finally, the international administrations in both countries never fought corruption within their own ranks, which only served to deepen the corruption problem in post-conflict BiH and Kosovo.

Party assistance organizations, despite having rather close contact with local political elites, were equally inept at addressing the issue of corruption. Closer examination of the potential causes behind this failure reveals that the organizations focused more on the form or technical aspects of political party organization rather than on content and the norms, values, attitudes and beliefs driving the politicians' behaviour. They did so partly out of ignorance of the local situation, but they also failed to recognize how deeply ingrained corruption and organized crime were in BiH and Kosovo. Next to this ignorance (or hubris?), the party assistance organizations also acted out of self-interest, choosing not to alienate their local partners (and thus eliminate their raison d'être) by lecturing them against corruption. Perhaps to ensure the continued funding of their assistance programmes, they opted to focus on 'safe' subjects such as increasing party membership, improving communication between headquarters and branches, and holding workshops on winning elections.

The post-conflict reconstruction and statebuilding work of the international community in BiH and Kosovo illustrates that ignoring corruption does not make it go away.

The extent of donations that disappeared into post-conflict reconstruction and state-building efforts is simply mindboggling: enormous sums ended up in the hands of those who were anything but beneficial for BiH's and Kosovo's democratic development. If post-conflict reconstructions are genuinely meant to build democratic societies, then the international community's intervening forces need to lead by example from the very beginning by embodying democratic values and norms. The international community still struggles with its response to various crises and conflicts in the world, and until a system is devised that rigorously promotes cooperation and accountability rather than allowing personal interests and misguided goodwill to prevail, corruption will continue to thwart statebuilding processes. This system must also stipulate checks on the organs charged with the oversight and governance of statebuilding and reconstruction activities. Similarly, until the international community acknowledges that they, too, have been a part of the problem rather than the solution, and until they decide to address the deeply ingrained corruption in BiH and Kosovo, these two countries will continue to suffer from the ills inherent in post-conflict democratization efforts.

Part III. Everyday Corruption in Russia

Elena Denisova-Schmidt

11. Informal Practices in Russia. State Influence on Foreign Companies Operating in Russia

11.1. Introduction

Before the current global economic crisis, Russia had a nine-year run of continuous rapid economic expansion (approximately 7% annually). It remains a very attractive market, presenting many promising investment opportunities with the potential for dynamic growth in sales and profits.

But despite its progress, Russia still clings to such informal Soviet-era practices as *blat*, bribes and double accounting. Transparency International ranked Russian corruption on a par with Cambodia, Kenya, and Papua New Guinea at 154th place in its 2010 index of 178 countries. Many Russian businesspeople continue to be influenced by their traditional culture, especially with respect to their management style, decision-making processes and performance.

Accordingly, foreign investors might face a number of significant challenges while working in Russia, because informal practices—i.e. the spoken and unspoken understandings that complement or contradict official procedures—often prevail over formal rules and laws. In this context, the primary aims of this chapter are to examine informal practices in modern Russia in the business environment and, based on these findings, to make recommendations on how foreign companies and individuals should operate in Russia.

Numerous in-depth interviews were conducted with academic and business representatives working closely with or for foreign companies operating in Russia, as well as with individuals involved in the 'technical' side of informal practices[1]. Due to the wealth of information provided by these interviews, this project could potentially increase the West's understanding of the Russian business environment considerably. It can also be read as a short practical guide for foreign investors.

11.2. Current State of Research

In each social community there are not only formal but also informal institutions in existence. Informal institutions visible to different degrees, but together with formal institutions, they influence the functions of a state and life in the state in gen-

---

1   The research was supported by the Kennan Institute of the Woodrow Wilson Center in 2008. Whenever possible, the data has been updated to reflect current practices.

eral. Informal institutions might include personal networks (Wang 2000[2]); corruption (Böröcz 2000[3]); clans and mafia (Lauth 2000[4], Collins 2002[5], Collins 2003[6]); *kompromat* (Ledeneva 2006[7]), *telefonnoe pravo*, or informal pressure from representatives of federal and regional authorities (Ledeneva 2006, 2008[8]); and legislative, judicial, and bureaucratic norms (Helmke/Levitsky 2004[9]). Informal institutions are 'socially shared rules, usually unwritten, that are created, communicated, and enforced outside of officially sanctioned channels' (Helmke/Levitsky 2004[10], p. 727).

The informal practices that shaped post-Soviet business such as *krugovaia poruka*, double accountancy and *blat* are explored by Ledeneva[11], Rahr[12], Vacroux[13] and have been described by Mi Lennhag in her chapter in this edited volume. More specific studies on corruption, have been conducted by Puffer/McCarthy[14], Roaf[15], Johnson/

2   Wang, Hongying: Informal institutions and foreign investment in China, in: Pacific Review, 2000, (vol. 13), no. 4, pp. 525–523.
3   Böröcz, Jószef: Informality Rules, in: East European Politics and Societies, 2000, (vol. 14), no. 2, pp. 348–380.
4   Lauth, Hans-Joachim: Informal Institutions and Democracy, in: Democratization, 2000, (vol. 7), no. 4, pp. 21–50.
5   Collins, Kathleen: Clans, Pacts and Politics in Central Asia, in: Journal of Democracy, 2002, (vol. 13), no. 3, pp. 137–152.
6   Collins, Kathleen: The Political Role of Clans in Central Asia, in: Comparative Politics, 2003, (vol. 35), no. 2, pp. 171–190.
7   Ledeneva, Alena: How Russia Really Works: The Informal Practices that Shaped Post-Soviet Politics and Business. Ithaca and London: Cornell University Press, 2006
8   Ledeneva, Alena: How Russia Really Works: The Informal Practices that Shaped Post-Soviet Politics and Business. Ithaca and London: Cornell University Press, 2006, Ledeneva, Alena: Telephone Justice in Russia, in: Post-Soviet Affairs 2008, (vol. 24) no. 4, pp. 324–350.
9   Helmke, Gretchen/ Levitsky, Steven: Informal Institutions ad Comparative Politics: A Research Agenda, in: Perspectives on Politics 2004, (vol. 2), no. 4, pp. 725–740.
10   Helmke, Gretchen/ Levitsky, Steven: Informal Institutions ad Comparative Politics: A Research Agenda, in: Perspectives on Politics 2004, (vol. 2), no. 4, p. 727.
11   Ledeneva, Alena: Russia's Economy of Favors: Blat, Networking and Informal Exchange, Cambridge and New York: Cambridge University Press, 1998; Ledeneva, Alena: How Russia Really Works: The Informal Practices that Shaped Post-Soviet Politics and Business, Ithaca and London: Cornell University Press, 2006; Ledeneva, Alena: From Russia with Blat: Can Informal Networks Help Modernize Russia?, in: Social Research 2009, (vol. 76), no. 1, pp. 257–288.
12   Rahr, Alexander: Russland gibt Gas. Die Rückkehr einer Weltmacht. München: Carl Hanser Verlag, 2008; Rahr, Alexander: Putin nach Putin. Das kapitalistische Russland am Beginn einer neuen Weltordnung, Wien: Universitas Verlag, 2009.
13   Vacroux, Alexandra: Formal and Informal Institutional Change: The Evolution of Pharmaceutical Regulation in Russia, 1991–2004, Ph.D. thesis, Boston: Harvard University, 2005.
14   Puffer, Sheila M./ McCarthy, Daniel J: Finding the Common Ground in Russian and American Business Ethics, in: California Management Review, 1995, (vol. 37), no. 2, pp. 29–42.
15   Roaf, James: Corruption in Russia, Washington DC: International Monetary Fund publications, 2000.

Kaufmann/McMillan/Woodruff[16], Cheloukhine/King[17]. The challenges that foreign companies might face in Russia were examined by Fey/Shekshnia[18]; country-based analyses on FDI and business activities in the Russian market were made from the Japanese perspective by Tokunaga[19], from the Japanese/Korean perspectives by Tomiyama[20] and from the Finnish perspective by Vahtra/Zashev[21].

Ledeneva[22] provides an excellent presentation of post-Soviet *tolkachi* ('pushers'), or people who 'push' for the company's interests by manipulating paperwork, networking with government officials, and 'thinking outside of their box in order to solve the problem'[23]. But she did not advise whether or not foreign companies operating in Russia need such *tolkachi* and, if so, how they should recruit them—and most importantly, how they should be trusted.

Johnson/Kaufmann/McMillan/Woodruff[24] not only describe corruption, but also estimate its size in Russia. By identifying common practices, Roaf[25] and Puffer/McCarthy[26] also indicate what is considered acceptable by Russians. Time is very crucial in working on projects covering the country, however. Some findings from 1995 and 2000 are virtually obsolete and need to be constantly updated.

16　Johnson, Simon/ Kaufmann, Daniel/ McMillan, John/ Woodruff, Christopher: Why Do Firms Hide? Bribes and Unofficial Activity after Communism, in: Journal of Public Economics, 2000, (vol. 76), no. 3, pp. 495–510.

17　Cheloukhine, Serguei/ King, Joseph: Corruption Networks as a Sphere of Investment Activities in Modern Russia, in: Communist and Post-Communist Studies, 2007, (vol. 40) no. 1, pp. 107–122.

18　Fey, Carl F./ Shekshnia, Stanislav: The Key Commandments For Doing Business in Russia, in: INSEAD Faculty & Research Working Paper, 2008, 16/EFE, Fey, Carl F./ Shekshnia, Stanislav: The Key Commandments For Doing Business in Russia, in: Organizational Dynamics, 2011 (vol. 40), no. 1, pp. 57–66.

19　Tokunaga, Masahiro: Delayed, but flourishing? Preliminary analysis of foreign direct investment of Japanese companies in Russia. Paper presented at VIII ICCEES World Congress, 26–31 July, 2010 Stockholm.

20　Tomiyama, Eiko: Entry and Marketing Strategies to Russian Market by Japanese, Korean Automobile Manufactures—Case Study of Entry to Russian market by Toyota, Hyundai & KIA Motor. Paper presented at VIII ICCEES World Congress, 26–31 July, 2010 Stockholm.

21　Vahtra, Peeter/ Zashev, Peter: Russian automotive manufacturing sector—an industry snapshot for foreign component manufacturers, in: Electronic Publications of the Pan-European Institute, 7, 2008; Vahtra, Peeter/ Zashev, Peter: Opportunities and strategies for Finnish companies in the Saint Petersburg and Leningrad region automobile cluster, in: Kymenlaakso University of Applied Sciences, Research and Report publication, 52, 2009.

22　Ledeneva, Alena: How Russia Really Works: The Informal Practices that Shaped Post-Soviet Politics and Business. Ithaca and London: Cornell University Press, 2006, pp. 164–189.

23　Ibid., p. 178

24　Johnson, Simon/ Kaufmann, Daniel/ McMillan, John/ Woodruff, Christopher: Why Do Firms Hide? Bribes and Unofficial Activity after Communism, in: Journal of Public Economics, 2000, (vol. 76), no. 3, pp. 495–510.

25　Roaf, James: Corruption in Russia. Washington DC: International Monetary Fund publications, 2000.

26　Puffer, Sheila M./ McCarthy, Daniel J: Finding the Common Ground in Russian and American Business Ethics, in: California Management Review, 1995, (vol. 37), no. 2, pp. 29–42.

Cheloukhine/King[27] conducted an impressive but very short examination of the Soviet roots of corruption and its transformation during the transitional period. The authors list the most corrupted spheres of the Russian economy, even specifying what can be achieved in one particular area. The researchers, however, did not give concrete recommendations for foreign companies on how to operate in Russia.

Holmes[28] claims that 'despite the significance of corruption … in Russia, the research and literature on [corruption] … has been less abundant in recent years than it was in the 1990s and at the start of the Putin era'. Holmes' statement concerning the 1990s is supported, for example, by significant studies in economic crime[29], corruption[30] and the informal economy (e.g. Kurkchiyan 2000, Radaev 2002)[31].

The books written by Rahr[32] might be considered 'pocket encyclopaedias' for understanding Russia. His monographs contain many examples of informal practices in modern Russia. Rahr rarely mentions his sources of information or methods of data collection, however, and some of his statements are questionable.

27   Cheloukhine, Serguei/ King, Joseph: Corruption Networks as a Sphere of Investment Activities in
      Modern Russia, in: Communist and Post-Communist Studies, 2007, (vol. 40), no. 1, pp. 107–122.
28   Holmes, Leslie: Corruption and Organized Crime in Putin's Russia, in: Europe-Asia Studies, 2008,
      (vol. 60), no. 6, pp. 1011–1031, here p. 1012.
29   Fituni, Leonid: Economic Crime in the Context of Transition to a Market Economy, in: Ledeneva,
      Alena/ Kurkchiyan, Marina (eds.): Economic Crime in Russia. London: Kluwer Law International,
      2000, pp. 17–30.
30   Ries, Nancy: Business, Taxes, and Corruption in Russia, in: Anthropology of East Europe Review,
      1999, (vol. 17), no. 1, pp. 59–62; Rose-Ackerman, Susan: Corruption and Government: Causes,
      Consequences and Reform, Cambridge: Cambridge University Press, 1999; Radaev, Vadim:
      Corruption and Violence in Russian Business in the Late 1990s, in: Ledeneva, Alena/ Kurkchiyan
      Marina (eds.): Economic Crime in Russia, London: Kluwer Law International, 2000, pp. 63–82;
      Pleines, Heiko: Large-Scale Corruption in the Russian Banking Sector, in: Ledeneva, Alena/
      Kurkchiyan, Marina (eds.): Economic Crime in Russia. London: Kluwer Law International, 2000,
      pp. 191–207; Pleines, Heiko: Corruption Networks in the Russian economy, in: Slovo (special
      issue), 2000, pp. 104–120; Pleines, Heiko: Korruption und organisierte Kriminalität, in: Höhmann,
      Hans-Hermann/ Schröder, Hans-Henning (eds.): Russland unter neuer Führung, Münster: Agenda
      Verlag, 2001, pp. 281–290; Pleines, Heiko: Korruptionsnetzwerke in der russischen Wirtschaft,
      in: Höhmann, Hans-Hermann (ed.): Kultur als Bestimmungsfaktor der Transformation im Osten
      Europas. Konzeptionelle Entwicklungen – Empirische Befunde. Bremen Edition: Temmen, 2001,
      pp. 141–156; Rahr, Alexander: Russland gibt Gas. Die Rückkehr einer Weltmacht. München: Carl
      Hanser Verlag, 2008; Rahr, Alexander: Putin nach Putin. Das kapitalistische Russland am Beginn
      einer einen Weltordnung. Wien: Universitas Verlag, 2009; Fey, Carl F./ Shekshnia, Stanislav: The
      Key Commandments For Doing Business in Russia, in: INSEAD Faculty & Research Working Paper,
      2008, 16/EFE.
31   Kurkchiyan, Marina: The Transformation of The Second Economy into the Informal Economy,
      in: Ledeneva, Alena/ Kurkchiyan, Marina (eds.): Economic Crime in Russia. London: Kluwer Law
      International, 2000, pp. 83–97; Radaev, Vadim: Corruption and Administrative Barriers for Russian
      Business, in: Kotkin, Stephen/ Sajo, Andras (eds.): Political Corruption in Transition: A Skeptic's
      Handbook. Budapest: Central European University Press, 2002, pp. 287–311.
32   Rahr, Alexander: Russland gibt Gas. Die Rückkehr einer Weltmacht, München: Carl Hanser Verlag,
      2008; Rahr, Alexander: Putin nach Putin. Das kapitalistische Russland am Beginn einer neuen
      Weltordnung, Wien: Universitas Verlag, 2009.

Though Fey/Shekshnia[33] provide their readers with the key commandments of doing business in Russia, including but not limited to some strategies on how to manage corruption in Russia in order to find a compromise between western ethical standards and Russian norms, both researchers present a very compact paper, and their study should have been supplemented with more concrete examples. The investigations by Tokunaga[34], Tomiyama[35], Vahtra/Zashev[36] are 'works in progress', but the studies' current results seem to be very promising and very close to the current research.

Several Russian and international country rankings and surveys also provide information on the Russian business climate and the role of informal practices and corruption. An overview is provided in the following table.

Table 11-1:   Country Rankings and Surveys

Study	Institution
International Sources	
Corruption Perception Index*	Transparency International
Worldwide Governance Indicators—Corruption control**	World Bank
Freedom House: Nations in Transit—Corruption Control***	Freedom House
Ease of Doing Business[†]	World Bank
Surveys on the Business Climate in Russia[††]	Deutsch-Russische Auslandshandelskammer
Survey on Russia Investment Destination 2006[†††]	The PBN Company
Business Environment and Enterprise Performance Survey (BEEPS)[‡]	EBRD and World Bank
Russian Sources	
Surveys on Corruption and Business Practices[‡‡]	The Levada-Center
Investigations of Corruption and Informal Practices in the Business Environment[‡‡‡]	The INDEM foundation
Russian Industrial Surveys[§]	Gaidar Institute

* *http://www.transparency.org/policy_research/surveys_indices/cpi, accessed 20 March 2011.*

33 Fey, Carl F./ Shekshnia, Stanislav: The Key Commandments For Doing Business in Russia, in: INSEAD Faculty & Research Working Paper, 2008, 16/EFE; Fey, Carl F./ Shekshnia, Stanislav: The Key Commandments For Doing Business in Russia, in: Organizational Dynamics, 2011 (vol. 40), no. 1, pp. 57–66.
34 Tokunaga, Masahiro: Delayed, but flourishing? Preliminary analysis of foreign direct investment of Japanese companies in Russia. Paper presented at VIII ICCEES World Congress, 26–31 July, 2010 Stockholm.
35 Tomiyama, Eiko: Entry and Marketing Strategies to Russian Market by Japanese, Korean Automobile Manufactures—Case Study of Entry to Russian market by Toyota, Hyundai & KIA Motor. Paper presented at VIII ICCEES World Congress, 26–31 July, 2010 Stockholm.
36 Vahtra, Peeter/ Zashev, Peter: Russian automotive manufacturing sector—an industry snapshot for foreign component manufacturers, in: Electronic Publications of the Pan-European Institute, 7, 2008; Vahtra, Peeter/ Zashev, Peter: Opportunities and strategies for Finnish companies in the Saint Petersburg and Leningrad region automobile cluster, in: Kymenlaakso University of Applied Sciences, Research and Report publication, 52, 2009.

** *http://info.worldbank.org/governance/wgi/index.asp, accessed 20 March 2011.*
*** *http://freedomhouse.org, accessed 20 March 2011.*
† *http://www.doingbusiness.org/economyrankings/, accessed 20 March 2011.*
†† *http://russland.ahk.de/publikationen/umfragen/konjunkturumfrage-dez-2009/, accessed 18 August 2010*
††† *http://www.pbnco.com/eng/news/presentation.php, accessed 17 January 2008.*
‡ *http://www.ebrd.com/pages/research/analysis/surveys/beeps.shtml, accessed 20 March 2011.*
‡‡ *http://www.levada.ru, accessed 20 March 2011.*
‡‡‡ *http://www.anti-corr.ru, accessed 20 March 2011.*
§ *http://www.iep.ru/index.php?option=com_bibiet&Itemid=50&catid=121&lang=ru&task=showallbib, accessed 20 March 2011.*

11.3. Research Design

Informal practices (spoken and unspoken understandings that complement official procedures) often balance formal rules (written, official regulation), especially in transition countries such as Russia. For this reason, empirical work yields valuable results both for specialists in the areas of Russian studies and informal networks and for practitioners.

I conducted semi-structured in-depth interviews with business representatives and other experts working closely with or for foreign companies operating in Russia, which provided much more detailed and in-depth information than that which is available through other data collection techniques—this is very important when examining such delicate topics. Moreover, the atmosphere of an in-depth interview, which is similar to, yet distinct from, everyday conversation, allows the collection of insights and perspectives that the respondents might reveal unconsciously, for example, the scope, context and roots of informal practices[37].

As the subject of informal practices is a very delicate topic, most of my interview partners did not wish to be cited. However, most of the information we discussed pertained to very famous cases in Russia and I found enough reliable sources in the mass media to validate the statements of my interview partners. In my paper, I do not cite my interview partners; I cite only major newspapers and other documents[38].

---

37   Johnson, John M.: In-Depth Interviewing, in: Gubrium, Jaber F./ Holstein, James A. (eds.) Handbook of Interview Research: Context & Method, London: SAGE, 2002, pp. 103-119; Lamnek, Siegfried: Qualitative Sozialforschung, Lehrbuch, Weinheim, Basel: Beltz Verlag, 2005; Seidmann, Irving: Interviewing as Qualitative Research: a Guide for Researchers in Education and the Social Science (3rd ed.), New York: Teachers College Press, 2006; Kvale, Steinar/ Brinkmann, Svend: Interviews: Learning the Craft of Qualitative Research interviewing. (2nd ed.). Thousand Oaks: Sage, 2009; Myers, Michael D..: Qualitative Research in Business & Management, London: Sage, 2009; Silverman, David: Doing Qualitative Research: a Practical Handbook (3rd ed.), Los Angeles: Sage, 2010.

38   For a similar approach see: Adachi, Yuko: Building Big Business in Russia: The Impact of Informal Corporate Governance Practices, London: Routledge, 2010.

11.4. Intellectual Property

Intellectual property protection has a long way to go in Russia. How do current practices in this arena affect foreign companies?

11.4.1. Trademark Piracy

International trademarks must be registered *in* Russia and renewed every ten years. If they are not used in commerce within a certain time frame (three years), they are subject to cancellation by Rospatent.[39]

Smelling an opportunity, Moscow lawyer Sergei A. Zuykov exploited loopholes in Russian legislation to sell foreign companies their own trademarks so that they could operate in Russia legally:

> Kodak, Forbes and Audi have all been targets of [Mr. Zuykov's ambushes] [...]. Zuykov said that in 2001, Audi paid him 25,000 USD for five brand names, including the Lamborghini Diablo. [...]
> Starbucks registered its trademark in Russia in 1997 but did not open any coffee shops here. In 2002 Mr. Zuykov filed to cancel the chain's trademark because it had not been used in commerce and registered it in the name of a Moscow company that he represents as a lawyer. [...][40]

Starbucks negotiated this issue for three long years. The company eventually won the legal proceedings and opened its first coffee house on Russian soil in Khimki (Moscow Region) in autumn 2007.

One of Starbucks' successful strategies was to establish and/or activate personal contacts with some well-known, well-connected decision-makers. The firm requested the help of US Secretary of Commerce Carlos M. Gutierrez, who took up Starbucks' cause in the IPR proceedings with Russian officials, and Arcadi Volski, at that time the president of the Russian Union of Industrialists and Entrepreneurs, who assisted Starbucks by calling the Russian Public Prosecutor's Office. In addition, Starbucks was lucky with the timing: in fall 2005, Russia applied to join the WTO, and the Starbucks case was sufficiently high profile to force Russia to address the coffee empire's grievances so as not to jeopardize its bid for membership.[41]

---

39   The Russian Federal Service for Intellectual Property, Patents, and Trademarks.
40   Kramer, Andrew: He Doesn't Make Coffee, but He Controls 'Starbucks' in Russia, in: The New York Times, 12 October 2005.
41   Kramer, Andrew: After Long Dispute, a Russian Starbucks, in: The New York Times, 7 September 2007.

11.4.2. Copyright Violations

Russians generally have a different concept of the term 'plagiarism': *Some Russians even think that copyrighted materials are part of the public domain, like the Bible: Something everyone knows about.*[42]

As a prime example, the research fellows at the Brookings Institute found that key sections of Vladimir Putin's Ph.D. thesis[43] 'were copied either word for word or with minute alterations from a management study, *Strategic Planning and Policy*, written by US professors William King and David Cleland'.[44]

I do not wish to make any assumptions on whether Putin wrote his dissertation by himself or if he asked somebody to do it, but this example shows a very common tendency for many academic papers written in Russia and other Post-Soviet Republics: the author proceeded from his/her assumption, that he/she is describing facts very well known by everyone working in a particular area, hence he/she 'forgets' to mention sources. This influences many areas of life in Russia.

Some Russian entrepreneurs might take 'inspiration' from well-established concepts. So, the Russian cosmetics chain *Dlia dushi i dusha* look very similar to the British cosmetics chain 'The Body Shop' (now under the L'Oreal brand) or the Russian consumer electronics chain *El'dorado* seems to be a subsidiary of the German 'Media Markt' (The Metro Group) because of the merchandising, the colours used, and even the logo—however, these are two different retailers[45].

Some Russians might also consider the appropriation of copyrighted materials to be a form of the 'learning-by-doing' process. Some Russian professional musicians are convinced that one can learn how to write a song simply by copying someone else's song. However, songwriting requires additional professional skills, for example musical notation and lyric writing.

This lax attitude toward copyrighted materials has dire consequences for foreign companies operating in Russia: pirated films, videos, sound recordings, books, and computer software are particularly rampant in Russia. In January 2006, German

---

42   Denisova-Schmidt, Elena: Cross-Cultural Communication in Russia. Current Trends in the Establishment of a Discipline. In: Haunreiter, Diego (ed.): *Kommunikation in Wirtschaft, Recht und Gesellschaft*. 5. Band der Schriftenreihe der Assistierenden der Universität St. Gallen (HSG), Bern: Stämpfli Verlag, 2010, pp. 123–140.

43   Putin, Vladimir: Strategicheskoye planirovaniye vosproizvodstva minera'lno-syr'yevoy bazy regiona v usloviyakh formirovaniya rynochnykh otnosheniy (Engl.: The Strategic Planning of the Reproduction of the Mineral Raw Materials Base of the Region under Conditions of the Formation of Market Relationships), State Mining Institute, St Petersburg, Russia, 1997.

44   Allen-Mills, Tony: Putin accused of plagiarizing his PhD thesis, in: The Sunday Times, 26 March 2006.

45   Seidel, Hagen: Russisches Eldorado, in: Welt Online, 25 August 2006, http://www.welt.de/print-welt/article147918/Russisches_Eldorado.html, accessed 20 March 2011.

Gref, at that time Economic Development and Trade Minister, put the value of pirated products in Russia at USD 4–6 billion per year[46].

11.4.3. Know-How 'Transfer'

According to the Russian Ministry of Energy and Industry, the longer-term goal of the United Aviation Building Corporation (UAC) is 'to become one of the world's leading players, to reach a minimum return of 6 billion USD and, by 2015, to match the sales volume of Airbus, Boeing, Bombardier and Embraer'[47].

However, the implementation of these ambitious plans is hampered by a shortage of (young) qualified staff. Some potential solutions and options have been discussed in the specialized literature. One suggestion is to create and update a database of potential employees and to follow closely the career of each candidate. In cases of emergency, these candidates could be contacted, invited, or even forced to work for the state[48]. Speaking about cooperation with EADS, President Putin made his position clear: 'If Airbus refuses to support modernizing the Russian national aerospace industry voluntarily, we will force it to do so'[49].

11.4.4. Recommendations for Foreign Companies

1. Before entering the Russian market, foreign companies should ensure the legal status of their own brands in Russia with Rospatent; otherwise, they could spend a lot of time and financial resources in Russian courts. Moreover, foreign firms should remember that the 'decisions of many Russian courts in commercial disputes are very susceptible to financial, political and other improper influence'[50].
2. If Russian employees working for foreign companies in Russia are recruited by the state, foreign investors could experience losses incurred through:
    a) costs for the education and development of these employees and
    b) costs resulting from infringements of intellectual property.
3. IPR in industry may be an important issue in Russia in the future.

---

46 Interfax, 31 January 2006, cited from Bush, Keith 2008: Russian Economic Survey, Washington D.C.: U.S.-Russia Business Council, January 2008.

47 Borodin, Vladislav: Russia. Aerospace and Defense. Russian Market Overview, The U.S. Commercial Service, U.S. Department of Commerce, 2006, p. 2

48 Isayev, Alexander: Vysshaya shkola perestroyki, in: Priamye investitsii, 2006 (vol. 50), no. 6, pp. 10–14.

49 Rahr, Alexander: Russland gibt Gas. Die Rückkehr einer Weltmacht, München: Carl Hanser Verlag, 2008, p. 17.

50 cf. Survey on Russia Investment Destination 2006, The PBN Company, http://www.pbnco.com/eng/news/presentation.php, accessed 17 January 2008.

11.5. Business vs. International Policy

The Russian government tends to use various business tools to regulate conflicts in international policy.

11.5.1.   Polish Exports to Russia

In November 2005, the Russian Ministry of Agriculture temporarily banned all Polish crop and cattle exports to Russia. The official reason was that the goods did not comply with sanitary standards. The unofficial reason is more likely that Poland opposes construction of the Nord Stream gas pipeline from Russia to Germany through the Baltic Sea—or Poland's active role in the Orange revolution in Ukraine. Losses for the Polish side: Polish agricultural exports to Russia were worth 347 million Euros annually prior to the ban.[51] Losses for the Russian side: in retaliation, Poland vetoed the opening of negotiations concerning Russian membership in the OECD and the agreement on strategic cooperation between the EU and Russia.

The ban on Polish meat exports was lifted in December 2007. The Polish veto on negotiations concerning Russian membership in the OECD was lifted in the same month. As soon as the Polish side was assured that Polish meat would reach Russian customers, they lifted the veto on negotiations about strategic cooperation between the EU and Russia[52].

11.5.2.   Georgian and Moldovan Wine Exports to Russia

In the spring of 2006, Rospotrebnadzor[53] prohibited Moldova and Georgia from exporting wine to Russia. As in the Polish agricultural ban, the official reason was that the goods did not comply with sanitary standards. The unofficial reason behind the ban on Moldovan wine was most likely to exert pressure on Vladimir Voronin, the Moldovan president, over his position on Transdniestrian independence[54] and possible cooperation with NATO. The unofficial reasons behind the ban on Georgian wine were similar: to rein in Mikhail Sakashvilli, the Georgian president, over his stance on South Ossetian and Abkhazian independence and to 'punish' him for his cooperation with NATO.

---

51   Vyse, Leah: Poland livid over Russia export ban, in: http://www.cee-foodindustry.com/, 13 December 2005.

52   Timofejchev, Aleksei: S chem priedet v Moskvu pol'skii prem'er?, in: BBCRussian.com, 7 February 2008.

53   The Russian Trade and Sanitary Inspection Authority.

54   Russia does not look kindly on the establishment of independent states. Russia did not support (and still does not recognize) the independence of Kosovo. The Russian government argued that Kosovan statehood would create a precedent and encourage other regions to declare independence, for example South Ossetia and Abkhazia, which became independent in August 2008.

The losses for Moldova and Georgia were substantial. Both countries have long traditions of exporting their products to Russia; correspondingly, the Russian market accounts for 80% of their exports. Russian consumers have very strong brand awareness and a long tradition of drinking Moldovan and Georgian wines. Due to the absence of Moldovan and Georgian products from the market for several months in 2006, wines from Europe, Australia, and New Zealand found new popularity among Russian consumers[55]. Moldovan and Georgian wine producers will have to work hard to win back Russian consumers. The ban on Moldovan imports was lifted in December 2007 after Moldova backed down from NATO involvement[56]. To date, the ban on Georgian imports has not been lifted[57].

11.5.3. Restriction of British Council Activities in Russia

In December 2006, the regional offices of the British Council were closed down by Russia's Ministry of Foreign Affairs. The official explanation was that the British cultural body had failed to comply with international and Russian regulations and had a questionable tax status. The unofficial reasons most likely had to do with the British request for the extradition of Andrei Lugovoi, the main suspect in the poisoning of Alexander Litvinenko in London. Russian officials refused to comply on the grounds of the Russian Constitution, which forbids the extradition of Russian citizens to foreign states[58]. Another unofficial reason for the closing of the British Council offices was very likely Britain's refusal to hand over Boris Berezovsky, a billionaire tycoon and outspoken critic of the Putin government, and Akhmed Zakayev, a former Chechen rebel wanted in Russia on charges of terrorism, to Moscow.

11.5.4. Estonia

In April 2007, the Red Army War Memorial was removed from the centre of the Estonian capital, Tallinn, to a military cemetery. While Estonian officials called the monument part of 'the internal affairs of Estonia'[59] and a 'symbol of a hated foreign occupation'[60], Russian officials condemned the removal as an act of 'blasphemy'. Russian Foreign

---

55 Doing Business in Russia: A Country Commercial Guide for U.S. Companies, US Commercial Service, United States of America Department of Commerce, 2007.

56 According to Vladimir Voronin, an oral agreement was concluded between Kishinev and Moscow, stipulating that Moldova would not apply for NATO membership. The Russian side denies this (cf. Kishinev obmenyayet NATO na Prednestrov'ye?, in: BBCRussian.com, 11 March 2008).

57 The last military conflict between Georgia and Russia certainly did not foster economic cooperation between the two countries.

58 Russia has carried out the extradition of Russian citizens to foreign states before, for example the extradition of Murad Garabayev to Turkmenistan.

59 Estonia memorial move 'blasphemy', in: BBC NEWS, 27 April 2007.

60 A cyber-riot. Estonia has faced down Russian rioters. But its websites are still under attack, in: The Economist, 10 May 2007.

Minister Sergei Lavrov promised to 'take serious steps'[61] against Estonia. Although the memorial was the official reason for his threat, the unofficial motives behind Russian sanctions against Estonia were more likely as follows:

1. Along with Poland, Estonia opposes the construction of the Nord Stream gas pipeline from Russia to Germany through the Baltic Sea[62].
2. The moment was ripe for President Putin to 'gain mileage' in his official successor's election campaign.

The consequences for business were not trivial:

- Several supermarket chains in the Moscow region (Seventh Continent, Samokhval and Kopeika) and some retail stores throughout Russia removed Estonian goods from their shelves.
- The Russian market was closed to Kalev, Estonia's leading confectionery maker. Its monthly sales to Russia had ranged from 190,000 to 250,000 Euros[63].
- Passenger rail services between Tallinn and St Petersburg were cut[64].
- Estonia's state (and some private) websites were the victims of cyber assaults and were disrupted for several weeks. Estonia's defence ministry compared the attacks to those initiated against America on 11 September 2001[65]. If a NATO member state is attacked with a missile, it is considered an act of war[66]; at the moment, there is no such legislation covering 'cyber-attacks', however.

Estonian businessmen are not especially welcome in Russia and they have to use lawyers or engage in informal practices to do business there. As a result of the tensions, some Russian investors ended up leaving Estonia; for example, Sergei Matvienko, general director of ZAO 'WTB-Capital' and the son of the governor of St Petersburg, Valentina Matvienko, sold his shares in this company.

11.5.5. Recommendations for Foreign Companies

The Russian government occasionally uses business instruments to regulate conflicts in international policy. Though Russian officials usually deny this, the two main concerns of the Russian government in the area of international policy seem to be:

- the presence of NATO member countries on the Russian border, and
- Russia's continuing status as a(n) (energy) superpower in the world.

---

61 Ibid.
62 Russia is not the only party annoyed by this opposition—Germany is, too. The internal problems within the European Union and discussions on whether or not the European Union should speak with one voice exceed the scope of this paper, however.
63 Dmitriyev, Sergei: Russian Retailers Boycott Estonian Goods, in: The Moscow News, no. 18, 2007.
64 A cyber-riot. Estonia has faced down Russian rioters. But its websites are still under attack, in: The Economist, 10 May 2007.
65 Ibid.
66 Article 5 of the NATO Charter.

Other countries not directly involved in a given conflict could nevertheless suffer as well; for example, the perennial gas conflicts between Ukraine and Russia can interrupt the supply of gas to Western Europe.

11.6. Corruption

Corruption is one of the main complaints of foreign companies operating in Russia. The tax authorities (32%), traffic police (28%), courts and judicial authorities (21%), customs officials (21%), and federal and regional licence authorities (21%) are the authorities most frequently named as being engaged in corruption[67].

Cheloukhine[68] identifies 'the most corrupted spheres of the Russian economy, starting with the most corrupt:
- licenses and quotas on exports (oil, metals, energy resources);
- Ministry of Finance tax offsets;
- social sphere (service of budgetary accounts);
- barter and natural offset of debts in regions (plundered 30–40% of total debts);
- railway transportation (the cost of transporting the same cargo can differ significantly, depending on the arrangements made with the local public official);
- agricultural sphere (preferential financing, write-off of debts).'

Corruption has a very long tradition in Russia; many Russians therefore have difficulty differentiating between a 'present' and a 'bribe'[69]. One Russian businessman describing the current situation in Russia observed, 'It used to be called bribery; now it is just called business'[70]. Some of the various forms of corruption in Russia will be discussed next.

---

67 cf. Survey on Russia Investment Destination 2006, The PBN Company, http://www.pbnco.com/eng/news/presentation.php, accessed 17 January 2008.
68 Cheloukhine, Serguei/ King, Joseph: Corruption networks as a sphere of investment activities in modern Russia, in: Communist and Post-Communist Studies, March 2007 (vol. 40), no. 1, pp. 107–122.
69 Ertelt-Vieth, Astrid/ Denisova-Schmidt, Elena: Kulturbedingte Unterschiede und Verstehensprobleme (»Lakunen«) zwischen russischen und deutschen Wissenschaftlern, in: Wolff, Armin/ Zollner, Reinhold (eds.): Umbrüche, Regensburg, 2006, pp. 185–206 and Ertelt-Vieth, Astrid/ Denisova-Schmidt, Elena: Kulturbedingte Unterschiede und Verstehensprobleme zwischen russischen und deutschen Wissenschaftlern, in: Bürgel, Matthias/ Umland, Andreas (eds.): Geistes- und sozialwissenschaftliche Hochschullehre in Osteuropa IV. Chancen und Hindernisse internationaler Bildungskooperation, Frankfurt a.M.: Peter Lang, 2009, pp. 244–263; Ledeneva, Alena: From Russia with *Blat*: Can Informal Networks Help Modernize Russia?, in: Social Research, 2009, (vol. 76), no. 1, pp. 257–288.
70 Myers, Steven Lee: Pervasive Corruption in Russia Is 'Just Called Business', in: New York Times, 13 August 2005.

11.6.1.   Express Application

Effective bureaucratic structures are still in development in Russia; for example, obtaining a business licence in Russia requires much more than the world average of 18 procedures and 218 days[71]. However, the process can be expedited by 'making gifts' to decision-makers. Excessive regulations for visas and work permits for foreign employees can be also alleviated by 'bringing presents' to local government officials.

Foreign companies are thus obliged to accept this informal practice of doing business in Russia and even participate in it if they wish to operate more effectively. Nevertheless, Russian authorities sometimes cross the line: when Transparency International applied to register its branch in 2000, an official in the Justice Ministry solicited a 300 USD 'fee' to correct supposed problems in the application[72].

11.6.2.   'Social Responsibility'

Russian local and federal officials try to convince foreign companies of the importance of social responsibility and often force them to invest in infrastructure, such as building roads, kindergartens, and hospitals.

11.6.2.1. IKEA in Russia[73]

Located in Khimki, Moscow Region, MEGA-2, an IKEA project, is the biggest mall in Europe. The grand opening was put off for two weeks because local government officials did not issue a permit[74]. The official reason was 'technical incompleteness of a shopping centre building'. The unofficial reason was the company's lack of 'social responsibility'. As soon as additional funds for the local children's sport activities hall were assured (one million USD), the grand opening was allowed to take place[75].

11.6.2.2. Lufthansa Cargo

In late 2007, Russian federal officials banned Lufthansa Cargo flights over its territory, disrupting service on 49 connections per week from Frankfurt to Astana, Kazakhstan.

---

71   cf. Index of Economic Freedom 2010. Russia, the Heritage Foundation, http://www.heritage.org/index/Country/Russia

72   Myers, Steven Lee: Pervasive Corruption in Russia Is 'Just Called Business', in: New York Times, 13 August 2005.

73   IKEA is facing many difficulties in its expansion into several Russian cities. For example, in Novosibirsk, IKEA spent two years trying to sign an agreement about leasing property to build a shopping centre. For four years, the administration in Yekaterinburg refused to support the opening of a supermarket, trying to force IKEA to invest money in some 'voluntary funds'.

74   Russian: 'Akt gosudarstvennoy priemki zaversheniya stroitel'stva ob''ekta'; English: 'state acceptance document about completion of building project'.

75   Valiullina, Elvira/ Valiullin, Radik: Managerwissen Kompakt, Russland, München, Wien: Carl Hanser Verlag, 2006.

The official reason for the ban was a 'disagreement with Russia about the royalties it charges for flights' above its territory. The unofficial reason behind the ban concerned investments for a new airport either in Krasnoyarsk or Novosibirsk[76]. Lufthansa Cargo officials called Russian demands 'blackmail' and refused to comply. In February 2008, Russian tax authorities froze Lufthansa's bank accounts (seven million USD) 'due to non-payment of turnover taxes, mainly the unified social tax and the roads usage tax'[77].

11.6.3. Personal Relationships

It is very important for anyone wishing to do business in Russia to establish and cultivate social networks with Russian decision-makers.

11.6.3.1. Two Retail Companies

In 1999, two West European companies were both trying to open new supermarkets in Moscow and the Moscow Region. The first company obtained permission to build from the Moscow city and regional governments rather quickly, while the second was forced to wait for almost two years. Why did this happen? The first had cooperated very closely with a Russian consulting agency, while the second had gone it alone. This consulting agency was very well connected to the Moscow city and regional governments and seems to have put these connections to very good use. The second retail company started its expansion in Moscow and the Moscow Region two years after the first retail company[78].

11.6.4. Recommendations for Foreign Companies

The Russian bureaucratic system is still evolving and modernization is progressing very slowly. Foreign companies therefore sometimes feel the need to make unofficial payments in order to speed up legal procedures. Unfortunately, Russian authorities sometimes abuse their power.

Entering and then operating in the Russian market can give rise to additional, unpredictable costs ranging from 1% to 15% of an entire project. According to other sources, such as Aslund (2008), kickback rates in Russia may range from 20% to 50%. Foreign companies refusing to participate in social projects could be 'punished' by legal means; for example, a western company, the major foreign investor in one Russian

---

76 Kazim, Hasnain: Russland erpresst Lufthansa, in: SPIEGEL ONLINE, 1 November 2007.
77 Pleshanova, Olga/ Ekimovsky, Alexei/ Egikyan, Seda: Lufthansa Taxed by Russia, in: Kommersant, 22 February 2008.
78 Valiullina, Elvira/ Valiullin, Radik: Managerwissen Kompakt. Russland, München, Wien: Carl Hanser Verlag, 2006.

region, faced numerous inspections after its refusal to participate in a certain social project. These inspections made life very difficult for the company.

Cooperation with local partners is certainly a must. Russian partners can, for example, take responsibility for all 'difficult contacts' with the Russian authorities. These contacts should be chosen carefully, however. For example, one business partner for the American sandwich chain Subway was recommended by the Yeltsin administration. A personal recommendation from the Kremlin is usually the best recommendation possible, but it did not help in this case—on the contrary, the American partners have struggled for almost 10 years to assert control over their own restaurants[79].

Many anti-corruption measures have recently been introduced, including the approval of the UN Convention against Corruption and the OECD Anti-Bribery Convention. Certain actors have also been replaced, such as the head of the Customs Service and several government officials (e.g. Vladimir Nikolaev, the mayor of Vladivostok) and various businessmen (Sergei Zuev, the head of Russia's largest furniture retailer, 'Tri kita' and 'Grand', and Vladimir Nekrasov, the head of Russia's largest cosmetic retailer, 'Arbat-Prestige') have been arrested. These are certainly the most significant anti-corruption campaigns to date[80]. Corruption has a very long tradition in Russia, however, and these actions amount to little more than 'Potemkin villages'.

11.7. Interpretation of Laws

11.7.1. Overlap or Conflict of Russian Laws

'Russian commercial regulations are contained in thousands of presidential, governmental and ministerial decrees. Often, these decrees and laws overlap or conflict'[81]. Law No. 160-FG of 09-July-1999 also states: 'Foreign investors have the same rights and obligations as the domestic ones have'[82]. In reality, however, foreign companies operating in Russia are subject to discrimination and many restrictions:

- Russian language: heads of foreign banks operating in Russia are required to be fluent in the Russian language.

- Individual income tax: non-residents are required to pay 30%, while residents pay only 13%. However, it is still one of the lowest rates in the world, and many indi-

---

79   Garcia, Shelley: Subway Restaurants, in: San Fernando Valley Business Journal, 19 July 2004.
80   Bush, Keith: Russian Economic Survey, Washington D.C.: U.S.-Russia Business Council, January 2008.
81   Doing Business in Russia. A Country Commercial Guide for U.S. Companies, US Commercial Service, United States of America Department of Commerce, 2007.
82   Valiullina, Elvira/ Valiullin, Radik: Managerwissen Kompakt. Russland, München, Wien: Carl Hanser Verlag, 2006.

viduals (depending on their contracts in Russia and countries of residence) are able to have their taxes refunded.

- The purchase of agricultural land by foreigners is prohibited.
- The purchase of land close to federal borders and in areas that the President determines as critical to national security is restricted for foreigners.
- Foreign direct investments are limited in certain sectors:[83] in the aerospace industry, foreign ownership is limited to 49% of an enterprise with Presidential approval, otherwise it is only 25%. In the insurance sector, foreign ownership of a firm is limited to 35%.

11.7.2. Constantly Changing Russian Laws

An additional obstacle for many foreign companies operating in Russia is the fact that the laws are constantly changing:

11.7.2.1. Production-Sharing Agreement (PSA)

The PSA provision was signed into law in December 1995. A PSA establishes the share of revenue or output between the host government and foreign investors. At the time the law was signed, it referred to three existing projects: Sakhalin I (ExxonMobil, Sodeco, Rosneft and ONGC), Sakhalin II (Shell, Mitsui and Mitsubishi) and the Timan Pechora project (TotalFinaElf and Norsk Hydro).

After the PSA law was approved, all necessary normative acts were delayed. The Russian side has made many attempts to rewrite this law and impose additional requirements. For instance, one amendment stipulates that 70% of equipment and services have to be supplied by Russian firms and 80% of the manpower engaged has to be Russian (1999). In another manoeuvre to thwart the legislation, it was claimed that as many as 1,700 separate approvals are needed to launch a PSA (2000).

In the end, the Russian government was not very successful with these threats; they therefore came up with a different solution involving Russia's licensing and environmental authorities. The state claimed that the above-mentioned Sakhalin II project would damage the ecosystem. In December 2006, the project was transferred to a new major shareholder, Gazprom. Gazprom took the issue of the ecological problems very seriously and, in 2008, was even recognized for its activities in the protection of the Western Gray Whale population by Yuri Trutnev, the Russian National Resources Minister.

---

83   For more information, see section 11.8. on 'Strategic Sectors'.

11.7.3. Selective Interpretation of Russian Laws

Foreign companies operating in Russia also complain about the 'selective interpretation of laws'[84]. Speaking about the Lugovoi case, Tony Brenton, then the British ambassador to Russia, mentioned that the Russian Constitution could be interpreted differently depending on circumstances:

> [The Russian Constitution] states that economic activities aimed at monopolization are prohibited (Article 34); [...] that Duma [the Russian Parliament] deputies cannot engage in paid work (Article 97) [85].

The Kremlin has indeed tended to establish monopolies over the past few years,[86] and Duma deputies are very successful in their paid activities outside of parliament; many examples are in direct violation of the Constitution.

11.7.4. Recommendations for Foreign Companies

Russian laws not only overlap and conflict with each other, but they may be enforced selectively. As noted in The Economist,

> ... if the [Russian] government with its high-profile spies and statists wants to change the ownership of an enterprise operating in a so-called strategic sector, it will find a way around any laws[87].

11.8. Strategic Sectors

The Heritage Foundation has stated that 'State involvement in the economy is increasing through large state-controlled enterprises in energy, shipping, shipbuilding and aerospace known as 'national champions''[88]:

* Aerospace sector: the United Aviation Building Corporation (UAC) brings together about 20 major Russian aviation enterprises;
* Automotive sector: the acquisition of AvtoVAZ by Rosoboronexport, OMZ by Gazprom or Silovye Mashiny by United Energy Systems;
* Metallurgical sector: the fusion of two large aluminium enterprises RusAl and SuAl, now working under the name RusAl (Russkii Aluminii);

---

84 cf. Survey on Russia Investment Destination 2006, The PBN Company, http://www.pbnco.com/eng/news/presentation.php, accessed 17 January 2008.

85 British Ambassador: 'Not an Everyday Incident'. Tony Brenton speaks about the 'Lugovoi case', in: Kommersant, no. 128 (3704), 23 July 2007.

86 For more information, see section 11.8. on 'Strategic Sectors'.

87 Sketching the limits for foreign investors. A new draft law has been approved, restricting foreign investment in Russia's strategic sectors, Business Eastern Europe, 5 February 2007, The Economist Intelligence Unit Limited 2007.

88 cf. Index of Economic Freedom 2008. Russia, the Heritage Foundation, http://www.heritage.org/index/country.cfm?id=Russia, accessed 17 January 2008.

- Oil sector: the acquisition of Severnaya Neft by Rosneft; the purchase of Sibneft by Gazprom.

In 2008, the Russian government approved a law that restricts foreign investment in 42 sectors of the Russian economy. On the one hand, this could help clarify the rules for many foreign companies; nevertheless, it could also precipitate renationalization in Russia[89]. Foreign companies working in strategic sectors could very likely suffer under this new law.

11.8.1. Recommendations for Foreign Companies

The establishment of 'national champions' in Russia is counterproductive for the country's economic development and would not 'attract' foreign investors. The new strategic law might indeed clarify the rules for many foreign companies, but it has not provided 'transparency in decision-making'[90]. Furthermore, it is not clear whether the business activities of foreign suppliers working for Russian strategic sectors are subject to this law or not.

Russian companies operating abroad could suffer retaliation for Russian protectionism. For example, the Russian government refused to sell Silovye Mashiny to the German company Siemens on the grounds that the engineering firm was in a 'strategic sector'; in response, the German government prevented the sale of Deutsche Bahn AG to Rossiiskie Zheleznye Dorogi (RZD) and Deutsche Telekom to Sistema, citing that these companies were in 'strategic sectors' as well[91].

11.9. General conclusions

During the last few years, the Russian government has regularly interfered in the business activities of foreign companies operating in Russia. This influence may be direct or indirect, but it is always technically legal. However, Russian laws seem to be enforced selectively and decision-making processes are still not transparent. This development will probably deter some foreign investors in the future and Russian companies operating abroad could suffer from retaliation by foreign governments.

Nevertheless, Russia is still a very attractive market. Before entering this market, though, a foreign company should:

---

89 Aslund, Anders: US-Russia Economic Relationship. Implications of the Yukos Affair, Testimony before the Committee on Financial Services, Subcommittee on Domestic and International Monetary Policy, Trade, and Technology, US House of Representatives, October 17, 2007, http://www.iie.com/publications/papers/paper.cfm?ResearchID=844

90 Sketching the limits for foreign investors. A new draft law has been approved, restricting foreign investment in Russia's strategic sectors. Business Eastern Europe, 5 February 2007, The Economist Intelligence Unit Limited 2007.

91 Rahr, Alexander: Russland gibt Gas. Die Rückkehr einer Weltmacht, München: Carl Hanser Verlag, 2008.

- do its homework and study the legal framework for operating in Russia.
- be aware of the loose definition of the term 'plagiarism' in Russia. Membership in the WTO would provide the framework for dealing with this issue, but some educational programs/campaigns would be needed in order to begin to alter the cultural attitude towards intellectual property rights in Russian minds.
- establish and cultivate personal relationships with Russian decision-makers.
- decide on a strategy for dealing with corruption.

US companies operating in Russia are subject to the FCPA (Foreign Corrupt Practices Act) of 1977, which prohibits them from engaging in informal practices while operating abroad; there is similar legislation for European companies.

Foreign businesses should be aware, however, of the following informal practices commonly used in Russia:

- (un-)official payments to expedite applications;
- gift-giving to decision-makers;
- pressure to participate in 'social responsibility' projects/activities;
- cooperation with local partners—corruption can be 'outsourced'.

Foreign companies should have a very flexible budget (sometimes up to two times the estimated costs) and allow enough time for dealing with the Russian bureaucracy. To survive, they need to be able to handle these common ways of doing business in Russia. If they follow these practices, their patience might be rewarded in the form of attractive sales markets and high profits.[92]

---

92   Denisova-Schmidt, Elena: Geschäftspartner Russland. Erfahrungen mit einem europäischen Land der besonderen Art. In: Tanner, Anne-Cathrine/ Siebeneck, Claudia/ Brändli, Beat (eds.): Schweiz und Europa – Auswirkungen auf Wirtschaft, Recht und Gesellschaft. 6. Band der Schriftenreihe der Assistierenden der Universität St. Gallen (HSG), Bern: Stämpfli Verlag, 2011, pp. 165–172.

Eduard Klein

12. Academic Corruption in Russia

12.1. Introduction

An education system that remains officially free while being fee-paying in practice corrupts both pupils and teachers.

Vladimir Putin, 03.04.2001

This quotation from former Russian president Vladimir Putin points at a problematic development in Russia's higher educational institutions after the collapse of communism: The education system—the international figurehead of the Soviet state—has become utterly corrupted.

Corruption in education is not a new phenomenon; it already existed in Soviet times.[1] However, after communism, its intensity and nature have reached new dimensions. In the old system, academic corruption occurred sporadically. In the present system, its character is systematic. The latest figures indicate that every second student[2] is confronted with corruption.[3] The market volume of corruption in education rose to 618 Million USD in 2008.[4] Even with the nationwide implementation of new standardised university admission exams in 2009 the amount has constantly increased.[5]

Corruption in higher education appears at three stages:

1. Before a course of study starts/at entrance examinations: to gain admission.
2. During a course of study: to ensure achievement on the course.
3. At the end of/after a course of study: to gain a degree or doctorate.

The admission procedure is generally the first point at which (future) students are involved in corruption.[6] An admission policy based on corrupt practices subverts the

---

1   As early as 1935, the Soviet magazine 'Krokodil' reported corruption during university admissions; see: Simis, Konstantin: USSR. Secrets of a Corrupt Society, London: Dent, 1982, here p. 43.

2   Out of a total of 7,513,000 students in 2008/2009—the largest student body in the history of Russia—more than 3,250,000 students were confronted with corruption. Federal State Statistics Service: Higher Education Institutions, in: gks.ru, 20.05.2010, http://www.gks.ru/bgd/regl/b09_12/IssWWW.exe/stg/d01/08-10.htm

3   Corruption process in Russia. Level, structure, trends. Corruption increase rate within four years' period as a result of the recent survey made by the INDEM Fund, in: INDEM.ru, 20.05.2010, http://www.indem.ru/en/Publicat/2005diag_engV.htm

4   Morar', Natal'ya: Korruptsiya v VUZakh. $ 618 Mio. i – nikakikh problem?, in: Newtimes.ru, 02.06.2008, http://newtimes.ru/articles/detail/4168/

5   Antikorrupcija.spb.ru, 27.05.2010, http://antikorrupciya.spb.ru/novosti/1329-2010-05-27-07-35-20.html

6   Sazonov, Dmitri: Korruptsiya v Sfere Vysshego Obrazovaniya. Regional'nyy Aspekt i Tendentsii Razvitiya (Na Primere Saratovskoy Oblasti), Saratov: State Academy of Law, 2007; Saborovskaya, Alina S. (et al.): Vysshee obrazovanie v Rossii. Pravila i realnost', Moscow: Independent Institute for Social Policy, 2004.

legally defined fair and free access to higher education.[7] Not the most talented students enter the universities but the wealthiest. This is also true for many universities in the Western hemisphere, but these institutions at least offer scholarships for poorer applicants. Scholarships at Russian universities are almost non-existent and students from deprived families are something of a rarity at prestigious Russian universities.

During their courses, students become involved in corruption in order to control their grades and to save time. At some universities, corrupt practices are highly institutionalised. The amount of the bribe may vary, but usually the price for grades or course exemptions is affordable for the majority of students.[8] The quality of education suffers seriously due to these informal practices[9] and the students—who learn that corrupt behaviour is very effective—are prepared for a later 'career of corruption'.

Finally, there is a rising demand for postgraduate degrees, resulting into an increasing amount of corruption in the field of postgraduate studies.[10] Because a doctorate has a positive impact on the holder's social prestige, job perspectives and salary, people are willing to bypass the time-consuming formal procedures by acquiring the title illegally. According to the Federal Education and Science Supervision Service (Rosobrnadzor) up to 25.000 postgraduate diplomas are sold illegally each year.[11]

Corruption in education has considerable ramifications for the society affected by it.[12] Economic and social prosperity are based on the education of the members of society. In the globalised world of the 21st century, higher education is essential for the future of a state. If the quality of education falls and unqualified graduates enter the labour market, Russia will lose its ability to compete in the international market.

The shortcomings in higher education have also been recognised by the Russian President Dmitri Medved'ev. In his speech to the nation in November 2008, he declared:

> [...] that the Russian education system should play a decisive role in shaping a new generation of professionals. Its previous successes were once recognised around the world. Today, despite some positive developments, the situation in education leaves much to be desired. Let us be frank: we were once in the vanguard and have now fallen behind. This has become a very serious threat to our competitiveness. *(President of Russia, Official Web Portal)*

---

7   Ibid.
8   Galitskiy, Yefim/ Levin, Mark: Zatraty Semey na Obrazovanie Detey. Informatsionnyy Byulleten', Moscow: Higher School of Economics, 2008; Galitskiy, Yefim/ Levin, Mark: Korruptsiya v Sisteme Obrazovaniya/Informatsionnyy byulleten', Moscow: Higher School of Economics, 2004.
9   Sazonov, Dmitri: Korruptsiya v Sfere Vysshego Obrazovaniya. Regional'nyy Aspekt i Tendentsii Razvitiya (Na Primere Saratovskoi Oblasti), Saratov: State Academy of Law, 2007.
10   Kalimullin, Tagir R.: Rossiyskiy Rynok Dissertatsionnykh Uslug, Moscow: Higher School of Economics, 2006; Osipian, Ararat L.: Corruption in Russia's Doctoral Education, Nashville: Vanderbilt University, 2008.
11   An estimated 20.000 diplomas are 'candidates of sciences' (PhD) and 5.000 are 'doctor of sciences' diplomas (similar to German 'Habilitation', post-doc).
12   Anti Corruption Research Center: Corruption in the Education Sector, in: U4.no, 20.05.2010, http://www.u4.no/themes/education/main.cfm

Two concrete examples illustrate the serious implications of academic corruption:

- How can an architect who bought the grades for his static exams be able to plan a building without constructional faults?
- Can you trust the moral integrity of a judge who only passed his entrance examinations because he bribed the university administration?

In order to combat academic corruption and its social consequences, the government implemented anti-corruption measures such as the new standardised entrance exam ('EGE'). The effectiveness of these measures is disputed.

12.2. Research Questions and Methodology

The primary research objective is the development of a catalogue of measures which will contribute to the reduction of corruption in Russian higher education. This objective is only achievable on the basis of a profound understanding of the structure of corruption. We must know in detail how academic corruption works if we want to develop effective countermeasures: The definition and description of corrupt practices at Russian universities is a precondition to the definition of anti-corruption tools.

In order to make up for the lack of empirical data concerning corruption in Russian higher educational institutions, the author carried out an empirical survey in Russia. 28 individuals—students, teachers and experts on corruption—were interviewed. The interviews took place in February and March 2009 in three Russian cities—Moscow, St Petersburg and Samara. Access was difficult as Russian universities are usually not interested in the disclosure of their corrupt practices.

The data collection was based on Andreas Witzel's[13] model of problem-centred interviews. This model allows for the reconstruction of social or biographical issues from an individual perspective. The focus is on the respondents' attitudes, actions and interpretations.

The interviewees were divided into three groups: students (16 individuals), faculty members (5 individuals) and experts on corruption (8 individuals).[14] Each group received a questionnaire created for that specific group. The students and the members of faculty were primarily asked about their attitudes towards corruption in education and about their personal experiences concerning corrupt practices. The questions for the experts were more aimed at the description of the social and structural context of academic corruption.

---

13 Witzel, Andreas: The Problem-Centered Interview, in: Forum: Qualitative Social Research, (Online Journal), (vol. 1), no. 1, http://www.qualitative-research.net/index.php/fqs/article/view/1132; Witzel, Andreas: Auswertung Problemzentrierter Interviews: Grundlagen und Erfahrungen, in: Strobl, Rainer/ Böttger, Andreas (eds.): Wahre Geschichten, Baden-Baden: Nomos, pp. 49–75, 1996.

14 See Appendix.

In order to gain an initial overview of the body of data, the interviews were encoded and categorised thematically. Based on the tabulated thematic blocks, a first outline of a hypothesis was possible. After a detailed analysis of the data, assumptions about the motives of corrupt students and teachers could be made and patterns and types of academic corruption elaborated. Gradually, reasons for the susceptibility of Russian higher educational institutions to corruption became more evident.

Finally, the results were interpreted in the context of existing research projects and empirical studies. Only then could a proposed catalogue of countermeasures be formulated.

12.3. Theoretical Framework

The research project is based on the theory of informal institutions.[15] Informal institutions are 'socially shared rules, usually unwritten, that are created, communicated, and enforced outside of officially sanctioned channels'.[16] Douglass North[17] describes them as 'the rules of the game' in a society. They coexist with formal institutions—constitutions, laws, regulations, decrees etc.—and to a considerable extent shape social interaction. Informal institutions are typical for post-Soviet societies, where practises such as clientelism[18], corruption[19] and 'blat'[20] already existed under the communist system.

Corruption is a subcategory of informal institutions. In our context, academic corruption is defined as 'the systematic use of public office for private benefit, whose

---

15   O'Donnell, Guillermo: Illusions about Consolidation, in: Journal of Democracy, 1996, (vol. 7), no. 2, pp. 34–51; Helmke, Gretchen/ Levitsky, Stephen: Informal Institutions and Comparative Politics: A Research Agenda, in: Perspectives on Politics, 2004, (vol. 2), no. 4, pp. 725–740; North, Douglas C.: Institutions, Institutional Change and Economic Performance, Cambridge: Cambridge University Press, 1990.

16   Helmke, Gretchen/ Levitsky, Stephen: Informal Institutions and Comparative Politics: A Research Agenda, in: Perspectives on Politics, 2004, (vol. 2), no. 4, pp. 725–740.

17   North, Douglass C.: Institutions, Institutional Change and Economic Performance, Cambridge: Cambridge University Press, 1990.

18   Lauth, Hans-Joachim: Informelle Institutionen politischer Partizipation und ihre demokratie-theoretische Bedeutung. Klientelismus, Korruption, Putschdrohung und ziviler Widerstand, In: Lauth, Hans-Joachim/ Liebert, Ulrike (eds.): Im Schatten demokratischer Legitimität. Informelle Institutionen und Politische Partizipation im Interkulturellen Demokratievergleich, Wiesbaden: Opladen, 1999, pp. 61–84.

19   Levin, Mark/ Satarov, Georgy: Corruption and Institutions in Russia, in: European Journal of Political Economy, 2000, (vol. 16), no. 1, pp. 113–132.

20   The Russian term 'blat' means reciprocal exchanges within informal networks which were used to gain personal advantage. See Ledeneva, Alena V.: Russia's Economy of Favours: Blat, Networking and Informal Exchange, Cambridge: Cambridge University Press, 1998; Ledeneva, Alena V.: How Russia Really Works: The Informal Practice that Shaped Post-Soviet Politics and Business, Ithaca [et al.]: Cornell University Press, 2006.

impact is significant on the availability and quality of educational goods and services, and, as a consequence on access, quality or equity in education'.[21]

The research on corruption offers different theoretical frameworks. Models from criminology,[22] psychology,[23] sociology,[24] economics,[25] the theory of governance[26] and the political sciences[27] compete with each other.

An orientation towards the political sciences narrows the choice of models to three approaches:

1. normative/traditional
2. functionalist
3. rational-choice

According to the normative or traditional approach, represented among others by Carl J. Friedrich,[28] corruption is a lack of political culture, a kind of moral 'disease' which leads to the decay of normative values: 'Corruption is a kind of behaviour which deviates from the norm actually prevalent or believed to be prevail in a given context, such as the political'.[29] The normative approach prioritises the mere description of behaviour, neglecting the motives and reasons for corrupt behaviour. It is therefore not adequate for our purposes.

Functionalist models stress the positive functions of corruption. Corruption is primarily defined by its ability to improve the performance of inflexible formal rules. 'Corruption can and does have numerous consequences that are anything but evil— providing welfare services for disadvantaged citizens that otherwise would be with-

21   Hallak, Jacques/ Poisson, Muriel: Corrupt Schools, Corrupt Universities: What can be Done?, Paris: International Institute for Educational Planing, 2007: here p. 29.

22   Bannenberg, Britta: Korruption in Deutschland. Ergebnisse einer kriminologisch-strafrechtlichen Untersuchung, in: von Arnim, Hans-Herbert (ed.): Korruption. Netzwerke in Politik, Ämtern und Wirtschaft, Munich: Droemer Knaur, 2003, pp. 204–234.

23   Richter, Horst-Eberhard: Die hohe Kunst der Korruption. Erkenntnisse eines Politik-Beraters, Hamburg: Hoffmann und Campe, 1989.

24   Luhmann, Niklas: Gesellschaftsstruktur und Semantik. Studien zur Wissenssoziologie der modernen Gesellschaft, Frankfurt a.M.: Suhrkamp, 1999; Höffling, Christian: Korruption als soziale Beziehung, Opladen: Leske & Budrich, 2002.

25   Shleifer, Andrei/ Vishny, Robert W.: Corruption, in: Quarterly Journal of Economics, 1993, (vol. 108), no. 3, pp. 599–617.

26   Homann, Karl: Unternehmensethik und Korruption, in: Zeitschrift für Betriebswirtschaftliche Forschung, 1997, (vol. 49), no. 3, pp. 187–209.

27   von Alemann, Ulrich/ Kleinfeld, Ralf: Begriff und Bedeutung der politischen Korruption aus politikwissenschaftlicher Sicht, in: Benz, Arthur/ Seibel, Wolfgang (eds.): Zwischen Kooperation und Korruption. Abweichendes Verhalten in der Verwaltung, Baden Baden: Nomos, 1992, pp. 259–282.

28   Friedrich, Carl J.: Corruption Concepts in Historical Perspective, in: Heidenheimer, Arnold J./ Johnston, Michael (eds.): Political Corruption. Concepts & Contexts, New Brundwick: Transaction Publishers, 2001, pp. 15–24.

29   Ibid., here p. 15.

out them'.[30] The functionalist approach, therefore, does not suit the research's focus on the negative effects of corrupt behaviour.

Recent research on corruption has been increasingly based on rational-choice models. These provide a value-free assessment of corruption and prioritise an examination of its causes. Hence they are a suitable theoretical framework for projects interested in the motives and causes of corruption and the development of countermeasures.

Table 12-1:   Political Science Approaches and their Assessment of Corruption

Approach	Assessment of corruption	Focus on
Normative/traditional approach	Negative	Continuous monitoring of corruption
Functionalist approach	Rather positive	Consequences of corruption (ex-post)
Rational Choice approach	Value-free	Causes of corruption (ex-ante)

Source: Höltge, Kristin: Governance in Transition: What Makes Georgia's Higher Education System so Corrupt?, Kassel: Kassel University Press, 2008, here p. 69.

Within the field of rational-choice-based research on corruption the stakeholder-specific principal-agent model proved to be the most suitable. It was originally developed by Rose-Ackerman.[31] She defines corruption as an exchange of goods between three participating actors—the principal/superior, the agent and a third person:

> While superiors would like agents always to fulfil the superior's objectives, monitoring is costly, and agents will generally have some freedom to put their own interests ahead of their principals'. Here is where the money enters. Some third person, who can benefit by the agent's action, seek to influence the agent's decision by offering him a monetary payment which is not passed on to the principal.[32]

Robert R. Klitgaard expanded upon Rose-Ackerman's model.[33] His theory involves the same actors changing their names only slightly—the third person is now called an *agent*. Klitgaard's *principal* is defined as the head of an institution who is supposed to embody the public interest. He employs several *agents* who are to act on his behalf when dealing with *clients*. An agent might not only serve public interests but also be tempted to misuse his position in order to pursue his/her private interests. The following example illustrates how Klitgaard's *principal-agent* model can be transferred to the object of this research:

---

30   Smelser, Neil J., quoted in: Höltge, Kristin: Governance in Transition. What Makes Georgia's Higher Education System So Corrupt?, Kassel: Kassel University Press, 2008, p. 68.
31   Rose-Ackerman, Susan: Corruption. A Study in Political Economy, New York [et al.]: Academic Press, 1978.
32   Ibid., here p. 6.
33   Klitgaard, Robert E.: Controlling Corruption, Berkeley [et al.]: University of California Press, 1991.

The *agent* is a university teacher who is employed by the *principal*, in our case the university rector. Several students—who take the role of the *clients* in our model—plan to make informal payments to influence the results of their course examinations. They offer money or gifts to their teacher in exchange for high marks. The teacher, who has to decide whether or not to act corruptly, makes the following considerations:

> If I am not corrupt, I get my pay and the moral satisfaction of not being a corrupt person.
> If I am corrupt, I get the bribe but 'pay' a moral cost. There is also some chance I will be caught and punished, in which case I will also pay a penalty, and lose my pay.
> So, I will be corrupt if: the bribe minus the moral cost minus [(the probability I am caught and punished) times (the penalty for being corrupt)] is greater than my pay plus the satisfaction I get from not being corrupt.[34]

If he refuses his students' offer, he guarantees his professional position and his salary and receives moral satisfaction for his exemplary behaviour. At the same time, he abandons the opportunity to receive extra payment. If he chooses the informal path, he makes a considerable profit but risks being caught and punished and experiencing feelings of guilt in the light of his moral failure.

We see that five determinants affect the agents and clients decision-making: 1. the salary of the teacher, 2. the sum of the bribe, 3. the moral attitude of the agent, 4. the risk of being caught and 5. the strictness of the sanctions/penalty.

The student (client) who has to decide whether to be or not to be corrupt makes similar considerations to his teacher:

> If I am not corrupt, I have to invest time and effort in order to receive credits. As a reward I acquire knowledge and the moral satisfaction of not being corrupt.
> If I am corrupt, I save time and effort, but I do not acquire knowledge and risk being caught and penalised.

Accordingly, the student will choose corruption if the time and effort saved minus the moral and economic costs minus the risk of being caught and penalised outweighs the satisfaction of having acquired knowledge and of not being corrupt.

The student's decision-making is also affected by the determinants named above, the only difference being the sum of the bribe: The *lower* the amount of the bribe, the higher the likelihood of corruption. In addition, the student's choice is influenced by a further determinant: the time and effort saved. The greater the value he places on an early diploma and the lower the value he places on the acquisition of knowledge, the higher the likelihood of corruption.

With its focus on the actors' personal motives, Klitgaard's theory provides a suitable framework for the explanation of the reasons for academic corruption in Russia. Klitgaard's model also deals with the problem of omnipresent informal institutions. It considers how informal institutions affect the choices made by the actors: According to Klitgaard, the moral costs of corruption can be zero if actors operate within a completely

---

34   Ibid., here p. 70.

corrupt environment.[35] Given the ubiquity of corrupt structures in Russia, this approach might enable an analysis of the ways in which pervasive informal institutions have an effect upon the social assessment and acceptance of corrupt behaviour. Finally, Klitgaard's model provides the following measures for controlling corruption:

1. Select agents for "honesty" and "capability"
2. Change the rewards and penalties facing agents (and clients)
3. Gather and analyse information in order to raise the chances that corruption will be detected
4. Restructure the principal-agent-client relationship to remove the corruption-inducing combination of monopoly power plus discretion plus little accountability
5. Change attitudes about corruption[36]

12.4. Empirical Results

An analysis of the answers in the survey reveals that the present problem of academic corruption in Russia is primarily a result of three developments:

1. *Economic reasons:* Most universities have lacked financial resources since the transformation period and the financial crisis of the 1990s.[37] As Tagir Kalimullin puts it:

   The scale of corruption we observe today is a logical consequence [of] the changes that have occurred since the 1990s. *(Interviewee 2, male, expert, Higher School of Economics, Moscow)*

2. *Structural reasons:* Corruption is firmly anchored in the educational system and already a part of it. Without corruption, the current system of higher education would not survive. Effective sanctions do not exist.

   If we were to eliminate corruption, many of the hierarchical structures that have already been created would disintegrate. [...] And then the whole higher education system would collapse. *(Interviewee 9, female, graduate, MGU State University, Moscow)*

3. *Historical/socio-cultural reasons:* Corruption has a long tradition in Russia, starting from the 11th century, where it was already known as 'kormlenye' ('feeding').[38] Informal institutions were established at universities during the Soviet era[39] and

---

35   Klitgaard, Robert E.: Controlling Corruption, Berkeley [et al.]: University of California Press, 1991, here p. 69.
36   Ibid., here p. 94.
37   Teichmann, Christine: Nachfrageorientierte Hochschulfinanzierung in Russland. Ein innovatives Modell zur Modernisierung der Hochschulbildung, in: HoFArbeitsberichte, no. 1, 2004.
38   Holm, Kerstin: Das korrupte Imperium, München: DTB, 2006; Schattenberg, Susanne: Die korrupte Provinz? Russische Beamte im 19. Jahrhundert, Frankfurt a.M. et al.: Campus, 2008
39   Konstantin Simis wrote in 1982: 'Corruption enters the life of the Soviet citizen at a very early age, even before he or she is old enough to be aware of it. [...] As they climb higher and higher up the pyramid of the education system [...] they are psychologically prepared for the corruption they encounter at this stage of their lives', in: Simis, Konstantin: USSR: Secrets of a Corrupt

are socially accepted today. Kirill Titaev sees the origin of academic corruption in the Soviet higher education system:

> The higher education system faced a situation in which formal procedures stopped to work … A large amount of people achieved diplomas without participating … different reasons forced professors to give marks: the main reason was blat *(Interviewee 26, male, expert, Higher School of Economics, Saint Petersburg)*

The omnipresence of corruption in social intercourse is one reason why experts question the effectiveness of anti-corruption measures. Most of them believe that a change is only possible if reforms are implemented in all social areas affected by corruption and not only in the education sector. Furthermore, they hold the lack of civil society participation responsible for the ineffectiveness of anti-corruption measures:

> It will not be effective because it was just decided, as everything is decided in Russia. This means that the law was not run past experts, it was not discussed in society [...] no academics or lawyers, but only officials [...] but without society, without journalists, without any media, a victory against corruption is impossible. *(Andrey Kalich, interviewee 5, expert, Centre for the Development of Democracy and Human Rights, Moscow)*

All respondents affirmed that education is of major importance, though the answers showed that the decision to study at university is mainly based on practical reasons. Experts have identified changing conditions in the labour market which they hold responsible for the students' attitudes: As long as employers give priority to formal criteria and value mere certificates more than expertise, students will undervalue the quality of education.

> Only 10 to 12% of the employers think it matters at which university your diploma was acquired … the majority of employers only want to know whether you have a degree or not … the way, the higher education system works, sends wrong signals to society. *(Interviewee 4, Leon Kosals, expert, Higher School of Economics, Moscow)*

Because they need formal records to enter the job market, more and more high school graduates register for university courses. Many Russian universities cannot cope with the increasing number of students. The basic conditions—financial resources, teaching staff etc.—are insufficient. It is a paradox that people are showing an increasing interest in education while the quality of education is continually worsening.

The high demand for university places—predominately for places that are state-subsidised—affects fair access to academic institutions negatively. Prestigious universities often choose students according to their financial means and/or their social standing and not their skills and ability. The greater the demand for places, the greater the value of the reward a student has to provide for his acceptance. A student reports:

> Not everyone has a right to higher education. I personally, as a man from the countryside, as well as my fellow students with whom I went to school in the village—just three went

---

Society, London: Dent, 1982, p. 163. See also: Friedberg, Maurice: How things were done in Odessa. Cultural and Intellectual Pursuits in a Soviet City, Boulder/CO: Westview, 1991.

> on to university out of 30. [...] currently, university entrance is undermined by corruption
> and not everyone can start a course. One must have connections, i.e. any personal con-
> tact to the university. [...] I've heard that our University will soon assume the status of a
> commercial university [...] and then only rich people who can afford it will study here.
> *(Interviewee 18, male, student, State Technical University, Samara)*

A graduate of a very prestigious faculty of the Lomonosov Moscow State University
adds:

> In practice, I can say, that at my faculty, this law [the right to free education and fair access,
> E.K.] has not been implemented. I know very well that when I began to study, there was
> not a single person who enrolled without money or relationships. *(Interviewee 9, female,
> graduate, MGU State University, Moscow)*

Universities that are less popular face a different situation: The number of applications
sometimes does not even meet the number of state-subsidised places.

The research dealt with academic corruption during entrance examinations and
during courses. Informal actions before the start of a course usually serve the purpose
of securing a state-subsidised place at a certain university or faculty. In Russia, this has
become a real 'business' (Georgy Satarov, interviewee 7, Expert, INDEM-Foundation,
Moscow). In the majority of cases, the parents of future students are the initiators. They
believe that a place at a popular university will help their children to succeed on the
job market. In order to achieve their objective, they use their economic capital (bribery) or social capital (blat). The so-called 'repetitorstvo', where parents engage university staff to 'prepare' their children for entrance examinations is very widespread[40]—
this practise seems dubious when the same tutors are simultaneously in the admission committees. Bribes for enrolment have become more prevalent over the last few
years. In Moscow, the average bribe for university admission amounts to around 5,000
USD[41] and may climb to 20,000 USD[42] or more. The total amount of corruption connected to entrance examinations was 520 million USD in 2008.[43]

To increase transparency during entrance examinations, the testing process was
reformed in 2009. Intransparent, corruption-prone procedures were replaced by the
standardised and computer-based Unified State Exam *EGE* (Yediniy gosudarstvenniy
ekzamen). Some respondents believe in the positive impact of the *EGE*, but most of

---

40   According to Galitskii and Levin, 36% of Russian parents paid between 18,600 roubles (on
     national average) and 54,700 roubles (in Moscow) for the 'repetitors' per annum. Galitskiy,
     Yefim/ Levin, Mark: Zatraty semey na obrazovanie detey. Informatsionnyy byulleten', Moscow:
     Higher School of Economics, 2008, here p. 33.
41   Ibid.
42   Interviewee 6, female, Professor, MGU State University, Moscow.
43   Morar', Natal'ya: Korruptsiya v VUZakh: $ 618 Mio. i – nikakikh problem?, in: Newtimes.ru,
     02.06.2008, http://newtimes.ru/articles/detail/4168/

them doubt its efficiency. Since the amount of corruption during entrance examinations has increased considerably in 2010[44], critics of the *EGE* seem to be right.

During their courses, students act corruptly to improve their performance. At certain universities, this form of corruption has become institutionalised to such an extent that students get price lists or remittance slips, which determine the bribes for high marks. Compared to the bribes paid for enrolment, the bribes that students pay during their courses are rather low and usually amount to between 3,000–4,000 roubles.[45] As gifts up to a value of 3,000 roubles are legal,[46] they are a frequent form of bribery.

> The best variant of corruption—is a bottle of cognac. It is a pleasant gift, it is fine, and it is innocent. *(Interviewee 9, female, Graduate, MGU State University, Moscow)*

In total, 98 million USD were spent in bribes during courses in 2008.[47]

Table 12-2 summarises the different forms of corruption that are present in Russian higher education.

Table 12-2:   A Typology of Education Corruption at Russian Universities

Before a University Course Goal: (State-subsidised) places at selected universities and departments	**During a University Course** Goal: Credits, exemption from classes
• 'Repetitorstvo' • Directly bribing selection committee members • 'Rektorskie/Dekanskie spiski'* • Preparatory classes • Purchasing the results of the standardised entrance exam 'EGE'	• Cash payments to teachers • Presents for teachers • 'Certified' corruption: payments to university pay offices (sometimes via bank transfer) • Optional preparatory classes (with costs) • Payments extracted from students

*   *These terms are used to describe the system of 'dean lists': Deans have the right to select students on their own initiative. Usually they sell university places or assign them to close friends, family members etc.*
Source: *author's own compilation based on interviews.*

At the majority of Russian universities, corruption is institutionalised. The dimension of corruption varies from university to university and between different departments at

44   Nasyrov, Evgeniy: Stoimost' «pyaterki» na EGE dostigla 150 tysyach rubley, in: GZT.ru, 18.06.2010, http://www.gzt.ru/topnews/education/-stoimostj-pyaterki-na-ege-dostigla-150-tysyach-/310865.html?from=linksfromsingle

45   Galitskiy, Yefim/ Levin, Mark: Zatraty Semey na Obrazovanie Detey. Informatsionnyy Byulleten', Moscow: Higher School of Economics, 2008, here p. 36.

46   Article 575 of the Civil Code of the Russian Federation legalises 'gifts, except for common gifts, whose value does not exceed the statutory five-fold amounts of the minimum wages or salaries: [...] to the workers of medical treatment, educational, social protection and other similar institutions by individuals who are treated, maintained or educated by them, and by spouses and relatives of these persons', 20.05.2010, http://www.russian-civil-code.com/PartII/SectionIV/Subsection1/Chapter32. html

47   Morar', Natal'ya: Korruptsija v VUZakh: $ 618 Mio. i – nikakikh Problem?, in: Newtimes.ru, 02.06.2008, http://newtimes.ru/articles/detail/4168/

the same university. In general, departments of the humanities show a higher degree of corruption than departments of natural sciences. Only a few universities—namely the Higher Schools of Economics in Moscow and St Petersburg, the New Economic School in Moscow and the European University St Petersburg—seem to have found measures to banish academic corruption.

Several interviewees have been told about cases of academic corruption by friends and acquaintances. Others have already been personally involved in corrupt acts. Some students buy their way out of classes if they believe that the effort for a class is not proportionate to its benefit. This is true especially for compulsory subjects, such as physical education, philosophy or history, which are considered irrelevant by many students.

One of the interviewed teachers admits, that her own work relations helped her younger sister to gain admission to the university where she worked: She presented a bottle of champagne to a member of the admission committee and "managed" the enrolment of her sister.[48] This incident is a typical example for the "closeness" at Russian universities (see also the following chapter by Elvira Leontyeva in this volume).

Academic corruption is seen as dysfunctional and affects Russian society negatively. The interviewees' main criticism is the unequal access to higher education, which sharpens the gap between the socially deprived and the privileged classes. It also damages the quality of higher education and is likely to create a shortage of well-educated specialist workers. Georgy Satarov speaks of a 'de-intellectualisation' and 'de-professionalization' of society (Interviewee 7, expert, INDEM-Foundation, Moscow). He fears, that Russian universities prepare their students for a 'career of corruption': They present corruption as a legitimate and socially acceptable way for the achievement of objectives.

12.5. Conclusions and Recommendations

Klitgaard's principal-agent-client model serves as a useful framework for analysing academic corruption in Russia. His model is based on the rational choices of the individuals involved in corruption.

A university teacher (agent) has two choices: to be corrupt or not to be corrupt. His decision is based on the calculation of the risks, costs and likely benefits. He will act corruptly if he comes to the conclusion that the benefits outweigh the risks and cost.

As specified in chapter 12-3, five determinants affect the teacher's decision-making:
- *The salary of the teacher:* The higher the pay, the lower the likelihood of corruption.
- *The sum of the bribe:* The higher the bribe, the greater the likelihood of corruption.
- *The moral attitude of the agent:* The fewer his objections to corruption, the greater the likelihood of corruption.

---

48   Interviewee 25, female, Professor, European University, St Petersburg.

- *The risk of being caught:* The higher this risk, the smaller the likelihood of corruption.
- *The strictness of the sanctions:* The less strict the sanctions, the greater the likelihood of corruption.

A student who offers his teacher a payment for high marks must have made similar considerations before he decided to adopt the informal approach. He weighed his personal costs and his likely benefits and came to the conclusion that high marks and saving time outweigh his payment, his sense of guilt and the potential hazard.

Due to economic, historical and cultural factors, informal institutions in Russia have become better established than in many other industrialised countries. In addition to economic and political corruption, the field of everyday corruption has expanded considerably and is now present in several social subsystems. Corruption is no longer a deviant act by particular individuals but rather a daily routine. Obviously the moral costs of corruption only play a subordinate part in the social conscience.

Higher education is a part of Russian society seriously affected by corruption. At many universities, corruption takes place in public. Apparently the fears of sanctions are minimal. Indeed, the risk of being caught and penalised is relatively modest. In 2007, only 500 cases of academic corruption which resulted in judicial proceedings were reported. Students, in particular, do not have to fear severe sanctions. If they exist at all, legal consequences apply to academic teachers. They often escape sanctions for taking bribes only in cases where they received non-monetary presents. Presents are legal if they are worth less than 3,000 roubles. This sum corresponds to the bribe for marks on courses (3,000 to 4,000 roubles) that is customary in the market of academic corruption. As it is affordable for most students (or at least for their parents), the amount of money demanded is usually no hindrance to corruption.

Apparently, the current situation regarding all determinants favours corrupt behaviour.

- University staff is usually underpaid.
- The amount of the bribes assures an appealing extra salary for the teachers. Yet, the sum is still affordable for the majority of students/parents.
- The moral objections to corruption are weak.
- The risk of being caught and penalised for academic corruption is minimal.
- Sanctioning mechanisms, for example, article 290 in the criminal code 'Acceptance of bribes', do exist but are ineffective.

As a result, the general likelihood of academic corruption in Russia is very high. To change the determinants in a way that will reduce academic corruption effectively, strict and intensive anti-corruption measures must be implemented. Regarding Klitgaards proposals and the empirical findings of this study, I suggest the following recommendations for action:

Effective sanctioning mechanisms: Academic corruption must have legal repercussions for all the parties involved. The strict application of the law and the removal of legal loopholes are obligatory. A compromise between hard and soft sanctions should be found.

Growing transparency: Non-transparent procedures, for example oral entrance examinations or 'dean lists' must be abolished. Standardised entrance exams, which have been introduced recently, could help fight corruption. Their actual success remains to be seen. Independent media should have a reporting and controlling function. Independent ombudsman need to be introduced as direct contact persons for students.

Deregulation: State control and influence must be reduced. Universities should be involved in important decisions in higher education policy.

Internationalisation: Significantly, universities with a strong international orientation face less problems with corruption. Their strategies (subsidies and teaching staff from abroad) could be adapted by other institutions. The integration into European education systems (through the Bologna Process) seems to be worthy of support.

Democratisation: The Russian education system is based on strict hierarchical structures. Most universities do not involve their students in decision-making. Student self-governing bodies are the exception. They must be strengthened to act as a counterbalance to the power of headmasters, administrations and teachers.

Downsizing: The Russian academic sector needs 'healthy downsizing'. Reduction is a precondition for improving learning conditions and a high quality education. A system of vocational training, similar to that in Germany for instance, could compensate the loss of university places.

Decoupling: Places that are state-subsidised and private places must be decoupled. Study programs with costs should be restricted to private universities.

'De-Sovietisation': Old-fashioned educational structures from the Soviet system (for example the status of physical education as a compulsory subject) must be finally abandoned.

Changing incentives for students: The current Russian labour market is, on the whole, only open to people with a degree. As a consequence, many students value exam results more than the quality of what they studied. If the conditions in the labour market are changed and courses are not only pursued in order to obtain certificates, there would be less incentive for corrupt practices.

Improving the financial framework: Public expenditure on education fell seriously after the collapse of the Soviet system. Universities had to deal with permanent underfunding which is still evident. All too often, the wages of academic teachers do not cover their living costs. If they cannot or do not want to take on more than one job at the same time, corruption becomes the easiest way out. A considerable pay rise and better retirement provisions would help to diminish the incentives for corruption among teachers.

A change of attitude: The social consciousness of the immoral and criminal aspects of corruption must be increased. Information campaigns which sensitise people to these aspects are needed. Non-governmental organisations, for example *Transparency International*, should be involved in this process.

All these measures cannot operate if the universities refuse to play an active part in the reform process. The Higher School of Economics in Moscow and St Petersburg or the European University in St Petersburg serve as positive examples for Russian academic institutions following a strict anti-corruption policy—with increasing success.

12.6. Appendix: Interviewees

Interviewee's Designation	Interviewee's Gender	Interviewee's Affiliation
Interviewee 1	female	Professor, University of Industry and Finance, Moscow
Interviewee 2	male	Tagir Kalimullin, expert, Higher School of Economics, Moscow
Interviewee 3	male	Andrey Kolesnichenko, expert, Newspaper 'Novye Izvestiya'
Interviewee 4	male	Leon Kosals, expert, Higher School of Economics, Moscow
Interviewee 5	male	Andrey Kalich, expert, Center for the Development of Democracy and Humand Rights, Moscow
Interviewee 6	female	Professor, MGU State University, Moscow
Interviewee 7	male	Georgy Satarov, Expert, INDEM-Foundation, Moscow
Interviewee 8	female	Student, MGU State University, Moscow
Interviewee 9	female	Graduate, MGU State University, Moscow
Interviewee 10	male	Student, MGU State University, Moscow
Interviewee 11	male	Mark Levin, expert, Higher School of Economics, Moscow
Interviewee 12	male	Student, State Technical University, Samara
Interviewee 13	male	Professor, State Technical University, Samara
Interviewee 14	male	Student, State Technical University, Samara
Interviewee 15	male	Student, State Technical University, Samara
Interviewee 16	male	Student, State Technical University, Samara
Interviewee 17	male	Student, State Technical University, Samara
Interviewee 18	male	Student, State Technical University, Samara
Interviewee 19	male	Student, State Technical University, Samara
Interviewee 20	male	Student, State Technical University, Samara
Interviewee 21	female	Student, State University, Samara
Interviewee 22	male	Lecturer, State University of Architecture and Civil Engineering, Samara
Interviewee 23	male	Student, ENGECON, St Petersburg
Interviewee 24	male	Aleksandr Sungurov, expert, Higher School of Economics, St Petersburg
Interviewee 25	female	Professor, European University, St Petersburg
Interviewee 26	male	Kirill Titaev, expert, Higher School of Economics, St Petersburg
Interviewee 27	male	Student, ENGECON, St Petersburg
Interviewee 28	male	Student, Higher School of Economics, St Petersburg

Elvira Leontyeva

13. Informal Ways of Obtaining Grades in Modern Russian Universities. How Daily Ties Become Corruption Networks

13.1. External Factors Determining the Growth of Informal Practices at Universities

Students and professors at Russian universities nowadays are finding it necessary to deviate from the formal rules of obtaining and providing an education (and thus to deviate from curricula, study plans, programmes). Due to increasing competition among universities for students and their tuition money, teachers have to provide favourable conditions to attract these students, e.g. by reducing the programme requirements and demands, inflating grades, simplifying the study material, etc. The first part of the chapter is devoted to the analysis of the influencing factors that have given rise to informal practices, which are becoming increasingly acceptable. To this end, three factors will be highlighted: the surge in the number of students in 1998–2008, the emergence of student strategies that are not oriented upon studying per se, and the 'closed' academic environment.

For the last ten years, the number of students in Russian universities has more than tripled, for an increase of more than seven million people in 2006.[1] Several factors contributed to this surge. First of all, starting in 2002–2003, the number of new, first-year students began to exceed the number of secondary school graduates. Nearly every secondary school student had decided to enter a higher education institution: according to estimates made in 2002–2003, 82–83% of secondary school graduates, 74–80% of technical school graduates and 39–60% of technical training college graduates planned to enter higher education institutions.[2] Finally, since 1998, the ratio between state-budget-funded and so-called 'commercial' slots for students (i.e. the places reserved for self-paying students) has steadily fallen at state universities; due to their shrinking budgets, they are taking more and more self-payers. These trends indicate that since 1998, swarms of students have been taking the opportunity to study on a commercial basis, i.e. are paying their own way. This means that students who have a low level of schooling—and who have not even taken the entrance examina-

---

1 Obrazovanie v Rossii: Statisticheckiy Ezhegodnik, Moskva, 2006 (Education in Russian Federation: Statistical yearbook, Moscow: State University of Higher Economic School, 2006).
2 Zaborovskaya, A./ Klyatchko, T./ Korolyov, I. et al.: Vysshee Obrazovanie v Rossii, Moskva, 2004 (Higher Education in Russia. Rules and reality, Moscow: Independent Institute of Social Policy, 2004), pp. 11–12.

                                    Elvira Leontyeva

tion—can enter universities. Academic administrations tend to support such students because they are the main source of extra-budget university funds.

Not surprisingly, the average base level of initial knowledge is falling as the number of paying students increases. At the same time, university programmes and curricula have not *officially* changed in terms of complexity and content. The curricula are supposed to conform to the high level of the state educational standard and should require students to master a broad scope of material in order to fulfil the minimum hours. Therefore, faced with the problem of training low-level students according to these high-level standards, teachers have only two choices, both of which entail bending the rules: they can adapt the programme materials to the decreasing quality of the students or they can use informal arrangements of a different character. Simply speaking, the choice is to make the educational material easier or to 'sell' grades in exchange for something else. It should also be noted that the boom in students has resulted in increased teaching loads. Our respondents reported this to be the case and statistical data distinctly support their assertion. In other words, the increase in the number of students in Russian higher educational institutions has not been accompanied by a corresponding increase in the quantity of teachers. For example, from 2001–2006, the number of students increased from 5.42 million to 7.06 million,[3] while the quantity of teachers increased from 265,200 thousand to only 322,100 thousand.[4] But if in 1995 there were 2.79 million students and 240,200 thousand teachers, or 12 students per teacher, then in 2006 the number of students per teacher nearly doubled, to 22 students per teacher. This increase was accompanied by a jump in teaching load: according to the same research, in 2006–2007 teachers were saddled with 22–23 educational hours per week. The surcharge for this excessive academic load is therefore the most common kind of additional payment in academia: according to the results of the Educational Economics Monitoring project, about 60% of teachers receive it. And, in spite of the fact that the majority of teachers are willing to work under these conditions, the heavy teaching loads undoubtedly erode their desire and ability to follow the rules.

The second factor is the emergence of non-study-oriented student strategies. Because almost every Russian secondary school student wants to enter university, the number of those who are focused not on learning but on simply obtaining diplomas and grades is constantly increasing too. According to various estimates, the share of such students now ranges from 15% to 30%. Basically, this figure includes those who go to university just to get a diploma, or, in other cases, 'university plays [the] role of a

---

3   Obrazovanie v Rossii: Statisticheckiy Ezhegodnik, Moskva, 2006 (Education in Russian Federation: Statistical Yearbook, Moscow: State University of Higher Economic School, 2006).
4   Prepodavateli na Rynke Obrazovatelnyh Uslug: Informatsionnyi Bulluten, Moskva, 2006 (Teachers in the Market of Educational Services: Information Bulletin. Moscow: State University of Higher Economic School, 2006).

social refuge for [a] certain circle of youth, relieving them both from army service and from low-skill work [in] manufacture and trade [or] in [the services sector]'.[5] As a rule, the lack of motivation goes hand in hand with a low initial level of knowledge, and these students have neither the desire nor the ability to study. This means that from the moment students enter university, the contingent of those intent on obtaining good grades by informal means has already formed.

The next factor is the so-called 'closeness' of the academic environment. The academic environment itself can be defined as 'a set of norms and rules of academic activity typical for the academic community, and also a set of resource, expert and status networks caused by these norms'.[6] In a 2008 study, E. Sivak and M. Yudkevich[7] developed the criteria for distinguishing between an 'open' and 'closed' environment: the hiring policy, the teachers' publication strategy and the structure of professional communications. First of all, a 'closed' environment is characterized by a hiring policy that is directed at attracting graduates of the same university. A second feature of a closed environment is that teachers publish papers primarily at the same university. Thirdly, 'professional communications are based mainly within the framework of the local community. [...] [Another parameter] of the closed academic environment is the significant distinctions in behavior of the teachers who [attended] the same university ('insiders') and who [attended another] ('outsiders')'.[8] In a closed academic environment, the university management tends to employ their own graduates; meanwhile, the teachers are mostly published by the same university and tend to pursue professional contacts in the immediate environment. All of these features support the author's assumption that Russian universities exhibit a closed academic environment. However, it is possible to add one more criterion: the intention of university employees to have their own children attend the same university at which they work.

Various means of attracting the teachers' and staffs' children to the universities (such as privileges and quotas) serve to perpetuate the closed model. In addition, this model reinforces the employees' motivation to engage in informal network interactions. As A. Osipyan argues,

> In countries where access to higher education and the financing of higher education are limited, high school teachers strive to enrol their children, grandsons, nephews, nieces and other close relatives in a given university, which promotes the transformation of some state and non-state universities into a kind of family business.[9]

---

5   Leybovich, O./ Sushkova, N.: Na semi vetrakh: institut vysshego obrazovaniya v post-sovets-kuyu epokhu in: Zhurnal sotsiologii i sotsial'noy antropologii, 2004 (vol. 7), no. 1, pp. 149–156, here p. 151.

6   Sivak, E./ Yudkevich, M.: «Zakrytaya» akademicheskaya sreda i lokal'nye akademicheskiye standarty, in: Foresight, 2008 (vol. 8), no. 4, pp. 32–41, here p. 33.

7   ibid.

8   Ibid., here p. 35.

9   Osipyan, A.: Corruption as a Legacy of the Medieval University, MPRA Paper No. 13250, pp. 23–24, http://mpra.ub.uni-muenchen.de/13250/

According to our data, more than 90% of Khabarovsk university teachers and staff members who have adult children teach them (or have recently taught them) in the same universities where they work. Last year, in fact, a special research project was conducted on the three largest faculties of one Khabarovsk university. Eleven departments were surveyed, whereby it was established that 77 of 253 members of these faculties (including teachers and other staff) had children between 17 and 30 years old; 115 of these children were studying (or had recently finished studying) at the same university. Only 13 children were studying (or had recently finished studying) elsewhere in the city, and only three children were studying at a university in a different city. Even this small sample reveals a strong tendency: 69 of the 77 teachers chose to have their children study at the university where they work. This figure does not include the faculty members' many other relatives studying at the university.

The majority of regional Russian universities tend to favour the closed academic community model, which generates a great deal of informal activity. It is probably not too much of an exaggeration to compare the management of academia by informal means to clan networks. These structures are organized as horizontal networks, and each position of this community is characterized by its own multi-role combination. In the closed environment generated by these sorts of network structures, all kinds of informal interactions take place.

13.2. Violating the Rules. Informal Ways of Obtaining Grades

This section focuses on the concrete informal practices of obtaining grades that are shaped by the factors analysed above. These informal methods were generated in the context of a specific strategy. Based on the information collected during the empirical phase of research, it is possible to divide these practices into two large groups: 'monetary' and 'non-monetary'. These groups differ with respect to the strategies employed for obtaining grades. 'Non-monetary' practices are based mainly on the use of personal communications or connections and network capital. 'Monetary' practices entail obtaining grades in exchange for monetary bribes or gifts. Both are accepted in international research as a criteria of corruption.[10] However; the use of personal contacts is considered as a form of corruption to a lesser degree. And in the Russian tradition, 'non-monetary' practices are perceived as informal, while only 'monetary' practices are seen as corruption.

The division of these strategies is relative, however, since in reality they are often used in combination, i.e. both personal connections and monetary bribes are employed at the same time. Some of the most interesting cases for research are the situations

---

10   Hallak, J./ Poisson, M.: Corrupt Schools, Corrupt Universities. What Can be Done?, Paris: International Institute for Educational Planing, 2007.

in which the monetary-corrupt strategy is represented as non-monetary—informal survival to some participants of action. This occurs when arrangements between a student and a teacher are carried out through a middleman, which could be another teacher or university employee, etc. In this scenario, the middleman takes money from the student but presents him- or herself as the student's friend or family member. This strategy has two advantages. First, such arrangements increase the profit for the middleman, who executes the action with minimal transaction costs. Second, this method serves to cloak the bribe in a socially acceptable framework. As researchers of corruption in Russia have shown, help that is given in response to personal requests is not condemned by the majority of Russians (i.e. it is not perceived as bribery), and frequently these practices are not associated with corruption in the mass consciousness. In the following, each of the designated strategies, including the most typical forms, will be examined in detail.

13.2.1. Guardianship as an Informal Strategy. The Use of Personal Ties for Obtaining Grades

Personal ties are used everywhere, including in the educational arena. In addition to the phenomena of 'trusteeship' and patronage, which will be discussed here, many other forms of personal ties come into play. Everyone knows someone who entered university and studied 'under the insurance' (i.e. with the help of powerful connections) or passed exams 'on a bell' (i.e. with help from above). Indeed, in a country where status and position were everything, dropping a name could solve any problem. A similar Soviet-era phenomenon, referred to as 'blat' in Russian, has been comprehensively investigated by A. Ledeneva.[11] 'Blat' entailed bypassing formal rules and using personal ties, contacts and networks to obtain access to resources, including goods, services, and even income. Ledeneva's works on educational establishments confirm that all modern practices, including trusteeship and patronage, have old traditions and a fundamentally social base. Obviously, 'blat' did not disappear after the Soviet epoch came to an end. It is still very much alive, and modern guardianship is embedded in the living 'tissue' of its networks.

In this chapter, 'guardianship' above students is understood as a complex of informal services for one person (or group of persons) to sidestep the requirements of the educational process which another person (or group) realizes *on a regular basis*. It entails steady and repeated contacts between the 'trustee' and his or her student. The guardianship consists of a standard set of 'services'—grades, credits, privileges, etc.—which are obtained as a result of an arrangement with colleagues.

---

11   Ledeneva, A.: Russia's Economy of Favours. Blat, Networking and Informal Exchange, Cambridge: Cambridge University Press, 1998; Ledeneva A.: Unwritten Rules. How Russia Really Works, London: Center for European Reform, 2001.

We will now scrutinize some types of guardianship ties according to special criteria. Before the reform of education and the transition to a market economy, guardianship and patronage had a different specificity. Their most important characteristic was the absence of market transactions and the mainly closed character of communications between the 'trustee' and student. Often the trustee was a friend or relative with a personal interest in the activity. Thus, such arrangements made use of pre-existing ties. 'Trusteeship' also took place via middlemen, but less frequently. For example, phenomena such as the 'loyal attitude' and the system of indulgences for students connected to a top party or administrative official have already been documented. The system of privileges dictated the rules of the game in higher education to a great extent.

In modern conditions, these practices have changed. It is obvious that they have become more widespread, and there is a reason for this: the mass requirement for higher education has triggered mass demand for similar sorts of services. The main difference is that in adapting to the market, these practices have become *more differentiated* with respect to the social roles involved. This differentiation, frequently expressed in subtle, vague details, determines whether the interaction falls under the category of traditional, relative- or friend-based personal participation or a monetary-corrupt interaction. That is why it is possible to assign different labels to what is externally the same phenomenon, but expressed in various role combinations: from 'participation' and 'sympathy' to 'under the roof' (i.e. under someone's protection).

To meet the increasing demand for higher education, the old 'blat' relations have to be modernized; the former, usual mode of communication is no longer sufficient. The 'trustee' strategy is thus becoming more and more popular, involving not only old ties, but also the active creation of new ones, which are directed to the realization of this purpose. V. Radaev has named this phenomenon the 'monetization of the Soviet blat'.[12]

For the purpose of classifying informal services, including the services of guardianship above students, we will utilize M. Granovetter's concept of strong and weak ties.[13] All informal practices emerge on the basis of personal ties according to one of these two strategies. In the case of strong ties, participants usually connect through existing relations and thus do not need to make special arrangements for a 'guardian'. Here problem-solving is carried out in clear and transparent conditions of mutual assistance for participants of a network.

---

12   Radayev, V.: Mozhno li predolet' korruptsiyu v obrazovanii? (Is it Possible to Overcome Corruption in Education?), accessed 21 June 2006, http://www.strf.ru/organization.aspx?CatalogId=221&d_no=10082
13   Granovetter, M.: The Strength of Weak Ties, in: American Journal of Sociology, 1973 (vol. 78), no. 6, pp. 1360–1380.

If the guardianship arrangement is based on weak ties, cooperation between participants is based on an oral agreement in which the conditions, volume of services and costs are fixed. In this scenario, the difference between the non-monetary practice of guardianship as a form of personal participation and the mixed strategy connecting corrupt contacts is clearly apparent. The problem is that these features can be clearly drawn only theoretically; in reality, it is nearly impossible to distinguish between these two interactions. Therefore, we can only draw a rough border between monetary and non-monetary practices, which have the basic character of a tie between a guardian and his or her ward.

In the event that the contacts between a 'trustee' and a 'ward' are based on strong ties, it is possible to characterize the guardianship as non-monetary informal practice. The purpose of the guardian's work is based on a sincere desire *to solve a problem as if it were his or her own*. If the arrangement is based on weak ties, however, something akin to an unwritten contract is made, whereby access to the guardian's social networks requires a sum of money (or some other good) to change hands. In this case, the guardian is motivated by material gain rather than by personal interest.

In our definition of guardianship, we identified the regular, systematic character of the services. Hence, repeatability and stability determine the time parameters and can also be considered as necessary attributes of this practice; they should therefore be included in the typology. Taking into account the frequency of contacts between the guardian and his or her ward, their communication can be periodic or continuous. Periodic contacts occur from time to time; their main feature is their suddenness and spontaneity. At first, such meetings arise spontaneously and according to necessity, acquiring a systematic character only after some time has elapsed. Contacts that take place on a continuous basis are distinguished by their initially well-thought-out character and scheduled arrangement. In this case relations are stable and meetings are planned throughout the arrangement period.

The above-mentioned criteria allow us to illustrate the types of guardianship services in a table (overleaf) based on examples taken from interviews.

                     Elvira Leontyeva

Table 13-1:   Classification of Guardianship

Characteristics of a network (Kinds of ties according to type and frequency)	Characteristics of social roles (depending on the types of connection)	
	Strong (relatives, close friends); the role of the guardian: insurer, sometimes assistant	*Weak* (acquaintances, distant friends, etc.) the role of the guardian: assistant (frequently paid)
Periodic (occurring spontaneously; unpredictable, from time to time)	Typical situation: from time to time a family member asks for assistance on behalf of a student who is struggling with his or her studies. *NON-MONETARY FORM*	Typical situation: 'I am frequently asked for help by different people. I don't always agree with the request, but I try to help. For the neighbour's girl, I sometimes agreed to help so that she wouldn't fail difficult subjects.' *(Senior lecturer, female, 42 years old)* *BOTH MONETARY AND NON-MONETARY FORM*
Constant (scheduled, designed for a long-term period)	Typical situation: a family member helps to teach the student under the guardianship. Frequently, acceptance into the university was due to the family member's clout. *NON-MONETARY FORM*	Typical situation: 'I decided to take a correspondence course only because I earn well, and although money is not a problem for me, it is still necessary to have time to get the diploma, i.e. I expected that I would come to an agreement with the teacher. But then our girls informed me that it is possible to approach teaching assistants and to talk. And they make the arrangements with the teachers themselves; it's more convenient that way. Last session I worked so hard and there was no time to go to university; so only documents with money were brought in.' *(Correspondence course student/ accountant, female, 32 years old)* *MONETARY FORM*

13.3. Monetary Form of Corruption Strategy. University Bribery

A great deal of empirical research on corruption in Russian universities has been conducted in recent years. Most of it provides a general picture of bribery and explores the issue by relying on quantitative data—such as the size of the corruption market, the motives for corruption, actual and potential participants, and so on. But these studies fail to explain how real corruption networks are organized, how they operate, what kinds of resources are exchanged, etc. These questions can be answered with qualitative data gathered from case studies. The following section presents a typical scheme of bribery interactions based on interviews with students and professors at universities in Khabarovsk.

The most clearly defined actors in corrupt interactions in the educational arena are teachers (tutors, professors) and students. One side has a resource; another is interested in getting it. The corrupt arrangement is initiated by the side that is more interested in obtaining the resource. Our research, as well as research conducted by some other authors, confirms that students tend to be the more interested party. In other words, the majority of contacts are initiated by students. In reality, however, the situation is a bit more complicated.

Assuming that the student is the more interested side of the equation, i.e. the initiator, we consider his or her position as forming a demand. The student is the consumer of services; accordingly, he or she acts as the tutor's or teacher's *customer*. In this case, the tutor is an *executor*. We will consider these roles as the main components of corrupt interactions.

Essentially, professors give students a choice: they can study (i.e. do the work necessary to pass courses) or they can pay to obtain grades (and thus not do the work). In other words, academically-inclined students can obtain their grades in the traditional way: by studying and taking exams. As for students who cannot or simply do not want to put in the effort, they can pay bribes in various ways. Professors often look to lower-level (i.e. less gifted) students as potential payers. Interestingly, students do not condemn professors for this practice; in fact, they even approve of it.

On the other side of the interaction is a student who is interested in obtaining a resource held by the executor. The student thus plays the role of the *customer* and *consumer*. Behavioural models of this side of corrupt interactions incorporate the course of study and speciality, the age of the student, employment, etc. Students combining work with study and students taking correspondence courses are more inclined to choose a corrupt strategy. As mentioned earlier, there are cases of students pursuing a higher education simply because they can afford to do so. In any case, the wholesale demand for grades boosts the demand for the guardianship services described above.

Corrupt arrangements come in two basic variants: direct arrangements and those involving a middleman or 'go-between'. According to the survey data, services involving a middleman are currently more popular. However, direct contacts are by no means rare; they are mainly established in cases when the teacher proposes a corrupt arrangement.

Teachers and students (*executors* and *customers*, respectively) are necessary links of the chain, but they are not the only ones. Employing middlemen is the most widespread approach to corrupt arrangements. The generalized data of all surveys show the distribution rate of corrupt contacts as follows:

- 49% of the students surveyed, speaking about known cases of bribery, reported that the executor and the customer had found each other through a middleman;
- 31% of the students surveyed reported that contact was initiated by students;
- 20% of the students surveyed reported that contact was initiated by teachers.

In terms of the structure of corrupt networks, there are two main types. The first exists to provide a procedure for the transfer of a bribe: it is the 'operational' parameter of a network. The second type promotes the dissemination of information about how the first can be used. These are crossed networks and mutual-aid structures, in which we can observe the different functions of middlemen: the roles of 'helper' and 'prompter'.

The first type (I) is formed by people who are part of a network of confidential contacts, and it is closed to the *executor*. As a rule, effectiveness and operability is provided by one initiator, whom we will call an *operator*. He (she) has two functions: coordinating arrangements and serving as the go-between. If the chain is short and simple, the operator only has to navigate between the *customer* and *executor*. If the network is more complex, he or she also becomes the coordinator between other intermediaries, clients and executors.

We can therefore conclude that in the mechanism of network operation where the information received in network II activates a chain of middlemen (network I), the structure of interaction can be divided according to a standard algorithm: client/prompter—middleman/executor.

The next section describes some typical situations according to this scheme.

13.4. The Schemes of Corruption Contacts

13.4.1. Situation 1: Contacts Through Go-Betweens

The 'intimidate and force to pay' scheme: the teacher is strict and rigid, demanding the highest standards of knowledge, and does not break rules and standards. Students cannot pass this teacher's exam, and start to search for middlemen/go-betweens. The go-betweens are found quickly and divide the income with the teacher.

Example given by a student:

> *It* was the most difficult subject. Even our A+ girls did not pass the exam on their first attempt. It was hopeless. Then we approached the teacher to talk about money. She told us that we mustn't come to her with such questions at all. Then we found out the person

through whom she takes money, and voilà: the money's in a document, the examination's in the bag. *(third-year student, female)*

Example given by a teacher:

My friend explained how she was taught by a friend—a teacher from faculty N—concerning bribes. She told me about her experience, i.e. how she prepares the students to get ready to offer bribes: 'First, it's absolutely necessary to conduct all planned lesson hours completely so that students cannot accuse you of failing to provide materials. It is necessary to prove that you are really very strict and students must believe that compromises are impossible. There are only two ways to succeed: learn by rote or pay. Second, it is necessary to repeat that you will give them all lecture materials and in addition you will give them questions from the textbook; you should name the textbooks. Then you announce that you will give them a minimum of material, less than is required, but this minimum should be learned by heart. Otherwise, if a student fails to answer a question, he or she will not pass. Upon hearing these instructions, most students will become interested in learning how and through whom they can pay for a passing grade. And because the senior students share the information, the way to go about it is quickly found out. Third, half of the students should be eliminated by means of a preliminary control test. When you work and teach in this way and state that you are demanding less than is necessary, you will not be accused. Students will think that you have truly done your best, and therefore they will not complain. And after that, you start to operate. It is always possible [to heap up obstacles (like asking difficult questions or being very strict with grading) so that students will have difficulty getting good grades on the exams]; then you let them search for ways [to get around these obstacles].' This teacher worked with a middleman called S. He took 3 thousand roubles, and they split it. *(Senior lecturer, female, 41 years old)*

This form of corruption combines the initiative of the teacher and the services of a go-between. This is not the only method, however. In some cases the *executor* initiates things directly, offering an array of 'services': go-betweens, prompters, helpers who can reduce the chain to a minimum number of participants, the arrangement of brief interactions, etc. Direct contact is the least popular method of obtaining a passing grade, but it has its advantages. Direct contacts are the most economical and mutually advantageous; they eliminate the go-betweens, and the minimal number of persons involved in the transaction reduces publicity and thus lowers the risk of being caught.

13.4.2. Situation 2: Direct Contact Initiated by the Teacher

The mechanism of this form of contact involves dropping a 'hint': the teacher chooses certain students (generally low-level) and informs them about the price of grades. This information is disclosed in various ways: figures are written on paper, on a blackboard, or shown on a calculator. In another variant, paid consultations are presented as an obligatory condition for obtaining a grade.

Example given by a pair of students:

A: A friend of mine and I failed the examination, and the teacher *hinted to us* that it was possible to pay 'a sponsor's payment' of 200 rubles and the problem would be solved.

Q: Did he tell you this directly or indirectly?

> A: *He gave us a really obvious hint.* He hinted in such a way that we understood immediately. (third-year student, male, 20 years old)

Example given by a teacher:

> I've heard that teachers write the sum of money on the blackboard or type it on a calculator to show how much a grade costs. I also heard from my student that a teacher told them that a particular subject is so difficult that no one can pass a test without additional consultation, and additional consultation costs a certain sum of money. I think that is a sort of bribe, too. *(Senior lecturer, female, 36 years old)*

Finally, the third way of establishing contact is also direct, but initiated by the student rather than by the teacher. This method is the second most popular form of obtaining a grade, but teachers frequently refuse to deal with the student directly. Nevertheless, around one third of such attempts usually result in agreement.

13.4.3. Situation 3

The 'teacher welfare' scheme: the student or group (generally those who are not serious students) offers material aid to the teacher. The money is inserted into a student's documents and thus transferred to the teacher, who takes the money, gives the student a passing grade, and returns the documents. In another variant, the 'welfare' (i.e. charity) is offered to the faculty, whereby the teacher accepts the money ostensibly on behalf of the faculty. Or, in yet another form, the teacher takes the money, but only after additional consultations with the student.

> Examples given by students:

> I had to leave town urgently, and I had no time to prepare for the examination. I approached the tutor and explained. He wrote a figure on a piece of paper silently, and I agreed. *(third-year student, female)*

> When I was a first-year student, I tried to give a hundred rubles to the tutor, but she said that she couldn't take the money just like that. She said I should come to a consultation and the problem would be solved. I attended the consultation and she gave me a five [the best grade on the Russian scale]. After I obtained the grade, I no longer needed to attend these consultations. *(fourth-year student, female)*

These mechanisms describe the main interactions, which can vary and combine different initiatives, but one of these three mechanisms constitutes the basis of each network.

13.5. Conclusion

We have studied the education process in a tertiary institution as a system based on informal ties. Taking into the account the unrealizability of academic programmes for certain students, the teacher can either decide to lower the requirements to suit the students' abilities or to present the material in full, knowing that the majority of students will not be able to master it. At this point, a student decides when and how to go about breaking the rules in order to obtain a passing grade. It is obvious that universities currently accept any and every mediocre applicant who is ready to pay his or her way. As long as this system exists, there can be no talk of integrity or honesty at our universities.

Dilorom Akhmedzhanova

14. Modern Russian Homeowners' Associations as Res Publicae. The Relationship between Commonwealth and Corruption

14.1. Introduction

According to the Russian Housing Code (passed in 2005), homeowners' associations are unions intended for the joint management of real estate (use, maintenance) in one or several multi-apartment buildings. These associations are non-profit organizations that may engage in entrepreneurial activities, but they must direct all profits to the maintenance of the housing and the adjacent territory.[1]

Actually, this form of collective housing management and maintenance is not a completely new phenomenon in Russia. But in its modern form, it has only existed since the new Housing Code was adopted in 2005. The creation and development of the maximum possible number of such associations is one of the most important steps toward housing reform in Russia conducted so far. The number of such associations has been growing steadily since the new Housing Code was introduced.[2]

Besides the Housing Code, a great corpus of legislation has been created to regulate the activities of homeowners' associations. These rules pertain to various aspects of housing relationships both inside and outside of the associations. The internal regulation (mostly described in the Housing Code) is directed at preventing corruption and abuse; some aspects of these crimes are also covered by the Russian Administrative and Criminal Law. All of these regulations and laws are intended to prevent and restrict any possibilities for abuse and corruption.

On the other hand, there have been lots of scandals about corruption, stealing and kickbacks in homeowners' associations in Russia in recent years. Most of the cases have involved infringements and abuses of power by chairpersons and board members.

The main goal of this article is to explain the reasons for corruption and its many forms in homeowners' associations. To achieve this objective, the following tasks will be undertaken:

1. a sociological description of homeowners' associations as a community-based entity designed to look out for the common interest;
2. an explanation of the theoretical basis of my research;
3. an analysis of the activities and collective organization in homeowners' associations;

---

1   Russian Housing Code. 2005. Article 135.
2   See Table 1.

4. an exploration and detailed explanation of corruption in homeowners' associations, including the reasons, bases and effect on the commonwealth.

The following empirical data will be presented in relation to the above-listed tasks: in-depth interviews with members and managers of homeowners' associations as well as with experts in the communal and housing sphere. The majority of the interviews were conducted during my dissertation research and are augmented by interviews conducted for the 'Homeowners' Support' project run by the New Eurasia Foundation (Moscow). These include expert interviews with municipal housing department officers and housing NGO representatives in Nizhniy Novgorod, Tver' and Perm'. Quantitative data from the questionnaires given to the associations were also used for the analysis. Russian housing law was a supplementary data source during the research.

The theoretical basis for my research is neo-republican theory. This choice was connected to an uncommon conception and understanding of the corruption phenomenon. In the republican tradition, 'corruption' is defined as the domination of private interests over common interests and non-participation in common deals and decision-making processes. Nowadays, the most common understanding of corruption is bribes obtained through position; possibilities and opportunities for corruption are also provided by legal loopholes, however, and the scale and dimensions of corruption varies in different countries and spheres. As Iseult Honohan observed, '[...] Corruption is not found only in illegal activities, but in engaging in political interaction to realise only individual or sectional interests in wealth, power or status.'[3] Republican theory explains corruption in a more detailed manner and reveals new aspects of corruption's appearance and development. The reasons and bases for corruption both lie in the organizational plane and concern moral and philosophical categories—civic virtue, 'life sense' production and individual freedom. All of these categories and aspects open new horizons in the analysis of the phenomenon of corruption.

This text contains the following parts: a sociological description of homeowners' associations as a specific type of community and organization, a theoretical section containing categories for analysis, field data characteristics, a re-evaluation of the field data according to theoretical concepts, an analysis of corruption in homeowners' associations, and conclusions.

14.2. The Homeowners' Association as a Specific Community

This section describes the specific aspects of homeowners' associations. Close attention will be paid to the social and sociological features of this type of human organization.

As mentioned above, the main goal of this type of association is to establish and develop a system of self-management in multi-apartment houses that addresses the

---

3   Honohan, Iseult: Civic Republicanism, London, New York: Routledge, 2002, p. 5.

quality of services, maintenance and building improvement. Owners and renters are integrated in the common property and they share the need for services. They supposedly participate in decision-making processes, pay fees for additional services and repairs, and in some cases pay fees for communal services.

The main basis for the classification of homeowners' associations is the year the building was constructed. The first law (entitled 'About homeowners' associations') on this subject was adopted in 1996.[4] The registration and creation of homeowners' associations is mandatory in newly constructed multi-apartment houses. Homeowners' associations can be categorized according to the way they are created. Roughly speaking, they fall into two large groups: those created in 'new' (after 1996) and 'old' houses. These types differ in terms of how they integrate and create community. In the 'new' houses, the registration of homeowners' associations is in many cases only a formality with no need to obtain consensus from residents. In the 'old' houses, it is not obligatory to register a homeowners' association on the basis of a common decision, which must be entered into the record properly.

But in the 'old' houses, the processes of integration are diverse and more complicated; the reasons for integration in these cases are also very different. One of the most common reasons for creating homeowners' associations is to resist raiders' (i.e. groups or companies attempting to capture a given property by means of illegal privatization, falsification of ownership documents, etc.) desires for basements, lofts and other common placements in multi-apartment houses. Another reason is unsatisfactory levels of maintenance and poor service quality; sometimes residents will try to create an association in order to increase the level of comfort in the building.

Two judicial reasons have also inspired the growth of homeowners' associations in 'old' houses. The first is the adoption of the Russian Land Code, which ordered the privatization of the land surrounding apartment houses. Homeowners' associations thereby received the opportunity to privatize the land under and around their houses.[5] The second law, entitled 'About the foundation (state corporation) toward promote reform of communal and housing industry', ordered capital repairs in multi-apartment houses constructed before 1991. Homeowners' associations have priority in applying for and receiving funding for capital repairs.

According to the Housing Code, there are various forms of ownership in multi-apartment houses: private, municipal and departmental (rare nowadays). But in 'new' houses, there is no mixture of ownership rights, a feature which also distinguishes 'old' and 'new' houses. The structure of ownership also depends on the year of construc-

---

4   This law was canceled after the adoption of the Housing Code, but this norm carried over to the new Code.
5   Except for driveways and lands designated for district technical communications (electricity transformers, etc.).

tion. Usually, there are more homogeneous ownership structures in newly constructed apartments, and communal flats are absent in 'new' houses.

The second criterion for classifying homeowners' associations is the size of the association. Obviously, it is easier to manage a small association than a large one.

Another classification criterion is the location of the apartment building, i.e. whether it is in the city centre or on the outskirts.

In general, there are more 'old', small, mixed social structure and ownership right associations in the centre of the city; the larger and more homogenous associations in the 'new' houses are mostly found in the suburbs.

There are two ways to manage building maintenance and service provision in homeowners' associations: via direct management or through a management company. In the case of direct management, associations hire their own staff and work as a small housing company. In the case of using a management company, the associations' members decide which company to hire and control its activities in their house(s).

Both forms of management imply collective decision-making. According to the Housing Code, each decision must be supported by at least 50 percent of the members plus one. The minimal meeting agendas include improving the annual report, election/re-election of the board, etc. But issues like the introduction of additional services, decisions about capital repairs and renting the common property are also subject to collective decision.

In the ideal model, collective decision-making leads to the effective distribution of payments, profitable disposal of common property and a rising level of residential comfort. These represent common goals for association members. However, the decision-making process is realized in different ways and sometimes by illegal means.

The process of decision-making and quorum gathering will be described and analysed in the chapter about homeowners' associations as res publicae. First, however, it is necessary to explain the general categories of res publicae. The next chapter introduces the theoretical framework for this research.

14.3. Theoretical Approach. The Res Publica as a Community and Method of Integration

In this chapter I will refer to two texts by Iseult Honohan, her book 'Civic Republicanism' and a collective article entitled 'Res Publica: Revival of the Interest'.

Following the demise of socialism in political philosophy, contemporary science suggests only one corpus of theories for common life (i.e. 'life together' in Laurent Thevenot's sense[6]): liberal theory. The republican tradition was revived as an alternative

---

6   Thevenot, Laurent: Nauka vmeste zhit' v etom mire, in: Neprikosnovenniy Zapas (Emergency Ration), 2004, no. 3 (35), http://magazines.russ.ru/nz/2004/35/teve2.html

approach toward public life. In contrast to libertarian theories, which are centred on individual interests, republican theory emphasizes responsibility for common goods.[7] One of the most important issues in republican theory is the provision of common goods, which entails creating social relationships that promote the collective interest over the individual yet protect individual freedom.

There are four key elements in the republican approach:

1. The realization of the *special concept of freedom*. This concept of freedom means not only freedom for mobility and activities, but freedom from the will of others. By accepting the limitations formulated within common decisions about law and rules, the individual remains free. The rules protect him/her from the arbitrariness of others.
2. *Civic Virtues*. To be a 'good citizen' means to participate in identifying the commonwealth and take care of it. Civic virtues are based on the conviction that the commonwealth is more important than individual benefits.
3. *Participation of citizens in common decisions* about common conditions of life, especially rules, and in common activities. Participation in the common decision-making process legitimates the rules within a community. The absence of these processes creates fertile ground for corruption.
4. *Recognition by the community of noticeable individual contributions to the common cause*. This practice creates a sense of individual efforts within the commonwealth.[8]

These four elements all create a special kind of community in which members are united by the goal of common good producing (commonweal) and strive to be 'good citizens'. This system not only has a large organizational basis in the technical sense but also pays great attention to the moral aspects of a community and its members. Thus, *a res publica* is a specific kind of community where participants are integrated into commonwealth production and support by means of a continuous decision-making and management process. In addition, the community is equipped with a set of civic virtues, and individual contributions and efforts are recognized.

How is *corruption* defined in republican theory? Corruption is the domination of individual interests over the collective interest. This domination might stem from that fact that political decisions are only temporary and involve a constantly evolving situation; furthermore, during the political process, 'people will always tend to be torn between their private interests and the common good'.[9] Therefore, various institutional tools are applied to foster the development and support of civic spirit: laws, the training of a citizen militia, civic education and civic religion.[10] The main goal for the republic is to create a system in which private interests cost less than the commonwealth.

7　Honohan, Iseult: Civic Republicanism, London, New York: Routledge, 2002, p. 10.
8　Ibid., p. 5.
9　Ibid., p. 6.
10　Ibid., p. 6.

It is therefore not only rules and management issues that are important; identity formation is equally critical.

In the next section, the individual elements of a republic are considered in detail.

Freedom. There two conventional types of freedom in political philosophy—negative and positive freedom. This distinction was introduced by Isaiah Berlin.[11] Positive freedom is the freedom to be the master of one's own life. Negative freedom is freedom from external interference. This distinction is not relevant for the republican sense of freedom. In the republican tradition, the concept of freedom includes both of these contradictory concepts in one category.[12] Freedom in the republican sense is non-slavery, e.g. freedom from tyranny and from the will of others. This brings us to the concept of non-domination, which is predicated upon the following condition: only those agree not to dominate others nor to be dominated by others can be considered free.[13] The main sense of republican freedom is preserving individual freedom, including under the law. Freedom in the republican sense is also preserved through obligatory collective decision-making about rules and the right to independence from the will of others.

Civic virtues are closely connected with the idea of a 'good citizen'. To preserve individual freedom, it is necessary to participate in a collective decision-making process and adopt or reject collective living rules as well as establish limits with respect to these rules. Only active participation in this process can ensure freedom, safety and the legitimization of existing rules and laws. Willingness to participate in collective action and to support the commonwealth are obligatory components of 'good citizenship'. But in a situation of rational choice, an individual selfishly tries to maximize his or her profits and minimize expenses. In what is known as the 'free rider' problem, individuals consume more than their fair share of a public good yet contribute less than their fair share to the production of this good. In other words, some individuals are only prepared to participate in collective action if it requires a minimal contribution or no individual efforts on their part.[14] This phenomenon has been described and investigated in numerous studies.[15] Olson's proposal for solving this problem consists of two methods: sanctions (from collective denunciation to physical punishment) and

---

11   Berlin, Isaiah: Dve Kontseptsii Svobody, Filosofiya Svobody. Evropa, Moscow: NLO, 2001 (1958), p. 133.
12   Akhmedzhanova, Dilorom/ Volkov, Vadim/ Gerasimova, Katerina/ Kaploun, Viktor/ Roschin, Yevgeniy/ Troyanovsky, Sergey/ Kharkhordin, Oleg/ Chyuikina, Sofia: Res Publica. Revival of the Interest, in: Kharkhordin, Oleg (ed.): What is Republican Tradition?, Saint Petersburg: EUSP press, 2009, pp. 7–22, here p. 10.
13   Ibid. p. 11.
14   Olson, Mancur: The Logic of Collective Action. Public Goods and the Theory of Groups, Cambridge, MA: Harvard University Press, 1965.
15   See for instance: Birnbaum, Pierre: States and Collective Action. European Experience, Cambridge, New York, Melbourne: Cambridge University Press, 1988; Fantasia, Rick: Culture of Solidarity. Consciousness, Action and Contemporary American Workers, Berkeley, Los Angeles, London:

creating a community ideology in which collective goods are dominant over individual interests. However, the costs for controlling access to common goods and imposing sanctions can be very high and incommensurate with individual contributions. In addition, the process of establishing a community ideology takes a long time and is therefore not a short-term solution to the problem of free riding.

In republican theory, the degradation of civic virtues and deliberate avoidance of the collective decision-making process gives rise to corruption. Corruption in this sense is the domination of private interests over collective aims. Compared to the more common concept of corruption (bribes, etc.), this definition is very basic. Corruption can only take root if collective aims are subordinated to individual goals and interests.

There are two arguments in the republican tradition regarding the development of civic virtues. The first one comes from Alexis de Tocqueville's book 'Democracy in America' and runs roughly as follows: if you live by your private interests and leave the community's management to others, you run the risk of losing the power to influence decisions that affect your interests.[16] According to de Tocqueville, civic virtues like education, freedom of the press and participation in municipal self-governing associations and other so-called 'schools of freedom' were the keys to preventing disenfranchisement.

The second republican argument with respect to the production and improvement of civic virtues entails elaborating recognition mechanisms in communities.

Recognition by a community is an important element of a republic. Public recognition and demonstration of individual contributions or civic virtues become the basis for participants' social identity and elevate the commonwealth over individual interests. This mechanism generates virtues competition in communities, a competition that is necessary to protect the community from degradation.

This idea also was developed by Alasdair MacIntyre.[17] He argued that constant public competition in the arts and politics as well as active citizenship is an obligatory condition for strong and sustainable community development. This competition must be transparent and realized only upon recognition of the participants' equality and after violence is unequivocally rejected as a tool for societal control. Through openness and transparency, the community creates new standards of virtue. How can one achieve recognition from the community? Only by participation.

Participation is one of the most crucial elements in community development. The participation process is rooted in the classical ancient republics of Athens and Rome. By including more and more social groups into the governing process, the necessity of

University of California Press, 1989; Oberschall, Anthony: Social Movements. Ideologies, Interests, and Identities, New Brunswick/NJ, London: Transaction Publishers, 1993.
16   De Tocqueville, Alexis: Democracy in America, trans. and eds. Mansfield, Harvey C./ Winthrop, Delba, Chicago: University of Chicago Press, 2000, p. 44.
17   MacIntyre, Alasdair: Posle Dobrodeteli (After Virtue), Moscow: Academicheskiy Proekt, 2000.

representative participation instead of direct democracy became increasingly important. The typical conception of direct democracy is common meeting, but indeed in the classical republics the practice of using lots to elect 'managers' was widespread. This mechanism provided equality among the formal participants. However, these elections had to be improved by a clearly defined and transparent procedure that excluded the possibility of cheating.

At the community level, the problem of participation concerns the size of the community; naturally, it is easier to gather 10 or 20 participants than two hundred. And in addition to the logistical problem of finding a convenient time and place for all to convene, there is also the issue of motivation and interest. The level of participation has a direct influence on whether or not corruption will take root and flourish.

Motivation and interest are derived from the commonweal. The level of the participants' access to a common good, as well as its structure and nature, are reasons for participation or non-participation in community activities. At this juncture it is necessary to extend our theoretical understanding of the res publica and explore the concept of 'common things'.

Common things in the republican case constitute the material cement for a community. Common ownership is more important and measurable than unclear and weak ideas about civic virtues. Shared ownership is an effective integrator and an individual financial interest may be more powerful and useful in community building.

Common good (or commonweal) in a community is 'good for each person as a member of a society or group'.[18] It is also important to emphasize that there is an 'inter-subjective-practical sense of the common good in which people who are intrinsically social as well as significantly separate benefit as members of a group'.[19] In this sense there are clear tensions between common goods producing and individual interests. Only a group that is able to provide common goods that exceed individual contributions can prevail over individual interests. This would entail regular contributions and the absence of oppressive and corrupt methods of government. Therefore, there are three tasks for any community wishing to engage in the production of common goods. First, the community must create common goods that are more valuable than the cost of individual contributions and efforts. The second task is to provide a means of collecting contributions and thus solve the free riders problem. The third task is to distribute the common goods, i.e. to provide equitable access for community members and restrict access for free riders.

However, it must be remembered that in the republican sense, the common good is first and foremost based on the value of joint self-governance. It is only after

---

18   Honohan, Iseult: Civic Republicanism, London, New York: Routledge, 2002, p. 151.
19   Ibid., p. 156.

this mechanism is established that other goods can be evaluated as important or unimportant for the community.

To conclude this part of the article, I will introduce the set of concepts that will be used in further stages of the analysis: *freedom (individual and community), civic virtues, community recognition, participation and common things*. All of these concepts are closely connected with *common goods (commonweal), community and individual interest* and will be considered in the following discussion on *corruption*.

How are these elements presented in modern homeowners' associations and how do they form the community? How does corruption arise and which factors enable it to exist in these associations? These two questions will be addressed in the following analysis.

14.4. Field Data

The field data were collected during two research projects. One project was my dissertation, which considers modern Russian homeowners' associations; the research was conducted within the collective research project 'Self-Governing Associations in North-Western Russia' (EUSP/Helsinki University) in 2005–2006.[20] More data were collected over the course of my individual research for my Ph.D.[21] The second research project, 'The Practical Methods of Housing Self-Governing in Nizhniy Novgorod, Perm' and Tver', was conducted within the framework of the 'Homeowners Support' project implemented by the New Eurasia Foundation (Moscow).[22]

Thirty-one interviews were conducted for the dissertation project, representing twelve cases of homeowners' associations in Saint Petersburg. Nine of these interviews were expert interviews. Information on legal regulations was collected from federal and regional databases.

The second research project focused on three target cities (Perm', Tver' and Nizhniy Novgorod) and addressed three target groups: homeowners, chairpersons of homeowners' associations and experts (municipal housing department heads, housing NGO representatives and housing journalists). Questionnaires were also distributed, with 856 questionnaires completed by homeowners in associations and 25 by association chairpersons. Additionally, six focus groups were carried out.

Not all of the above-mentioned data are directly connected with the present topic; only relevant data will be discussed here. The quantity of field data is, however, sufficiently representative for the present analysis of corruption in homeowners' associations.

---

20   The project was supported by the Academy of Finland.
21   The project was supported by the EUSP Interdisciplinary Centre 'Res Publica' and funded by Dynasty Foundation (Russia).
22   This project was funded by USAID.

14.5. The Res Publica in Modern Homeowners' Associations

Is the modern homeowners' association a republican community? In which sense and according to which criteria could it be viewed as a republican community? The next section will address these questions.

The theoretical scheme is refined in this analysis. We will start by considering *common things*. Theoretically, this concept is the weakest from the critics' point of view. How should we define common things? Is the formal recognition of common property the only basis for considering this property as a 'common thing'? In this part of the analysis, I understand *common thing* to mean a material or non-material object which is subject to common ownership rules. It is the reason for the development of management practices and promotes integration/disintegration of a community, primarily in the form of self-management and community identity forming.

According to the Housing Code, the common property in multi-apartment buildings consists of common stairs, stairwells, roofs, basements, the land under the building and the lands around the building (if these lands were privatized by the homeowners' association). Besides these items there could be additional common things, such as playground equipment, fences, guards and video-monitoring systems, trees and plants, benches, etc.

The most important issue for this part of the analysis is the distribution of responsibility for building parts and access to common use.

In 'old' houses, there are sometimes problems with the basements and roofs. The legal status of these quarters, especially in buildings in the city centre, remains a very hotly debated issue in Russia. During the privatization process in the 1990s, these buildings were privatized (regardless of their technical status as multi-apartment buildings), with legal restrictions imposed upon them, and re-rented by different commercial firms and municipalities. This problem has a double effect on homeowners' associations. On the one hand, the owners of these quarters established and registered homeowners' associations as a forum to fight for their full rights. On the other hand, some owners were scared off by the associations because they did not want to be part of the community.

However, on the basis of the field data, I can conclude that the presence of an external threat is a strong factor for integration. In most cases, common things became the subject of all of the homeowners' interactions. There are at least two reasons for this. First, these things constitute the minimal set of items that support building functionality and thus represent a 'subsistence minimum' in any multi-apartment building exploitation. Second, the 'manifestation' of these objects happens regularly in most buildings due to breakage.[23] This breakage indeed creates the need for homeowner communication, but how should the financial responsibility for repairs be divided and how should these repairs be organized?

The most striking illustration of relationships based on common property concerns the allocation and governing of parking places. The first reason for conflict is the fact that not all homeowners own cars nowadays. The second reason is that there are not enough parking places at most apartment buildings. Thus, the decision on how much land should be allocated to parking places forms the core of the debate between car owners and others, e.g. the parents of small children interested in playgrounds, pet owners, pensioners who prefer to plant flowers around the building, etc. The distribution of parking places is also a very acute issue for homeowners' associations. Many different decisions are involved: whether to expand parking lots via construction work, introduce a parking time-table, etc.

In two cases in my sample, a republican solution for distribution was used. Lots were drawn to division parking spaces. However, this mechanism must be executed with procedural norms to ensure the legitimation of the community's decision. A special commission consisting of homeowners must be established to monitor the procedure, the procedure itself must be maximally transparent, and the result must be codified immediately. The correct execution of this procedure could help associations to prevent corrupt practices. In reality, however, this procedure is not widespread, or it is executed with various violations. Conflicts about parking places are sometimes solved by means of informal practices of a different character. In some cases a physical altercation (such as fighting or vandalism) or the 'law of the jungle' might be involved, while in other cases interested car owners can give bribes to the association's manager.

In conclusion, private interests prevail over common interests in the distribution of limited resources. The 'common thing' thus did not become a common cause and an object for joint care, but a resource that all members of the community fought over.

Ideally, the whole community must be integrated around *common goods* producing. What is commonweal in homeowners' associations? The answer resides in its judicial definition: joint management of common property in a multi-apartment building. But as the analysis of participation will show, this common good is not universally recognized by homeowners. For many homeowners, common goods produced by associations are significant. Among such common goods is comfortable living. As one homeowner said, 'What is the main issue? That our house is clean and beautiful.' But producing this kind of common good also entails obstacles in the form of non-payers and free riders. As we shall see, there are two forms of participation: political

---

23   Such breakages take place not only in 'old' buildings but in 'new' buildings, too. The breakage is due to the poor quality of construction; Russia still lacks a certification system for construction companies.

and practical. In the political sense, there is participation in common meetings and the use of self-government to develop the association. In the practical sense, financial contributions to the production of functional common goods can be made. How these common goods are supported and provided by association members will be described later in the chapter on participation.

The next republican characteristic is the special concept of *freedom* realization. This concept is very important for a republican community, but in the case of homeowners' associations, members' freedom is a very philosophical question. Are owners free in their decisions about common property? How does the community constrain them? All of these questions are very serious and are the object of large-scale separate research. For this analysis it is important to remember that formally, all homeowners are equal in their rights and their votes depend on the size of their quarters. On the other hand, the minority must accept the majority's decision. This does not contradict republican principles.

Recognition of members' contributions at the level of homeowners' associations can be judicial and ideological. First of all, it is necessary to clarify what effect a contribution has on community development and functioning. Where are the two kinds of contributions. The first kind is official: payments for services, voluntary donations for additional equipment, and participation in decision-making processes. These kinds of contributions are described and regulated by the Housing Code and Russian law. The second kind of contribution is informal: volunteer work and initiatives for building improvement and mediation in conflict situations. The first kind of contribution is rewarded by the absence of judicial problems in most cases. The second kind could be rewarded by other members' respect.

But for a classical republic with its constant competition in civic virtues, recognition has an additional effect: it contributes to the community's ability to commemorate and immortalize its members, i.e. to honour them as a standard of virtue for future generations. However, this aspect poses a problem in homeowners' associations. People do not seek meaning in their lives from this kind of community. It would be strange to dedicate one's life to such a community. The ideas of motherland, religion and patriotism are more important to most people than their apartment. This phenomenon is influenced by community ideology. The process of establishing a community identity and forming symbolic significance is a very long and complicated process. In certain cases this has taken place to some extent. For example, some homeowners' associations have produced their own symbols, such as flags, logos, etc. Some multi-apartment buildings constructed in the 19th and early 20th centuries have a very rich history, and this history has become the basis for identity development. It is nevertheless difficult to conduct a monosemantic evaluation on identity and ideology in homeowners' associations because they have not been around for very long.

Civic virtues are very important in homeowners' associations. As mentioned above, two kinds of contributions constitute representations of 'good citizens' in these groups. In a technical sense, the most important virtue is regular payment for services. But the problem of non-payers and free riders is a typical problem for any homeowners' association—in 'old' and 'new', large and small, average and even elite houses.[24]

The second kind of contribution (volunteer work, mediation in conflicts) is fairly uncommon and not widely recognized by community members. One of the reasons for this lack of recognition is that these contributions have not been defined as important for associations.

The most important kind of civic virtue within homeowners' associations is participation in decision-making processes. This kind of contribution plays an important role in this analysis and therefore needs to be examined in more detail.

Russian housing law stipulates that at least one common meeting must be conducted per year. The formal purpose of these meetings is to present the association board's annual report and re-elect the board; these activities are mandatory. Additionally, the introduction of new services, distribution of payments, identification of non-payers, etc. could also take place at these annual meetings.

If the association takes a vote, the decision is legitimate if it is supported by at least 50% +1 member of the association. The special procedure of absentee voting was officially adopted only two years ago. This format was introduced due to difficulties with quorum gathering in annual meetings and technical problems with holding unscheduled meetings, such as renting a large hall, mailing official invitations, and preparing certain documentation.

At this point we can move on to the main part of this analysis: *participation*. There are different ways to evaluate participation in homeowners' associations.

Over the course of the research for the 'Homeowners' Support Project', a special 'participation index' was created. Based on the answers for 11 questions in the questionnaire for homeowners in Tver', Perm' and Nizhniy Novgorod,[25] the index characterizes the residents' level of participation, readiness for participation, and degree of interest in association activities.

The index exhibited a dispersion from minus 9 to 10 (potentially from minus 13 to 11), indicating an average tendency favouring participation over non-participation.

---

24   A more detailed description of this process is given in: Akhmedzhanova, Dilorom: The Problem of Collective Action Inside Homeowners' Associations in Russia, paper presented at the Changing Europe Summer School IV. Civil Society in Central and Eastern Europe before and after the End of Socialism, Kyiv (Ukraine), 27–31 July 2009, http://www.changing-europe.org/download/Summer_School_2009/Akhmedzhanova.pdf

25   The list of these questions can be found in Section 14.8, Appendix 2. The statistical analysis was made by Lev Shilov, project analyst. Part of the report is published in Russian at: http://www.tsj.ru/forum.asp?ForumID=502&id=261510&showtext=0&act=view&page=1&pagenum=8&print=1, accessed 27 May 2010.

This index was configured into five groups, from total non-participation to full participation. The index spreads in interval and group expressions are shown in Section 14.9, Appendix 3.[26]

As the graphs show, the 'high participation' group is larger than the 'medium participation' group (38.08% vs. 31.78%).[27] Note that the value of 'medium' tends to 'high', with the highest limit of interval 2 significantly higher than the lowest value of interval 0.

The dependence of the index on the general respondents' characteristics was also analysed. There was no correlation with the homeowners' sex, but there was a correlation with their age. The group under 30 had a low value in this index; the highest values were in the groups aged 30–40, 40–50 and 60–70. We can therefore conclude that the older the homeowners were, the more disposed they were to take part in homeowners' association activities.

Salary level and the size of payments to homeowners' associations did not influence the index values. However, household size was significant for participation level: singles were found to be less inclined to participate. The length of residency in multi-apartment buildings also influenced the level of participation; the highest value was assigned to groups living in the building for more than 20 years, while the lowest value was exhibited by groups who had lived in their multi-apartment building for less than 5 years. There was no significant correlation of the level of participation and the level of the respondents' education and profession, but as expected, pensioners were more inclined to exhibit a high level of participation.

The general conclusion from the analysis of this index is that pensioners are more likely to participate due to their age and length of residency in the house.

How is participation determined in homeowners' associations?

There were two assumptions for this part of the analysis. The first supposition was that homeowners who are more interested and informed about the associations' activities would be more given to high participation; this assumption was confirmed by statistical tests. The second assumption, concerning dependence between the level of solidarity (readiness to help neighbours solve small problems, loyalty to non-payers) and the level of participation, was not confirmed by the analysis.

How did the homeowners' opinion of the management as well as their view of the level of transparency and efficiency in their homeowners' association correlate to 'high' and 'low' levels of participation? The following trends emerged:

---

26 The index groups were formed in the following way: [-9;-5] was the lowest level of participation, followed by the intervals [-4; -1], [0; 2] and [3;6], with [7;9] being the highest level of participation.

27 It is important to emphasize that for participation in this project, there was a special tender both for target regions and homeowners' associations involved in the research. It means that the sample was filled by the more advantaged homeowners' associations.

1. Respondents with a high level of participation thought that there were small allowable difficulties during common meetings; respondents with a low level of participation thought that the common meeting was a waste of time.
2. Respondents with a high level of participation were satisfied with the information provided about the associations' activities; respondents with a low level of participation held the opposite opinion.
3. Respondents with a high level of participation judged the maintenance of their buildings as 'satisfactory' or 'good'; homeowners with a low level of participation said that they were unable to pass judgment on the maintenance work ('don't know', 'difficult to say').
4. Homeowners with a high level of participation evaluated the association chairpersons' qualifications as sufficient for their functions; homeowners with a low level of participation held the opposite view.
5. Homeowners with a high level of participation were more likely to entrust multi-apartment maintenance and association management to the association chairperson; in contrast, homeowners with a low level of participation were more inclined to entrust these tasks to special housing management companies.

In general, I can conclude that the higher level of participation correlated to the level of information about overall building activities and to the level of satisfaction with the building maintenance. Participation was less connected with financial position, number of common meetings per year or access to specific information. An additional discriminant analysis showed that there were no clear factors capable of influencing the values of the participation index.

How was the homeowners' participation evaluated by the associations' chairpersons? To answer this question, data from the chairpersons in the same homeowners' association survey were analysed. Most of the chairpersons felt that the problem of participation was the most acute for associations. Thus, 88% of the chairpersons responded that 'indifferent attitude to common property and association activities from the side of the homeowners' was a serious problem for their association, while 76% of the chairpersons supposed that more active involvement of the homeowners in association activities could improve the efficiency of the associations. But with respect to the homeowners' behaviour, the most pressing problems were cited as non-payment (33%), non-participation in common meetings (24%) and lack of participation in common works (16%).[28] In other words, the chairpersons felt that most problems were due to the homeowners' lack of participation (either financial or in terms of activities).

Why were there such strong contradictions within the same associations? There are two sources for this asymmetry. The first source is the fact that people prefer to make themselves look good, and are therefore unlikely to criticize their own level of

---

28   See Section 14.9, Appendix 3.

activity. The second reason concerns the asymmetry in information and evaluations: the chairpersons sometimes did not have complete knowledge about their associations' members or had different concepts about the homeowners' levels of activity and participation.

Remarkably, the experts polled for this research held the common opinion that the best role for homeowners is to simply pay for services without actively participating in decision-making processes. The experts explained that the communication costs in decision-making are very high, especially because homeowners are not experts in specific technical matters.

Why are there so many contradictions? Let us consider three components of participation: regular payments, taking part in common meetings and participation in common works.

The first form of participation is currently a very acute problem for homeowners' associations and housing cooperatives, as well as for any multi-apartment houses. For example, the population's debt for housing/communal services in the Leningrad region alone in 2008 was more than 1 billion rubles (approximately 22.7 million euros).[29] There are various reasons for non-payment, of course: tardiness/disorganization, poverty, dissatisfaction with the quality of received services, etc. As the expert data in my dissertation research show, the non-payer problem became increasingly perceptible not only because of rising levels of non-payers, but also, and maybe even mostly, because there are no effective methods to force non-payers to pay that are permissible in Russian law.

The second kind of participation concerns not only the homeowners but also the board. There have been cases in which common meetings were deliberately organized to occur when the majority of homeowners could not attend. For instance, meetings have been held in an inconvenient location (such as across town), or invitations to the meetings were not sent two weeks beforehand, as required by law, but at the last moment. Such violations usually take place to arrange a vote to approve a decision that will only benefit certain groups, or to falsify the annual report as 'satisfactory' despite numerous violations in association activities.

In most cases, however, the homeowners themselves are simply not interested in attending these common meetings. Typical excuses for skipping the meetings include 'I hadn't enough time', 'My opinion doesn't matter' and 'There are enough people without me to make decisions.' There are deeper reasons for the absenteeism at common meetings, however.

---

29   http://www.newspb.ru/allnews/462829/ data from Leningrad regional governance. Total statistics for all of Russia have not been gathered. It is therefore only possible to estimate the level of non-paying in the communal-housing sector in a fragmentary way.

One of the reasons for non-participation concerns the weakness of the management system itself. Indeed, it is not possible for the homeowners' associations to influence most of the fees for communal services; services like water (hot and cold), heating and electricity are sold by monopolistic companies.[30] The procedure to change service companies is also usually very complicated, and it is not popular to change companies even if the services provided are poor.

And of course, the behaviour of the associations' managers and chairpersons is not transparent in all cases. There could be different forms of violations from their side, such as collusion with suppliers resulting in kickbacks or ineffective or criminal distribution of payments.

One of the most common reasons for replacing chairpersons is misappropriation of association finances. There were three such cases in my dissertation research. These events tend to follow a standard scenario. Most homeowners are not control of their board; in the cases I observed, an initiative group collected and initiated an audit procedure after two or three years. After that common meetings were conducted and evidence of fraud was presented to the homeowners. But even when such scandals occur, it is still difficult to gather a quorum for a common meeting.

The second cause of non-participation resides in the nature of the homeowners' associations. In terms of day-to-day significance, these associations are not really organizations or communities, but simply entities pertaining to housing. When people come home, they want to relax and enjoy their private lives, not participate in common meetings and discussions. This conflict between public and private life is a very big reason for the low level of participation in decision-making processes.

Additionally, the residents' conception of physical borders provides a very good index of attitudes toward the associations. Homeowners find it difficult to define the borders of their courtyards—where does home end and the street begin? Enclosed courtyards are more often defined as a middle ground between home and the street, but for many of my informants, the doors of their apartments constituted the border between their territory and the outside world. In most cases the owners' concepts of 'their' territory are limited to the physical confines of their apartments. However, they consider the courtyards, which they formally share with the other tenants, to belong to others. Given this attitude, it is not surprising that many homeowners are not interested in association activities or membership.

This is very common for all home-owners' associations. But nevertheless we observe various levels of participation in different home-owners' associations. How can these differences be explained? And what kind of measures can associations use to increase participation levels?

---

30   This monopolism is not so much due to political and economic interests, but to technical reasons. To some extent, these companies are natural monopolies.

First, an effective management system within homeowners' associations promotes managers who do not need to conceal their activities and who are interest in high levels of participation. Second, the significance of membership in the community has to be demonstrated. If membership is considered to be important, the level of participation is high. In 'republican' terms this means that the recognition of individual contributions to the communities' common good is one of the most important aspects for such communities as home-owners' associations. In this context the communication system in homeowners' associations plays a noticeable role. As our research in three Russian regions has shown, there is a strong correlation between a positive assessment of the communication system on the one hand and satisfaction with the work of the chairperson and high participation levels on the other hand.

The third explaining factor for different levels of participation and corruption in home-owners' association is the nature of the community. In general home-owners' associations are seen as the community of real estate owners who are united by common goals, like organisation of building maintenance, accomplishment and comfort of living in multi-apartment buildings. However, in many cases home-owners have both common interests as well as individual interests. And taking these individual interests into consideration, the community consists of sub-communities and individuals who have divergent and also conflicting interests.

A good example for this is the conflict over the distribution of courtyard territory. The conflict 'grass-plot versus parking place' evokes very hot discussions either inside the community of home-owners or between home-owners and their association's board. This conflict also became a cause for corruption, as in some cases this issue has been solved through manipulation of the decision-making process, voting without quorum and ignoring one side. This dilemma shows that non-coordination between common and individual interests is conductive to the appearance of corruption and with that to low levels of participation.

In conclusion, participation in homeowners' associations is a process that is influenced by many different factors, including the management system, individual features, and the conflict between one's public duty to take part in decision-making and the wish to simply enjoy one's private life.

14.6. Conclusion

Modern homeowners' associations in Russia do not have a long history and have not yet formed a perfect management system or instilled a common value system. The notion of 'common things', i.e. common property, is easy for residents to grasp, but there is still no common understanding of 'civic virtues' within these associations. Some attempts have been made in this regard, but even if these virtues are shown to be valuable, the mechanisms for establishing community recognition of these virtues and for recognizing contributions toward community improvement are not sufficient. Homeowners' associations have not yet succeeded in creating a strong 'sense of meaning' or a group identity for which members would be willing to forget about private interests. It is difficult to speak of 'citizenship' in these associations; in most cases only 'membership' is involved. And thus far, 'civic virtues' are merely understood as 'responsibilities to the association'.

These associations exhibit commonweal in the form of joint self-government, but not all homeowners share this common good. The associations produce common goods like a comfortable living environment, but there are a lot of free riders taking advantage of these goods. Why does this happen?

The main basis for corruption in these associations is the lack of participation. There are a lot of structural reasons for the low level of participation—from poverty to ineffective management of the common meetings. But one of the main problems for any homeowners' association is the constant tension between the desire to simply enjoy one's *private life* at home and the necessity to conduct a *public life*. The real republicans prefer an active public and political life. But when there are attempts to forcibly plant this public life into the private sphere, civic virtues and recognition by the community depreciates; home is the last place where political activity should have to take place. Thus, because of this unique tension between private and public, homeowners' associations cannot be viewed as republics in the full sense.

In the republican view, the domination of private life over common interests is tantamount to corruption. This domination is expressed in the distinction between individual and common interests. Not all home-owners share the association's interests and if these interests do not correspond with their individual goals and intensions, they let private interests dominate over common goals in cases related to the distribution of common and limited recourses. Indeed, this domination paves the way for all sorts of corruption, from falsified common decisions to bribes and kickbacks.

The challenge now is to create a kind of management and control system that does not require total and constant participation yet protects associations from degradation processes.

14.7. Appendix 1: Statistical Data

Table 14-1:   Homeowners' Associations in Russia 1993–2006

Year	Number of multi-apartment buildings
1993	9
1994	80
1995	325
1996	615
1997	1,875
1998	3,351
1999	4,100
2000	4,800
2001	5,500
2002	6,500
2003	7,500
2004	9,740
2005	12,244
2006	18,467
2007	no data available in open sources
2008	no data available in open sources
2009 (9 September)	55,864

Source: 2009: The Association of NGOs to Promote the Development of Homeowners' Associations and Housing Cooperatives, http://tsg-rf.ru/library/509, accessed 8 May 2010; 1993–2006: The Practice of Russian Federation Housing Code Realization. The Urban Economics Institute, www.urbaneconomics.ru, accessed 8 May 2010.

Comment 1. Growth since 1996 is due to the adoption of the 'About Homeowners' Associations' law (this law was cancelled after the passage of the new Housing Code).

Comment 2. Growth from 2007 to the present is due to the passage of Federal Law 185 'About the Foundation to Housing and Communal Reforming Promotion' 21 July 2007. Based on this law, a special programme for capital repairs funding was adopted.

14.8. Appendix 2: The Participation Index

Questions used to create the 'Participation Index'.

1. Do you discuss problems with your homeowners' association with your neighbours? ('Yes': +1)

2. Are common meetings between homeowners and members of your homeowners' association conducted? ('Don't know': -1)

3. Do you participate in these common meetings? ('Yes': +2, 'Sometimes take part': +1, 'Have never participated because not interested': -1)

4. Do you receive information about common property maintenance? ('I'm not interested in this information and do not receive it': -1)

5. Are there plans for common property maintenance and repairs discussed in common meetings? ('Don't know': -1)

6. Do ordinary homeowners' association members participate in decisions about the salary levels of association chairpersons, managers and personnel? ('Don't know': -1)

7. Do homeowners have opportunities to find out how money collected for services was spent? ('Don't know': -1)

8. Do homeowners participate in decisions on how much money is spent on common property maintenance? ('Don't know': -1)

9. What is the role of a homeowner? ('Only to pay for maintenance and building repair, without participating in decision-making about the kind and amount of work for maintenance, the cost of this work and form of payment': -1)

10. Describe the level of your personal activity in your homeowners' association development and functioning. ('Very active': +2; 'Active': +1; 'Fairly inactive': -1; 'Totally inactive': -2)

11. Would you like to take part more actively in your homeowners' association's activities? ('Yes, I would like to take a more active part' or 'Yes, I would like to give consultations': +1; 'No': -1)[31]

Figure 14-1: 'Participation index'. Statistical Distribution. Data from the Research within 'Homeowners' Support Project' (Line Chart)

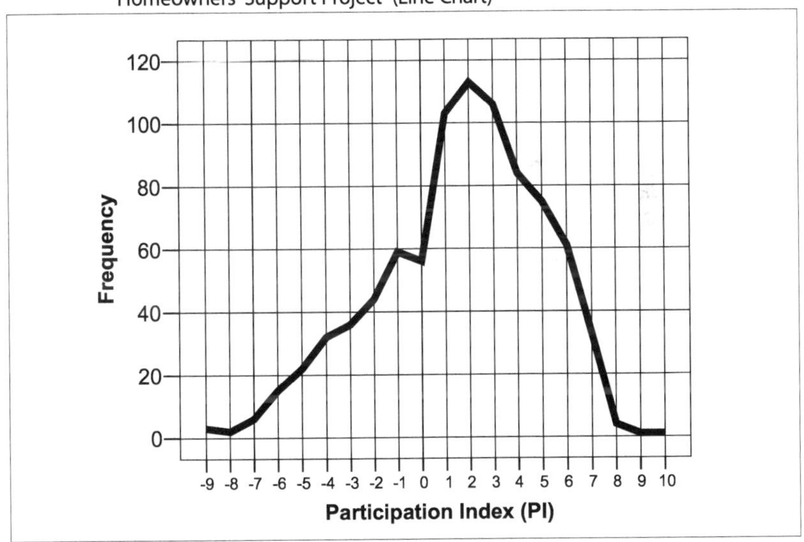

---

31 Questions about potential participation are characterized as indirect readiness to participate. These questions are therefore also included, but with the weight minus 1, because they are subjective.

Figure 14-2: 'Participation index'. Statistical Distribution. Data from the Research within 'Homeowners' Support Project' (Pie Chart)

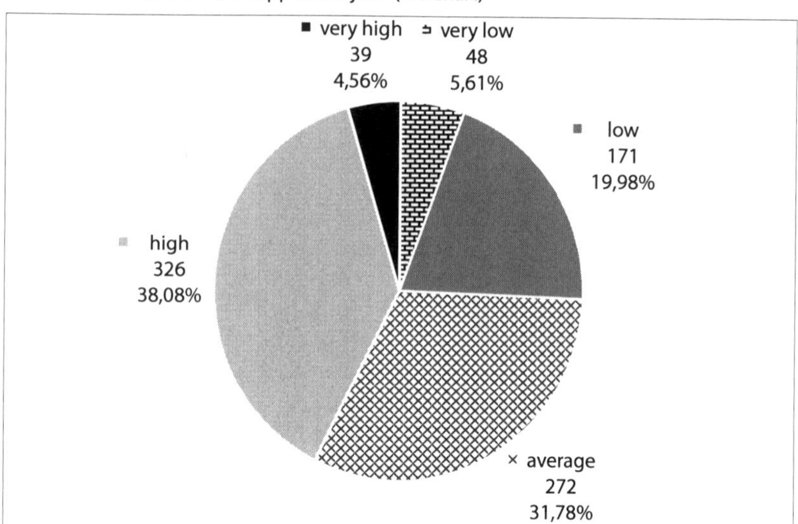

14.9. Appendix 3: The Biggest Problems for Associations

Table 14-2: Distribution of Answers From Homeowners' Association Chairpersons to the Question: 'Which Homeowner Behaviour Creates the Biggest Problems for the Association?'

Behaviour	Percent*
Late or non-payment of compulsory fees for common property maintenance	33
Use of apartments for purposes other than living	3
Prohibited renovation of apartments (e.g. replacing internal walls)	8
Use of common property for private needs	3
Use of land for private needs	6
Improper maintenance of apartments	3
Non-participation in common meetings	24
Non-participation in common works projects approved at the common meeting	16
Disorderly conduct	2
Complaints about the board and chairperson	2
Total	100

*   This question offered multiple answers; the averages were standardized to 100%.

Bibliography

Adachi, Yuko: Building Big Business in Russia: The Impact of Informal Corporate Governance Practices, London: Routledge, 2010.

Afanasyev, Mikhail N.: Klientelizm i rossiyskaya gosudarstvennost', Moscow: MONF, 2000.

Ajani, Gianmaria: La Circulation de Modèles Juridiques Dans le Droit Post-socialiste, in: Revue Internationale de Droit Comparé, 1994, no. 4, pp. 1087–1106.

Ajani, Gianmaria: Chance and Prestige. Legal Transplants in Russia and Eastern Europe, in: The American Journal of Comparative Law, 1995 (vol. 43), no. 1, pp. 93–117.

Ajani, Gianmaria: Diritto dell'Europa Orientale, Torino: Utet, 1996.

Ajani, Gianmaria: Il Modello Post-Socialista, Torino: G. Giappichelli Editore, 2008.

Akhmedzhanova, Dilorom/ Volkov, Vadim/ Gerasimova, Katerina/ Kaploun, Viktor/ Roschin, Yevgeniy/ Troyanovsky, Sergey/ Kharkhordin, Oleg/ Chyuikina, Sofia: Res Publica. Revival of the Interest, in: Kharkhordin, Oleg (ed.): What is Republican Tradition?, Saint Petersburg: EUSP press, 2009, pp. 7–22.

Akhmedzhanova, Dilorom: The Problem of Collective Action Inside Homeowners' Associations in Russia, paper presented at the Changing Europe Summer School IV. Civil Society in Central and Eastern Europe before and after the End of Socialism, Kyiv (Ukraine), 27–31 July 2009, http://www.changing-europe.org/download/Summer_School_2009/Akhmedzhanova.pdf

Alexander, Jeffrey: The Paradoxes of Civil Society, in: International Sociology, 1997 (vol. 12), no. 2, pp. 115–133.

Alionescu, Ciprian: Parliamentary Representation of National Minorities in Romania, in: Southeast European Politics, 2004 (vol. 5), no. 1, pp. 60–75.

Amin, Ash: An Institutionalist Perspective on Regional Economic Development, in: International Journal of Urban and Regional Research, 1999 (vol. 23), no. 2, pp. 365–78.

Anderson, James/ Gray, Cheryl: Anticorruption in Transition 3. Who Is Succeeding … And Why? Washington D.C.: World Bank, 2006.

Andreescu, Gabriel: Ruleta. Romani si maghiari, 1990–2000 (The Roulette. Romanians and Hungarians. 1990–2000), in: Editura Polirom, 2001.

Andreev, Svetlozar: What is the Convention Method? London: Centre for the Study of Democracy, University of Westminster, 2006.

Anheier, Helmuth: What Kind of Nonprofit Sector, What Kind of Society?, in: American Behavioral Scientist, 2009 (vol. 52), no. 7, pp. 1082–1094.

Ansell, Chris: The Networked Polity. Regional Development in Western Europe, in: Governance. An International Journal of Policy and Administration, 2000 (vol. 13), no. 3, pp. 303–333.

Arato, Andrew/ Cohen, Jean, L.: Civil Society and Political Theory. Cambridge and London: MIT, 1990.

Arendt, Hannah: Human Condition. Chicago: University of Chicago Press, 1998.

Auyero, Javier: The Logic of Clientelism in Argentina: An Ethnographic Account, in: Latin American Research Review, 2001 (vol. 35), no. 3, pp. 55–81.

Bachtler, John/ McMaster, Irene: EU Cohesion Policy and the Role of the Regions. Investigating the Influence of Structural Funds in the New Member States, in: Government and Policy, 2008 (vol. 26), no. 2, pp. 398–428.

Baez-Camargo, Claudia. Accountability for Better Health Care Provision: a framework and guidelines to define, understand and assess accountability in health systems, Basel Institute on Governance Working Paper 10.

Bailey, David/ Lisa de Propris: A Bridge to Phare? EU Pre-Accession Aid and Capacity-Building in the Candidate Countries, in: Journal of Common Market Studies 2004 (vol. 42), no. 1, pp. 77–98.

Baldassarri, Delia/ Diani, Mario: The Integrative Power of Civic Networks, in: American Journal of Sociology, 2007 (vol. 113), no. 3, pp. 735–780.

Banchoff, Thomas/ Smith, Mitchell: Legitimacy and European Union: The Contested Polity, London: Routledge, 1999.

Bannenberg, Britta: Korruption in Deutschland und ihre strafrechtliche Kontrolle, Neuwied: Luchterhand, 2002, pp. 109–111.

Bannenberg, Britta: Korruption in Deutschland. Ergebnisse einer kriminologisch-strafrechtlichen Untersuchung, in: von Arnim, Hans-Herbert (ed.): Korruption. Netzwerke in Politik, Amtern und Wirtschaft, Munich: Droemer Knaur, 2003, pp. 204–234.

Batory, Agnes: Post-accession Malaise? EU Conditionality, Domestic Politics and Anticorruption Policy in Hungary, in: Global Crime, 2010 (vol. 11), no. 2, pp. 178–209.

Bayart, Jean Francois: The State in Africa: The Politics of the Belly, New York: Longman, 1993.

Bayart, Jean Francois/ Ellis, Stephen/ Hibou, Beatrice: The Criminalization of the State in Africa, Bloomington: Indiana University Press, 1999.

Becker, G.: Nobel Lecture: The Economic Way of Looking at Behavior. The Journal of Political Economy, 1993 (vol. 101), no. 3.

Beetham, David: The Legitimation of Power. London: MacMillan, 1991.

Beetham, David/ Lord, Christopher: Legitimizing the EU: Is there a Post-Parliamentary Basis for its Legitimation?, in: Journal of Common Market Studies, 2001 (vol. 39) no. 3. pp. 433–462.

Bellamy, Richard/ Castiglione, Dario: Between Cosmopolis and Community: Three Models of Rights and Democracy within the European Union, in Archibugi, Daniele/ Held, David/ Koehler, Martin (eds.): Reimagining Political Community: Studies in Cosmopolitan Democracy. Oxford: Polity Press, 1998, pp. 152–178.

Bellamy, Richard/ Warleigh, Alex (eds.): Citizenship and Governance in the European Union. London: Continuum, 2001.

Bellamy, Richard: The 'Right to Have Rights': Citizenship Practice and the Political Constitution of the EU, in: Bellamy, Richard, Warleigh, Alex (eds.): Citizenship and Governance in the European Union. London: Continuum, 2001, pp. 41–70.

Bennett, Robert/ Krebs Günter: Local Economic Developments Partnerships. An Analysis of Policy Networks in EC-LEDA Local Employment Development Strategies, in: Regional Studies, 1994 (vol. 28), no. 2, pp. 119–140.

Benz, Arthur/ Fürst, Dietrich: Policy learning in regional networks, in: European Urban and Regional Studies, 2002 (vol. 9), no. 1, pp. 21–36.

Berlin, Isaiah: Dve Kontseptsii Svobody, Filosofiya Svobody. Evropa, Moscow: NLO, 2001 (1958).

Berman, Harold J.: Law and Revolution. The Formation of the Western Legal Tradition, Harvard: Harvard University Press, 1983.

Birnbaum, Pierre: States and Collective Action. European Experience, Cambridge, New York, Melbourne: Cambridge University Press, 1988.

Bjuremalm, Helena: Power Analysis—Experiences and Challenges, Swedish International Development Agency (SIDA), Stockholm, 2006.

Bloom, Gerard/ Han, Leiya/ Li, Xiang: How health workers earn a living in China, Brighton: Institute for Development Studies, 2000, IDS Working Paper 108.

Boerzel, Tania: Paradox of Double Weakness, Research Report for the Project New Modes of Governance, 2007.

Booth, David: Elites, Governance and the Public Interest in Africa: Working With the Grain? Africa Power and Politics Programme, 2009 Discussion Paper 6.

Borén, Thomas: What are Friends for? Rationales in Informal Exchange in Russian Everyday Life, in Arnstberg, Karl-Olov/ Borén, Thomas (eds.): Everyday Economy in Russia, Poland and Latvia. Stockholm: Södertörns högskola, 2003.

Borodin, Vladislav: Russia. Aerospace and Defense. Russian Market Overview, The U.S. Commercial Service, U.S. Department of Commerce, 2006.

Börzel, Tanja A./ Buzogány, Aron: Governing EU Accession in Transition Countries. The Role of Non-state Actors, in: Acta Politica, 2010 (vol. 45), nos. 1–2, pp. 158–182.

Börzel, Tanja A./ Stahn, Andreas/ Pamuk, Yasemin: The European Union and the Fight Against Corruption in its Near Abroad: Can it Make a Difference?, in: Global Crime, 2010 (vol. 11), no. 2, pp. 122–144.

Bozóki, Andraś/ Ishiyama, John T. (eds.): The Communist Successor Parties of Central and Eastern Europe, Armonk/NY, London: M.E. Sharpe, 2002.

Bratton, Michael/ Van de Walle, Nicolas (eds.): Democratic Experiments in Africa: Regime Transitions in Comparative Perspective, Cambridge: Cambridge University Press, 1997.

Brinkerhoff, Derick W./ Goldsmith, Arthur A. Clientelism, Patrimonialism and Democratic Governance: An Overview and Framework for Assessment and Programming. Prepared for USAID by Abt Associates Inc., December 2002.

Brinkerhoff, Jennifer/ Brinkerhoff, Derrick: Government-Nonprofit Relations in Comparative Perspective. Evolution, Themes, and New Directions, in: Public Administration and Development, 2002 (vol. 22), no. 1, pp. 3–18.

Brinkerhoff, Derick W/ Bossert, Thomas J: Health Governance: Concepts, Experience, and Programming Options. Bethesda: Abt Associates Inc, 2008.

Brioschi, Alberto: Breve Storia della Corruzione. Dall'Età Antica ai Giorni Nostri, Milano: TEA, 2004.

Brugha, R./ Varvasovsky, Z.: How to do (or not to do)… A Stakeholder analysis. Health Policy and Planning, 2000 (vol. 15), no. 3, pp. 338–345.

Bruszt, Laszlo/ Stark, David: Who Counts? Supranational Norms and Societal Needs, in: East European Politics and Societies, 2002 (vol. 17), no. 1, pp. 74–82.

Bruszt, Laszlo/ Vedres, Balazs: The Politics of Civic Combinations, in: Perez Diaz, Victor (ed.): Markets and Civil Society, New York: Berghahn Books, 2006.

Bruszt, Laszlo: Multi-level Governance. The Eastern Version. Emerging Patterns of Regional Development Patterns in the New Member States, EUI Working Papers, 2007/13.

Bruszt, Laszlo/ Vedres, Balazs: Fostering Developmental Agency from Without, paper prepared for the EUSA Eleventh Biennial International Conference Los Angeles/ CA, 23–25 April 2009.

Bryant, Christopher, G. A.: Social Self-Organisation, Civility and Sociology: A Comment on Kumar's 'Civil Society, in: The British Journal of Sociology, 1993 (vol. 44), no. 3, pp. 397–401.

Bryant, Christopher, G. A./ Mokrycki, Edmund (eds.): Democracy, civil society and pluralism. Warsaw: IFis Publishers, 1995.

Buisson, Antoine: State-Building, Power-Building and Political Legitimacy: The Case of Post-Conflict Tajikistan, in: China and Eurasia Forum Quarterly, 2007 (vol. 5), no. 4, pp. 115–147.

Bukowski, Charles/ Racz, Barnabas (eds.): The Return of the Left in Post-Communist States. Current Trends and Future Prospects, Cheltenham, Northampton/MA: Edward Elgar, 1999.

Bush, Keith 2008: Russian Economic Survey, Washington D.C.: U.S.-Russia Business Council, January 2008.

Cain, Bruce E./ Gash, Alison L./ Oleszek, Mark J.: Conflict-of-Interest Legislation in the United States. Origins, Evolution, and Inter-Branch Differences, in: Trost, Christine/ Gash, Alison L. (eds.): Conflict of Interest and Public Life, Cambridge: Cambridge Univ. Press, 2008, pp. 101–123.

Calhoun, Noel: The Ideological Dilemma of Lustration in Poland, in: East European Politics and Societies, 2002 (vol. 16), no. 2, pp. 494–520.

Candland, Christopher/ Sil, Rudra (eds.): The Politics of Labour in a Global Age. Continuity and Change in Late-Industrializing and Post-Socialist Economies, Oxford, New York: Oxford University Press, 2001.

Carothers, Thomas: Confronting the Weakest Link. Aiding Political Parties in New Democracies, Washington D.C.: Carnegie Endowment for International Peace, 2006.

Cars, Thorsten: Mutbrott, bestickning och korruptiv marknadsföring: corruption in Swedish law. Stockholm: Norstedts juridik, 2001.

Casale, Giuseppe: Evolution and Trends in Industrial Relations in Central and Eastern European Countries, in: International Journal of Comparative Labour Law and Industrial Relations, 2003 (vol. 19), no. 1, pp. 5–32.

Casalegno, Paolo: Introduzione alla Filosofia del Linguaggio, Firenze: Carrocci, 1997.

Chabal, Patrick/ Daloz, Jean-Pascal: Africa Works: Disorder as Political Instrument. Bloomington: Indiana University Press, 1999.

Cheloukhine, Serguei/ King, Joseph: Corruption Networks as a Sphere of Investment Activities in Modern Russia, in: Communist and Post-Communist Studies, 2007, 40 (1), 107–122.

Cinalli, Manilion: Between Horizontal Bridging and Vertical Governance, in: Osborne, Steven (ed.): The Third Sector in Europe. Prospects and Challenges, Abingdon, Oxon: Routledge, 2008, pp. 88–108.

Clapham, Christopher: Third World Politics: An Introduction, London: Routledge, 1985.

Clarke, Simon: Russian Trade Unions in the 1999 Duma Election, in: The Journal of Communist Studies and Transition Politics, 2001 (vol. 17), no. 2, pp. 43–69.

Coleman, William D.: Business and Politics. A Study of Collective Action, Kingston/ON.: McGill-Queen's University Press, 1988.

Collier, David/ Levitsky, Steven: Democracy 'With Adjectives': Conceptual Innovation in Comparative Research, in: World Politics, April 1997 (vol.49), No.3, pp.430–451.

Cook, Linda J.: Labor and Liberalization. Trade Unions in the New Russia, New York: Twentieth Century Fund Press,1997.

Cook, Linda J.: Trade Unions, Management, and State in Contemporary Russia, in: Rutland, Peter (ed.): Business and State in Contemporary Russia, Boulder/CO: Westview Press, 2001, pp. 151–172.

Cotta, Maurizio: Building Party Systems After the Dictatorship. The East European Cases in a Comparative Perspective, in: Pridham, Geoffrey/ Vanhanen, Tatu (eds.): Democratization in Eastern Europe. Domestic and International Perspectives, London, New York: Routledge, 1994, pp. 99–127.

Coulon, Christian/ Cruise O'Brien, Donal B.: Senegal, in Cruise O'Brien, Donal B./ Dunn, John/ Rathbone, Richard (eds.) Contemporary West African States. Cambridge: Cambridge University Press, 1989.

Crowley, Stephen/ Ost, David (eds.): Workers After Workers' States. Labor and Politics in Postcommunist Eastern Europe, Lanham et al.: Rowman and Littlefield Publishers, 2001.

Crowley, Stephen: The Social Explosion That Wasn't: Labor Quiscence in Postcommunist Russia, in Crowley, Stephen/ Ost, David (eds.): Workers After Workers' States. Labor and Politics in Postcommunist Eastern Europe, Lanham et al.: Rowman and Littlefield Publishers, 2001, pp. 199–218.

Csanádi, Maria: Party-States and Their Legacies in Post-Communist Transformation, Cheltenham, Northampton/MA: Edward Elgar, 1997.

Curry, Jane L./ Urban Joan B. (eds.): The Left Transformed in Post-Communist Societies. The Cases of East Central Europe, Russia and Ukraine, Lanham et al.: Rowman and Littlefield Publishers, 2003.

Curry, Jane L.: Poland's Ex-Communists. From Pariahs to Establishment Players, in: Curry Jane L./ Urban, Joan B. (eds.): The Left Transformed in Post-Communist Societies. The Cases of East Central Europe, Russia and Ukraine, Lanham et al.: Rowman and Littlefield Publishers, 2003, pp. 19–60.

Darden, Keith: The integrity of corrupt states: Graft as an informal state institution, in: Politics & Society, 2008 (vol. 36), pp. 35–59.

David, René/ Brierley, John E.C.: Major Legal Systems in the World Today. An Introduction to the Comparative Study of Law, New York: Free Press, 1985.

Davies, Jonathan: The Governance of Urban Regeneration. A Critique of the 'Governing Without Government' Thesis, in: Public Administration, 2002 (vol. 80), no. 2, pp. 301–322.

Davis, Jennifer: Corruption in Public Service Delivery: Experience from South Asia's Water and Sanitation Sector, World Development, 2004 (vol. 32), no. 1, pp. 53–71.

Davis, Michael: Introduction, in: Davis, Michael/ Stark, Andrew (eds.): Conflict of Interest in the Professions, Oxford, New York: Oxford University Press, 2001, pp. 3–19.

De Boer Buquicchio, Maud: Legislative Measures of the Council of Europe to Adress Corruption and Money-Laundering in the International Financial System, in: UNODC (ed.): Global Action against Corruption. The Mérida Papers, Vienna: United Nations, 2004, pp. 109–112.

De Sardan, Olivier/ Jean Pierre: Researching the practical norms of real governance in Africa. Africa Power and Politics Programme 2009, Discussion Paper 5.

De Savigny, Don/ Adam, Taghreed (eds.): Systems thinking for health systems strengthening. World Health Organization, Geneva, Switzerland. 2009.

De Sousa Santos, Boaventura: Toward a New Legal Common Sense. Law, Globalization, and Emancipation, Cambridge: Cambridge University Press, 2002.

De Sousa, Luís: Clientelism and the Quality(ies) of Democracy. Public and Policy Aspects, in: DISC Working Paper Series, DISC WP/2008/2, Central European University, Center for the Study of Imperfections in Democracy, pp. 1–19, http://pdc.ceu.hu/archive/00004462/01/discwp-2008-02.pdf

De Tocqueville, Alexis: Democracy in America, trans. and eds. Mansfield, Harvey C./ Winthrop, Delba, Chicago: University of Chicago Press, 2000.

Decker, Christopher D.: The Use of Cultural Autonomy to Prevent Conflict and Meet the Copenhagen Criteria. The Case of Romania, in: Ethnopolitics, 2007 (vol. 6), no. 3, pp. 437–450.

Delanty, Gerard/ Rumford, Chris: Rethinking Europe. Social theory and the implications of Europeanization. London and New York: Routledge, 2005.

Della Porta, Donatella/ Vannucci, Alberto: Corrupt Exchanges. Actors, Resources, and Mechanisms of Political Corruption, New York: Aldine de Gruyter, 1999.

Della Porta, Donatella/ Caiani, Manuela: The Europeanization of Public Discourse in Italy: A top-down Process, in: European Union Politics, 2006 (vol. 7), No.1, pp. 77–112.

Della Porta, Donatella: Democracy in Social Movements, New York: Palgrave Macmillan, 2009.

Denisova-Schmidt, Elena: Cross-Cultural Communication in Russia. Current Trends in the Establishment of a Discipline, in: Haunreiter, Diego (ed.): Kommunikation in Wirtschaft, Recht und Gesellschaft. 5. Band der Schriftenreihe der Assistierenden der Universität St. Gallen (HSG), Bern: Stämpfli Verlag, 2010, pp. 123–140.

Denisova-Schmidt, Elena: Geschäftspartner Russland. Erfahrungen mit einem europäischen Land der besonderen Art, in: Tanner, Anne-Cathrine/ Siebeneck, Claudia/ Brändli, Beat (eds.): Schweiz und Europa – Auswirkungen auf Wirtschaft, Recht und Gesellschaft. 6. Band der Schriftenreihe der Assistierenden der Universität St. Gallen (HSG), Bern: Stämpfli Verlag, 2011, pp. 165–172.

Denissen, Ingeborg: New Forms of Political Inclusion: Competitive Clientelism. The case of Iztapalapa, Mexico City. MinBuZa: A Rich Menu for the Poor: Food for Thought on Effective Aid Policies Essay Series, 2009, no. 33.

Diamond, Larry/ Gunther, Richard: Types and Functions of Parties, in: Diamond, Larry/ Gunther, Richard (eds.): Political Parties and Democracy, Baltimore/London: The Johns Hopkins University Press, 2001.

Diani, Mario/ McAdam, Doug (eds.): Social Movements and Networks, Oxford: Oxford University Press, 2003.

DiMaggio, Paul/ Powell, Walter W.: The Iron Cage Revisited. Institutional Isomorphism and Collective Rationality in Organizational Fields, in: American Sociological Review, 1983 (vol. 48), no. 2, pp. 147–160.

Dimitrova-Grajzl, Valentina/ Simon, Eszter: Political Trust and Historical Legacy. The Effect of Varieties of Socialism, in: East European Politics & Societies, 2010 (vol. 24). no. 2, pp. 206–228.

Dininio, Phyllis: Warlords and corruption in post-conflict governments, in: New Routes, Pilfering the Peace. The nexus between corruption and peacebuilding, 2009 (vol. 14), no. 3–4.

Dionisie, Dan/ Checchi, Francesco: Corruption and Anti-Corruption Agencies in Eastern Europe and the CIS. A Practitioners' Experience, 2008, http://ancorage-net.org/content/documents/dionisie-checchi-corruption_in_ee.pdf

Draude, Anke: How to Capture Non-Western Forms of Governance. In Favour of An Equivalance Functionalist Observation in Areas of Limited Statehood. SFB Working Paper Series 2, January 2007, pp 1–16.

Duff, Andrew. A Liberal Reaction to the European Convention and the Intergovernmental Conference. Federal Trust Papers, July. London: Federal Trust, 2003.

Easter, Gerald: Reconstructing the state: personal networks and elite identity in Soviet Russia, Cambridge: Cambridge University Press, 1999.

Eisenstadt, Shmuel N: Traditional Patrimonialism and Modern Neopatrimonialism. Beverly Hills: Sage Publications, 1973.

Emanuel, Ezekiel J./ Steiner, Daniel: Institutional Conflict of Interest, in: New England Journal of Medicine, 1995 (vol. 332), no. 4, pp. 262–268.

Eriksen, Erik, O./ Fossum, John, E: Europe in Search of its Legitimacy: The Strategies of Legitimation Assessed. International Political Science Review, 2004 (vol. 25), no. 4, pp. 435–459.

Erne, Roland: European Unions: Labors' Quest for Transnational Democracy. Ithaca: Cornell University Press, 2008.

Ertelt-Vieth, Astrid/ Denisova-Schmidt, Elena: Kulturbedingte Unterschiede und Verstehensprobleme (»Lakunen«) zwischen russischen und deutschen Wissenschaftlern, in: Wolff, Armin/ Zollner, Reinhold (eds.): Umbrüche, Regensburg, 2006, pp. 185–206.

Ertelt-Vieth, Astrid/ Denisova-Schmidt, Elena: Kulturbedingte Unterschiede und Verstehensprobleme zwischen russischen und deutschen Wissenschaftlern, in: Bürgel, Matthias/ Umland, Andreas (eds.): Geistes- und sozialwissenschaftliche Hochschullehre in Osteuropa IV. Chancen und Hindernisse internationaler Bildungskooperation, Frankfurt a.M.: Peter Lang, 2009, pp. 244–263.

Etzioni, Amitai: The Third Sector and Domestic Missions, in: Public Administration Review 1973 (vol. 33), no. 1, pp. 314–323.

Evans, Peter B./ Rueschemeyer, Dietrich/ Skocpol, Theda (eds.): Bringing the State Back in. Cambridge: Cambridge University Press, 1985.

Evans, Peter: Development as Institutional Change: The Pitfalls of Monocropping and the Potentials of Deliberation, in: Studies in Comparative International Development, 2004 (vol. 38), pp. 30–52.

Everson, Michelle: 'Subjects', or 'Citizens of Erewhon'? Law and Non-Law in the Development of a 'British Citizenship'. In: Citizenship Studies, 2003 (vol.7), no. 1, pp. 57–83.

Fairclough, Norman: Language and Power, London: Longman, 1989.

Fantasia, Rick: Culture of Solidarity. Consciousness, Action and Contemporary American Workers, Berkeley, Los Angeles, London: University of California Press, 1989.

Fazi, Elodie/ Smith, Jeremy: Civil dialogue: making it work better, Brussels: Civil Society Contact Group, 2006.

Fey, Carl F./ Shekshnia, Stanislav: The Key Commandments For Doing Business in Russia, in: INSEAD Faculty & Research Working Paper, 2008, 16/EFE.

Fituni, Leonid: Economic Crime in the Context of Transition to a Market Economy, in: Ledeneva, A./ Kurkchiyan, M. (eds.): Economic Crime in Russia. London: Kluwer Law International, 2000, 17–30.

Fitzpatrick, Sheila: Everyday Stalinism: Ordinary Life in Extraordinary Times: Soviet Russia in the 1930s, New York: Oxford University Press, 1999.

Fornasari, Gabriale/ Luisi, Demetrio (eds.): La Corruzione. Profili Storici, Attuali, Europei e Sopranazionali, Padova: CEDAM, 2003.

Fossum, John E./ Trenz, Hans-Joerg: The EU's Fledgling Society: From Deafening Silence to Critical Voice in European Constitution Making. in: Journal of Civil Society, 2006 (vol. 2), no. 1, pp. 57–77.

Foster, Mary/ Meinhard, Agnes: A Regression Model Explaining Predisposition to Collaborate, in: Nonprofit and Voluntary Sector Quarterly, 2002 (vol. 31), no. 4, pp. 549–564.

Freizer, Sabine: Tajikistan Local Self Governance: A Potential Bridge Between Government and Civil Society, in: Di Martino, Luigi (ed.): Tajikistan at a Crossroads: the Politics of Decentralisation, Cimera: Geneva, 2004.

Fric, Pavol: The Uneasy Partnership of the State and he Third Sector in the Czech Republic, in: Osborne, Steven (ed.): The Third Sector in Europe. Prospects and Challenges, Abingdon, Oxon: Routledge, 2008, pp. 230–255.

Friedberg, Maurice: How Things were Done in Odessa. Cultural and Intellectual Pursuits in a Soviet City, Boulder/CO: Westview, 1991.

Friedrich, Carl J.: Corruption Concepts in Historical Perspective, in: Heidenheimer, Arnold J./ Johnston, Michael (eds.): Political Corruption. Concepts & Contexts, New Brundwick: Transaction Publishers, 2001, pp. 15–24.

Fukuyama, Francis: State-Building. Governance and World Order in the 21st Century, New York: Cornell University Press, 2004.

Gadowska, Kaja: National and International Anti-Corruption Efforts: the Case of Poland, in: Global Crime, 2010 (vol. 11), no. 2, pp. 178–209.

Galdia, Marcus: Comparative Law and Legal Translation, in: The European Legal Forum, 2003 (vol. 1), pp. 1–4.

Gallagher, Tom: A Feeble Embrace: Romania's Engagement with Democracy, 1989–1994, in: Journal of Communist Studies and Transition Politics, 1996 (vol. 12), no. 2, pp. 145–172.

Gay, Robert: Community Organization and Clientelist Politics in Contemporary Brazil. A Case Study from Suburban Rio de Janeiro, in: International Journal of Urban and Regional Research, 1990 (Vol. 14), no. 4, pp. 648–665.

Gazley, Beth: Intersectoral Collaboration and the Motivation to Collaborate. Toward an Integrated Theory, in: O'Leary, R./ Bingham, L.B.: Big Ideas in Collaborative Public Management, Armonk/NY: Sharpe, M. E., 2008.

Geddes, Mike: Neoliberalism and Local Governance. Cross-National Perspectives and speculations, in: Policy Studies, 2005 (vol. 26), no. 3–4, pp. 359–375.

Gellner, Ernest: Civil Society in Historical Context, in: International Social Science Journal, 1991 (vol. 129), pp. 415–510.

Gellner, Ernest: Podmínky svobody: Občanská společnost a její rivalové. Brno: Centrum pro studium demokracie a kultury, 1995

Getman, Karen/ Karlan, Pamela S.: Pluralists and Republicans, Rules and Standards. Conflict of Interest and the California Experience, in: Trost, Christine/ Gash, Alison L. (eds.): Conflict of Interest and Public Life. Cross-National Perspectives, Cambridge: Cambridge University Press, 2008, pp. 56–74.

Giddens, Anthony: The Constitution of Society, Cambridge: Polity Press, 1984.

Gilson, Lucy: Trust and the development of health care as a social institution, in: Social Science & Medicine, 2003 (vol. 56), no. 7, pp. 1453–1468.

Goldman, David B.: Globalisation and the Western Legal Tradition. Recurring Patterns of Law and Authority, Cambridge: Cambridge University Press, 2007.

Golosov, Grigorii V.: Partiinye sistemy Rossii i stran Vostochnoi Evropy, Moscow: Ves' mir, 1999.

Górski, Andrzej: Tendencje do komercjalizacji w nauce i dydaktyce wymagają pilnych uregulowań administracyjno-prawnych, Forum Akademickie, 2002, no. 2.

Granovetter, Mark.: The Strength of Weak Ties, in: American Journal of Sociology, 1973 (vol. 78), no. 6, pp. 1360–1380.

Green, Andrew, T: Občanská společnost, ideje a utváření politiky, in: Sociologický časopis, 1997 (vol. 33), no. 3, pp. 309–320.

Green, Jeffrey: History of Conflicts Law, in: Hamline Law Review, 2002 (vol. 26), no. 3, pp. 556–600.

Greenwood, Justin: Interest Representation in the European Union, New York: Palgrave Macmillan, 2003.

Gregory, Paul R.: Restructuring the Soviet Economic Bureaucracy, Cambridge: Cambridge University Press, 1990.

Grzymala-Busse, Anna: Beyond Clientelism. Incumbent State Capture and State, in: Comparative Political Studies, 2008 (Vol. 41), no. 4/5, pp. 638–673.

Grzymala-Busse, Anna: Redeeming the Past. The Regeneration of Communist Parties in East Central Europe, Cambridge: Cambridge University Press, 2002.

Grzymala-Busse, Anna: The Programmatic Turnaround of Communist Successor Parties in East Central Europe, 1989–1998, in: Communist and Post-Communist Studies, 2002 (vol. 35), no. 1, pp. 51–66.

Guzin, Bayar: Corruption and Intermediaries—A Game Theoretical Approach, in: Middle East Technical University Studies in Development, 2009 (vol. 36), no. 1, pp. 25–49.

Haas, Ernst. B.: Beyond the Nation State. Functionalism and International Organizations. Stanford: Stanford University Press, 1964.

Habermas, Juergen: Between Facts and Norms: Contributions to the Discourse Theory of Law and Democracy. Cambridge: MIT, 1996.

Habermas, Juergen: The Future of Human Nature. Oxford: Polity Press, 2003.

Hallak, Jacques/ Poisson, Muriel: Corrupt Schools, Corrupt Universities: What Can be Done?, Paris: International Institute for Educational Planing, 2007.

Hasselmo, Nils: Individual and Institutional Conflict of Interest. Policy Review by Research Universities in the United States, in: Science and Engineering Ethics, 2002 (vol. 8), no. 3, pp. 421–427.

Hausner, Jerzy (ed.): Evolution of Interest Representation and Development of the Labour Market in Post-Socialist Countries, Cracow: Cracow Academy of Economics, 1994.

Hausner, Jerzy/ Pedersen, Ove/ Ronit, Karsten (eds.): Evolution of Interest Representation and Development of the Labour Market in Post-Socialist Countries, Cracow: Cracow Academy of Economics, 1994.

Hausner, Jerzy: Organizacje interesu i stosunki przemysłowe w krajach postsocjalisty-cznych, in: Przegląd Socjologiczny, 1994, no. 43, pp. 9–26.

Haveman, Roelof/ Kavran, Olga/ Nicholls, Julian: Supranational Criminal Law. A System *Sui Generis* (vol. 1), Schoten: Intersentia, 2003.

Hedlund, Stefan: Institutionell teori: ekonomiska aktörer, spelregler och samhällsnormer, Lund: Studentlitteratur, 2007.

Helmke, Gretchen/ Levitsky, Steven: Informal Institutions and Comparative Politics: A research Agenda, in: Perspectives on Politics, 2004 (vol. 2), pp. 725–740.

Henning, Peter J.: Public Corruption A Comparative Analysis of International Corruption Conventions and United States Law, in: Arizona Journal International & Comparative Law, 2001 (vol. 18), no. 3, pp. 793–846.

Héretier, Adrienne: Elements of democratic legitimation in Europe: an alternative perspective, in: Journal of European Public Policy, 1999 (vol. 6), no. 2, pp. 269–282.

Herod, Andrew: Theorizing Trade Unions in Transition, in: Pickles, John/ Smith, Adrian: Theorizing Transition: The Political Economy of Post-Communist Transformations, New York, London: Routledge, 1998, pp. 197–217.

Herrigel, Gary: Emerging Strategies and Forms of Governance in High-wage Component Manufacturing Regions, in: Industry and Innovation, 2004 (vol. 11), no. 1/2, pp. 45–79.

Heyneman, Stephan P.: Education and Corruption, in: International Journal of Educational Development, 2004 (vol. 24), no. 6, pp. 637–648.

Hix, Simon: What's Wrong with the European Union and How to Fix it. Cambridge: Polity, 2008.

Höffling, Christian: Korruption als Soziale Beziehung, Opladen: Leske & Budrich, 2002.

Holm, Kerstin: Das Korrupte Imperium, München: DTB, 2006.

Holmes, Leslie: Rotten states?, Durham: Duke University Press, 2006.

Holmes, Leslie: Corruption and Organized Crime in Putin's Russia, in: Europe-Asia Studies, 2008 (vol. 60), no. 6, pp. 1011–1031.

Höltge, Kristin: Governance in Transition. What Makes Georgia's Higher Education System So Corrupt?, Kassel: Kassel University Press, 2008.

Homann, Karl: Unternehmensethik und Korruption, in: Zeitschrift für Betriebswirtschaftliche Forschung, 1997, (vol. 49), no. 3, pp. 187–209.

Honohan, Iseult: Civic Republicanism, London, New York: Routledge, 2002.

Hooghe, Liesbet/ Marks, Gary: Multi-Level Governance and European Integration, Lanham/MD: Rowman and Littlefield, 2001.

Horvath, Istvan/ Scacco, Alexandra: From the Unitary to the Pluralistic. Fine-Tuning Minority Policy in Romania, in: Biro, Anna-Maria/ Kovacs, Petra (eds.): Diversity in Action. Local public management of multi-ethnic communities in Central and Eastern Europe, Budapest: Open Society Institute, 2001, pp. 241–272.

Howard, Marc M: The Weakness of Civil Society in Post-Communist Europe, Cambridge: Cambridge University Press, 2003.

Howard, Marc, M: Variations in Dual Citizenship Policies in the Countries of the EU, in: International Migration Review, 2005 (vol. 39), No.3, pp 697–720.

Huber, Barbara: La Lotta alla Corruzione in Prospettiva Sovranazionale, in Rivista Trimestrale di Diritto Penale dell'Economia, 2001 (vol. 2), no. 3, pp. 475–489.

Humphrey, Caroline: The Unmaking of Soviet Life. Everyday Economies After Socialism, London: Cornell University Press, 2002.

Huyse, Luc/Salter, Mark Traditional Justice and Reconciliation after Violent Conflict: Learning from African Experiences, Stockholm: IDEA 2008.

Hyden, Goran: Informal Institutions, Economy of Affection, and Rural Development, in: Tanzanian Journal of Population Studies and Development, Special Issue: African Economy of Affection, 2002 (vol. 11), no. 2.

Hyden, Goran: African Politics in Comparative Perspective, Cambridge: Cambridge University Press, 2006.

Hyden, Goran: Beyond Governance: Bringing Power into Development Policy Analysis, paper presented to the Danida/GEPPA Conference on Power, Politics and Change in Weak States, Copenhagen, 1–2 March 2006, online at www.geppa.dk/files/activities/Conference%202006/Goran%20Hyden.pdf

Hyden, Goran Governance and Poverty Reduction in Africa, in: Proc. Natl. Acad. Sci. USA, 2007 (vol. 104) no. 43, pp. 16751–16756.

Hyden, Goran Institutions, Power and Policy Outcomes in Africa. Africa Power and Politics Programme 2008, Discussion Paper 2.

Ilkhamov, Alisher: Neopatrimonialism, Interest Groups and Patronage Networks: The Impasses of the Governance System in Uzbekistan, in: Central Asian Survey, 2007 (vol. 26), no. 1, pp. 65–84.

Isaev, Alexander: Vysshaia shkola perestroiki, in: Priamye investicii, 2006 (vol. 50), no. 6, pp. 10–14.

Ishiyama, John T.: The Communist Successor Parties and Party Organizational Development in Post-Communist Politics, in: Political Research Quarterly, 1999 (vol. 52), no. 1, pp. 87–112.

Ishiyama, John T./ Shafqat, Sahar: Party Identity Change in Post-Communist Politics: The Cases of the Successor Parties in Hungary, Poland, and Russia, in: Communist and Post Communist Studies, 2000 (vol. 33), no. 4, pp. 439–455.

Ishiyama, John.T./ Bozóki, Andraś: Adaptation and Change. Characterizing the Survival Strategies of the Communist Successor Parties, in: Journal of Communist Studies and Transition Politics, 2001 (vol. 17), no. 3, pp. 32–51.

Ivanov, Kalin: The 2007 Accession of Bulgaria and Romania: Ritual and Reality, in: Global Crime, 2010 (vol. 11), no. 2, pp. 210–219.

Janoski, Thomas: Citizenship and Civil Society: A Framework of Rights and Obligations in Liberal, Traditional, and Social Democratic Regimes. Cambridge: Cambridge University Press, 1998.

Jaworski, Adam/ Coupland, Nikolas (eds.): The Discourse Reader, London: Routledge, 1999.

Jenei, Gyorgy/ Kuti, Eva: The Third Sector and Civil Society, in: Osborne, Steven (ed.): The Third Sector in Europe. Prospects and Challenges, Abingdon, Oxon: Routledge, 2008.

Jessop, Bob: The Rise of Governance and the Risks of Failure. The Case of Economic Development, in: International Social Science Journal, 1998 (vol. 50), no. 155, pp. 29–46.

Johnson, J. M.: In-Depth Interviewing, in: Gubrium, Jaber F./ Holstein, James A. (eds.) Handbook of Interview Research: Context & Method, London: SAGE, 2002, pp. 103–119.

Johnson, Simon/ Kaufmann, Daniel/ McMillan, John/ Woodruff, Christopher: Why Do Firms Hide? Bribes and Unofficial Activity after Communism, in: Journal of Public Economics, 2000 (vol. 76), no. 3, pp. 495–510.

Johnston, Michael: Syndromes of Corruption: Wealth, Power, and Democracy, Cambridge: Cambridge University Press, 2005.

Jones, B./ Chandran, R. et al.: Concepts and Dilemmas of State Building in Fragile Situations: From Fragility to Resilience, OECD/DAC, Discussion Paper, 2008.

Kalimullin, Tagir R.: Rossiyskiy Rynok Dissertatsionnykh Uslug, Moscow: Higher School of Economics, 2006.

Kamiński, Antoni Z.: Korupcja jako system instytucjonalnej niewydolności państwa i zagrożenie dla rozwoju polityczno-gospodarczego polski, in: Popławska, Ewa (ed.): Dobro wspólne, władza, korupcja. Konflikt interesów w życiu publicznym, Warsaw: ISP, 1997, pp. 23–74.

Karasimeonov, Georgi: Differentiation Postponed: Party Pluralism in Bulgaria, in: Wightman, Gordon (ed.): Party Formation in East Central Europe. Post-Communist Politics in Czechoslovakia, Hungary, Poland, and Bulgaria, Aldershot: Edward Elgar, 1995, pp. 154–179.

Karklins, Rasma: Typology of Post-Communist Corruption, in: Problems of Post-Communism, July/August 2002 (vol. 49), no. 4, pp. 22–32.

Karklins, Rasma: The System Made Me Do It: Corruption in Post-Communist Societies, New York: M.E. Sharp, 2005.

Kaufman, Robert: The Patron-Client Concept and Macro-Politics: Prospects and Problems, in: Comparative Studies in Society and History, 1974 (vol. 16), no. 3. 284–308.

Kaufmann, Daniel/ Kraay, Aart/ Mastruzzi, Massimo: Governance Matter VIII: Aggregate and Individual Governance Indicators, 1996–2008. World Bank Policy Research Working Paper 4978, 29 June 2009.

Keane, John: Democracy and Civil Society. London: Verso, 1988.

Kelsall, Tim. Game-theoretic models, social mechanisms and public goods in Africa: a methodological discussion. Africa Power and Politics Programme 2009 Discussion Paper 7.

Kelsall, Tim: Going with the grain in African development? Africa Power and Politics Programme, 2008 Discussion Paper 1.

Kettering, Sharon: The Historical Development of Political Clientelism, in: Journal of Interdisciplinary History, 1988 (vol. 18), no. 3, pp. 419–447.

Kideckel, David A.: Winning the Battles, Losing the War: Contradictions of Romanian Labor in the Postcommunist Transformation, in: Crowley, Stephen/ Ost, David (eds.): Workers After Workers' States. Labor and Politics in Postcommunist Eastern Europe, Lanham et al.: Rowman and Littlefield Publishers, 2001, pp. 102–132.

King, Iain/ Whit Mason: Peace at Any Price. How the World Failed Kosovo, New York: Cornell University Press, 2006.

Kitschelt, Herbert et al.: Post-Communist Party Systems. Competition, Representation, and Inter-Party Cooperation, Cambridge, New York: Cambridge University Press, 1999.

Kitschelt, Herbert: Constraints and Opportunities in the Strategic Conduct of Post-Communist Successor Parties. Regime Legacies as Causal Argument, in: Bozóki, Andraś/ Ishiyama, John T. (eds.): The Communist Successor Parties of Central and Eastern Europe, Armonk/NY, London: M.E. Sharpe, 2002, pp. 14–40.

Klaus, Vaclav. Predmluva. in Coughlan, Anthony/ Louzek, Marek et al. Krach evropske ustavy: Sbornik textu. Praha: Centrum pro ekonomiku a politiku, 2005.

Klitgaard, Robert E.: Controlling Corruption, Berkeley: University of California Press, 1991.

Kohler-Koch, Beate: European Networks and Ideas. Changing National Policies?, in: European Integration Online Papers, 2002 (vol. 6), no. 6, http//eiop.or.at/eiop/texte/2002–006a.htm

Kohler-Koch, Beate/ Rittberger, Berthold (eds.): Debating the Democratic Legitimacy of the European Union. Lanham: Roman and Littlefield, 2007.

Kohler-Koch, Beate/ De Biévre, Dirk/ Maloney, William: Opening EU Governance to Civil Society—Gains and Challenges, CONNEX Report Series no. 5, 2008.

Kohler-Koch, Beate/ Larat, Fabrice: Efficient and Democratic Governance in the European Union. CONNEX Report series no. 9. Mannheim: MZES, 2008.

Kohler-Koch, Beate/ Quittkat, Cristine/ Buth, Vanessa: Civil Society Organisations under the Impact of the European Commission's Consultation Regime, Paper presented at the CONNEX Final Conference, Workshop 5: Putting EU civil society involvement under scrutiny, Panel: Civil Society Organisations in EU, 2008.

Komter, Aafke: Social Solidarity and The Gift, Cambridge: Cambridge University Press, 2004.

Kostelecký, Tomas: Political Parties After Communism. Developments in East-Central Europe, Washington, D.C.: Woodrow Wilson Center Press, 2002.

Kriesi, Hans Peter: The Political Opportunity Structure of New Social Movements. Its Impact on Their Mobilization, in: Jenkins, J. C./ Klandermans, B. (eds.): The Politics of Protest Comparative Perspectives on States and Social Movements, London: UCL Press, 1995, pp. 167–199.

Krimsky, Sheldon: Science in the Private Interest: Has the Lure of Profits Corrupted Biomedical Research?, Lanham: Rowman and Littlefield, 2003.

Kubicek, Paul: Organized Labor in Postcommunist States. From Solidarity to Infirmity, Pittsburgh: University of Pittsburgh Press, 2004.

Kumar, Krishan. Civil Society: An Inquiry into the Usefulness of the Historical Term. in The British Journal of Sociology, 1993 (vol. 44), no. 3, pp. 375–395.

Kumar, Krishan: Civil Society Again: A Reply to Christopher Bryant's 'Social Self-organization', Civility and Sociology', in: The British Journal of Sociology, 1994 (vol. 45), no. 1, pp. 127–131.

Kumar, Krishna: Reflections on International Political Party Assistance, in: Democratization, 2005 (vol. 12), no. 4, pp. 505–527.

Kurkchiyan, M.: The Transformation of The Second Economy into the Informal Economy, in: Ledeneva, A./ Kurkchiyan, M. (eds.): Economic Crime in Russia. London: Kluwer Law International, 2000, pp. 83–97.

Kvale, Steinar/ Brinkmann, Svend: Interviews: Learning the Craft of Qualitative Research interviewing. (2nd ed.). Thousand Oaks: Sage, 2009.

Lamnek, Siegfried: Qualitative Sozialforschung, Lehrbuch, Weinheim, Basel: Beltz Verlag, 2005.

Lauth, Hans-Joachim: Informelle Institutionen Politischer Partizipation und Ihre Demokratietheoretische Bedeutung. Klientelismus, Korruption, Putschdrohung und ziviler Widerstand, In: Lauth, Hans-Joachim/ Liebert, Ulrike (eds.): Im Schatten Demokratischer Legitimität. Informelle Institutionen und Politische Partizipation im interkulturellen Demokratievergleich, Wiesbaden: Opladen, 1999, pp. 61–84.

Ledeneva, Alena V.: Russia's Economy of Favours: Blat, Networking and Informal Exchange, Cambridge: Cambridge University Press, 1998.

Ledeneva, Alena: Unwritten Rules. How Russia Really Works, London: Center for European Reform, 2001.

Ledeneva, Alena V.: How Russia Really Works: The Informal Practice that Shaped Post-Soviet Politics and Business, Ithaca, NY: Cornell University Press, 2006.

Ledeneva, Alena V.: Blat and Guanxi: Informal Practices in Russia and China, in: Comparative Studies in Society and History, 2008 (vol. 50), No.1, pp. 118–144.

Ledeneva, Alena: From Russia with Blat: Can Informal Networks Help Modernize Russia?, in: Social Research 2009, 76, 1, 257–288.

Levin, Mark/ Satarov, Georgy: Corruption and Institutions in Russia, in: European Journal of Political Economy, 2000, (vol. 16), no. 1, pp. 113–132.

Lévi-Strauss, Claude: The Principle of Reciprocity, in: Komter, Aafke (eds.): The Gift: An Interdisciplinary Perspective, Amsterdam: Amsterdam University Press, 1996.

Lewicka-Strzałecka, Anna: Teoretyczne i praktyczne aspekty identyfikacji i ograniczania konfliktu interesów, in: Węgrzecki, Adam (ed.): Konflikt interesów – konflikt wartości, Cracow: Wydawnictwo Akademii Ekonomicznej, 2005, pp. 7–23.

Lewis, Maureen: Governance and Corruption in Public Health Care Systems, Center for Global Development, Washington, 2006, Working Paper 78.

Lewis, M./ Pettersson, G.: Governance in Health Care Delivery: Raising Performance, Unpublished draft, July 2009.

Lewis, Paul G.: Political Parties in Post-Communist Eastern Europe, London, New York: Routledge, 2000.

Leybovitch, O./ Sushkova, N.: Na semi vetrah: Institite Vysshego Obrasovaniya v Post-sovetskuyu Epohu in: Journal of Sociology and Social Anthropology, 2004 (vol. 7), no. 1, pp. 149–156.

Liebert, Ulrike: Structuring political conflict about Europe: Media, parliaments and constitutional treaty ratification. ConstEPS internal material no. IV. Outline for country case studies. Bremen: CeUS, 2006.

Liebert, Ulrike: The European citizenship paradox: Renegotiating equality and diversity in the New Europe. in: Siim, Birte/ Squires, Judith (eds.): Contesting Citizenship. London: Routledge, 2008.

Linz, Juan J./ Stepan, Alfred C.: Problems of Democratic Transition and Consolidation. Southern Europe, South America and Post-Communist Europe, Baltimore, London: Johns Hopkins University Press, 1996.

Locati, Giovanni: Le Convenzioni del Consiglio d'Europa in Materia di Lotta alla Corruzione e gli Adempimenti di Alcuni Stati ad esse Aderenti, Liuc Papers no. 123, Serie Impresa e Istituzioni, 2003.

Lombardo, Emanuela: The Participation of Civil Society in the European Constitution-making Process. Paper for the CIDEL Workshop London, 2004.

Lord, Christopher: Democracy in the European Union. Sheffield: Sheffield Academic Press, 1998.

Lord, Christopher/ Magnette, Paul: E Pluribus Unum? Creative Disagreement about Legitimacy in the EU. in: Journal of Common Market Studies, 2004 (vol. 1), no. 42, pp. 183–202.

Lord, Christopher/ Harris, Erika: Democracy in the New Europe. London: Palgrave Macmillan, 2006.

Lovell, S./ Ledeneva, A./ Rogachevskii, A.: Bribery and Blat in Russia: Negotiating Reciprocity from the Early Modern Period to the 1990s, Houndmills, Basingstoke: Macmillan Press Ltd, 2000.

Lubecki, Jacek: Echoes of Latifundism? Electoral Constituencies of Successor Parties in Post-Communist Countries, in: East European Politics and Societies, 2004 (vol. 18), no. 1, pp. 10–44.

Luhmann, Niklas: Gesellschaftsstruktur und Semantik. Studien zur Wissenssoziologie der modernen Gesellschaft, Frankfurt a.M.: Suhrkamp, 1999.

MacIntyre, Alasdair: Posle Dobrodeteli (After Virtue), Moscow: Academicheskiy Proekt, 2000.

Magnette, Paul/ Lequesne, Christian/ Jabko, Nicolas/ Costa, Olivier: Conclusion: Diffuse Democracy in the European Union: The Pathologies of Delegation. Journal of European Public Policy, 2003 (vol. 10) no. 5, pp. 834–840.

Magnette, Paul: Will the EU be More Legitimate after the Convention?, in: Shaw, Jo/ Magnette, Paul/ Hoffman, Lutz/ Vergés Bausili, Anna. The Convention on the Future of Europe Working Towards and EU Constitution. London: The Federal Trust, 2003.

Mahr, Allison/ Nagle, John D.: Resurrection of the Successor Parties and Democratization in East Central Europe, in: Communist and Post Communist Studies, 1995 (vol. 28), no. 4, pp. 393–409.

Majone, Giandomenico: Deficit Democratico: Instituzioni Non-Maggioritarie ed il Paradosso dell'Integrazione Europea. in: Stato e Mercato, 2003 (vol. 67), no. 1, pp. 3–38.

Majone, Giandomenico: Federation, Confederation, and Mixed government: A EU-US Comparison, in: Menon, Anand/ Schain, Martin A. (eds.): Comparative Federalism: The European Union and the United States in Comparative Perspective, Oxford: Oxford University Press, 2007. pp. 121–46.

Maloney, William/ Rossteutscher, Sigrid (eds.): Social Capital and Associations in European Democracies. A Comparative Analysis, London: Routledge, 2007.

Mandell, Myrna/ Keast, Robert: Evaluating the Effectiveness of Interorganizational Relations through Networks, in: Public Management Review, 2008 (vol. 10), no. 6, pp. 715–731.

Manning, Carrie: The Making of Democrats. Elections and Party Development in Postwar Bosnia, El Salvador and Mozambique, New York: Palgrave MacMillan, 2008, pp. 79–81.

Marada, Radim: Civil Society: Adventures of the Concept before and after 1989, in: Czech Sociological Review, 1997 (vol. 5), no. 1, pp. 3–22.

March, Luke: For Victory? The Crises and Dilemmas of the Communist Party of the Russian Federation, in: Europe-Asia Studies, 2001 (vol. 53), no. 2, pp. 263–290.

March, Luke: The Communist Party in Post-Soviet Russia, Manchester, New York: Manchester University Press, 2002.

Marin, Bernd: Generalized Political Exchange, Antagonistic Cooperation and Integrated Policy Circuits, Boulder/CO: Westview Press, 1990.

Markowski, Radoslaw: The Polish SLD in the 1990s. From Opposition to Incumbents and Back, in: Bozóki, Andraś/ Ishiyama, John T. (eds.): The Communist Successor Parties of Central and Eastern Europe, Armonk/NY, London: M.E. Sharpe, 2002, pp. 51–88.

Matveeva, Anna: The Perils of Emerging Statehood: Civil War and State Reconstruction in Tajikistan. An Analytical Narrative on State-Making. Crisis States Research Centre 2009. Working Paper 46.

Mauss, Marcel: The Gift: The Form and Reason for Exchange in Archaic Societies, London: Routledge, 1990.

McCarthy, John D./ Zald, Mayer N.: Resource Mobilization and Social Movements: A Partial Theory, in: American Journal of Sociology, 1977, (vol. 82), no. 6, pp. 1212–1241.

McDermott, Gerry: Institutional Change and Firm Creation in East-Central Europe. An Embedded Politics Approach, in: Comparative Political Studies, 2004 (vol. 37), No.2, pp. 188–217.

Meehan, Elizabeth: Europeanization and Citizenship of European Union. in: Harmsen, Robert/ Wilson, Thomas, M.: Yearbook of European Studies, 2000 (vol. 14), pp. 157–177.

Melucci, Alberto: Getting Involved: Identity and Mobilization in Social Movements, in: Kriesi, Hanspeter/ Tarrow, Sidney (eds.): From Structure to Action: Comparing Social Movements Across Cultures, International Social Movement Research I, Greenwich, CT: JAI, 1988, pp. 329–48.

Migdal, Joel S.: Strong Societies and Weak States: State-Society Relations and State Capabilities in the Third World, Princeton: Princeton University Press, 1988.

Millard, Frances: Polish Politics and Society, London, New York: Routledge, 1999.

Mishler, William/ Rose, Richard: What are the Origins of Political Trust? Testing Institutional and Cultural Theories in Post-Communist Societies, in: Comparative Political Studies, 2001 (vol. 34), no. 1, pp. 30–62.

Moravcsik, Andrew. In Defence of the Democratic Deficit: Reassessing Legitimacy in European Union, in: Journal of Common Market Studies, 2002 (vol. 40), no. 4, pp. 603–624.

Moroffa, Holger/ Schmidt-Pfister, Diana: Anti-corruption movements, mechanisms, and machines—an introduction, in: Global Crime, 2010 (vol. 11), no. 2, pp. 89–98.

Müller, Karel: Koncept občanské společnosti: konceptualizace, dilemata a nebezpečí. in: Politologická revue, 2001, no. 1, pp. 3–26.

Murer, Jeffrey S.: Mainstreaming Extremism. The Romanian PDSR and the Bulgarian Socialists in Comparative Perspective, in: Bozóki, Andraś/ Ishiyama, John T. (eds.): The Communist Successor Parties of Central and Eastern Europe, Armonk/NY, London: M.E. Sharpe, 2002, pp. 367–396.

Myers, Michael D..: Qualitative Research in Business & Management, London: Sage, 2009.

Nardin, Terry: Private and Public Role in Civil Society, in: Waltzer, Michael (ed.): Towards a Global Civil Society. Providence: Berghahn Books, 1998, pp. 29–33.

Nash, Robert/ Hudson, Alan/ Lutrell, Cecilia: Mapping Political Context: A Toolkit for Civil Society Organisations, Overseas Development Institute, 2006.

Nenadović, Maja: An Uneasy Symbiosis. The Impact of International Administrations on Political Parties in Post-Conflict Countries, in: Democratization, 2010 (vol. 17), no. 6, pp. 1153–1175.

Neocleous, Mark: From Civil Society to the Social. In: The British Journal of Sociology, 1995 (vol. 46), no. 3, pp. 395–408.

Noonan, John T.: Bribes, New York: Macmillan, 1984.

Norris, Pippa/ Krook, Mona L.: One of Us. Multilevel models examining the impact of descriptive representation on civic engagement, paper presented at the APSA 2009 Toronto Meeting, http://papers.ssrn.com/sol3/papers.cfm?abstract_id=1451149, accessed 21 May 2010.

North, Douglas C.: Institutions, Institutional Change and Economic Performance, Cambridge: Cambridge University Press, 1990.

North, Douglass C.: Institutions, in: The Journal of Economic Perspectives, 1991 (vol. 5), no. 1, pp. 97–112.

O'Donnell, Guillermo/ Schmitter, Phillipe C.: Transitions from Authoritarian Rule: Tentative Conclusions about Uncertain Democracies, Baltimore: Johns Hopkins University Press, 1986.

O'Donnell, Guillermo: Illusions About Consolidation, in: Journal of Democracy, 1996 (vol. 7), no. 2, pp. 34–51.

O'Neill, William G.: Kosovo. An Unfinished Peace, London: Lyne Rienner Publishers, 2002.

Oberschall, Anthony: Social Movements. Ideologies, Interests, and Identities, New Brunswick/NJ, London: Transaction Publishers, 1993.

Obradovic, Daniela: Policy Legitimacy and European Union. Journal of Common Market Studies, 1996 (Vol.34), No.2, pp. 191–219.

Obradovic, Daniela: Civil Society and the Social Dialogue in European Governance. in: Yearbook on European Law, 2005 (vol. 24), pp 261–328.

Obradovic, Daniela/ Alonso Vizcaino, Jose M: Good Governance Requirements for the Participation of Interest Groups in EU Consultations, in: Pleines, Heiko (ed.): Participation of Civil Society in New Modes of Governance. The Case of the New EU Member States. Part 3: Involvement at the EU Level, Forschungsstelle Osteuropa an der Universität Bremen. Arbeitspapiere und Materialien, no. 76, 2006, pp. 19–44.

OECD DAC: Service Delivery in Fragile Situations. Key Concepts, Findings and Lessons, in: Journal of Development, 2008 (vol.9), no. 3.

Olson, Mancur: The Logic of Collective Action. Public Goods and the Theory of Groups, Cambridge, MA: Harvard University Press, 1965.

Orenstein, Mitchell A.: A Genealogy of Communist Successor Parties in East-Central Europe and the Determinants of Their Success, in: East European Politics and Societies, 1998 (Vol. 12), no. 3, pp. 472–499.

Orenstein, Mitchell A./ Hale, Lisa E. Corporatist Renaissance in Postcommunist Central Europe?, in: Candland, Christopher/ Sil, Rudra (eds.): The Politics of Labour in a Global Age. Continuity and Change in Late-Industrializing and Post-Socialist Economies, Oxford, New York: Oxford University Press, 2001.

Osipian, Ararat L.: Corruption in Russia's Doctoral Education, Nashville: Vanderbilt University, 2008.

Osipyan A.: Corruption as a Legacy of the Medieval University, MPRA Paper no. 13250, 2004, pp. 23–24, http://mpra.ub.uni-muenchen.de/13250/

Ost, David: Labour, Class, and Democracy; Shaping Political Antagonisms in Post-Communist Society, in: Crawford, Beverly: Markets, States, and Democracy: The Political Economy of Post-Communist Transformation, Boulder: Westview, 1995, pp. 177–203.

Ost, David: The Weakness of Strong Social Movements: Models of Unionism in the East European Context, in: European Journal of Industrial Relations, 2002 (vol. 8), no. 1, pp. 79–96.

Ost, David: The Defeat of Solidarity. Anger and Politics in Postcommunist Europe, Ithaca/NY: Cornell University Press, 2005.

Ostrom, Eleanor: Understanding Institutional Diversity, Princeton, NJ: Princeton University Press, 2005.

Paolini, Giulia: The Legitimacy Deficit of the European Union and the Role of National Parliaments. Fiesole: EUI Dissertation, 2007.

Pap, András L.: Human Rights and Ethnic Data Collection in Hungary, in: Human Rights Review, 2008 (vol. 9), no. 1, pp. 109–122.

Parssons, Talcott/ Shills, Edward E.: Toward a General Theory of Action. Theoretical Foundations for the Social Sciences, New Brunswick, NJ: Transaction Publishers. Abridged edition, 2001.

Paul, S.: Accountability in Public Services: Exit, Voice and Control, in: World Development, 1992 (vol. 20), no. 7, pp. 1047–1060.

Peregudov, Sergey P.: Korporatsii, Obshchestvo, Gosudarstvo. Evolutsiya Otnosheniy, Moscow: Nauka, 2003.

Petrova, Tsveta/ Tarrow, Sidney: Transactional and Participatory Activism in the Emerging European Polity. The Puzzle of East-Central Europe, in: Comparative Political Studies, 2007 (vol. 40), no. 1, pp. 74–94.

Pfeffer, Jeffrey/ Salancik, Gerald R.: The External Control of Organizations. A Resource Dependence Perspective, New York: Harper and Row Inc, 1978.

Piattoni, Simona: Clientelism, Interests and Democratic Representation, Cambridge and New York: Cambridge University Press, 2001.

Pierson, Paul: Politics in Time. History, institutions, and Social Analysis, Princeton: Princeton University Press, 2004.

Piirainen, Timo: Learning to Live with the Market. Urban Households in Russia and the Official and Informal Economies, in Månson, Per (ed.): East Europe Ten Years After Communism. Transforming Power and Economy, Forskning om Europafrågor, no. 9, 2000.

Pitkin, Hanna F.: The Concept of Representation, Berkeley, Los Angeles, London: University of California Press, 1972.

Pitkin, Hanna: Representation and Democracy: Uneasy Alliance, in: Scandinavian Political Studies, 2004, (vol.27), p.336.

Pleines, Heiko: Large-Scale Corruption in the Russian Banking Sector, in: Ledeneva, A./ Kurkchiyan, M. (eds.): Economic Crime in Russia. London: Kluwer Law International, 2000, pp. 191–207.

Pleines, Heiko: Corruption Networks in the Russian economy, in: Slovo (special issue), 2000, pp. 104–120.

Pleines, Heiko: Korruption und organisierte Kriminalität, in: Höhmann, H.-H./ Schröder, H.-H. (eds.): Russland unter neuer Führung, Münster: Agenda Verlag, 2001, pp. 281–290.

Pleines, Heiko: Korruptionsnetzwerke in der russischen Wirtschaft, in: Höhmann, H.-H. (ed.): Kultur als Bestimmungsfaktor der Transformation im Osten Europas. Konzeptionelle Entwicklungen – Empirische Befunde. Bremen Edition: Temmen, 2001, pp. 141–156.

Pleines, Heiko : Czech Environmental NGOs in EU governance. Challenges of Accountability. Case study of NewGov project, 2007.

Pleines, Heiko: Czech Environmental NGOs: Actors or agents in EU multi-level governance?, NewGov Policy Brief no. 20, 2008.

Pound, Roscoe: Law in Books and Law in Action, in: American Law Review (vol. 44), no. 12, pp. 12–18.

Pradel, Jean: Droit Penal Compare, 3rd edn., Paris: Dalloz, 2008.

Pridham, Geoffrey: The EU's Political Conditionality and Post-Accession Tendencies: Comparisons from Slovakia and Latvia, in: Journal of Common Market Studies, 2008 (vol. 46), no. 2, pp. 365–387.

Puffer, Sheila M./ McCarthy, Daniel J: Finding the Common Ground in Russian and American Business Ethics, in: California Management Review, 1995 (vol. 37), no. 2, pp. 29–42.

Putin, Vladimir: Strategicheskoye Planirovaniye Vosproizvodstva Minera'lno-syr'yevoy Bazy Regiona v Usloviyakh Formirovaniya Rynochnykh Otnosheniy (Engl.: The Strategic Planning of the Reproduction of the Mineral Raw Materials Base of the Region under Conditions of the Formation of Market Relationships), State Mining Institute, St Petersburg, Russia, 1997.

Putnam, Robert: Making Democracy Work: Civic Traditions in Modern Italy, Princeton: Princeton University Press, 1993.

Radayev, Vadim: Corruption and Violence in Russian Business in the Late 1990s, in: Ledeneva, A./ Kurkchiyan, M. (eds.): Economic Crime in Russia, London: Kluwer Law International, 2000, pp. 63–82.

Radayev, V.: Corruption and Administrative Barriers for Russian Business, in: Kotkin, S./ Sajo, A. (eds.) Political Corruption in Transition: A Skeptic's Handbook. Budapest: Central European University Press, 2002, pp. 287–311.

Radayev, V.: Mozhno li predolet' korruptsiyu v Obrazovanii? (Is it Possible to Overcome Corruption in Education?), 21 June 2006, http://www.strf.ru/organization. aspx?CatalogId=221&d_no=10082

Radnitz, Scott: It Takes More than a Village: Mobilisation, Networks and the State in Central Asia. PhD Thesis, Massachusetts Institute of Technology, February 2007.

Radnitz, Scott/ Wheatly, Jonathan/ Zürcher, Christopher: The Origins of Social Capital. Evidence from a Survey in Post-Soviet Central Asia, in: Comparative Political Studies, 2009 (vol. 42), pp. 707–732.

Rahr, Alexander: Russland gibt Gas. Die Rückkehr einer Weltmacht, München: Carl Hanser Verlag, 2008.

Rahr, Alexander: Putin nach Putin. Das kapitalistische Russland am Beginn einer einen Weltordnung. Wien: Universitas Verlag, 2009.

Rhodes, Robert A. W.: Policy Networks. A British Perspective, in: Journal of Theoretical Politics, 1990 (vol. 2), no. 3, pp. 292–331.

Rhodes, Robert: The New Governance. Governing without Government, in: Political Studies, 1996 (Vol. 44), no. 1, pp. 652–67.

Richter, Horst-Eberhard: Die hohe Kunst der Korruption. Erkenntnisse eines Politik-Beraters, Hamburg: Hoffmann und Campe, 1989.

Ries, Nancy: Business, Taxes, and Corruption in Russia, in: Anthropology of East Europe Review, 1999 (vol. 17), no. 1, pp. 59–62.

Roaf, James: Corruption in Russia. Washington DC: International Monetary Fund publications, 2000.

Roberts, Andrew: The Quality of Democracy, in: Comparative Politics, 2005 (vol. 37), no. 3, pp. 357–376.

Roberts, Marc/ Hsiao, William/ Berman, Peter/ Reich, Michael: Getting Health Reform Right, Oxford: Oxford University Press, 2002.

Roberts, Peter: Partnerships, programmes and the promotion of regional development. An evaluation of the operation of the structural funds regional programmes, in: Programme Planning, 2003 (vol. 59), pp. 1–69.

Roniger, Luis: Political Clientelism, Democracy, and Market Economy, in: Comparative Politics, 2004 (vol. 36), no. 3, pp. 353–375.

Rose, Richard: Living in an Anti-Modern Society, in: East European Constitutional Review, 1999 (vol. 8), no. 1–2, pp. 68–75.

Rose-Ackerman, Susan: Corruption. A Study in Political Economy, New York: Academic Press, 1978.

Rose-Ackerman, Susan: Corruption and Government: Causes, Consequences and Reform, Cambridge: Cambridge University Press, 1999.

Rothstein, Bo: Social Trust and Honesty in Government: A Causal Mechanisms Approach, in: Kornal, Janos/ Rothstein, Bo/ Rose-Ackerman, Susan (eds.): Creating Social Trust in Post-Socialist Transition, N.Y.: Palgrave Macmillan, 2004.

Ruger, Jennifer Prah: Global Health Governance and the World Bank, in: The Lancet, 2007 (vol. 370) Issue 9597, pp. 1471–1474.

Ruzza, Carlo et. al: Final report of the project 'Organized Civil Society and European Governance'. Trento: Universita degli studii Trento, 2005.

Ruzza, Carlo: Organized Civil Society and the EU. Paper presented at the 3rd ECPR general Conference in Budapest, 2005.

Saborovskaya, Alina S. (et al.): Vysshee Obrazovanie v Rossii. Pravila i Realnost', Moscow: Independent Institute for Social Policy, 2004.

Sakwa, Richard: Russia's 'Permanent' (Uninterrupted) Elections of 1999–2000, in: Journal of Communist Studies and Transition Politics, 2000 (vol. 16), no. 3, pp. 85–112.

Sakwa, Richard: Russian Politics and Society, London, New York: Routledge, 2002.

Sakwa, Richard: The 2003–2004 Russian Elections and Prospects for Democracy, in: Europe-Asia Studies, 2005 (vol. 57), no. 3, pp. 369–398.

Salamon, Lester M.: Partners in Public Service: Government-Nonprofit Relations in the Modern Welfare State. Baltimore: The Johns Hopkins University Press, 1995.

Salamon, Lester/ Helmuth, Anheier: The Nonprofit Sector. A New Global Force, Working Paper of the Johns Hopkins Comparative Nonprofit Sector Project no. 21, Baltimore/ MD: The Johns Hopkins Institute for Policy Studies, 1996.

Sampson, Steven: The anti-corruption industry: from movement to institution, in: Global Crime, 2010 (vol. 11), no. 2, pp. 261–278.

Santambrogio, Marco: Introduzione alla Filosofia Analitica del Linguaggio, Bari: Laterza, 1992.

Savona, Ernesto U./ Curtol, Federica: The Contribution of Data Exchange Systems to the Fight against Organised Crime in the See Countries, Transcrime Reports no. 10, Trento: Transcrime, 2004.

Sazonov, Dmitri: Korrupcija v Sfere Vysshego Obrazovanija. Regional'nyj Aspekt i Tendencii Razvitija (Na Primere Saratovskoj Oblasti), Saratov: State Academy of Law, 2007.

Scharbatke-Church, Cheyanne/ Kirby Reilin: Lilies that fester. Seeds of corruption and peacebuilding, in: New Routes, Pilfering the Peace. The nexus between corruption and peacebuilding, 2009 (vol. 14), no. 3–4.

Scharpf, Fritz: Games Real Actors Play, Boulder/CO: Westview Press, 1997.

Scharpf, Fritz: Governing in Europe. Effective and Democratic?, Oxford: Oxford University Press, 2002.

Schattenberg, Susanne: Die Korrupte Provinz? Russische Beamte im 19. Jahrhundert, Frankfurt a.M. et al.: Campus, 2008.

Schattschneider, E.E.: Party Government, New York: Rhinehart & Co., 1942.

Scheuch, Erwin Kurt: Die Mechanismen der Korruption, in: von Arnim, Hans Herbert/ Bannenberg, Britta (eds.): Korruption. Netzwerke in Politik, Ämtern und Wirtschaft, München: Droemer Knaur, 2003, pp. 31–75.

Scheuch, Erwin Kurt: Korruption als Teil einer freiheitlichen Gesellschaftsordnung. Oder: Die Kriminogenese eines kommunalen 'Klüngels', in: Kriminalistik, 2002, (vol. 56), no. 2, pp. 79–91.

Schiffer, Eva/ Waale, Douglas: Tracing Power and Influence in Networks, IFPRI 2008, Discussion Paper 00772.

Schmitter, Philippe: How to Democratize the EU … and why bother? Oxford: Rowman & Littlefield Publishers, 2000.

Schmitter, Philippe: What is there to Legitimize in the European Union and how this might be accomplished, Mimeo, Fiesole: EUI, 2000.

Schmitter, Philippe: Organized Labor between the Practice of Democracy and the Prospect of Democratization of Europe. in Magnusson, Lars/ Ottosson, Jan (eds.): Europe—One Labour Market?, Bruxelles: PIE-Peter Lang, 2002.

Schmitter, Philippe: Democracy in Europe and Europe's Democratization. In: Journal of Democracy, 2003 (vol. 14), no. 4, pp. 71–85.

Scott, Robert: Institutions and Organizations, Thousand Oaks/CA: Sage, 1995.

Seidmann, Irving: Interviewing as Qualitative Research: a Guide for Researchers in Education and the Social Science (3rd ed.), New York: Teachers College Press, 2006.

Seligman, Adam. B.: The Idea of Civil Society, New York: Free Press, 1992.

Sharpf, Fritz: Governing in EU: Effective and democratic? Oxford: Oxford University Press, 1999.

Shefter, Martin: Party and Patronage. Germany, England, and Italy, in: Politics & Society, 1977 (vol. 7), no. 4, pp. 403–451.

Shelley, Louise: Organized Crime and Corruption in Ukraine. Impediment to the Development of a Free Market Economy, in: Demokratizatsiya, 1998 (vol. 6), no. 4, pp. 648–663.

Shelley, Louise: Can Russia Fight Organized Crime and Corruption, in: The Tocqueville Review, 2002 (vol. 23), no. 2, pp. 37–55.

Shelley, Louise: Crime and Corruption. Enduring Problems of Post-Soviet Development, in: Demokratizatsiya, 2003 (Vol. 11), no. 1, pp. 110–114.

Shleifer, Andrei/ Vishny, Robert W.: Corruption, in: Quarterly Journal of Economics, 1993, (vol. 108), no. 3, pp. 599–617.

Shugart, Matthew S./ Carey, John T.: Presidents and Assemblies. Constitutional Design and Electoral Dynamics, Cambridge: Cambridge University Press, 1992.

Silverman, David: Doing Qualitative Research: a Practical Handbook (3rd ed.), Los Angeles: Sage, 2010.

Simis, Konstantin: USSR. Secrets of a Corrupt Society, London: Dent, 1982.

Simon, Rick: Labour and Political Transformation in Russia and Ukraine, Aldershot: Ashgate, 2000.

Sivak, E./ Yudkevich, M.: Zakrytaya Akademicheskaya Sreda i Localnye Akademicheskie Standarty, in: Foresight, 2008 (vol. 8), no. 4, pp. 32–41.

Sjöstrand, Glenn: Gåvoinstitutionen i det moderna samhället, in: Sociologisk Forskning, 2001, no. 2, pp. 44–66.

Skocpol, Theda: Advocates Without Members. The Recent Transformation of American Civic Life, in: Skocpol, Theda (ed.): Civic Engagement in American Democracy, Washington D.C.: Brookings Inst., 1999, pp. 461–509.

Smith, Michael, E.: Toward a Theory of EU Foreign Policy Making: Multi-level Governance, domestic Politics, and national Adaptation to Europe's Common foreign and security Policy, in: Journal of European Public Policy 2004 (vol. 11), no. 4, pp. 740–758.

Somers, John/ Bradford, David: Discourses of Partnership in Multi-agency Working in the Community and Voluntary Sectors in Ireland, in: Irish Journal of Sociology, 2006 (vol. 15), no. 2, pp. 67–85.

Stark, Andrew: Conflict of interest in American public life, Cambridge/MA: Harvard University Press, 2000.

Stark, David/ Vedres, Balazs/ Bruszt, Laszlo: Rooted Transnational Publics. Integrating Foreign Ties and Civic Activism, in: Theory and Society, 1996 (vol. 35), no. 3, pp. 323–349.

Stigler, George J.: The Economics of *Conflict of Interest*, in: Journal of Political Economy, 1967 (Vol. 75), no. 1, pp. 100–101.

Strazzari, Francesco: The Decade Horribilis. Organized violence and Organized Crime along the Balkan Peripheries, 1991–2001, in: Meditteranean Politics, July 2007 (Vol. 12), pp. 185–209.

Strazzari, Francesco: L'Oeuvre au Noir. The Shadow Economy of Kosovo's Independence, in: International Peacekeeping, 2008 (vol. 15), no. 2, pp. 155–170, p. 161.

Struyk, Raymond J.: Nonprofit Organizations as Contracted Local Social Service Providers in Eastern Europe and the Commonwealth of Independent States, in: Public Administration and Development, 2002 (vol. 22), no. 5, pp. 429–437.

Suarez, David/ Hwang, Hokyu: Find a Partner. Nonprofit Organizations and the Culture of Collaboration, paper prepared for the Consortium on Collaborative Governance Mini-Conference, Santa Monica/CA, 10–12 April 2008.

Suwaj, Patrycja Joanna: Konflikt interesów w administracji publicznej, Warsaw: Wolters Kluwer Polska, 2009.

Szajkowski, Bogdan (ed.): Political Parties of Eastern Europe, Russia and Successor States, London: Longman,1994.

Szczerbiak, Aleks: Poles Together? Emergence and Development of Political Parties in Post-Communist Poland, Budapest: Central University Press, 2001.

Szczerbiak, Aleks: Old and New Divisions in Polish Politics. Polish Parties Electoral Strategies and Bases of Support, in: Europe-Asia Studies, 2003 (vol. 55), no. 5, pp. 729–746.

Teichmann, Christine: Nachfrageorientierte Hochschulfinanzierung in Russland. Ein innovatives Modell zur Modernisierung der Hochschulbildung, in: HoF-Arbeitsberichte, no. 1, 2004.

Teorell, Jan: Corruption as an Institution: Rethinking the Nature and Origins of the Grabbing Hand, QoG Working Papers Series, The Quality of Government Institute, 2007.

Tesser, Lynn M.: The Geopolitics of Tolerance. Minority Rights under EU Expansion in East-Central Europe, in: East European Politics and Societies, 2003 (vol. 17), no. 3, pp. 483–532.

Thevenot, Laurent: Nauka vmeste zhit' v etom mire, in: Neprikosnovenniy Zapas (Emergency Ration), 2004, (vol. 35), no. 3, http://magazines.russ.ru/nz/2004/35/teve2.html

Thompson, R./ Rittmann, J.: A Review of Specialty Provision: Urology Services, in: Thompson, R./ Ensor, Tim/ Rittmann, J. (eds.): Health care Reform in Kazakhstan, Compendium of Papers Prepared for the World Bank Health Reform Technical Assistance Project, 1995–1996, 1997.

Tiihonen, Seppo (ed.): The History of Corruption in Central Government, Amsterdam: IOS Press, 2003.

Tilly, Charles: From Mobilization to Revolution, Reading/MA: Addison-Wesley, 1978.

Timofeychev, Aleksey: S chem priyedet v Moskvu pol'skiy prem'yer?, in: BBCRussian.com, 7 February 2008.

Tokunaga, Masahiro: Delayed, but flourishing? Preliminary analysis of foreign direct investment of Japanese companies in Russia. Paper presented at VIII ICCEES World Congress, 26–31 July, 2010 Stockholm.

Tomiyama, Eiko: Entry and Marketing Strategies to Russian Market by Japanese, Korean Automobile Manufactures—Case Study of Entry to Russian market by Toyota, Hyundai & KIA Motor. Paper presented at VIII ICCEES World Congress, 26–31 July, 2010 Stockholm.

Trost, Christine/ Gash, Alison L.: Conflict of Interest and Public Life. Cross-national Pperspectives, Cambridge: Cambridge University Press, 2008.

Tsebelis, George: Nested Games. Rational Choice in Comparative Politics, Berkley, Los Angeles, London: University of California Press, 1990.

Unsworth, Sue: Understanding Pro-Poor Change: a Discussion Paper, London: Department for International Development, 2001.

Urban, Joan B./ Solovej, Valerij D.: Russia's Communists at the Crossroads, Boulder/CO: Westview Press, 1997.

Vachudova, Milada A.: Corruption and Compliance in the EU's Post-Comunist Members and Candidates, in Journal of Common Market Studies, 2009 (vol. 47), Annual Review, pp. 43–62.

Vacroux, Alexandra: Formal and Informal Institutional Change: The Evolution of Pharmaceutical Regulation in Russia, 1991–2004, Ph.D. thesis. Boston: Harvard University, 2005.

Vahtra, Peeter/ Zashev, Peter: Russian automotive manufacturing sector—an industry snapshot for foreign component manufacturers, in: Electronic Publications of the Pan-European Institute, 7, 2008.

Vahtra, Peeter/ Zashev, Peter: Opportunities and strategies for Finnish companies in the Saint Petersburg and Leningrad region automobile cluster, in: Kymenlaakso University of Applied Sciences, Research and Report publication, 52, 2009.

Valiullina, Elvira/ Valiullin, Radik: Managerwissen Kompakt, Russland, München, Wien: Carl Hanser Verlag, 2006.

Van Oorschot, Wim/ Arts, William: The Social Capital of European Welfare States. The Crowding Out Hypothesis Revisited, in: Journal of European Social Policy, 2005 (vol. 15), no. 1, pp. 5–26.

Vettori, Barbara/ Zanella, Marco: Tra Nuove e Vecchie Fattispecie Penali, in: Di Nicola, Andrea (ed.): Contro la Criminalità Organizzata in Europa. Una Prima Valutazione delle Politiche Penali ed Extra-penali, Milano: Franco Angeli, in press.

Vlan, Taryn. Corruption in the Health Sector, in: U4, 2008 no. 10, pp. 31–41.

Vian, Taryn: Review of Corruption in the Health Sector: Theory, Methods and Interventions, in: Health Policy and Planning, 2008 (vol. 23), no. 2, pp. 83–94.

Von Alemann, Ulrich/ Kleinfeld, Ralf: Begriff und Bedeutung der politischen Korruption aus politikwissenschaftlicher Sicht, in: Benz, Arthur/ Seibel, Wolfgang (eds.): Zwischen Kooperation und Korruption. Abweichendes Verhalten in der Verwaltung, Baden Baden: Nomos, 1992, pp. 259–282.

Walker, Neil: The White Paper in Constitutional Context, Jean Monnet Working Paper no. 6/01, 2001.

Walker, Neil: Constitutionalising Enlargement, Enlarging Constitutionalism, in: European Law Journal, 2003 (vol. 9), no. 3, pp. 365–385.

Waller, Michael: Adaptation of the Former Communist Parties of East Central Europe. A Case of Democratization?, in: Party Politics, 1995 (vol. 1), no. 3, pp. 373–390.

Waller, Michael: Starting-up Problems: Communists, Social-Democrats and Greens, in: Wightman, Gordon (ed.): Party Formation in East Central Europe. Post-Communist Politics in Czechoslovakia, Hungary, Poland, and Bulgaria, Aldershot: Edward Elgar, 1995, pp. 218–237.

Wallström, Margot: A Note, in: Fazi, Elodie/ Smith, Jeremy: Civil Dialogue—Making it work better,Civil Society Contact Group, 2006. p. 2.

Waltzer, Michael: The Civil Society Argument in: Beiner, Ronald (ed.): Theorizing Citizenship, New York: SUNY Press, 1995.

Waltzer, Michael: The Concept of Civil Society in: Waltzer, Michael (ed.) Towards a Global Civil Society, Providence: Berghahn Books, 1998, pp. 7–27.

Warleigh, Alex: Purposeful Opportunists? EU Institutions and the Struggle over European Citezenship, in: Bellamy, Richard/ Warleigh, Alex (eds.): Citizenship and Governance in the European Union. London: Continuum, 2001, pp. 19–40.

Warrener, Debbie: The Drivers of Change Approach. Overseas Development Institute. November 2004. Synthesis Paper.

Wästerfors, David: Berättelser om mutor, Eslöv: Symposion, 2004.

Wendel, Janine: The Private Poland. Oxford: Oxford University Press, 1986.

Williams, Paul: The Competent Boundary Spanner, in: Public Administration, 2002 (vol. 80), no. 1, pp. 103–124.

Williamson, Oliver E.: The New Institutional Economics: Taking Stock, Looking Ahead, in: Journal of Economic Literature, 2000 (vol. 38), pp. 595–613.

Witzel, Andreas: Auswertung problemzentrierter Interviews: Grundlagen und Erfahrungen, in: Strobl, Rainer/ Böttger, Andreas (eds.): Wahre Geschichten, Baden-Baden: Nomos, 1996, pp. 49–75.

Witzel, Andreas: The Problem-Centered Interview, in: Forum: Qualitative Social Research, (Online Journal), 2000 (vol. 1), no. 1, http://www.qualitative-research.net/index.php/fqs/article/view/1132

Wolf, Sebastian: Assessing Eastern Europe's Anti-Corruption Performance: Views from the Council of Europe, OECD, and Transparency International, in: Global Crime, 2010 (vol. 11), No 2, pp. 99–121.

Wolfgram, Mark A.: When the Men with Guns Rule. Explaining Human Rights Failures in Kosovo since 1999, in: Political Science Quarterly, Fall 2008 (vol. 123), no. 3, pp. 461–484.

World Bank: Anticorruption in Transition. A Contribution to the Policy Debate, Washington D.C.: World Bank, 2000.

Zaborovskaya, A./ Klyatchko, T./ Korolyov, I. et al.: Vysshee Obrazovanie v Rossii, Moskva, 2004 (Higher Education in Russia. Rules and Reality, Moscow: Independent Institute of Social Policy, 2004), pp. 11–12.

Zimmer, Annette/ Freise, Matthias: Bringing Society Back In. Civil Society, Social Capital, and Third Sector, in: Maloney, William A./ Deth, Jan van (ed.): Civil Society and Governance in Europe, Cheltenham: Edward Elgar, 2007, pp. 19–42.

Zimmerman, William: Mobilized participation and the nature of the Soviet dictatorship, in Millar, James (ed.): Politics, work, and daily life in the USSR, Cambridge: Cambridge University Press, 1987.

Zubek, Voytek: The Reassertion of the Left in Post-Communist Poland, in: Europe-Asia Studies, 1994 (vol. 46), no. 5, pp. 801–837.

Zweigert, K./ Kötz, H.: Introduction to Comparative Law, Broadbridge: Clarendon Press, 1998.

Zybertowicz, Andrzej: Demokracja jako fasada. Przypadek III RP, in: Mokrzycki, Edmund/ Rychard, Andrzej/ Zybertowicz, Andrzej (eds.): Utracona dynamika? O niedojrzałości polskiej demokracji, Warsaw: Wydawnictwo IFiS PAN, 2002, pp. 173–214.

Zybertowicz, Andrzej: Kontrola społeczna trzeciego stopnia, in: Kwaśniewski, Jerzy/ Winczorek, Jan (eds.): Idee naukowe Adama Podgóreckiego, Warsaw: Wydawnictwo UW, 2009, pp. 152–178.

About the Authors

Dilorom Akhmedzhanova has a master's degree in sociology (European University at Saint Petersburg). She currently works at the European University at Saint Petersburg, Russia.

Stanislaw Burdziej received his Ph.D. in 2008. He is an assistant professor at Warmia and Mazury University in Olsztyn, Poland.

Andreea Carstocea is a Ph.D. student at the School of Slavonic and East European Studies, University College London. Her thesis focuses on a series of unexpected effects of the post-1990 public policies for the protection of national minorities in Romania grouped together under the journalistic tag of 'ethno-business'. She worked as a senior expert at the Department for Interethnic Relations of the Romanian Government between 2001 and 2010.

Elena Denisova-Schmidt, MBA, Ph.D., teaches and conducts research at the University of St. Gallen, Switzerland. Her main research interests cover informal business practices, corruption and cross-cultural management with a focus on Russia. Before changing to an academic career, she worked for the VSMPO-AVISMA Corporation, Russia.

Tomasz Gabor holds a master's degree in international relations as well as an MA in sociology from the Jagiellonian University in Cracow, Poland. Currently, he is enrolled in the Ph.D. programme at the Department of Social and Political Science of the European University Institute in Florence, Italy.

Dr. **Petra Guasti** is a researcher in the Department of Political Sociology in the Institute of Sociology of the Academy of Sciences of the Czech Republic and in the Institute for Political and Social Research of the University of Würzburg, Germany. She focuses on the workings of modern democracies at the national and European levels and democratic institutions from a comparative perspective and mostly using international comparative approaches. Her current research interests are the effects of informal institutions, including corruption, clientelism and elite agreements on the rule of law in Central and Eastern Europe. As part of the international project RECON, she is studying the question of legitimacy and democratic governance in the EU.

Eelco Jacobs is part of the research team of the Governance of Health Systems Project jointly run by the Basel Institute on Governance and the Swiss Tropical and Public Health Institute, which investigates case studies in Tajikistan and Tanzania. Alongside the project, he has been working on his Ph.D. in political sociology at the University of Basel since September 2009. His doctorate examines power relations in the governance of Tajikistan's health system.

Eduard Klein is currently writing his doctoral thesis 'Academic Corruption in Russia and Ukraine' at the University of Bremen, Germany, with a grant from the Heinrich Böll Foundation.

Mi Lennhag is a second year Ph.D. student in political science at Lund University, Sweden. She holds degrees in political science and East European studies. Her Ph.D. project examines the informal economy and petty corruption involving ordinary citizens (i.e. not companies and politicians) in contemporary post-Soviet Europe. The main focus is on individuals' descriptions and explanations of, as well as their justifications for, their ongoing participation in the grey economy in the post-Soviet context.

Elvira Leontyeva is a senior lecturer in the sociology department of the Pacific National University in Khabarovsk, Russia as well as a candidate of science (the Russian equivalent of a Ph.D.).

Dr. **Zdenka Mansfeldová** is a senior researcher and head of the Department of the Sociology of Politics of the Institute of Sociology, Academy of Sciences of the Czech Republic. Her research focuses on political institutionalization and the representation of interests in both political terms (parties and parliament) and the non-political meso-structures of social interests.

Maja Nenadović is a Ph.D. candidate at the European Studies Department of the University of Amsterdam, the Netherlands. She is in the final (fourth) year of her Ph.D. programme and is scheduled to complete her research on democracy promotion and international political party assistance in Bosnia-Herzegovina (1996–2008) and Kosovo (1999–2008) in the summer of 2011. In her free time, she teaches debate at universities throughout Europe.

Veronika Pasynkova holds a candidate of political sciences (Ph.D.) degree. She is a research fellow in the Department of Political Science and Sociology of the European University at Saint Petersburg and a lecturer in the Intercultural Communication Department at the Saint Petersburg State University of Service and Economics, Russia.

Dr. **Heiko Pleines** is head of the Department of Politics and Economics of the Research Centre for East European Studies (Forschungsstelle Osteuropa) and lecturer in comparative politics at the University of Bremen, Germany. His major research interest is the role of non-state actors in political decision-making processes and the resulting impact on political regimes.

Piotr Stankiewicz received his Ph.D. in 2008. He is an assistant professor at Nicolas Copernicus University in Torun, Poland. He is currently working on the issue of conflict of interest in science and technology development.

Marco Zanella is a Ph.D. candidate on the XXIV cycle of the International Ph.D. Programme in Criminology at the Catholic University of Milan, Italy. His research interests are economic organized crimes and corruption.

ibidem-Verlag / *ibidem* Press
Melchiorstr. 15
70439 Stuttgart
Germany

ibidem@ibidem.eu
www.ibidem-verlag.com
www.ibidem.eu